KUROGANE 3

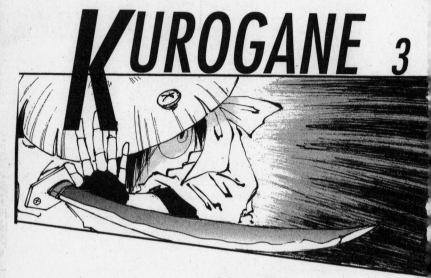

Kei Toume

Translated by Ikoi Hiroe
Lettered by Takka Takka

DEL REY

Ballantine Books ★ New York

Kurogane volume 3 copyright © 1996 by Kei Toume
English translation copyright © 2006 by Kei Toume

All rights reserved.

Published in the United States by Del Rey Books, an imprint of
The Random House Publishing Group, a division of Random House, Inc.,
New York.

DEL REY is a registered trademark and the Del Rey colophon is a trademark
of Random House, Inc.

Publication rights arranged through Kodansha Ltd.

First published in Japan in 2003 by Kodansha Ltd., Tokyo.

ISBN 978-0-345-49205-0

Printed in the United States of America

www.delreymanga.com

2 4 6 8 9 7 5 3 1

Translator—Ikoi Hiroe
Lettering—Takka Takka

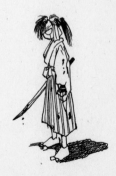

CONTENTS

A NOTE FROM THE AUTHOR

Eternal Recurrence

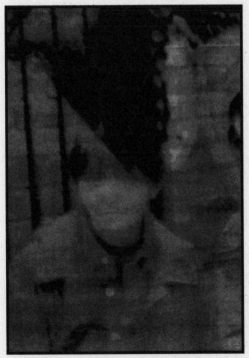

Recent photograph of the author

HONORIFICS EXPLAINED

Throughout the Del Rey Manga books, you will find Japanese honorifics left intact in the translations. For those not familiar with how the Japanese use honorifics and, more important, how they differ from American honorifics, we present this brief overview.

Politeness has always been a critical facet of Japanese culture. Ever since the feudal era, when Japan was a highly stratified society, use of honorifics—which can be defined as polite speech that indicates relationship or status—has played an essential role in the Japanese language. When addressing someone in Japanese, an honorific usually takes the form of a suffix attached to one's name (example: "Asuna-san"), or as a title at the end of one's name, or in place of the name itself (example: "Negi-sensei" or simply "Sensei!").

Honorifics can be expressions of respect or endearment. In the context of manga and anime, honorifics give insight into the nature of the relationship between characters. Many English translations into English leave out these important honorifics, and therefore distort the feel of the original Japanese. Because Japanese honorifics contain nuances that English honorifics lack, it is our policy at Del Rey not to translate them. Here, instead, is a guide to some of the honorifics you may encounter in Del Rey Manga.

-san: This is the most common honorific and is equivalent to Mr., Miss, Ms., Mrs. It is the all-purpose honorific and can be used in any situation where politeness is required.

-sama: This is one level higher than "-san" and is used to confer great respect.

-dono: This comes from the word "tono," which means "lord." It is even a higher level than "-sama" and confers utmost respect.

-kun: This suffix is used at the end of boys' names to express familiarity or endearment. It is also sometimes used by men amongst friends, or when addressing someone younger or of a lower station.

-chan: This is used to express endearment, mostly toward girls. It is also used for little boys, pets, and even amongst lovers. It gives a sense of childish cuteness.

Bozu: This is an informal way to refer to a boy, similar to the English terms "kid" or "squirt."

Sempai/
Senpai: This title suggests that the addressee is one's senior in a group or organization. It is most often used in a school setting, where underclassmen refer to their upperclassmen as "sempai." It can also be used in the workplace, such as when a newer employee addresses an employee who has seniority in the company.

Kohai: This is the opposite of "-sempai," and is used toward underclassmen in school or newcomers in the workplace. It connotes that the addressee is of a lower station.

Sensei: Literally meaning "one who has come before," this title is used for teachers, doctors, or masters of any profession or art.

-[blank]: This is usually forgotten in these lists, but it is perhaps the most significant difference between Japanese and English. The lack of honorific means that the speaker has permission to address the person in a very intimate way. Usually, only family, spouses, or very close friends have this kind of permission. Known as *yobisute*, it can be gratifying when someone who has earned the intimacy starts to call one by one's name without an honorific. But when that intimacy hasn't been earned, it can be very insulting.

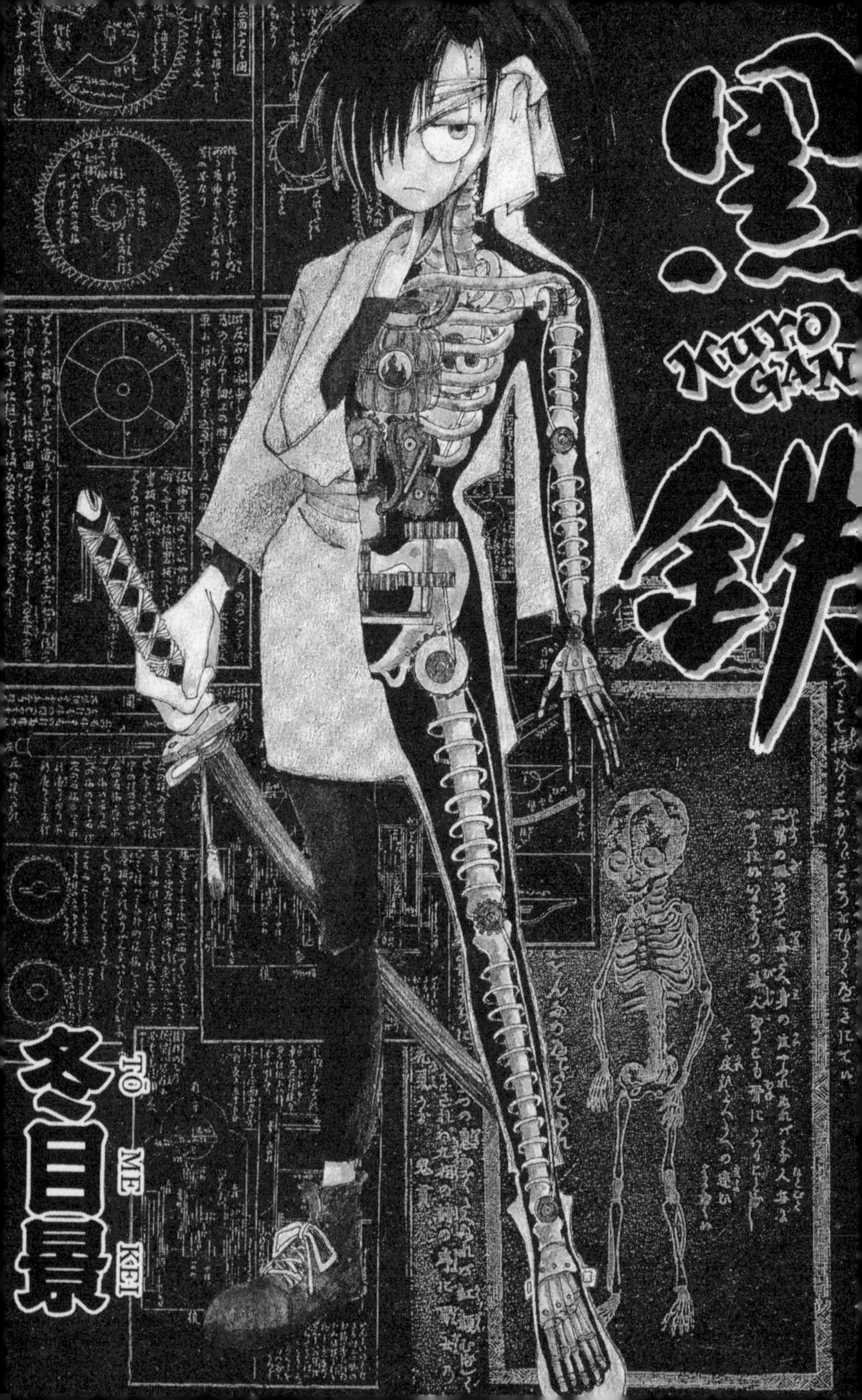
黒鉄
KURO
GAN
冬目景
TŌ ME KEI

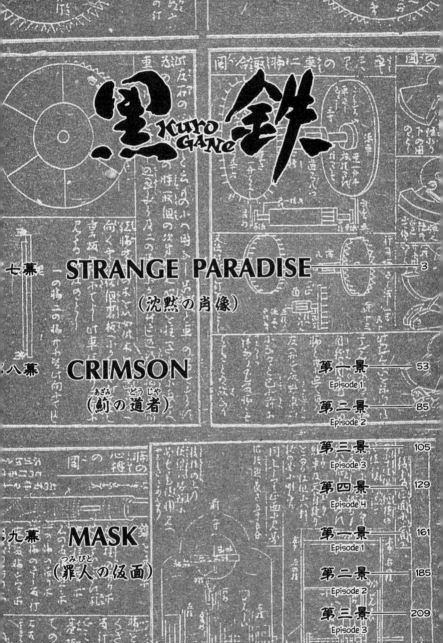

黒 *KURO GANE* 鉄

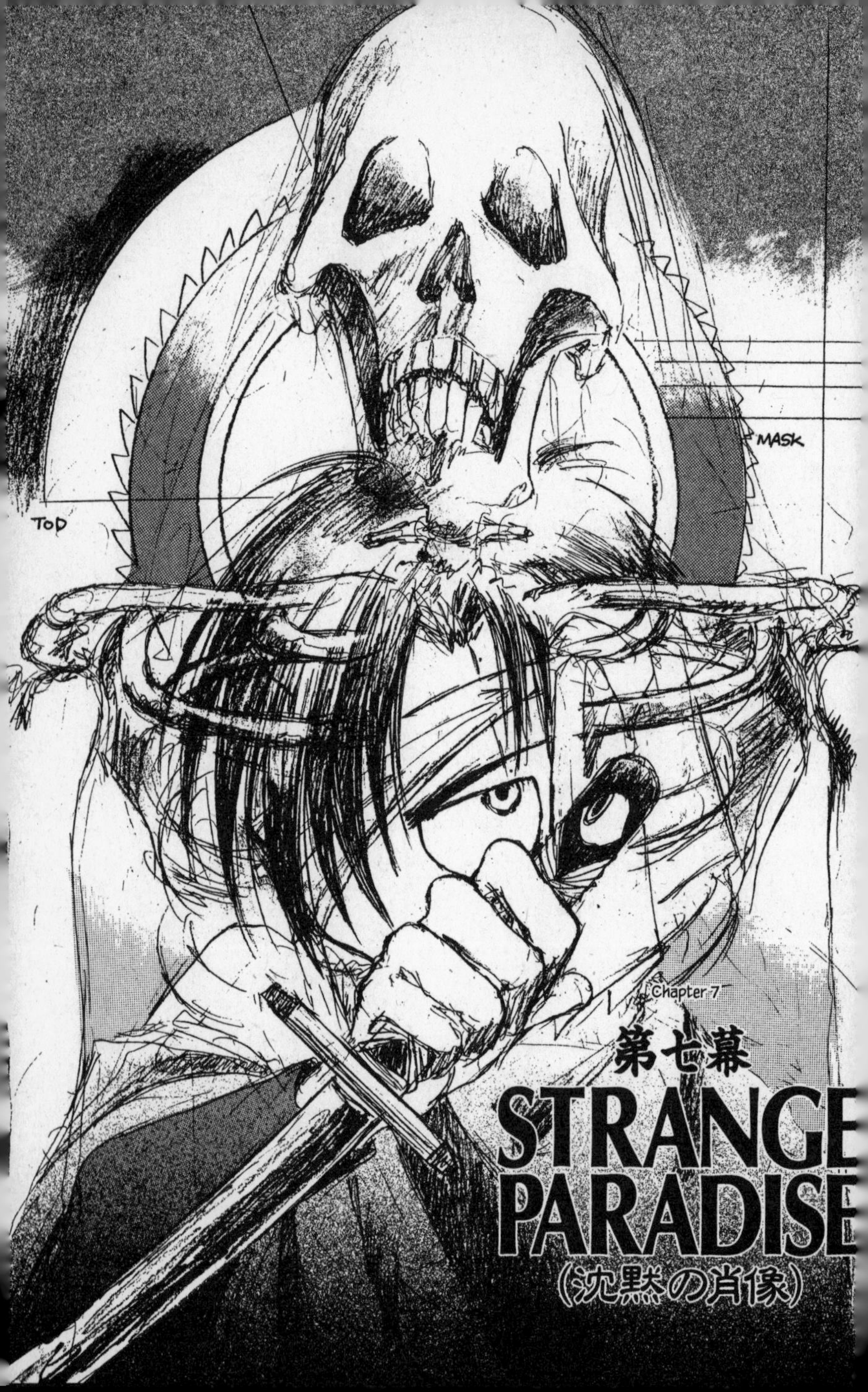
MASK
TOD
Chapter 7
第七幕
STRANGE PARADISE
(沈黙の肖像)

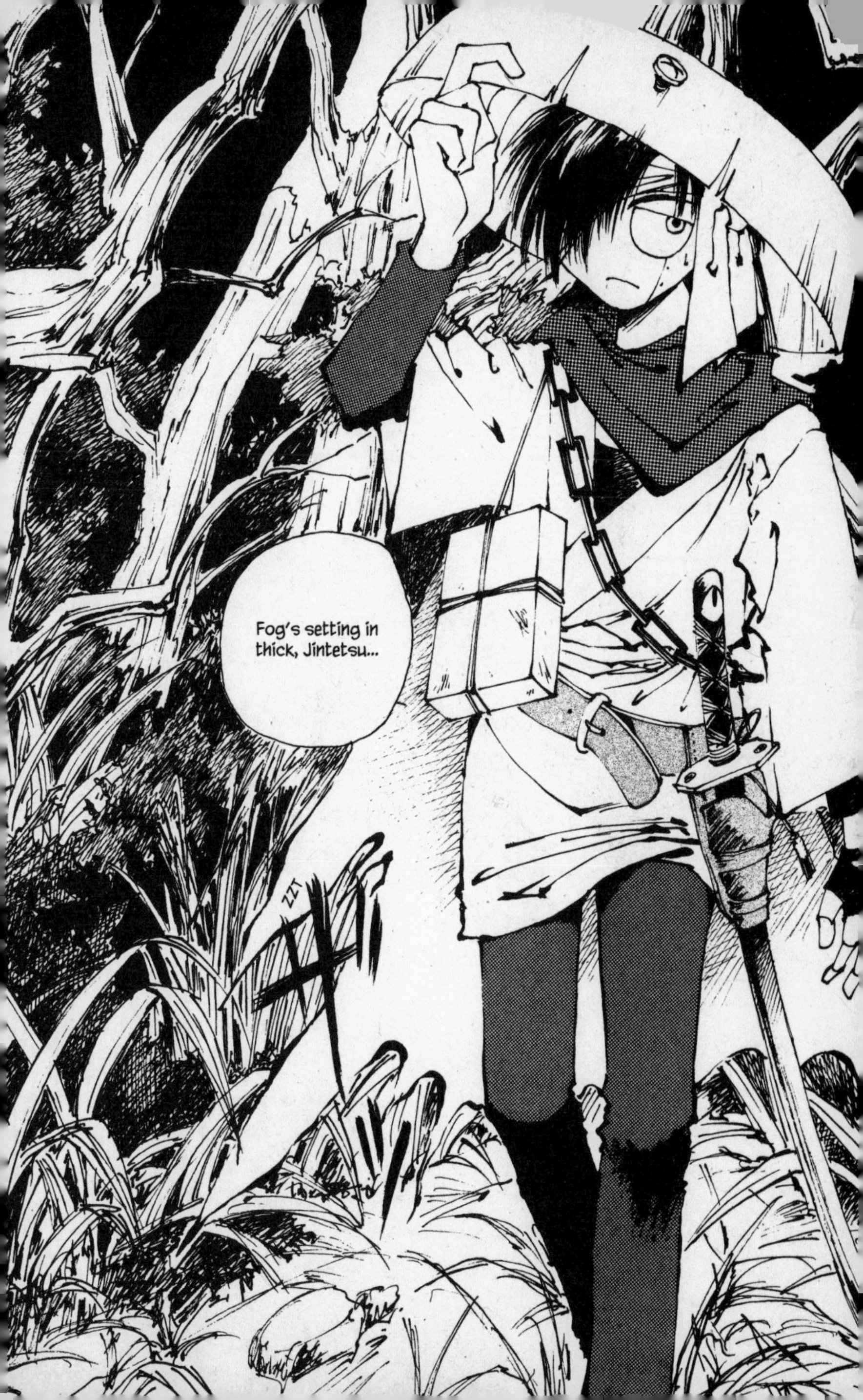
Fog's setting in thick, Jintetsu...

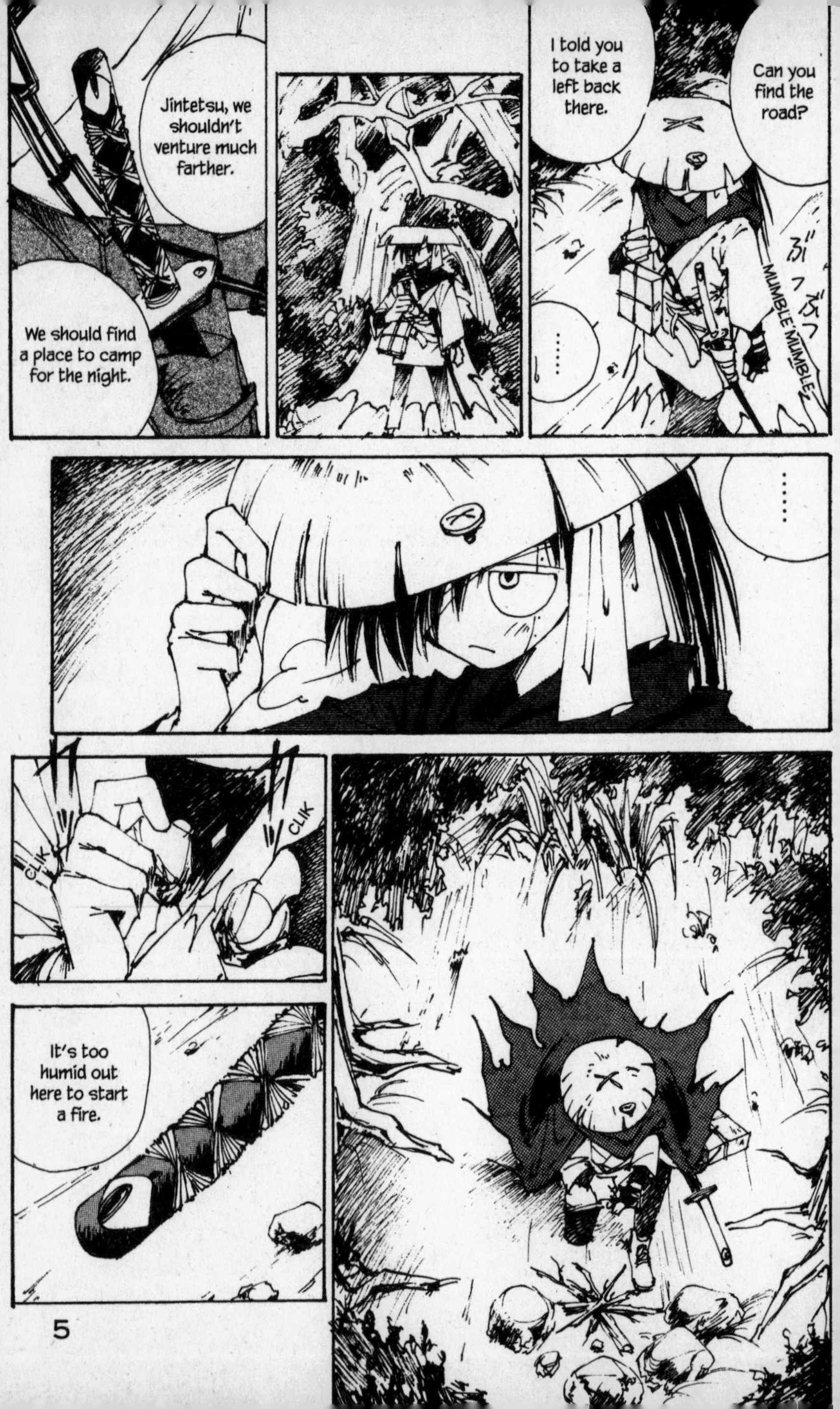

Can you find the road?
I told you to take a left back there.
......
MUMBLE MUMBLE
Jintetsu, we shouldn't venture much farther.
We should find a place to camp for the night.
......
CLIK
CLIK
It's too humid out here to start a fire.

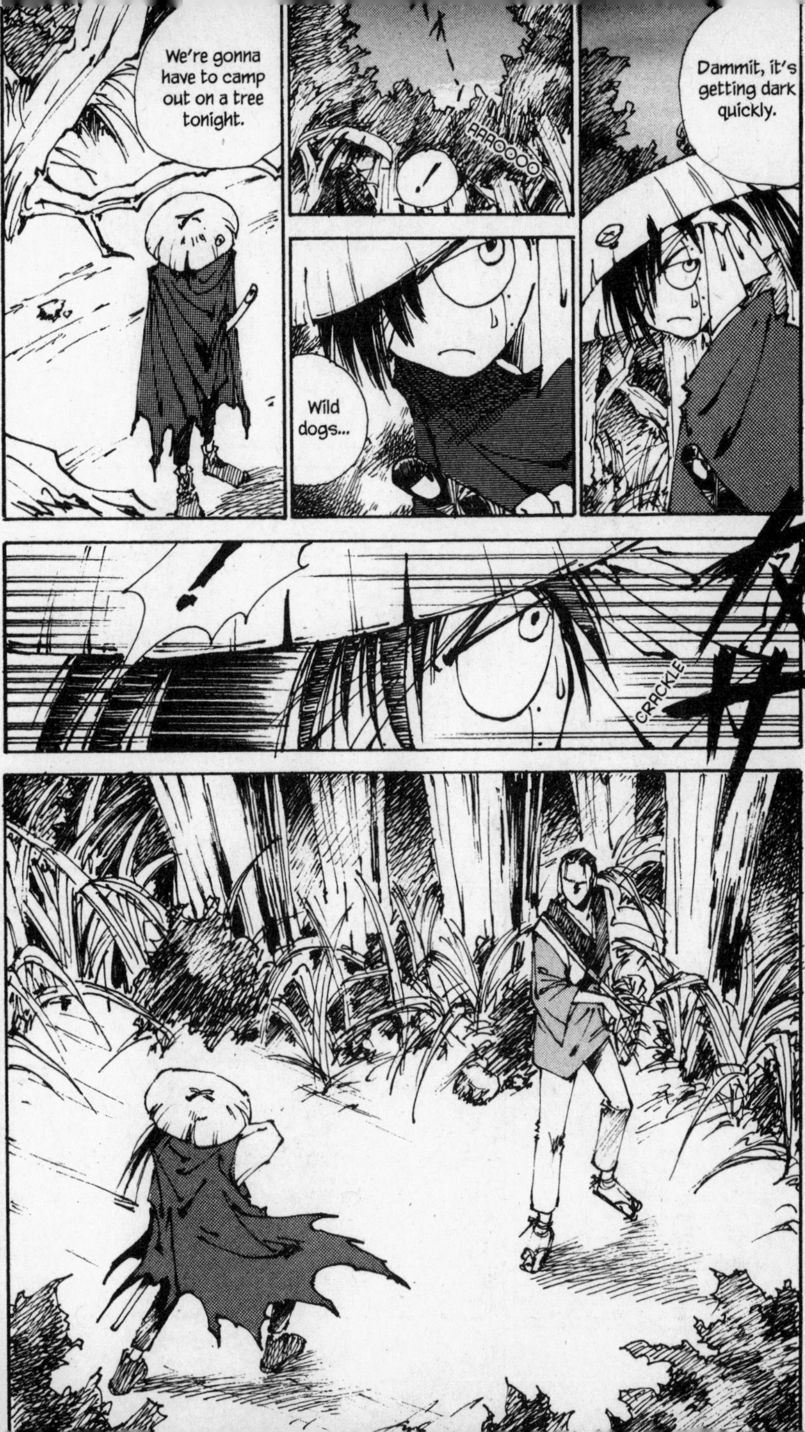
Dammit, it's getting dark quickly.
AAAOOOO
Wild dogs...
We're gonna have to camp out on a tree tonight.
CRACKLE

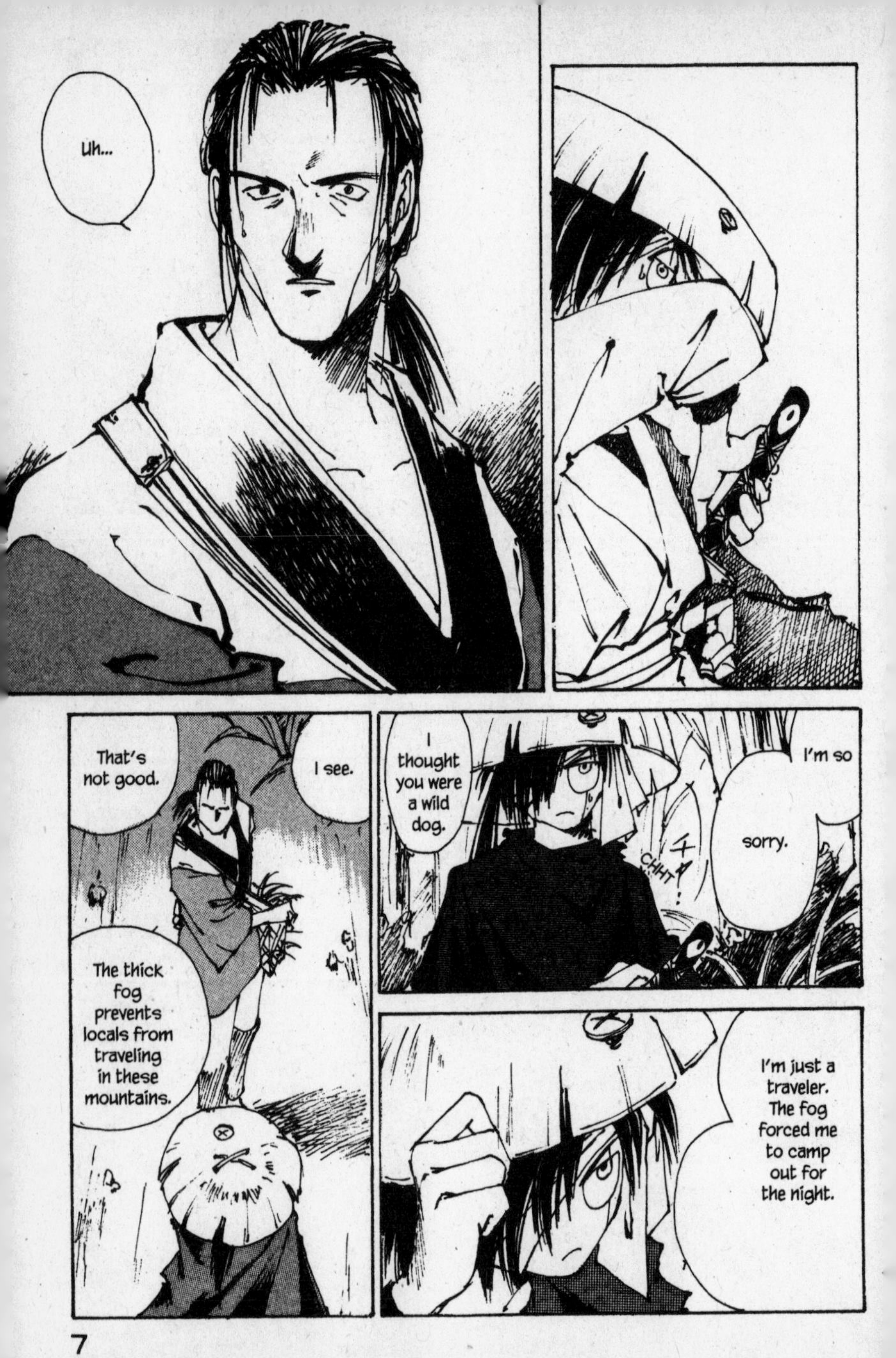
Uh...
I'm so sorry.
CHHT
I thought you were a wild dog.
I'm just a traveler. The fog forced me to camp out for the night.
I see.
That's not good.
The thick fog prevents locals from traveling in these mountains.

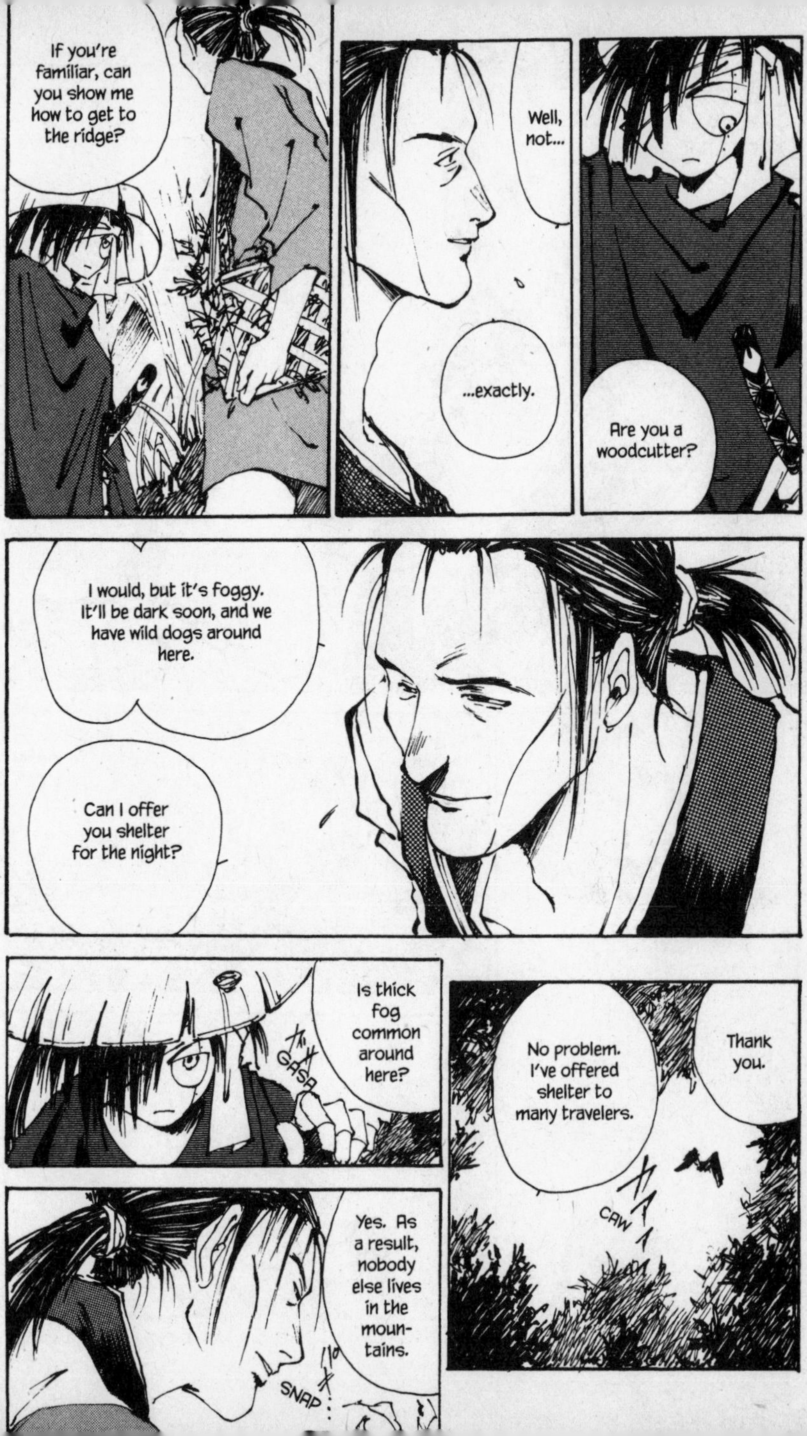
Are you a woodcutter?
Well, not...
...exactly.
If you're familiar, can you show me how to get to the ridge?
I would, but it's foggy. It'll be dark soon, and we have wild dogs around here.
Can I offer you shelter for the night?
Thank you.
No problem. I've offered shelter to many travelers.
CAW
Is thick fog common around here?
GASA
Yes. As a result, nobody else lives in the moun-tains.
SNAP

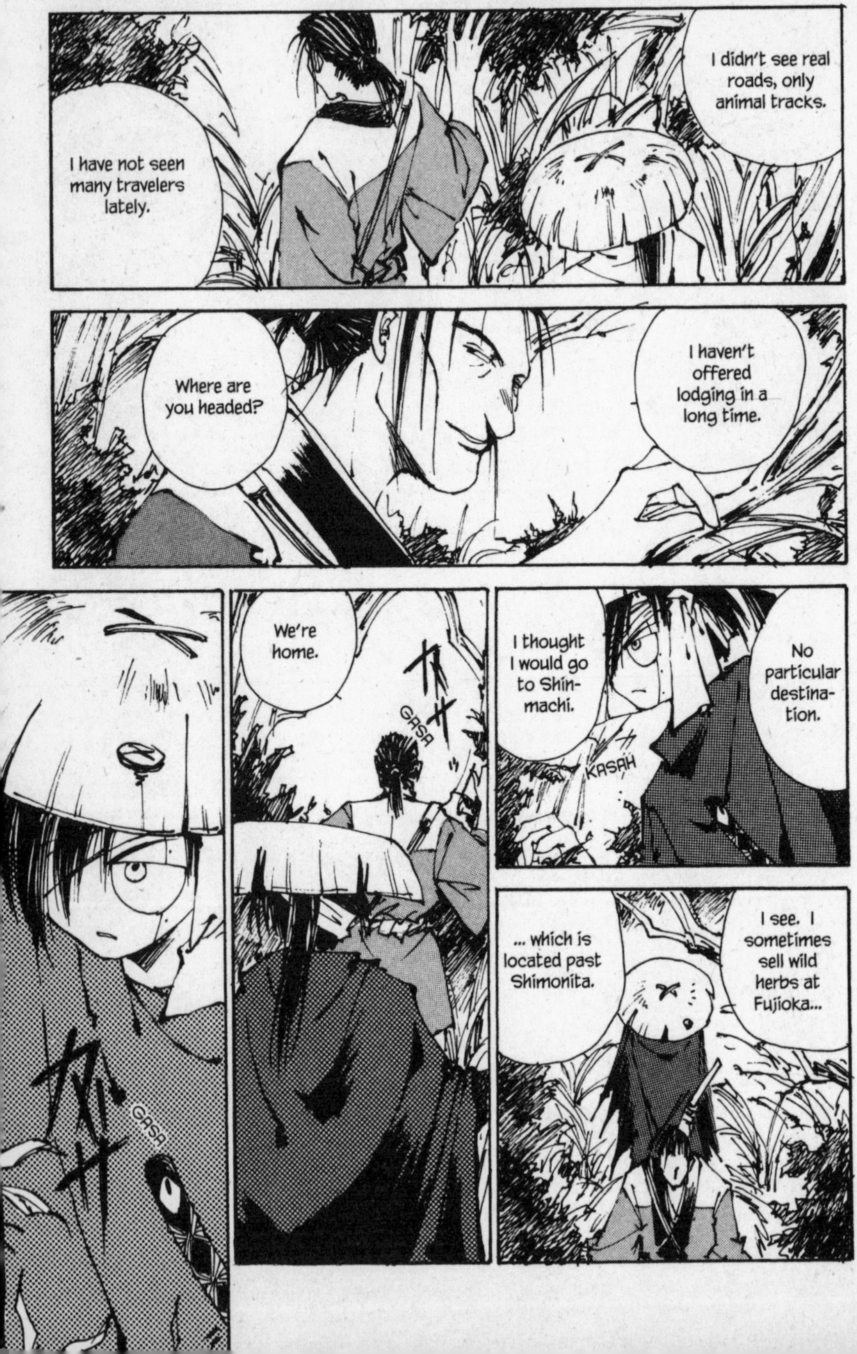
I didn't see real roads, only animal tracks.
I have not seen many travelers lately.
I haven't offered lodging in a long time.
Where are you headed?
No particular destination.
I thought I would go to Shin-machi.
KASAH
I see. I sometimes sell wild herbs at Fujioka...
... which is located past Shimonita.
We're home.
GASA
GASA

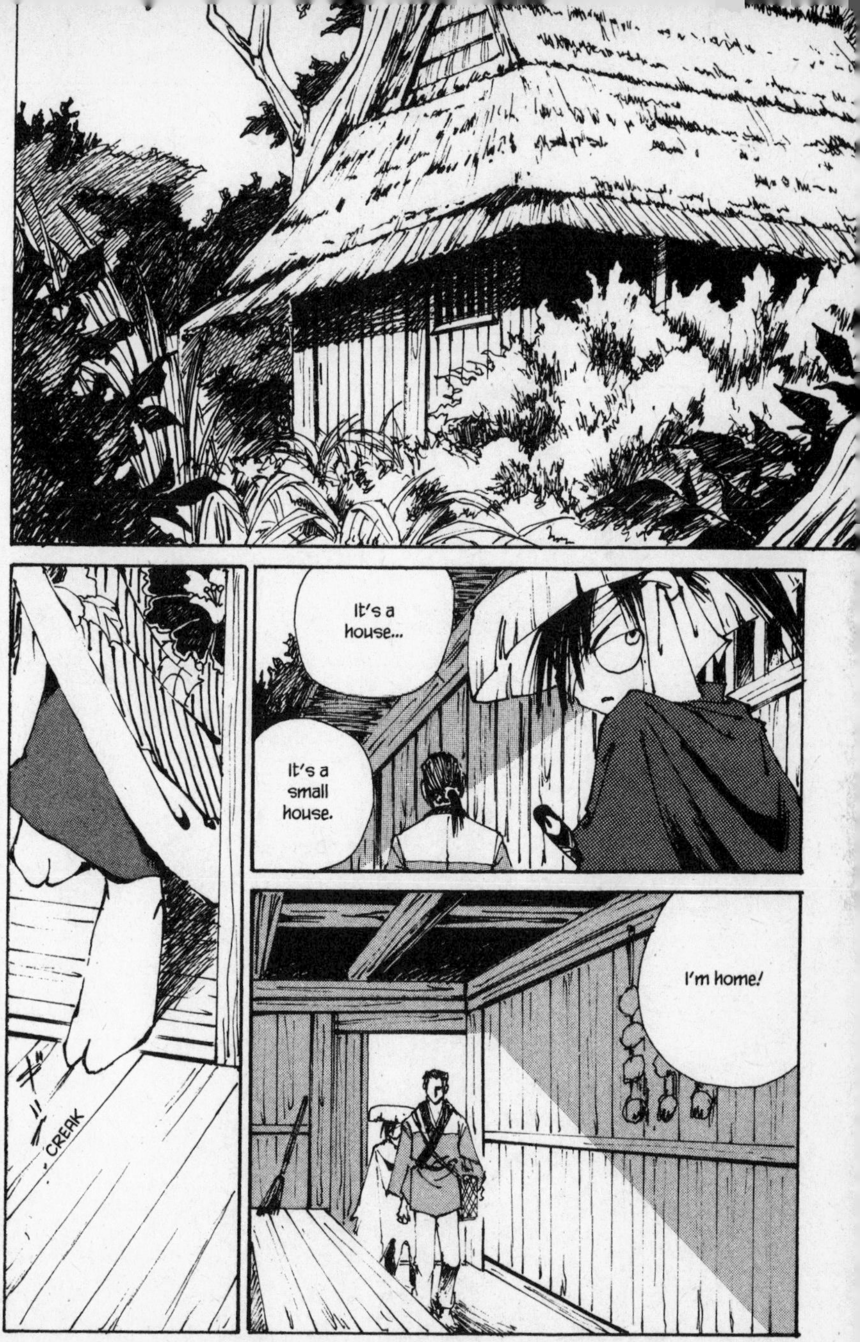
It's a house...
It's a small house.
I'm home!
CREAK

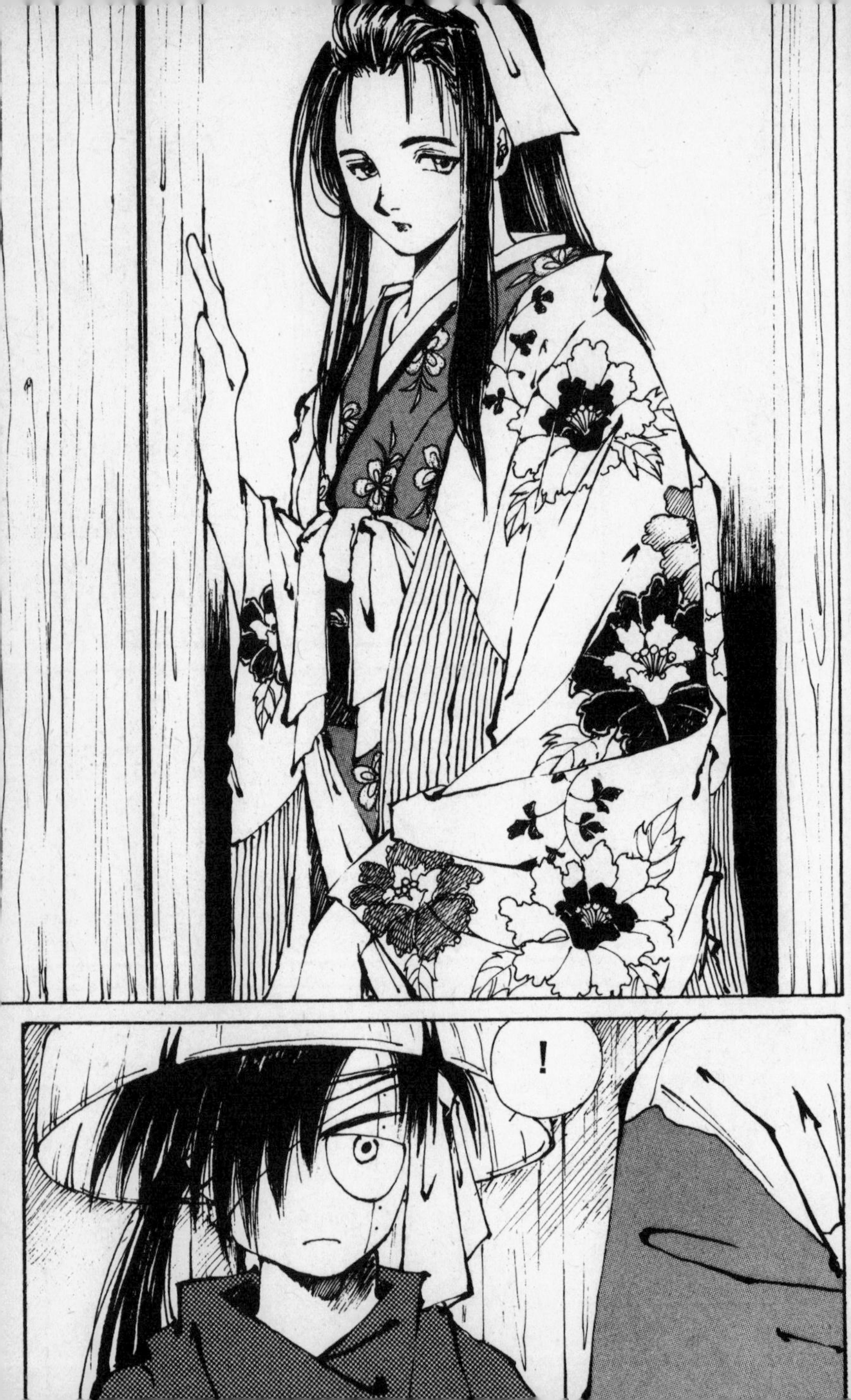
!

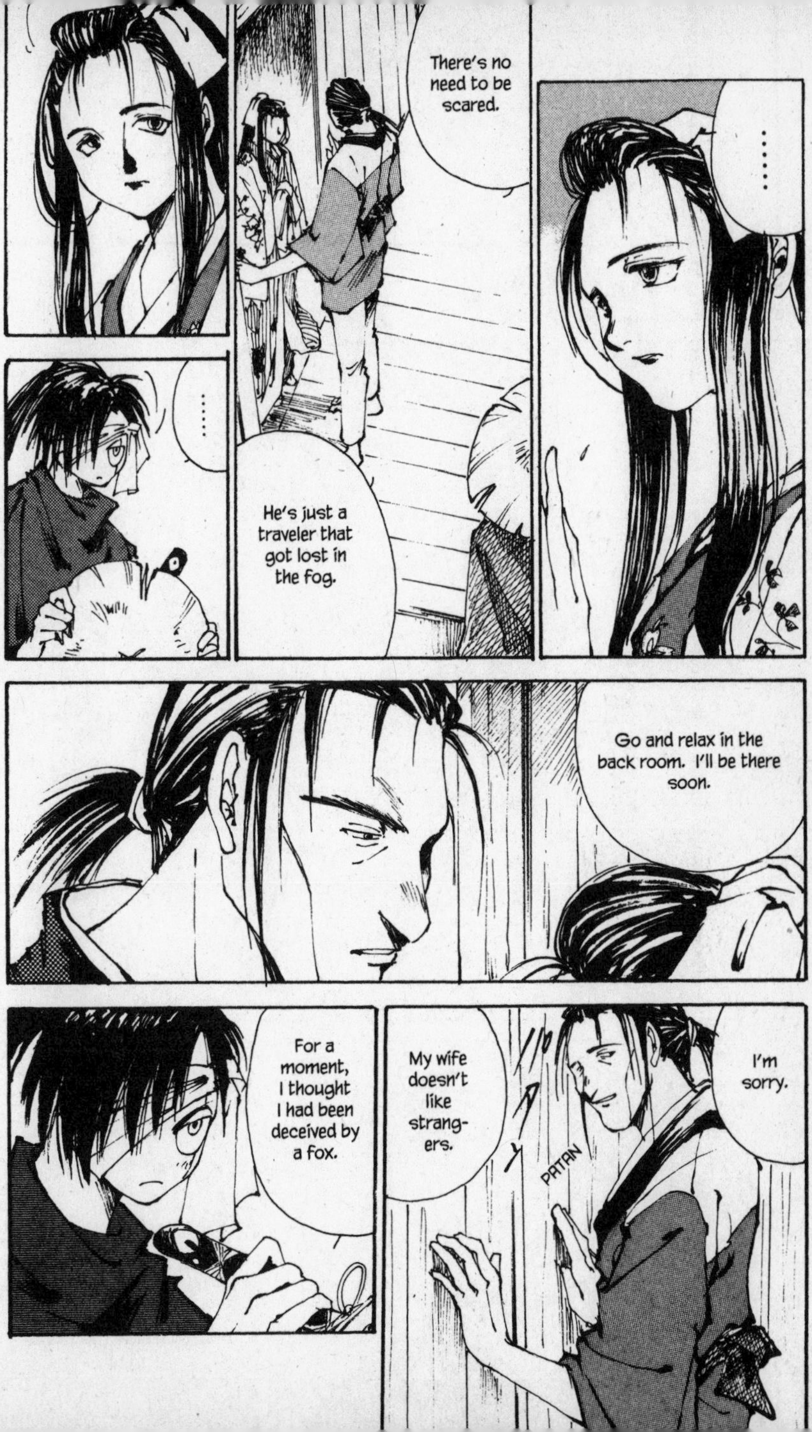
……
There's no need to be scared.
He's just a traveler that got lost in the fog.
……
Go and relax in the back room. I'll be there soon.
I'm sorry.
My wife doesn't like strangers.
PATAN
For a moment, I thought I had been deceived by a fox.

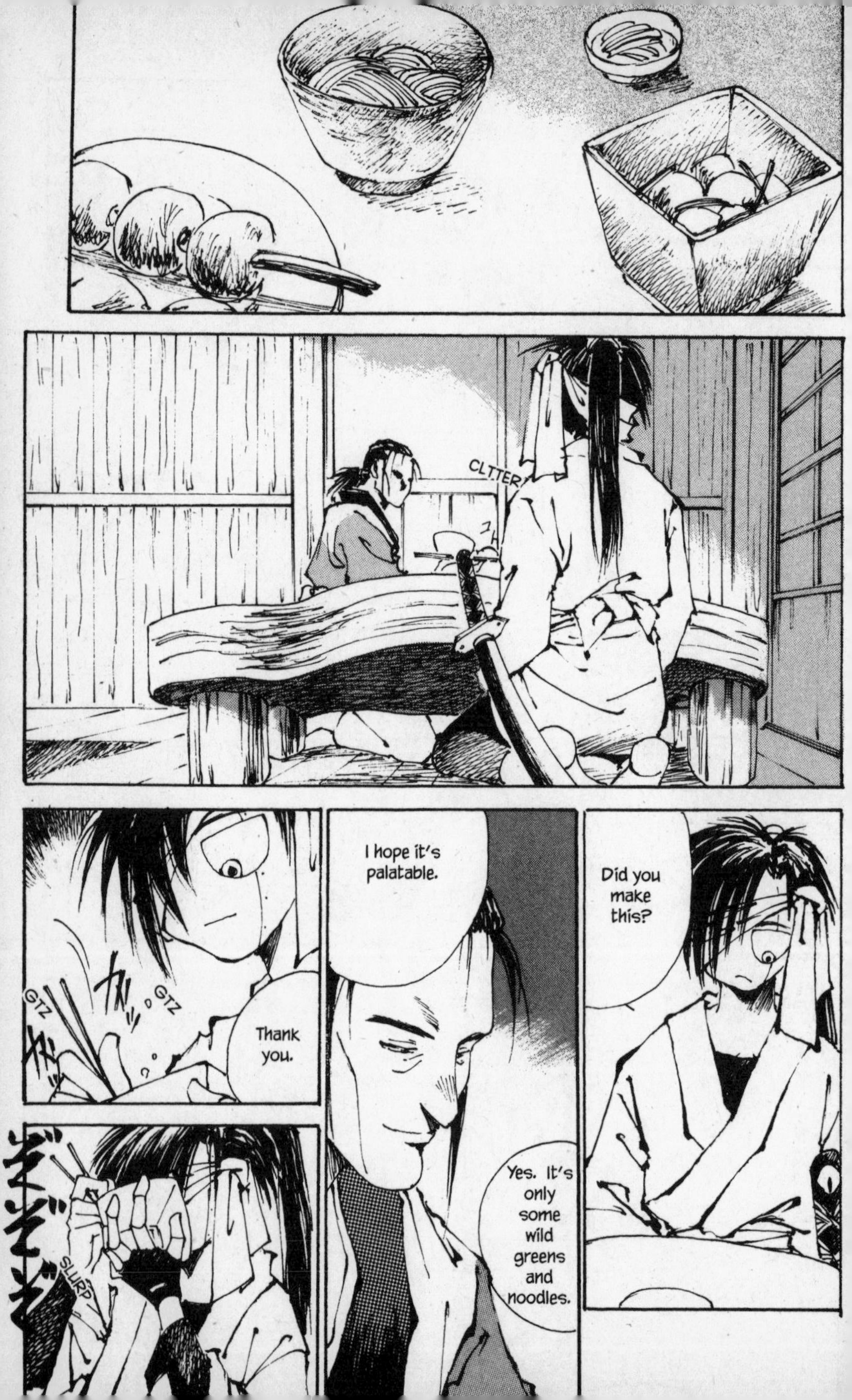
CLTTER
Did you make this?
I hope it's palatable.
Yes. It's only some wild greens and noodles.
GTZ
GTZ
Thank you.
SLURP

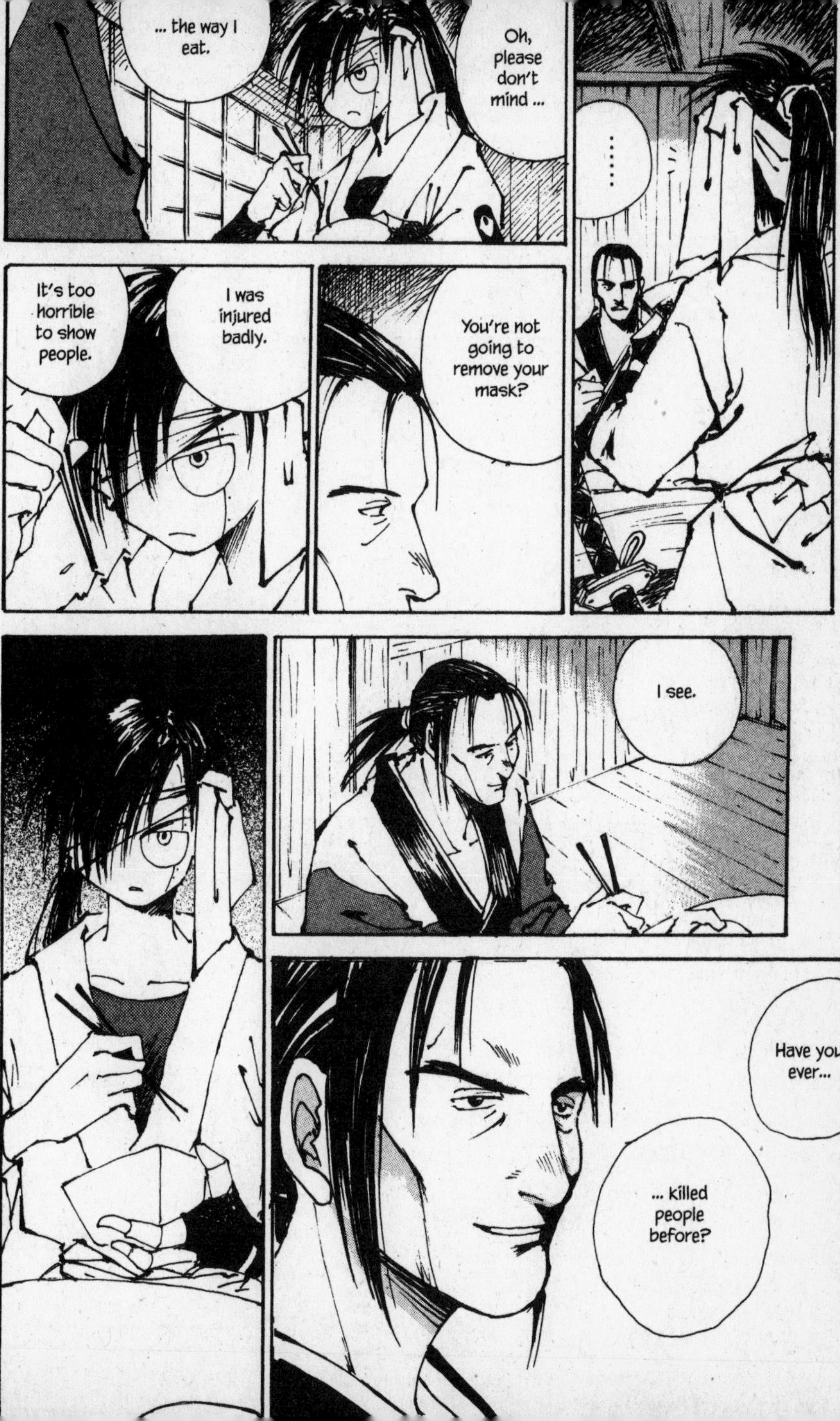
……
Oh, please don't mind ...
... the way I eat.
You're not going to remove your mask?
I was injured badly.
It's too horrible to show people.
I see.
Have you ever...
... killed people before?

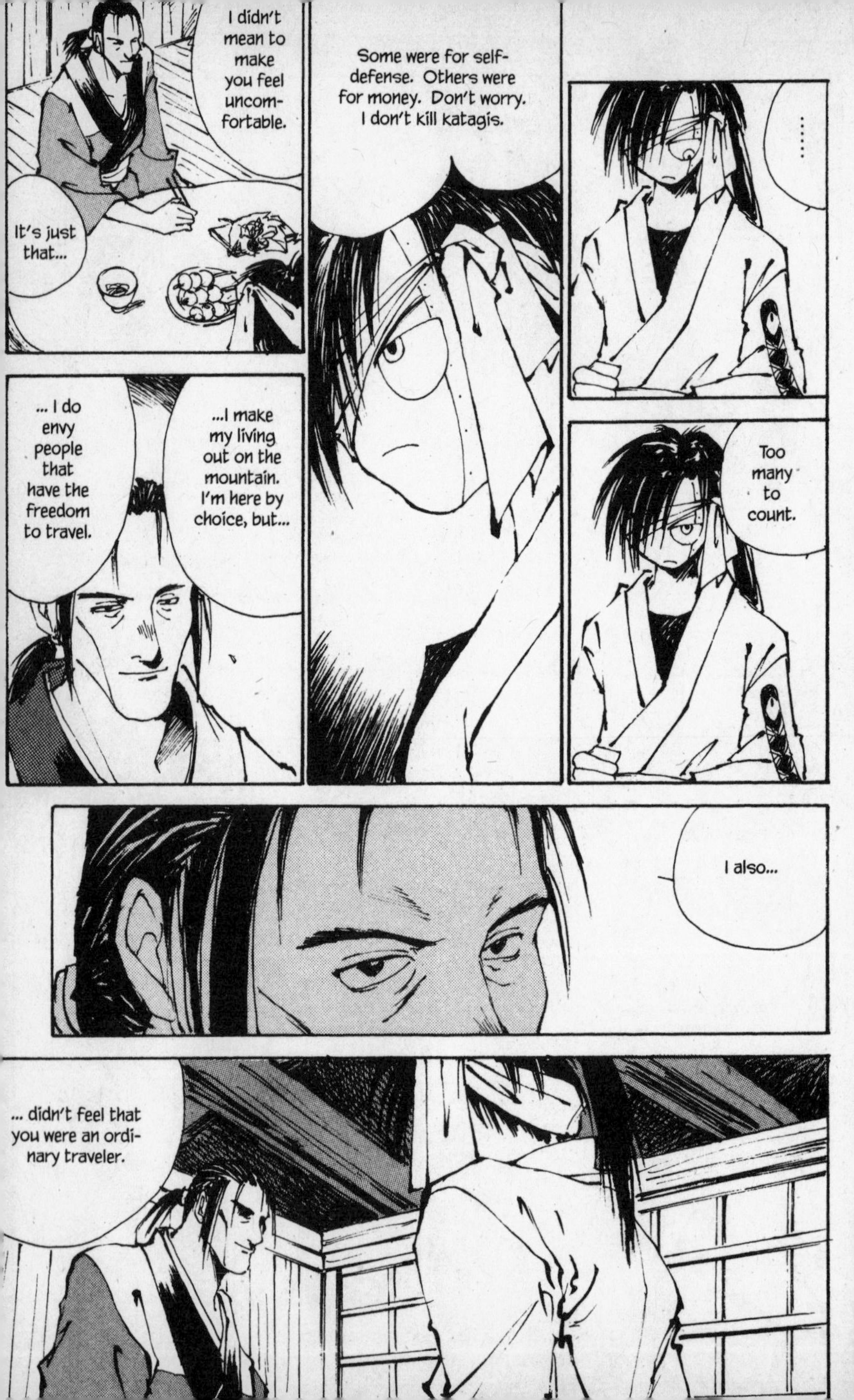
......
Too many to count.
Some were for self-defense. Others were for money. Don't worry. I don't kill katagis.
I didn't mean to make you feel uncomfortable.
It's just that...
...I make my living out on the mountain. I'm here by choice, but...
... I do envy people that have the freedom to travel.
I also...
... didn't feel that you were an ordinary traveler.

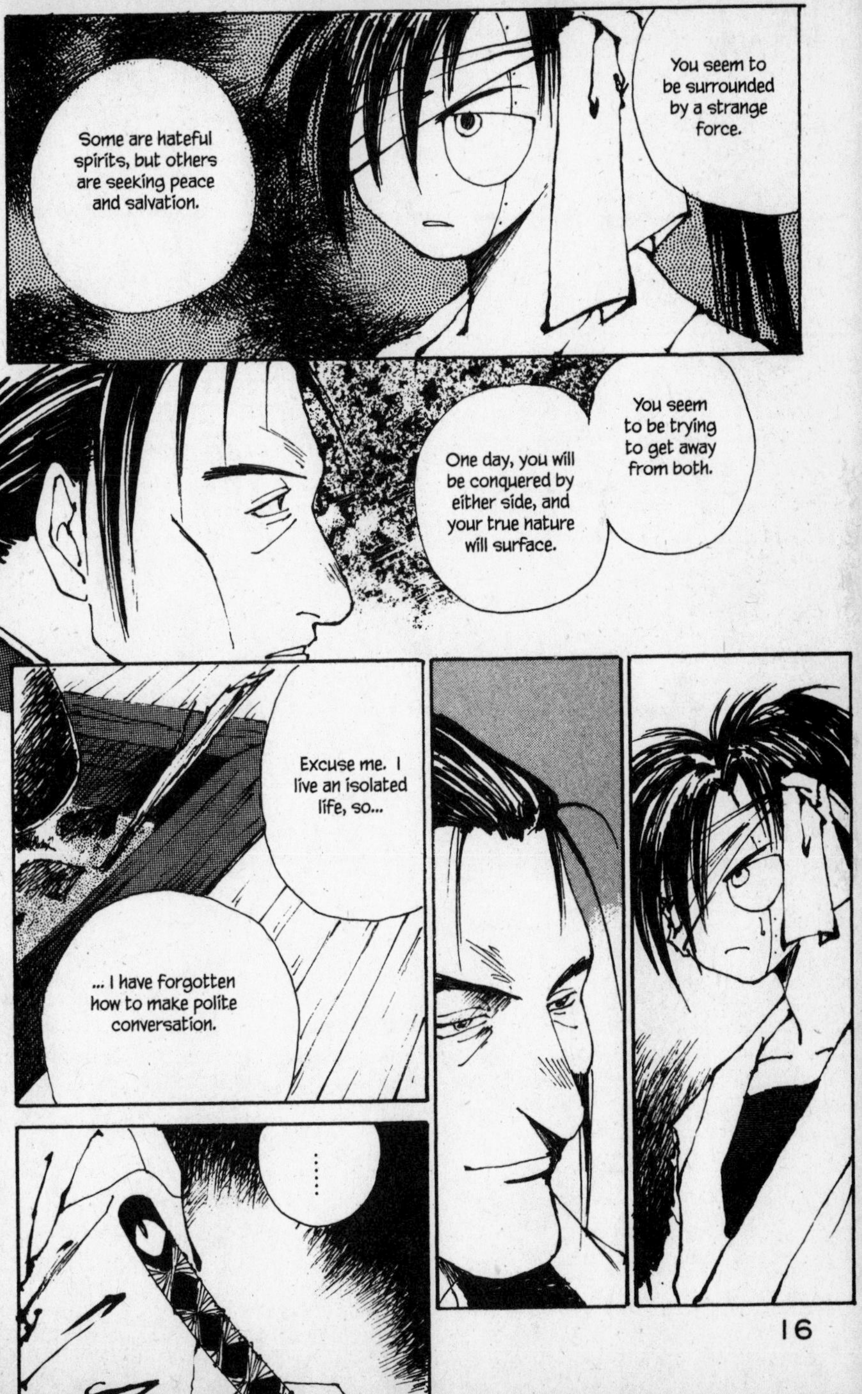
You seem to be surrounded by a strange force.
Some are hateful spirits, but others are seeking peace and salvation.
You seem to be trying to get away from both.
One day, you will be conquered by either side, and your true nature will surface.
Excuse me. I live an isolated life, so...
... I have forgotten how to make polite conversation.
......

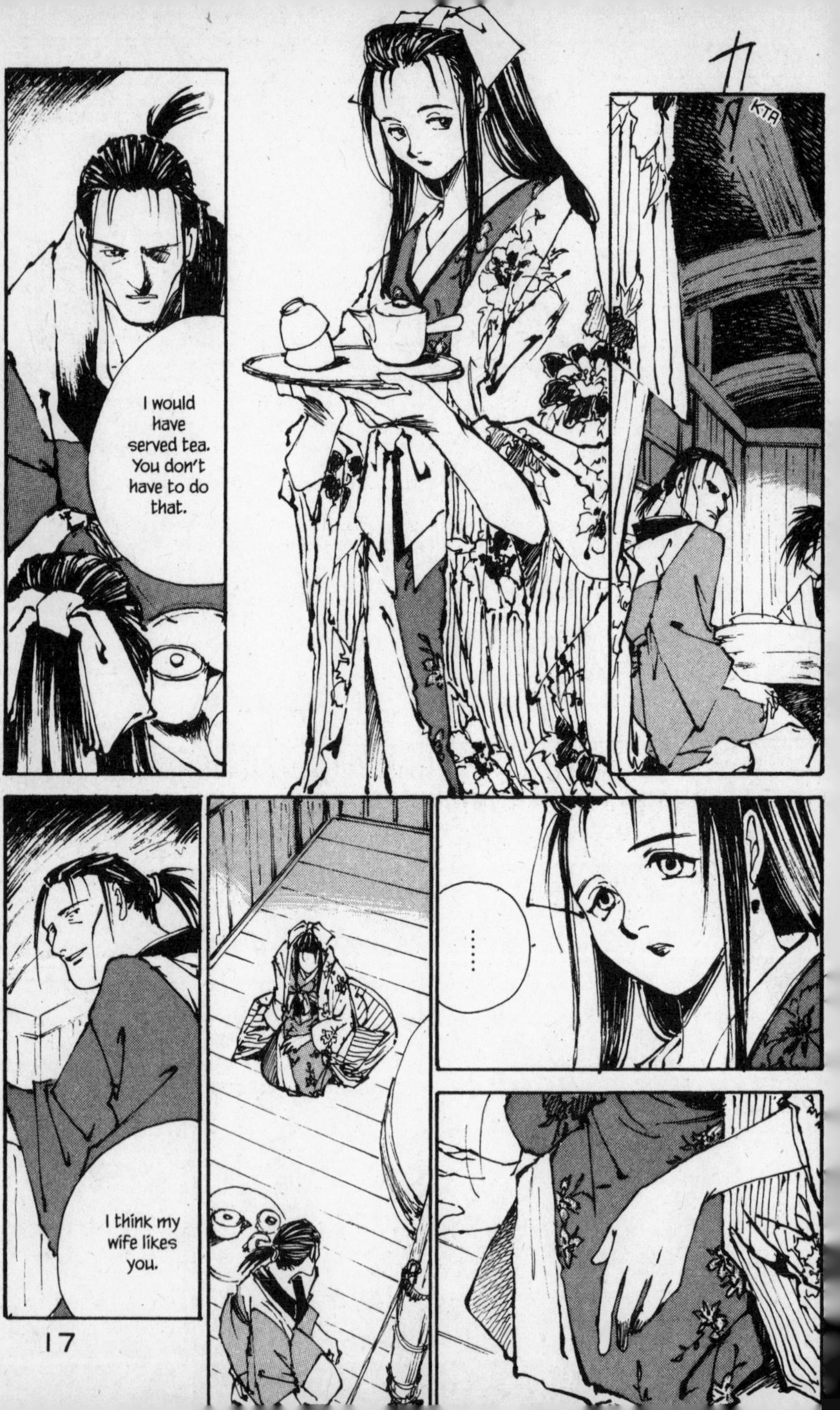
カ
KTA
I would have served tea. You don't have to do that.
......
I think my wife likes you.

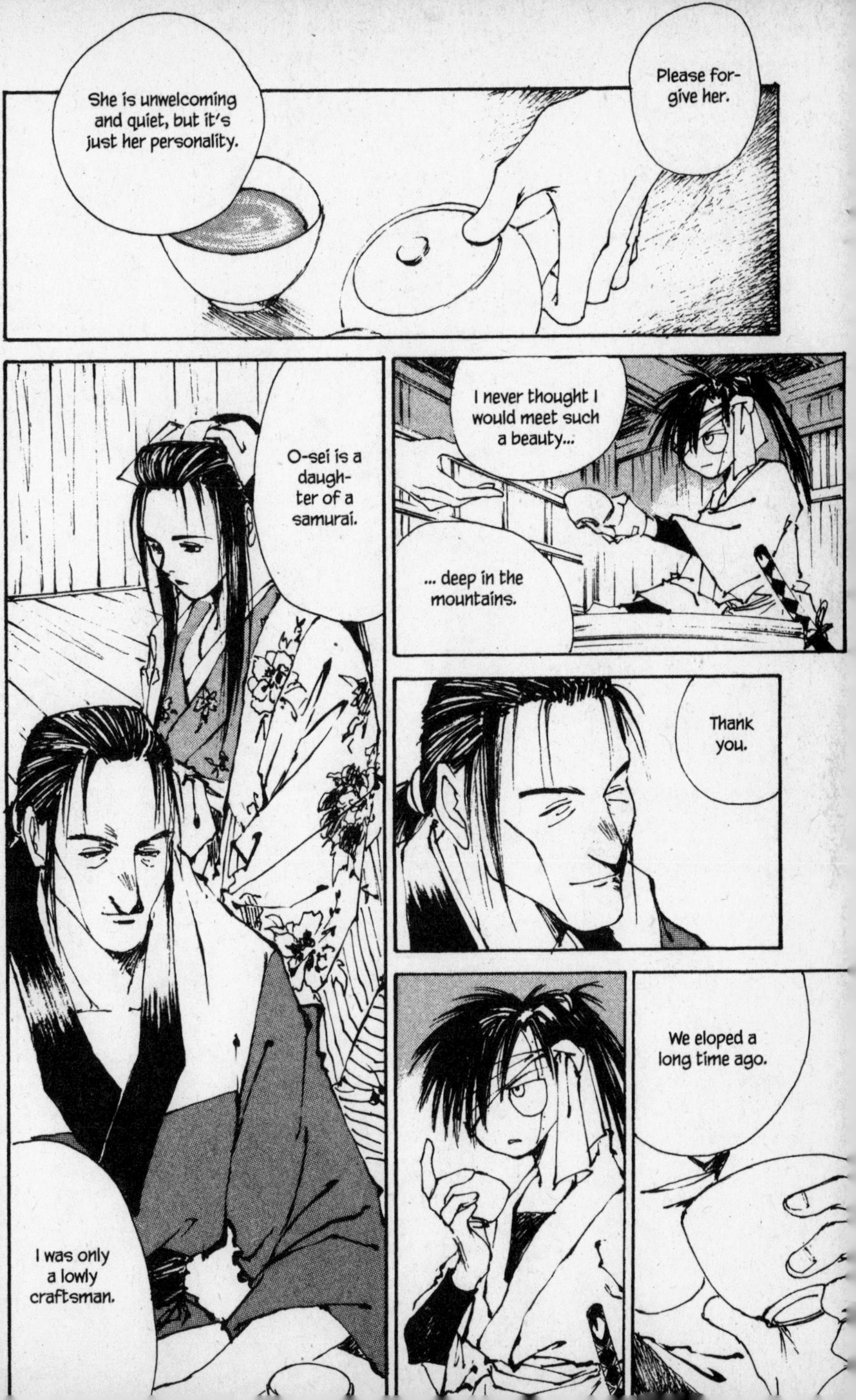
Please forgive her.
She is unwelcoming and quiet, but it's just her personality.
I never thought I would meet such a beauty...
... deep in the mountains.
Thank you.
We eloped a long time ago.
O-sei is a daughter of a samurai.
I was only a lowly craftsman.

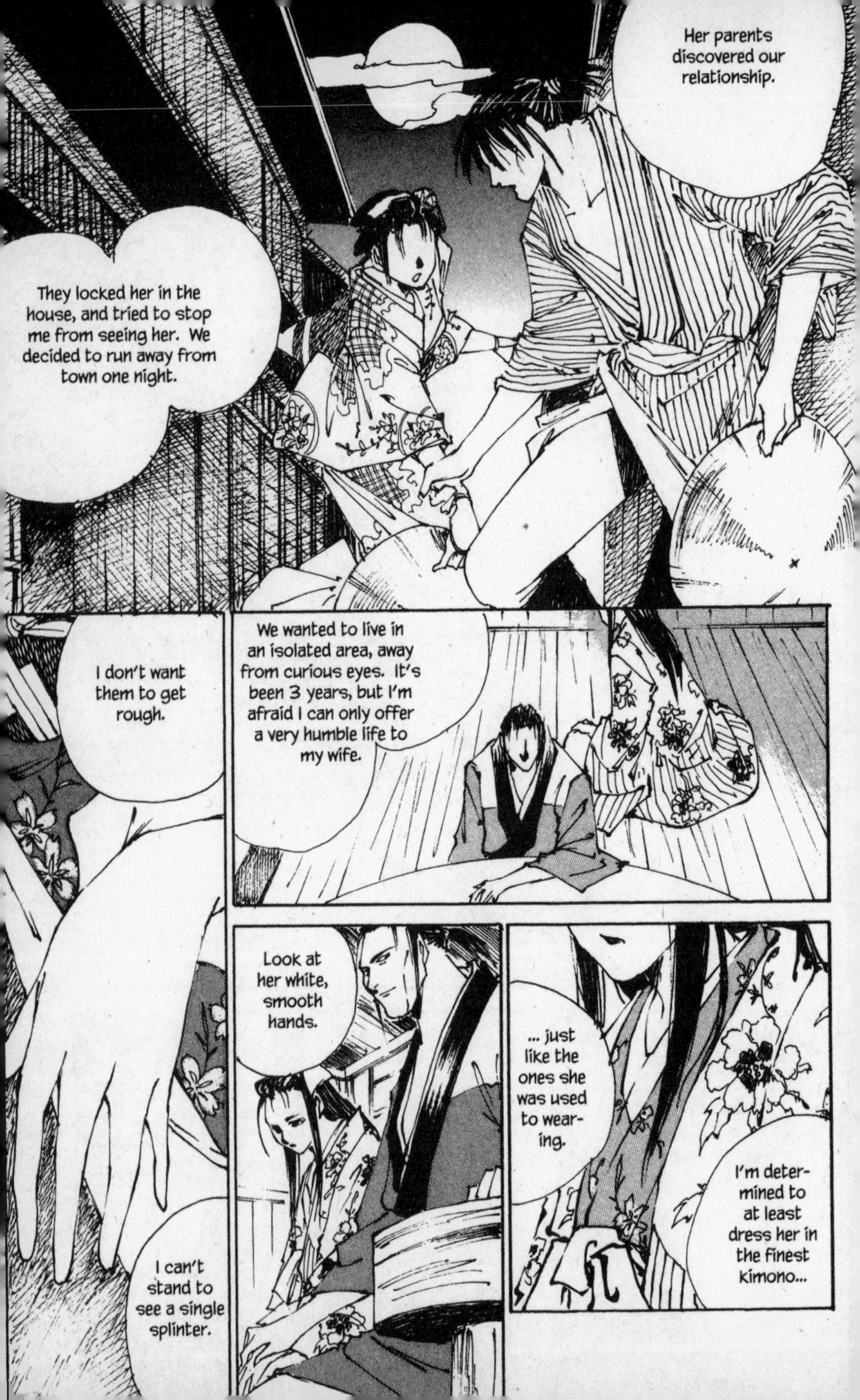
Her parents discovered our relationship.
They locked her in the house, and tried to stop me from seeing her. We decided to run away from town one night.
We wanted to live in an isolated area, away from curious eyes. It's been 3 years, but I'm afraid I can only offer a very humble life to my wife.
I'm determined to at least dress her in the finest kimono...
... just like the ones she was used to wear-ing.
Look at her white, smooth hands.
I don't want them to get rough.
I can't stand to see a single splinter.

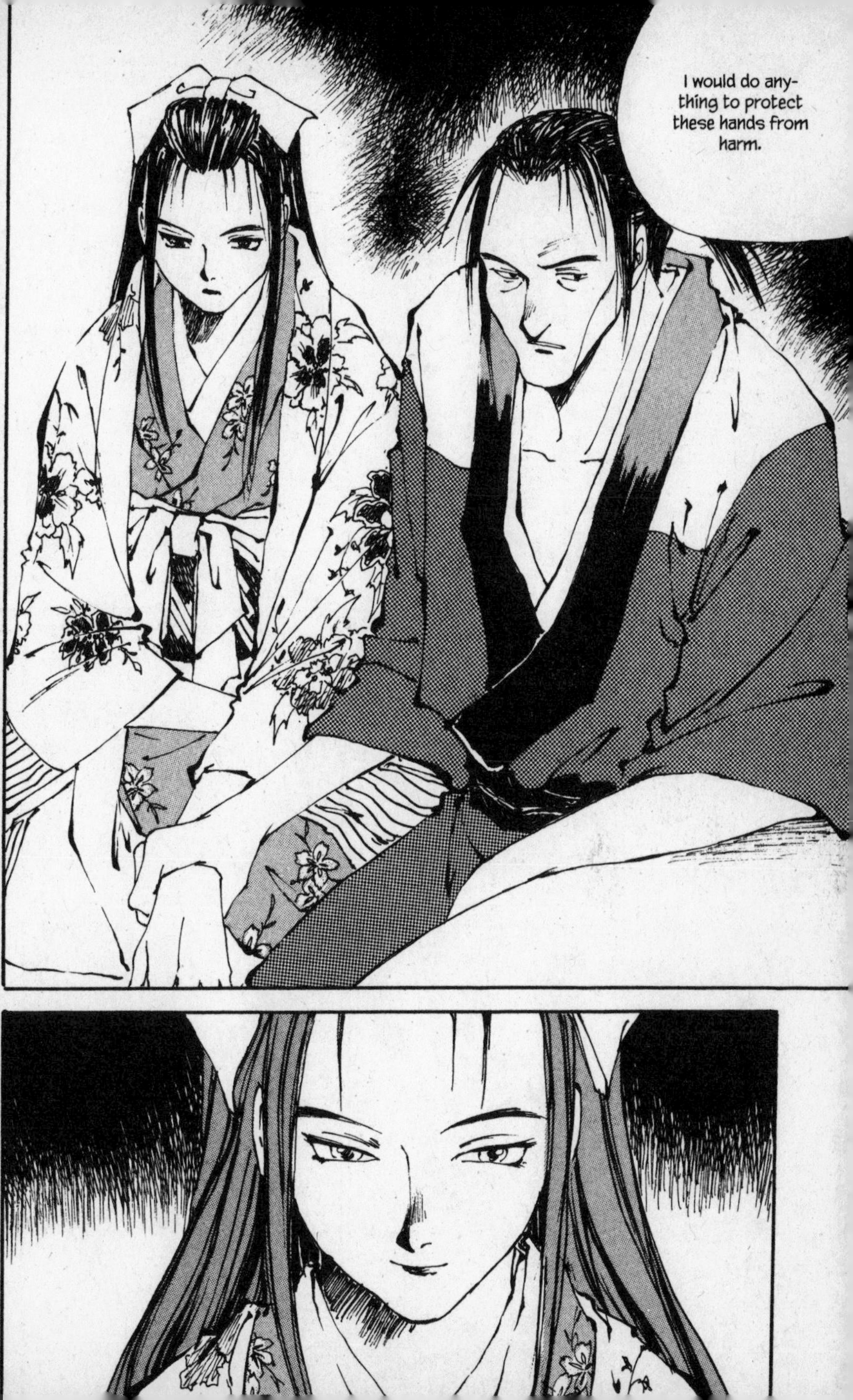
I would do anything to protect these hands from harm.

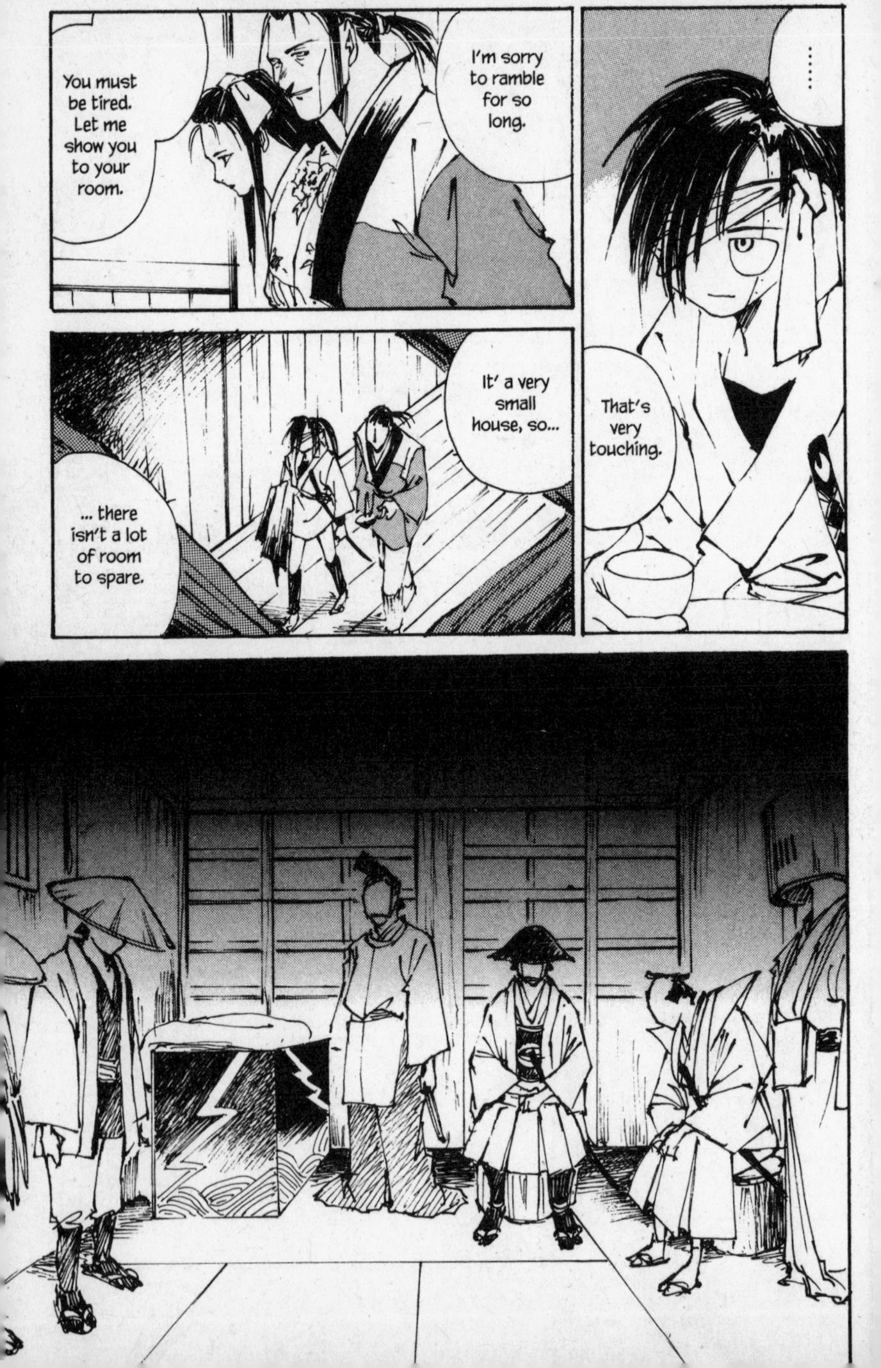
……
That's very touching.
I'm sorry to ramble for so long.
You must be tired. Let me show you to your room.
It' a very small house, so...
... there isn't a lot of room to spare.

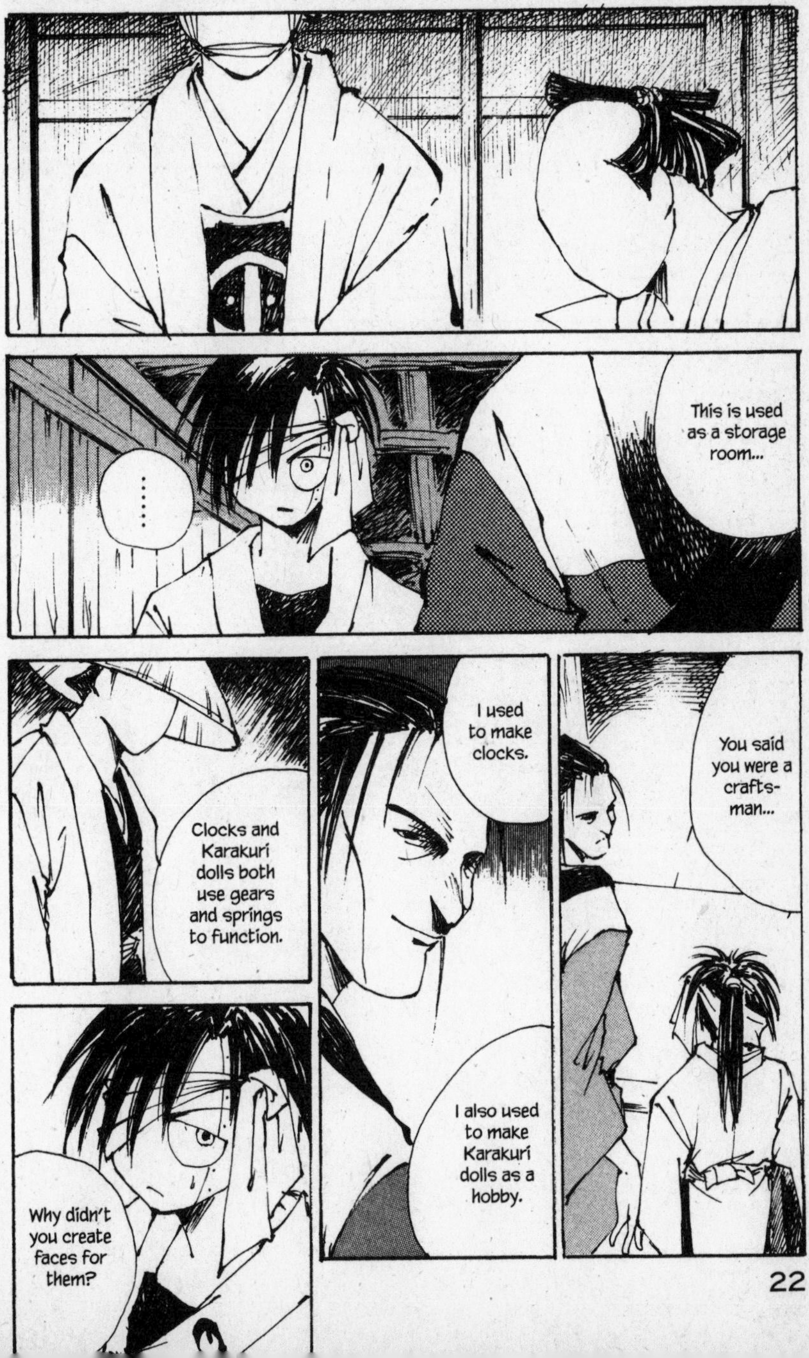
This is used as a storage room...
......
You said you were a crafts-man...
I used to make clocks.
I also used to make Karakuri dolls as a hobby.
Clocks and Karakuri dolls both use gears and springs to function.
Why didn't you create faces for them?

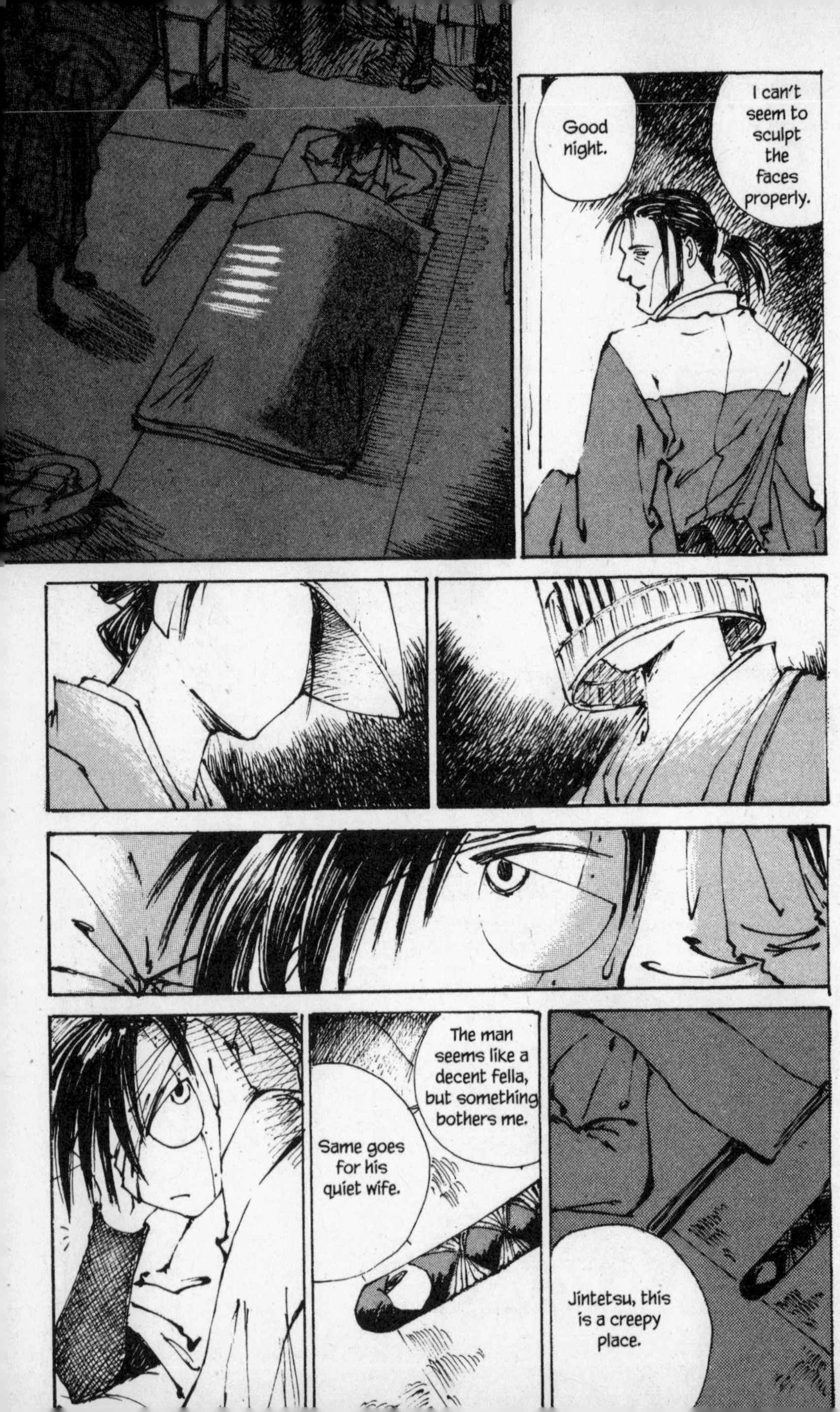
I can't seem to sculpt the faces properly.
Good night.
Jintetsu, this is a creepy place.
The man seems like a decent fella, but something bothers me.
Same goes for his quiet wife.

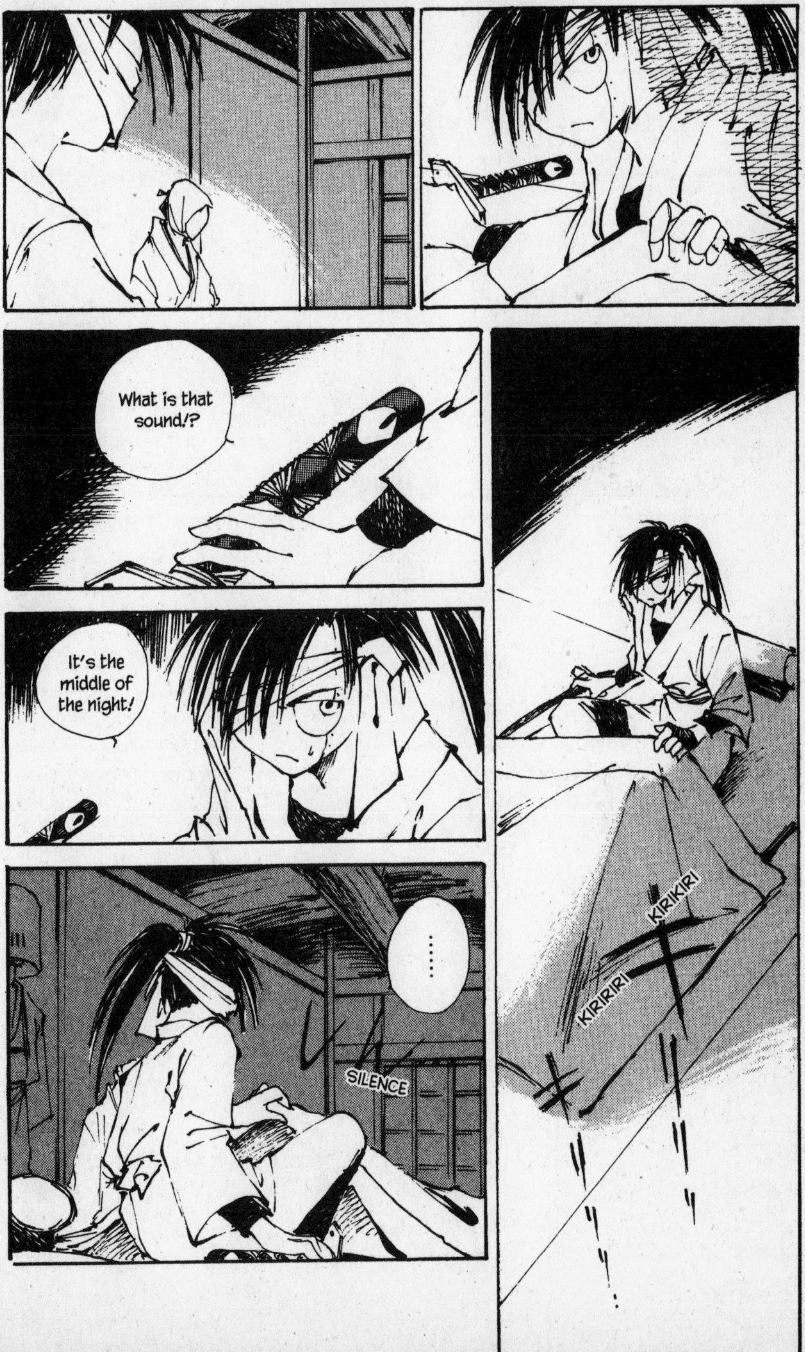
KIRIKIRI
KIRIRIRI
What is that sound!?
It's the middle of the night!
......
SILENCE

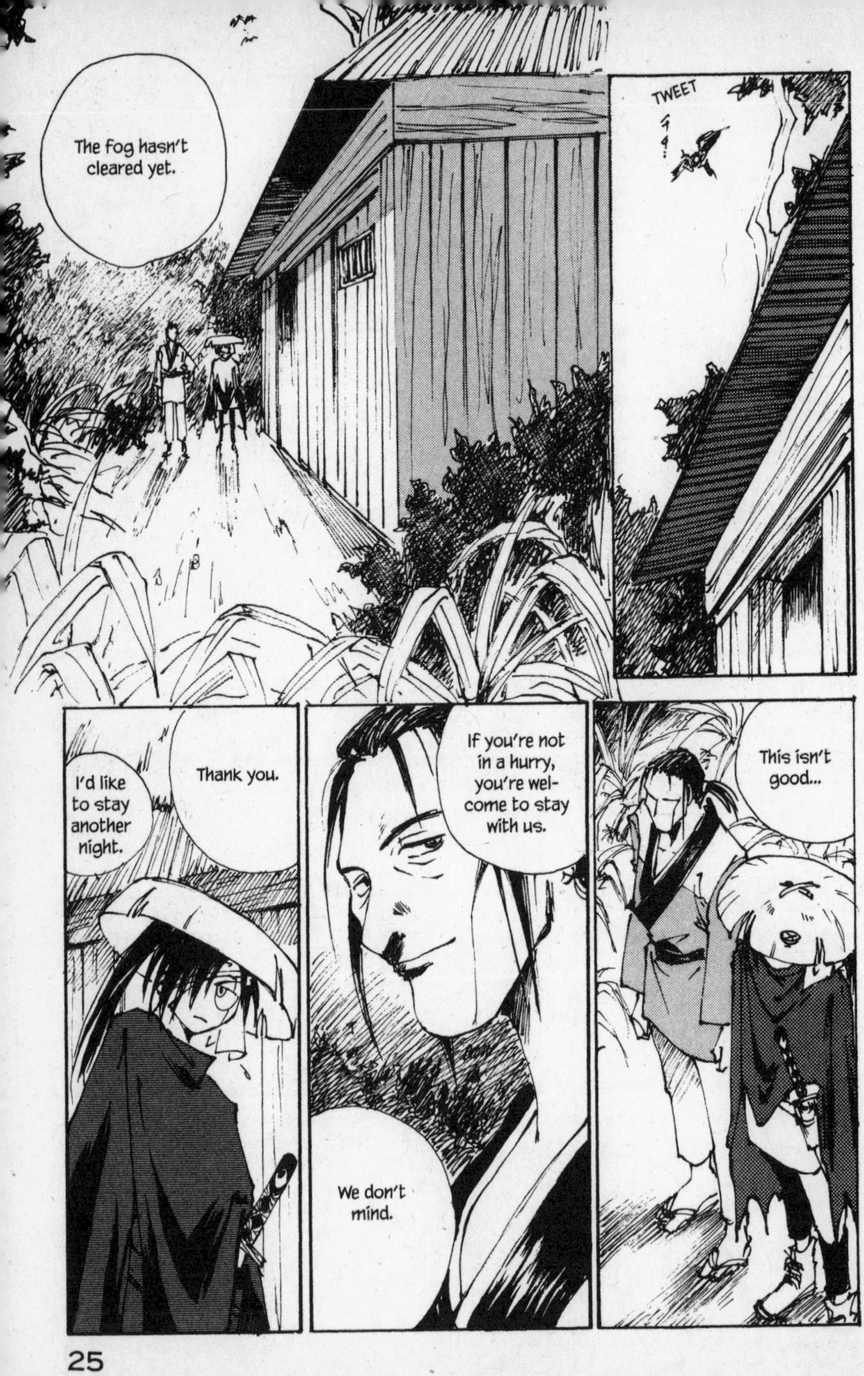
TWEET
The fog hasn't cleared yet.
This isn't good...
If you're not in a hurry, you're wel-come to stay with us.
We don't mind.
Thank you.
I'd like to stay another night.

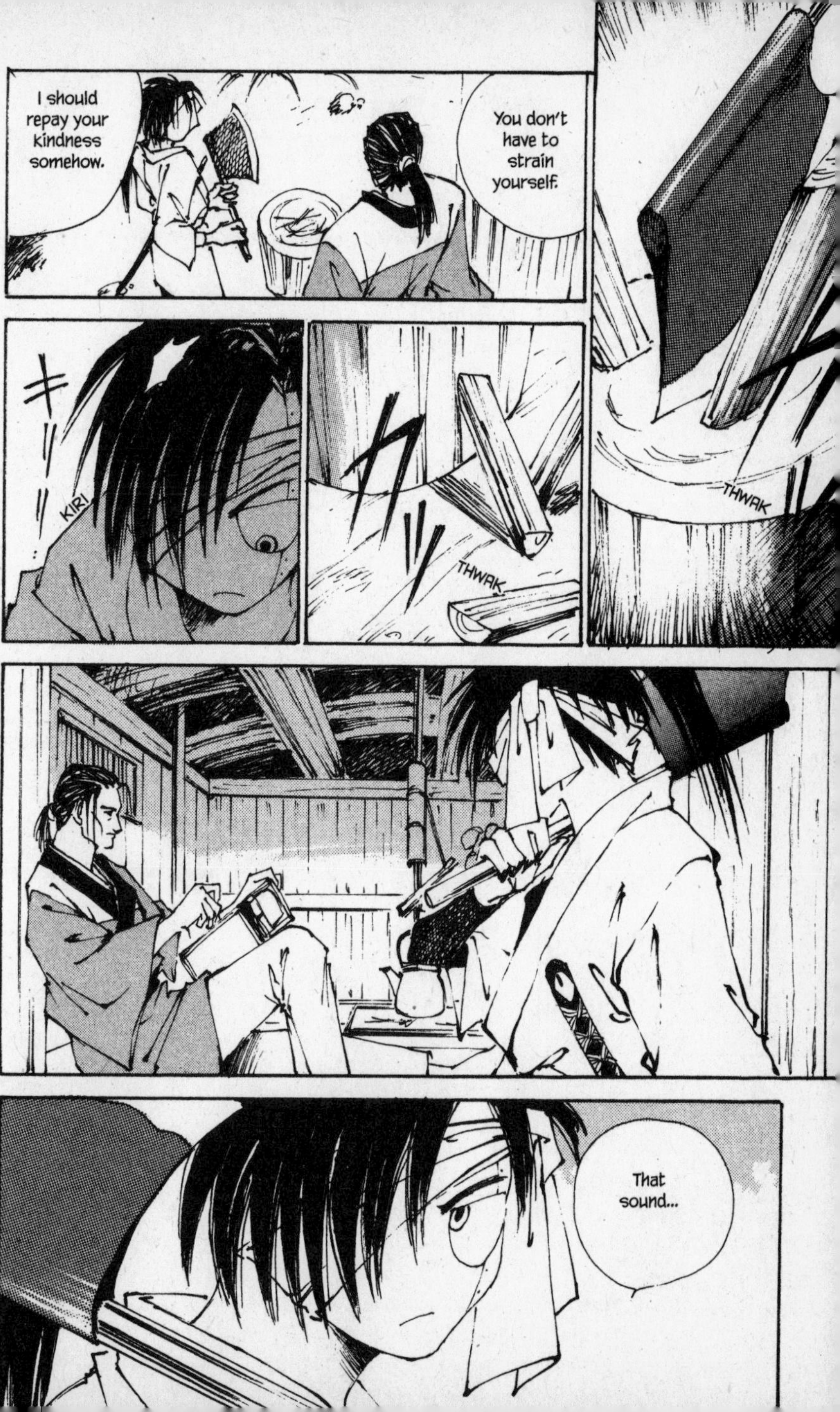
THWAK
You don't have to strain yourself.
I should repay your kindness somehow.
THWAK
KIRI
That sound...

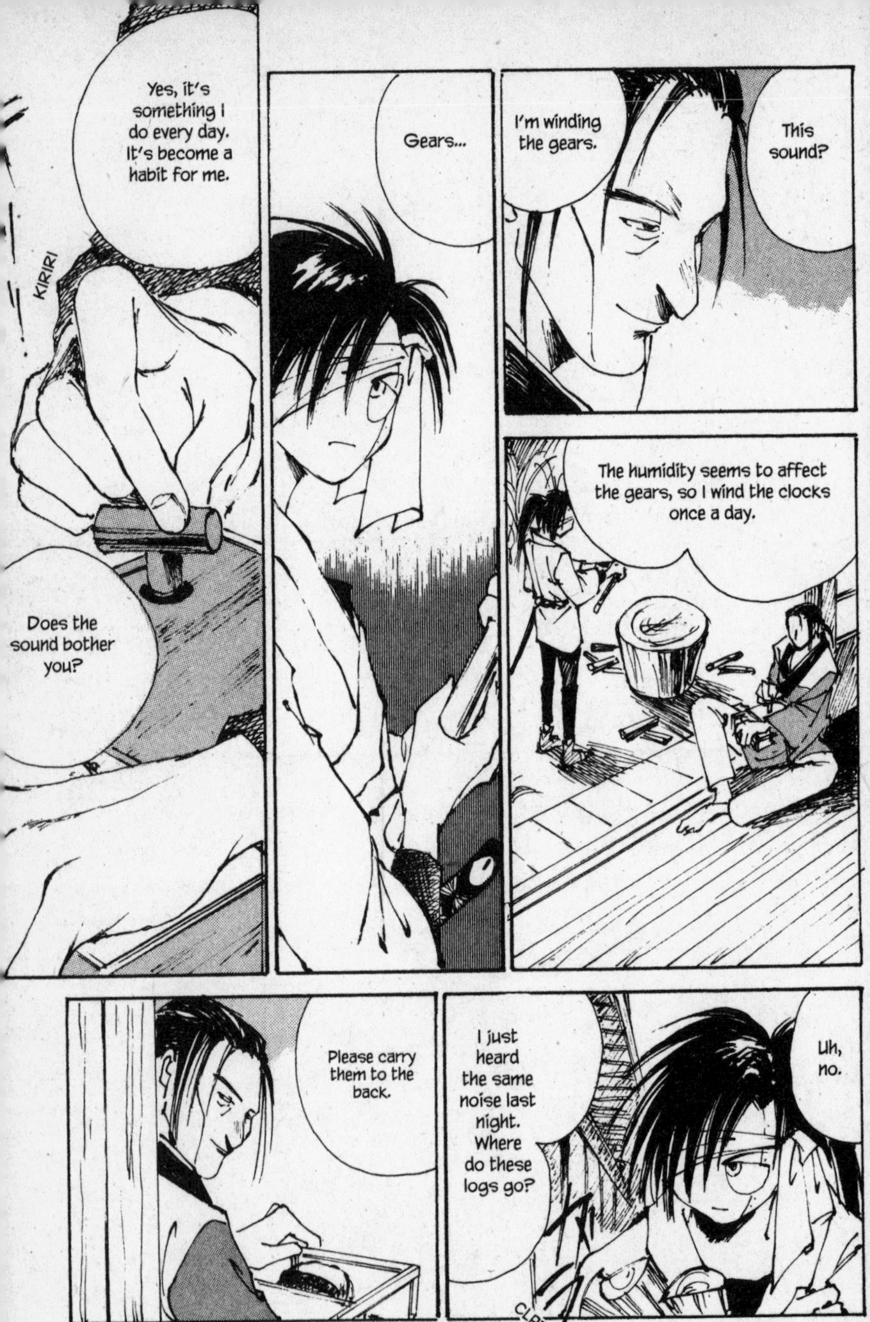
This sound?
I'm winding the gears.
The humidity seems to affect the gears, so I wind the clocks once a day.
Gears...
Yes, it's something I do every day. It's become a habit for me.
KIRIRI
Does the sound bother you?
Uh, no.
I just heard the same noise last night. Where do these logs go?
CLATTER
Please carry them to the back.

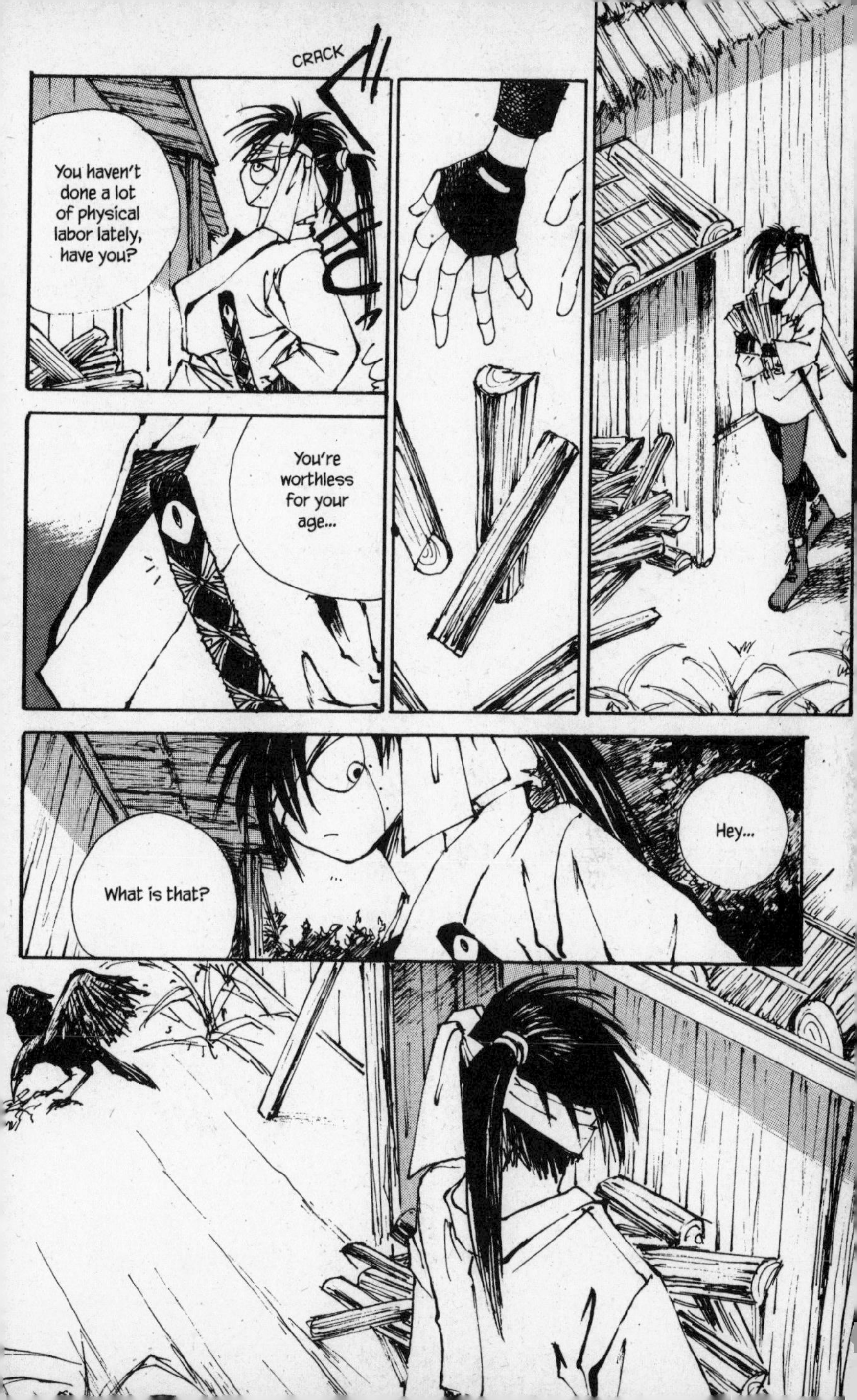
CRACK
You haven't done a lot of physical labor lately, have you?
You're worthless for your age...
Hey...
What is that?

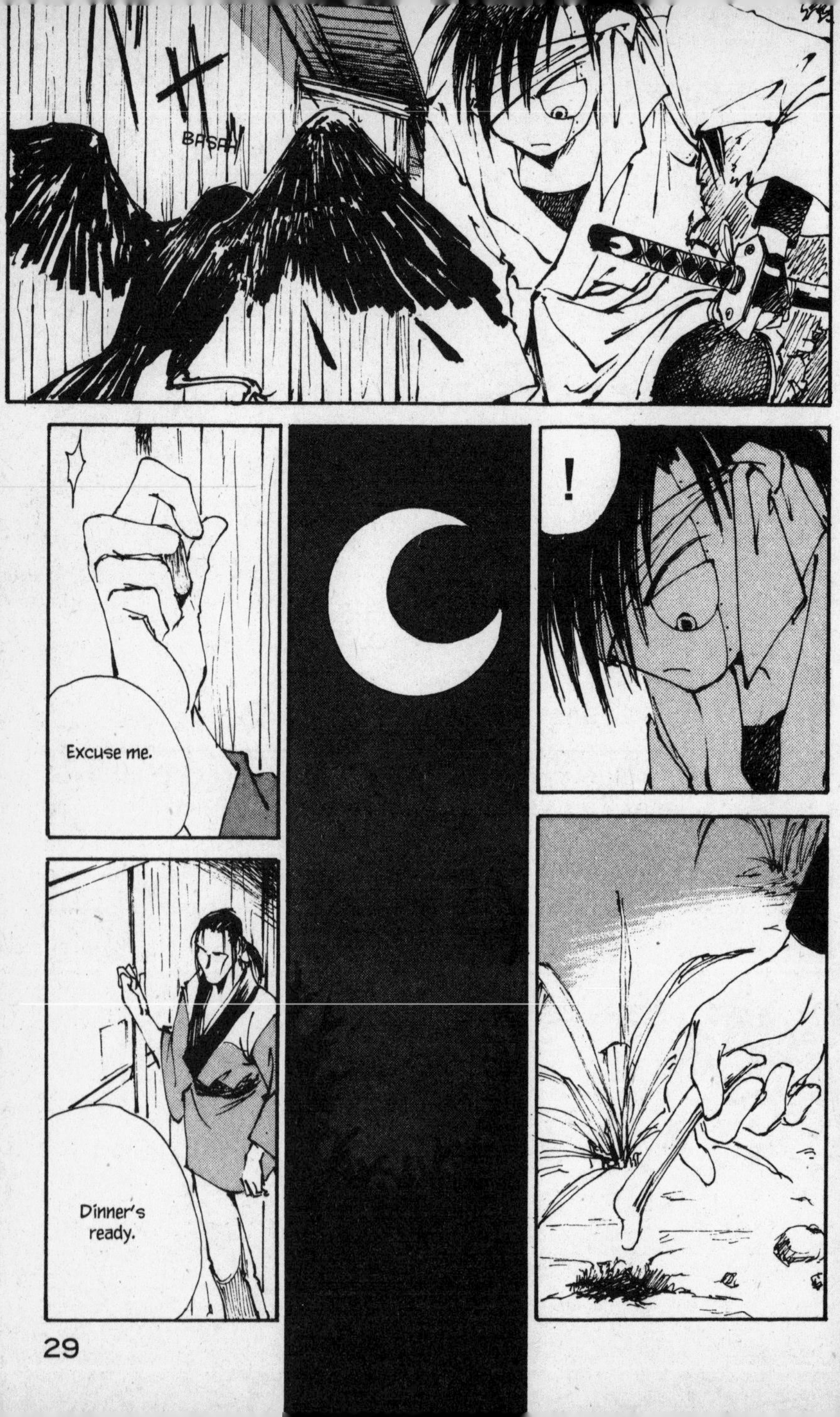
BASAH
!
Excuse me.
Dinner's ready.

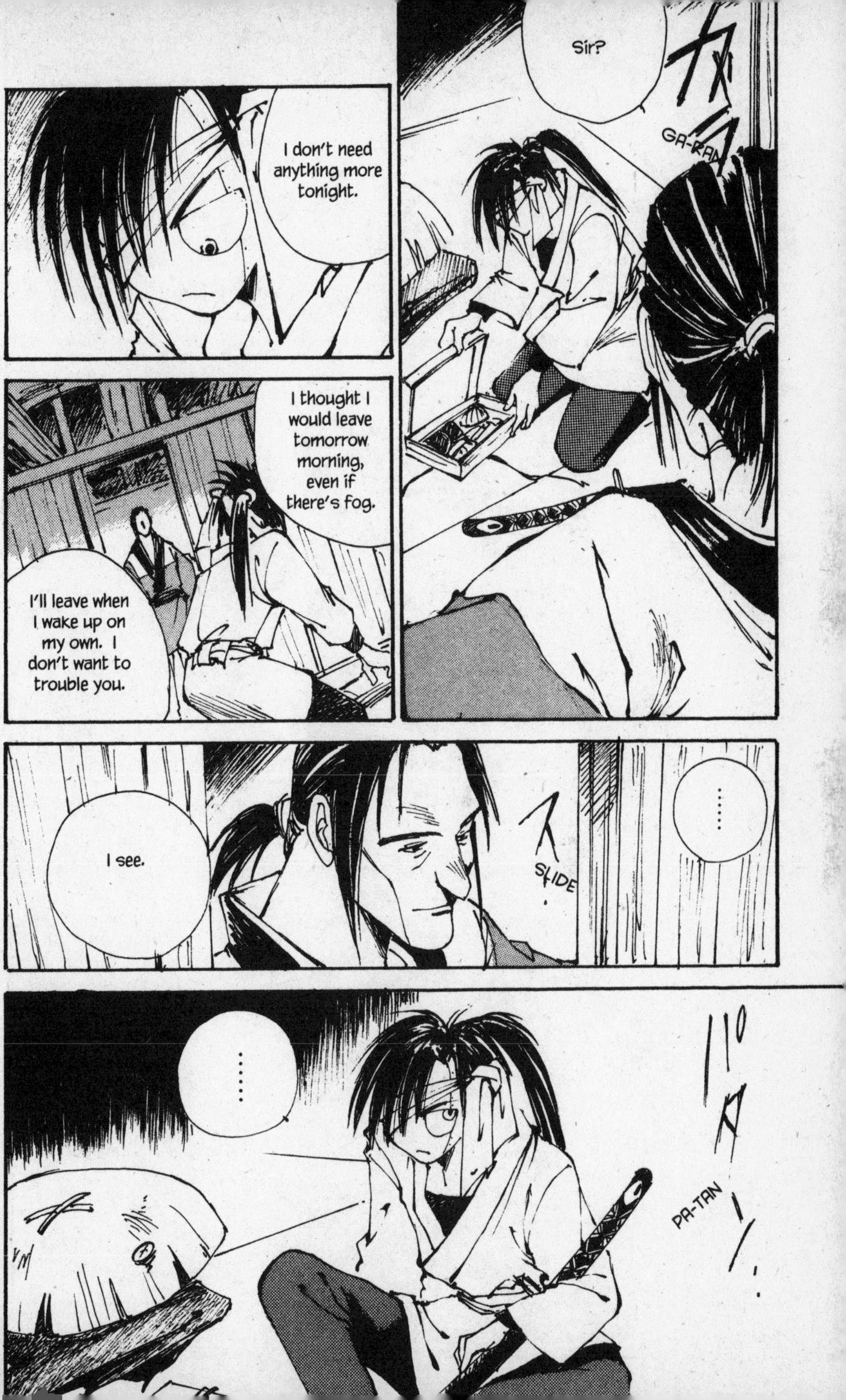
Sir?
GA-RAN
I don't need anything more tonight.
I thought I would leave tomorrow morning, even if there's fog.
I'll leave when I wake up on my own. I don't want to trouble you.
......
SLIDE
I see.
......
PA-TAN

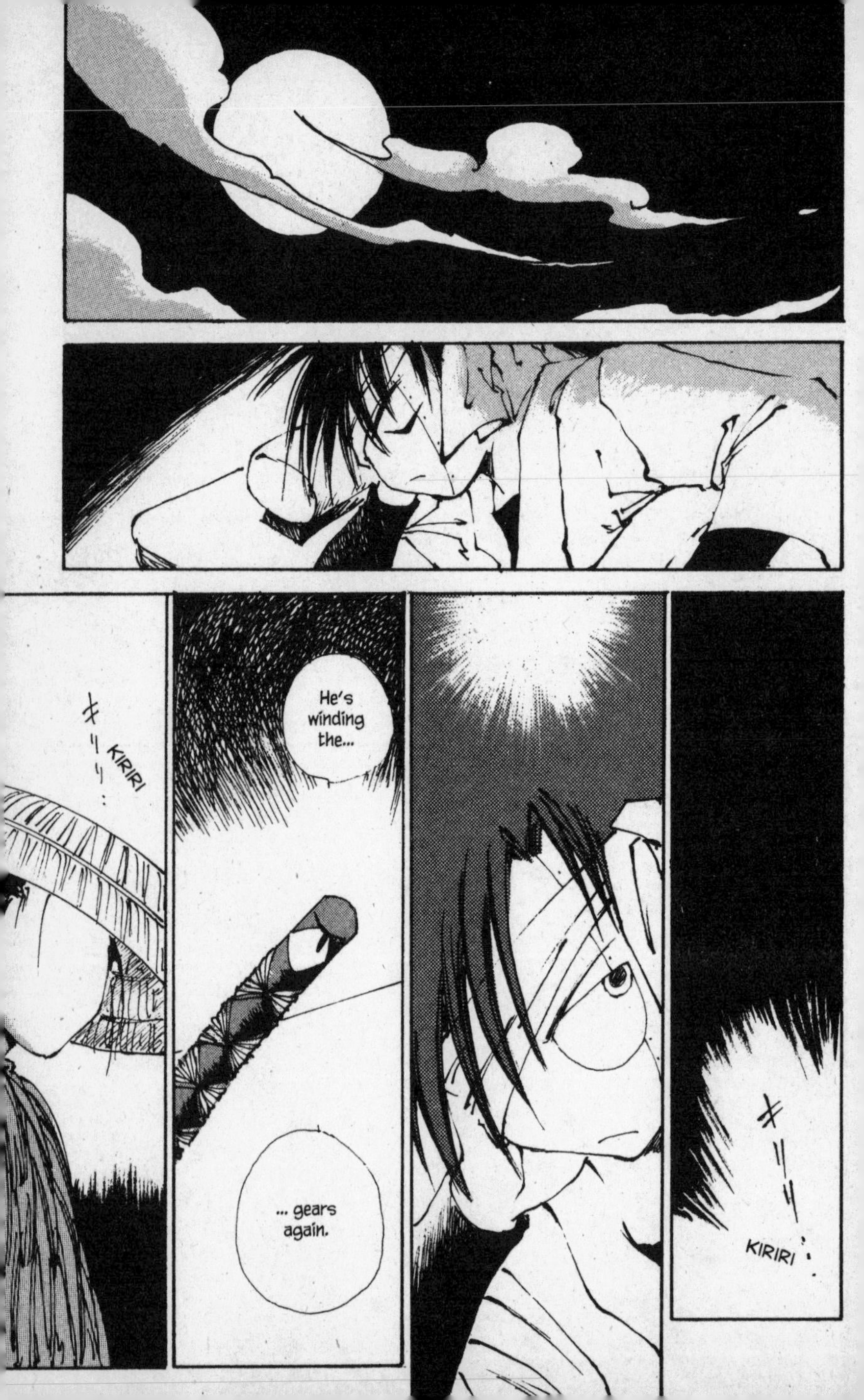
キリリ
KIRIRI
He's winding the...
... gears again.
キリリ
KIRIRI

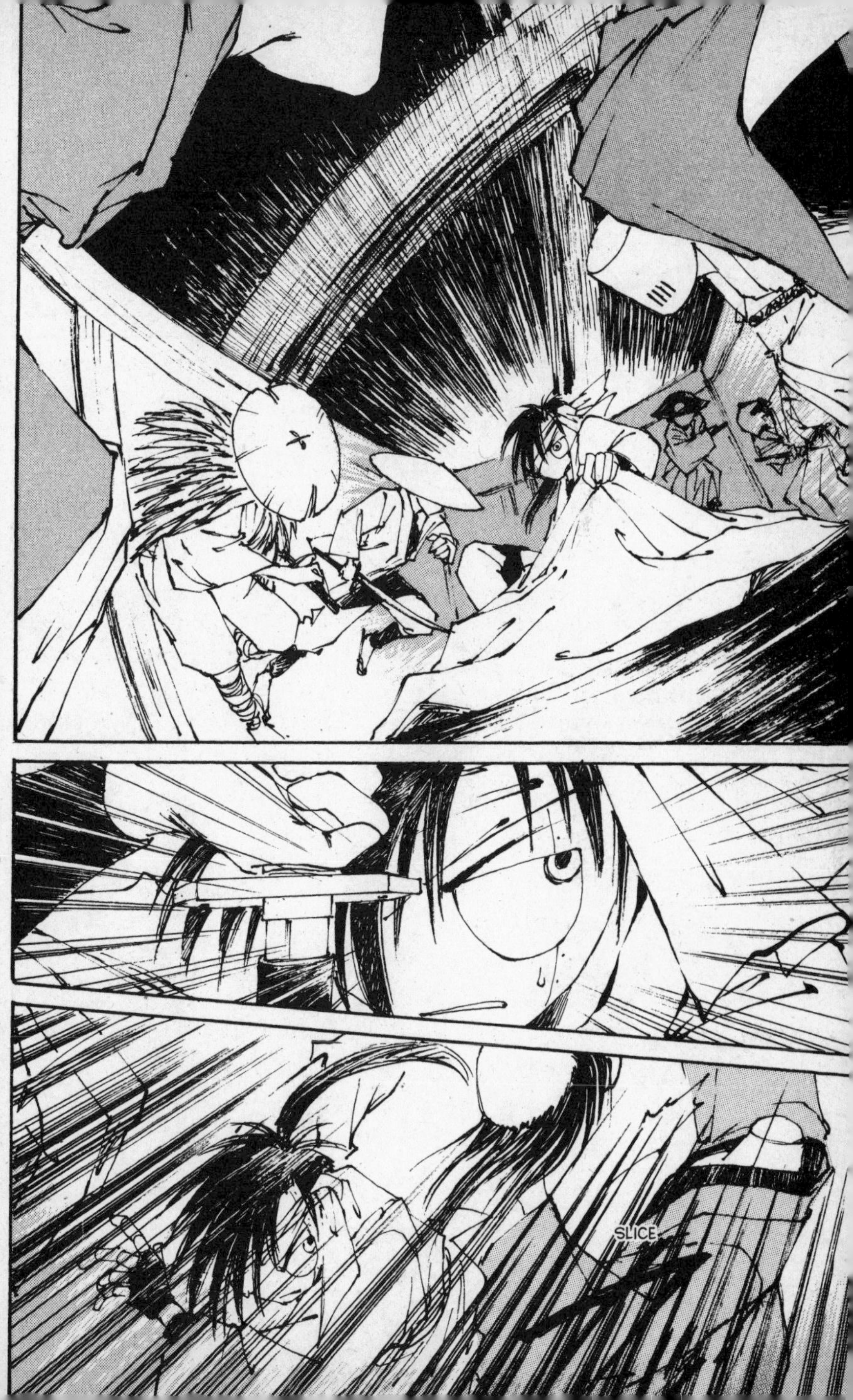
SLICE

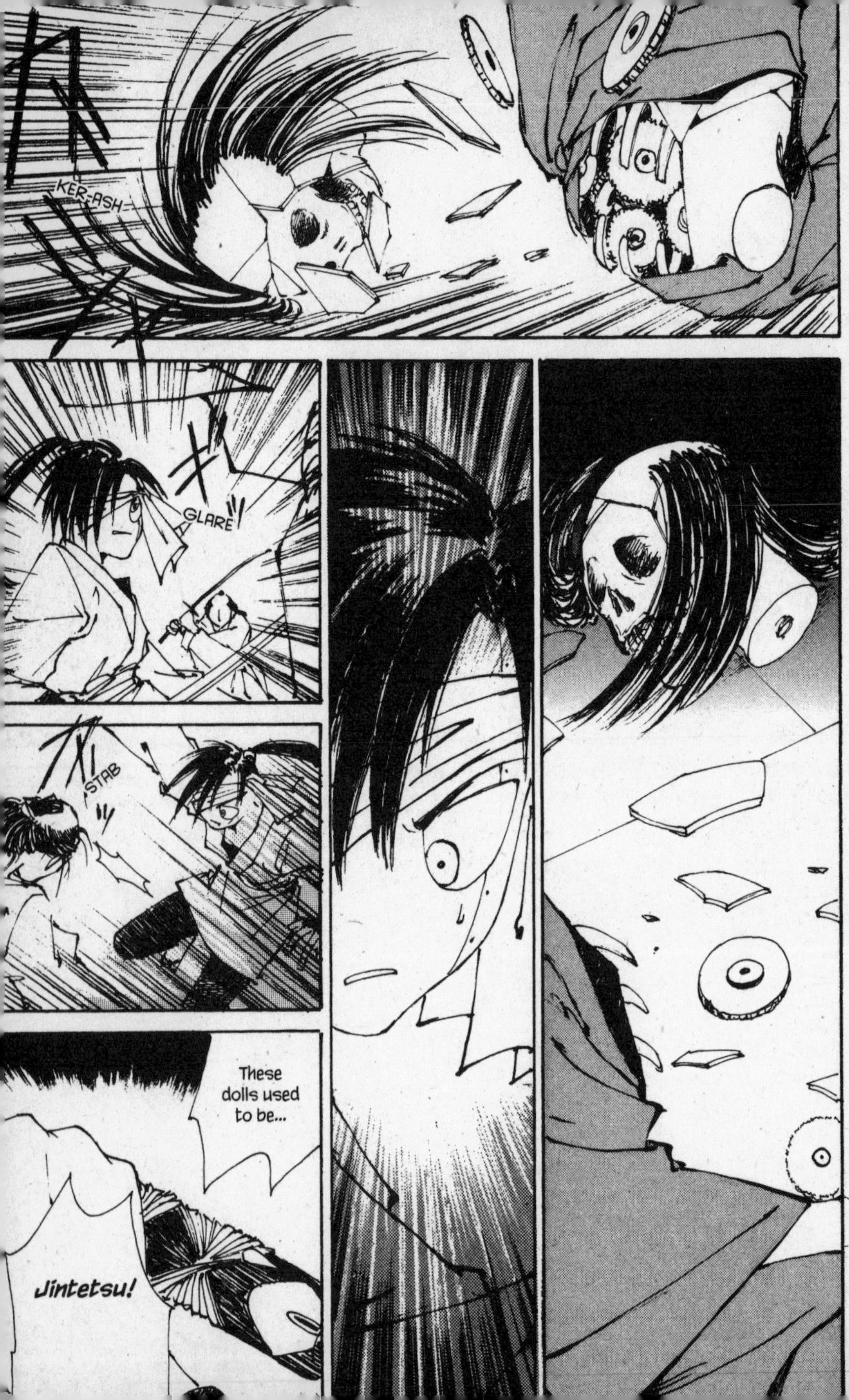
KER-ASH
GLARE
STAB
These dolls used to be...
Jintetsu!

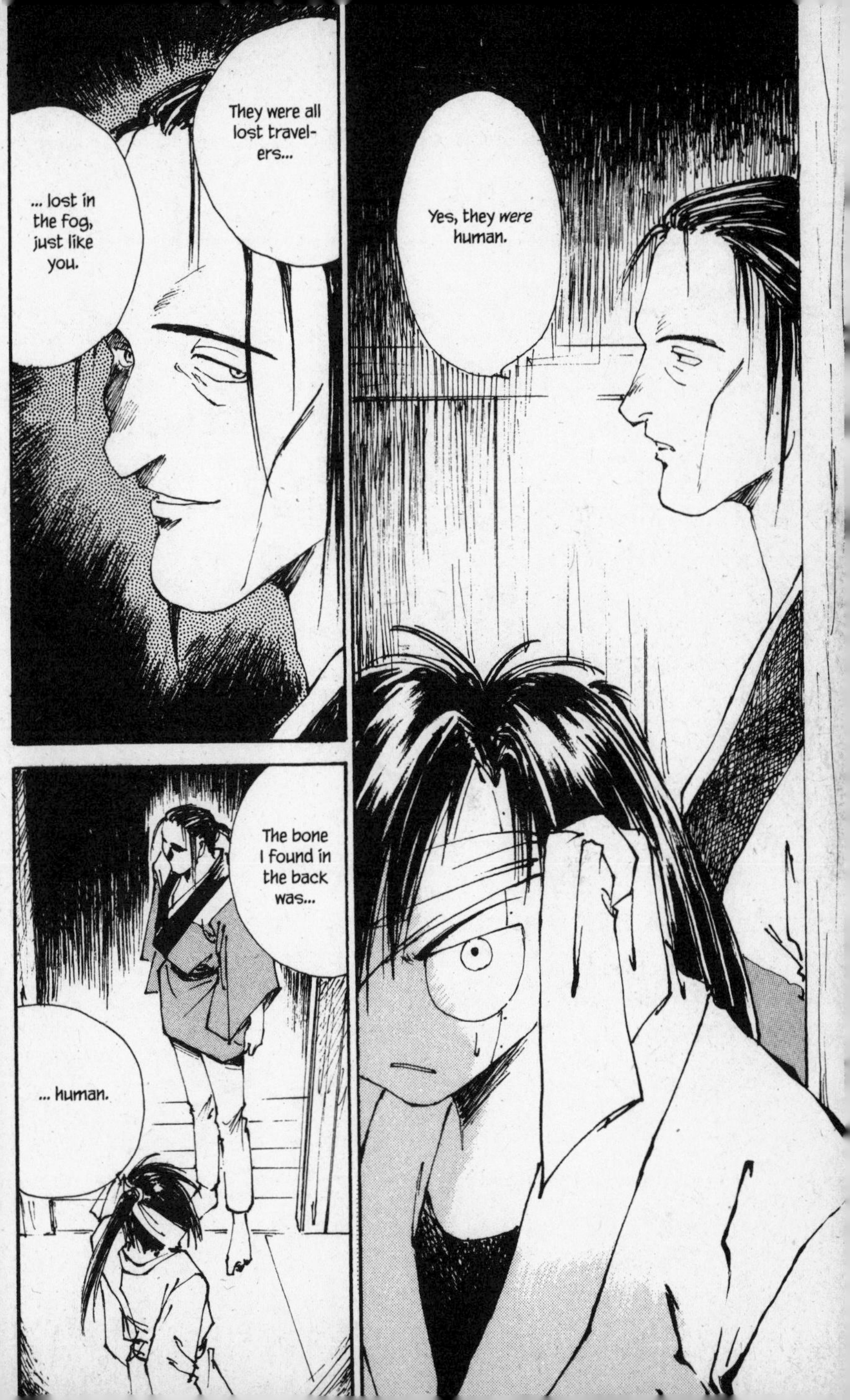
They were all lost travelers...
... lost in the fog, just like you.
The bone I found in the back was...
... human.
Yes, they *were* human.

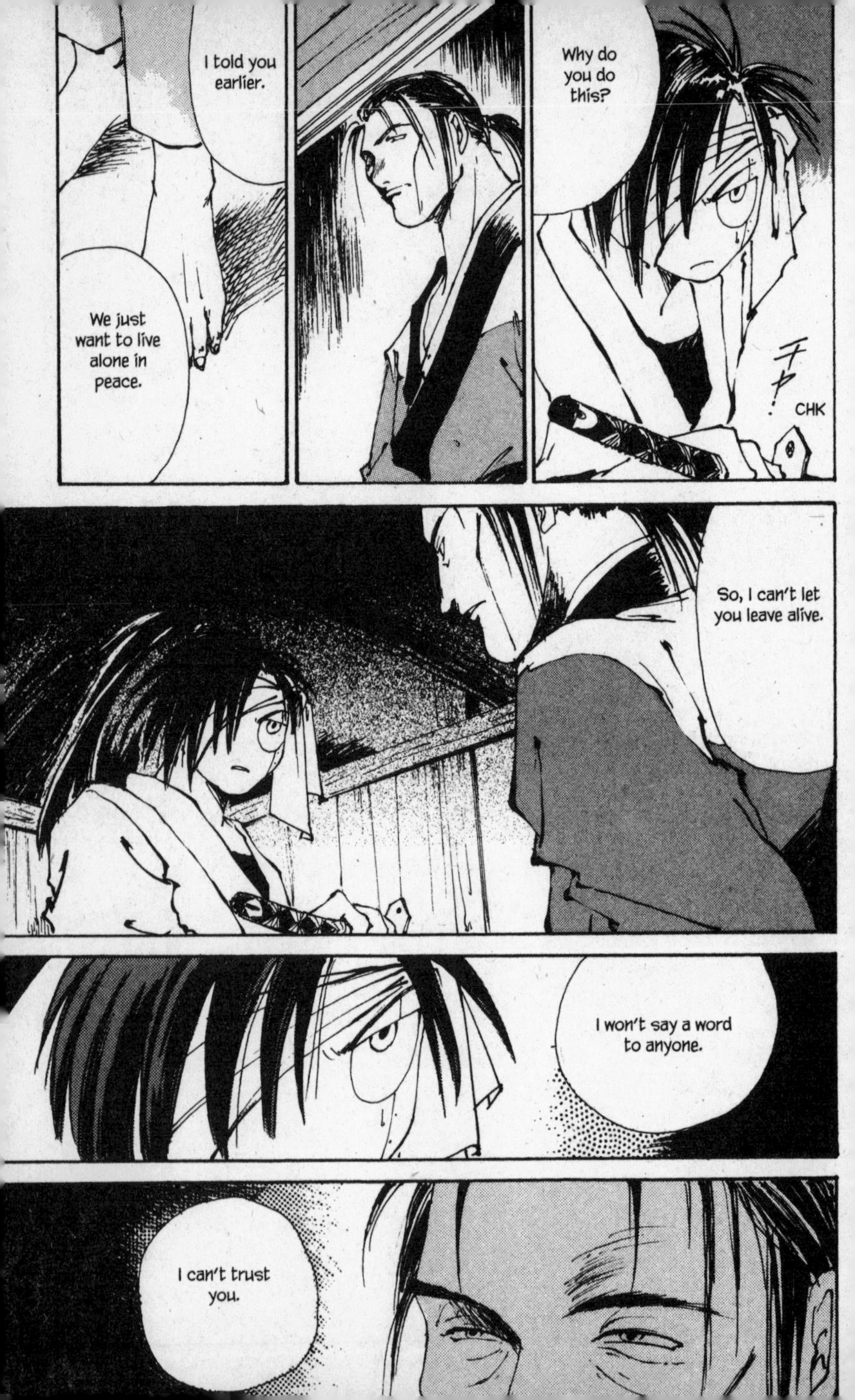
Why do you do this?
CHK
I told you earlier.
We just want to live alone in peace.
So, I can't let you leave alive.
I won't say a word to anyone.
I can't trust you.

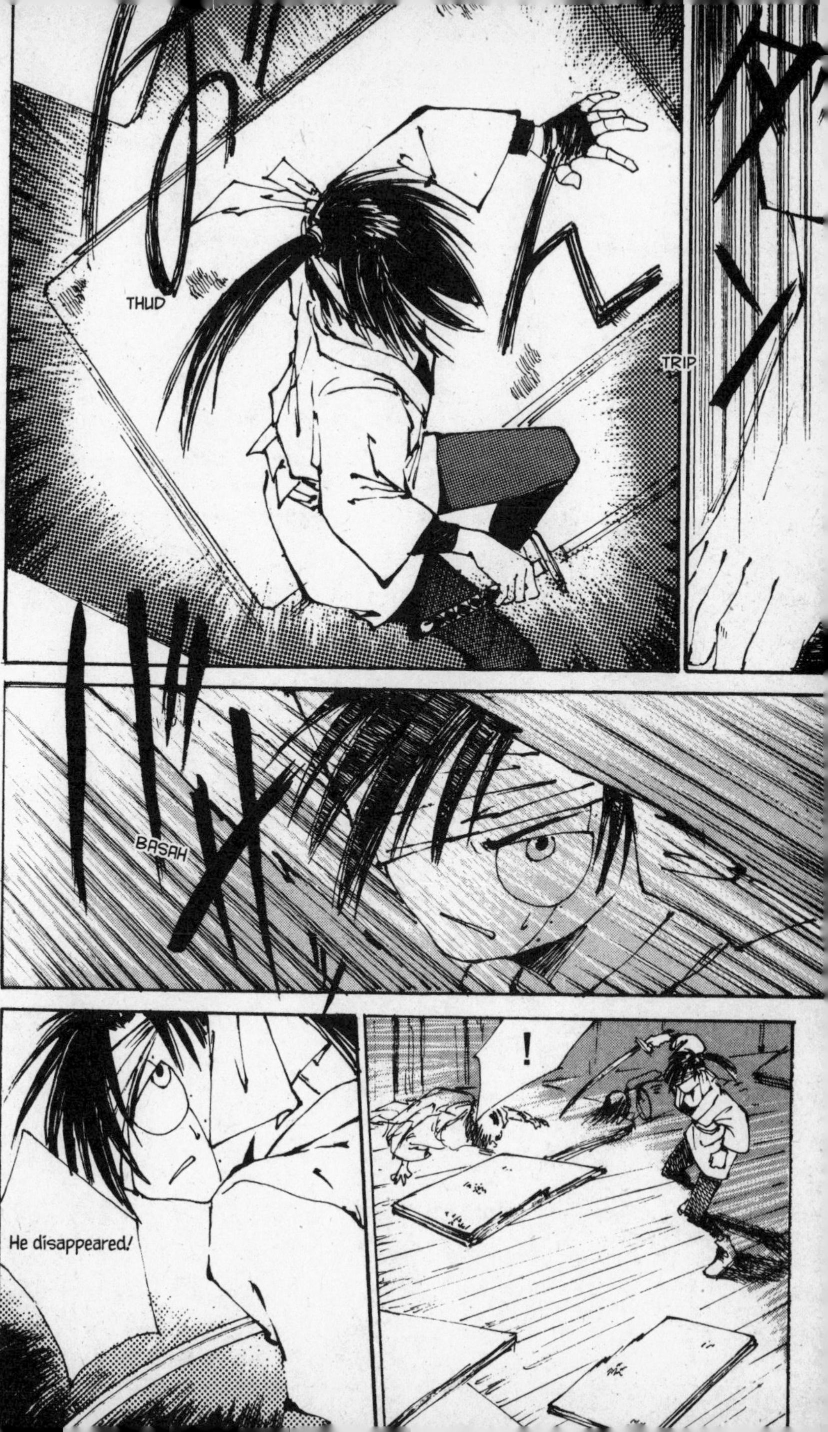
TRIP
THUD
BASAH
!
He disappeared!

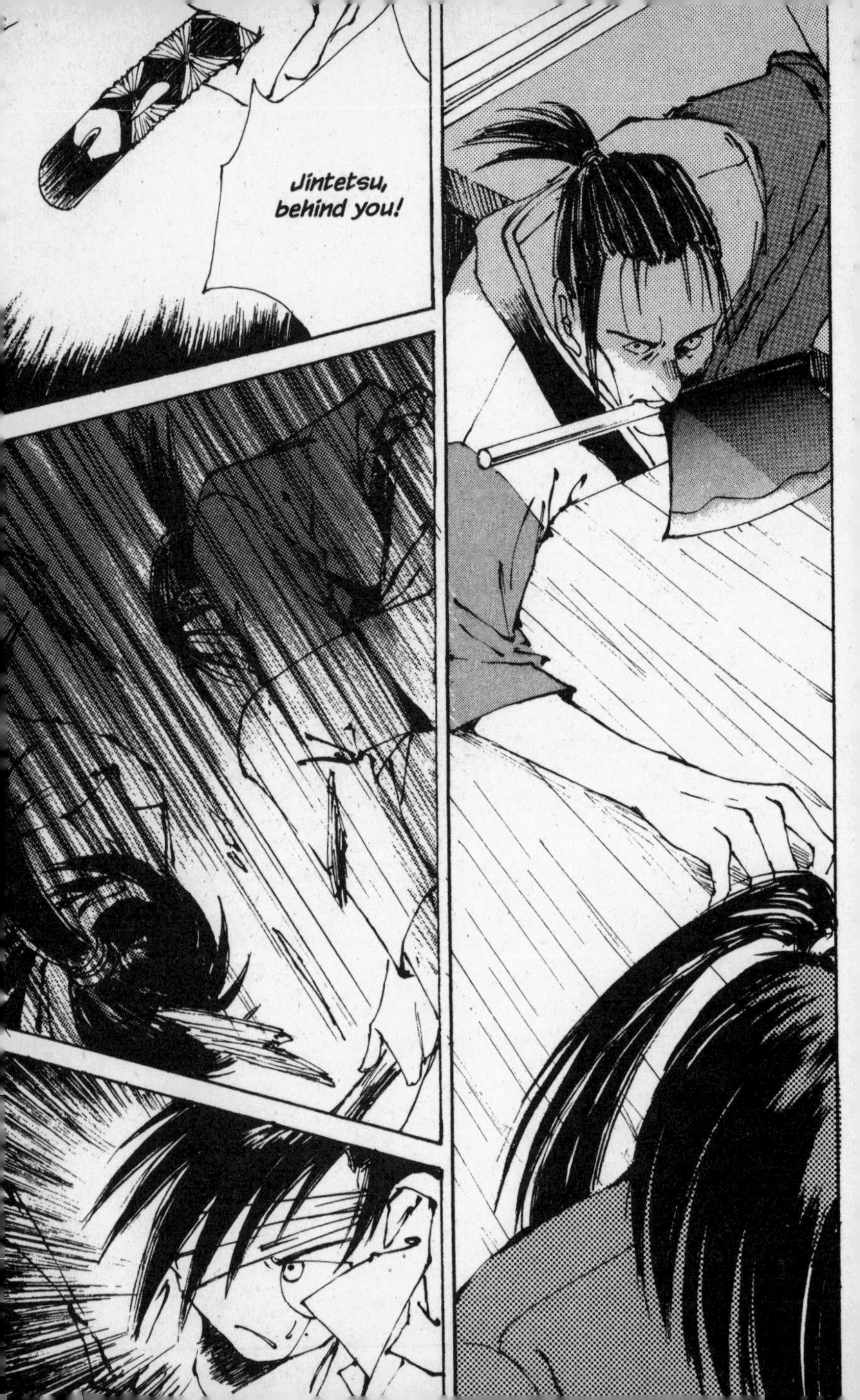
Jintetsu, behind you!

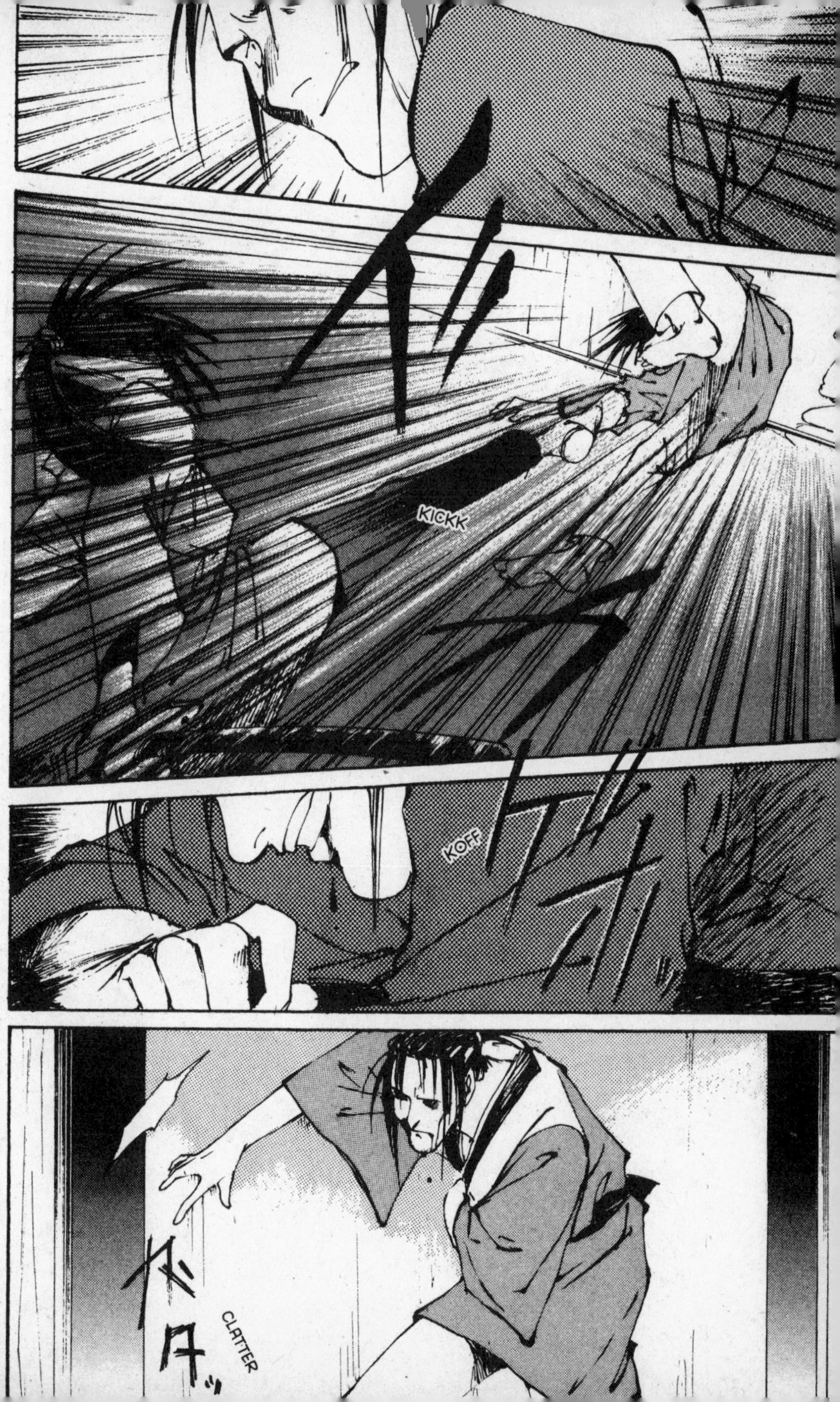
KICKK
KOFF
CLATTER

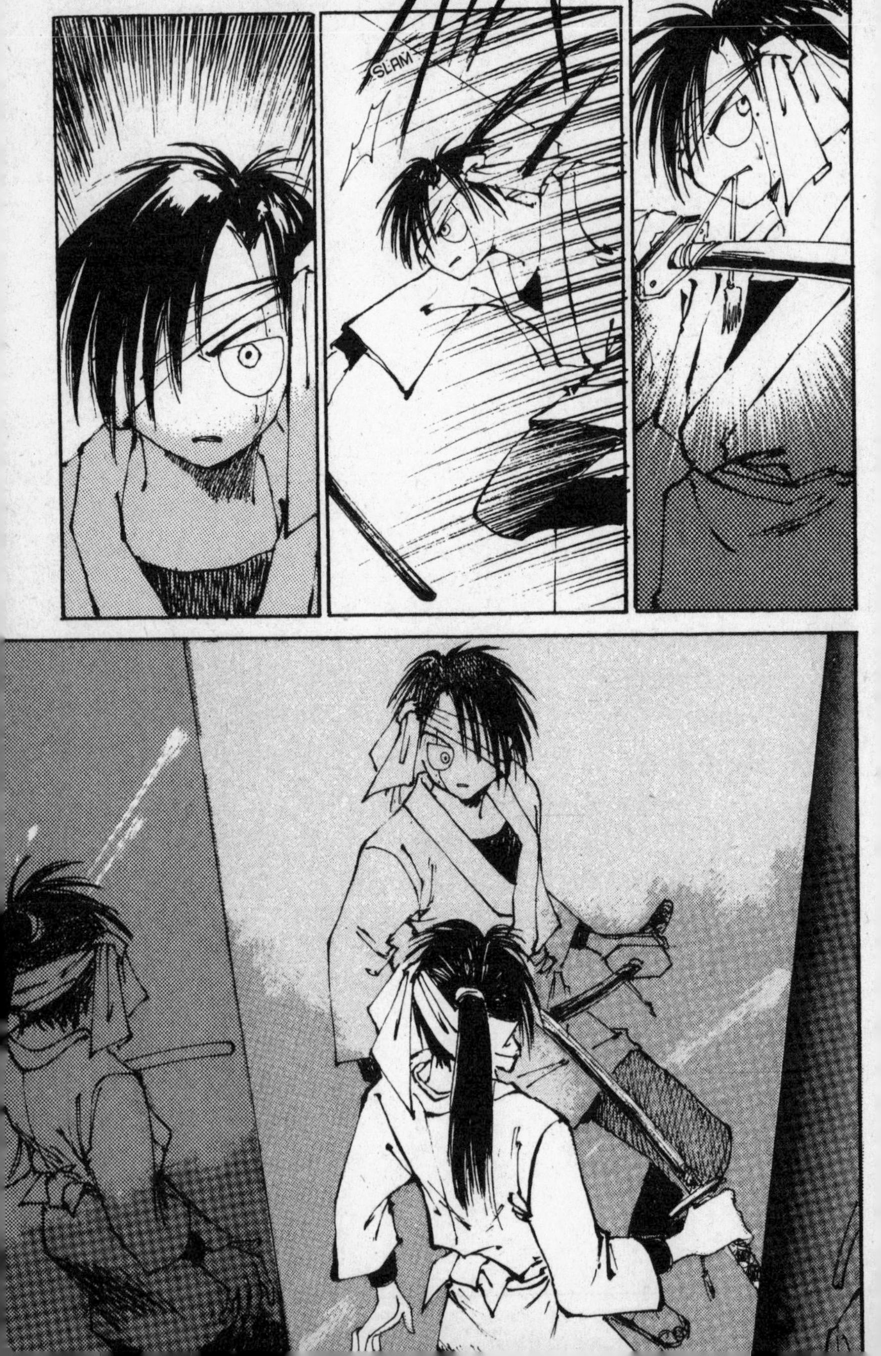
SLAM

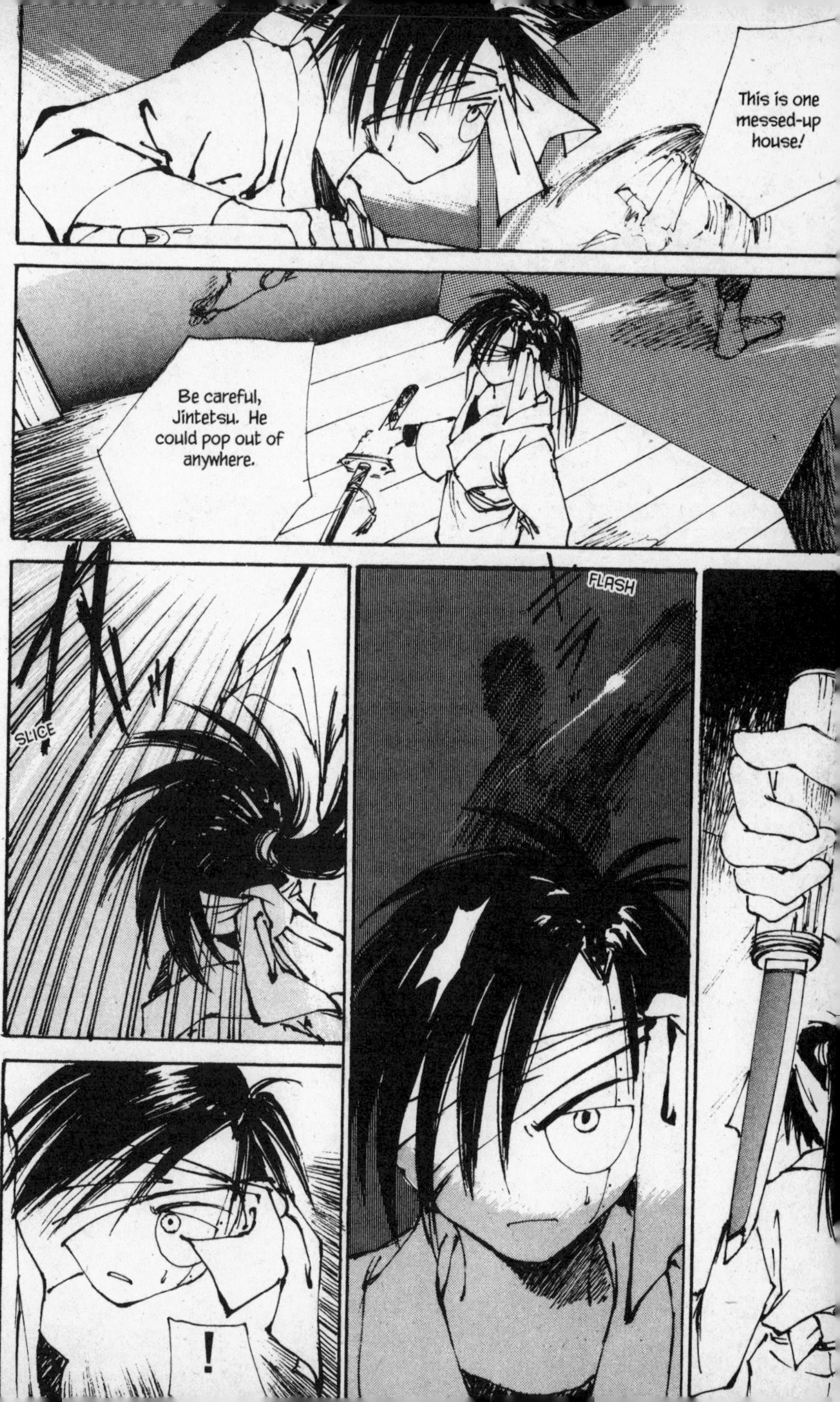
This is one messed-up house!
Be careful, Jintetsu. He could pop out of anywhere.
FLASH
SLICE
!

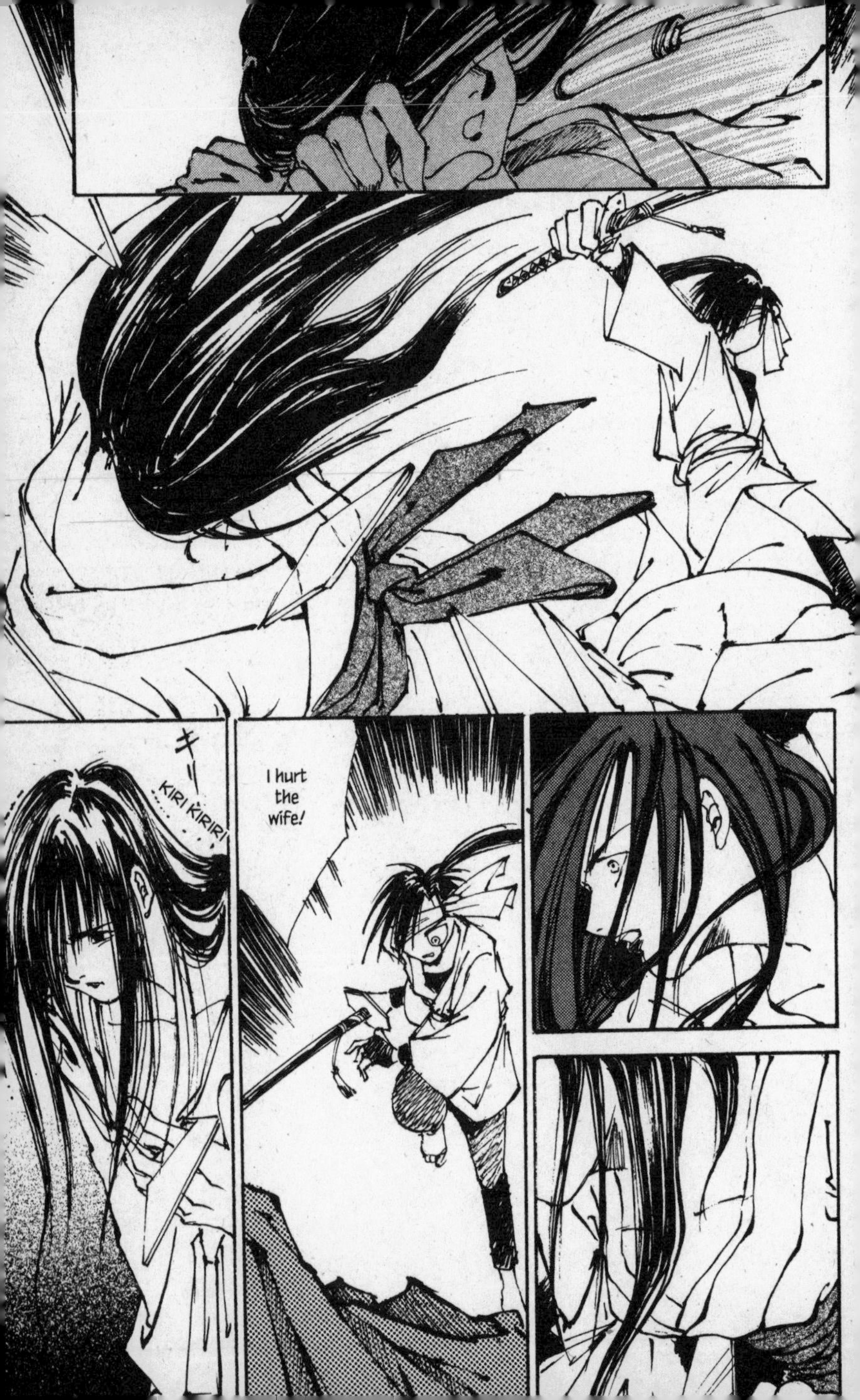
I hurt the wife!
キリ
KIRI KIRIRI

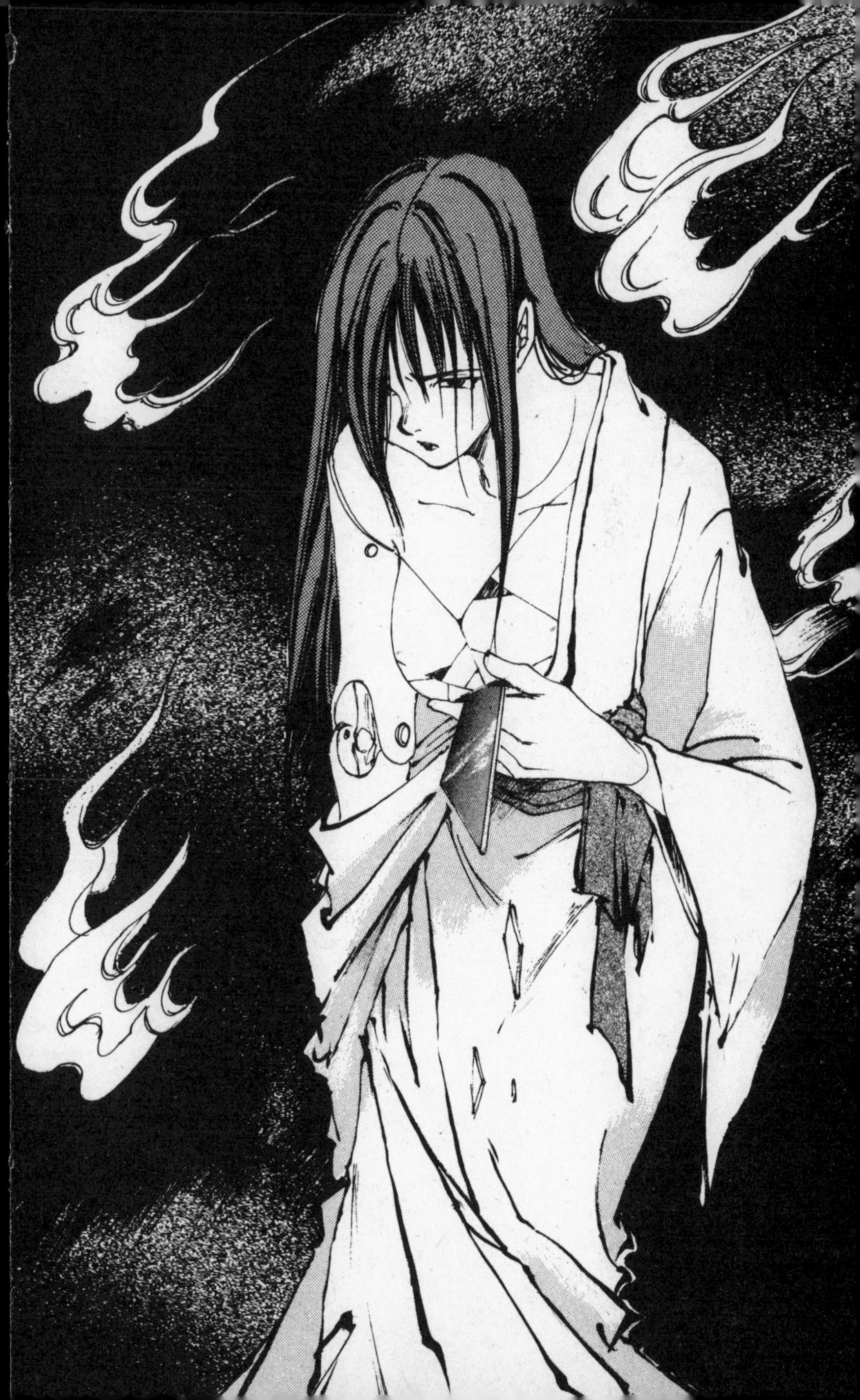

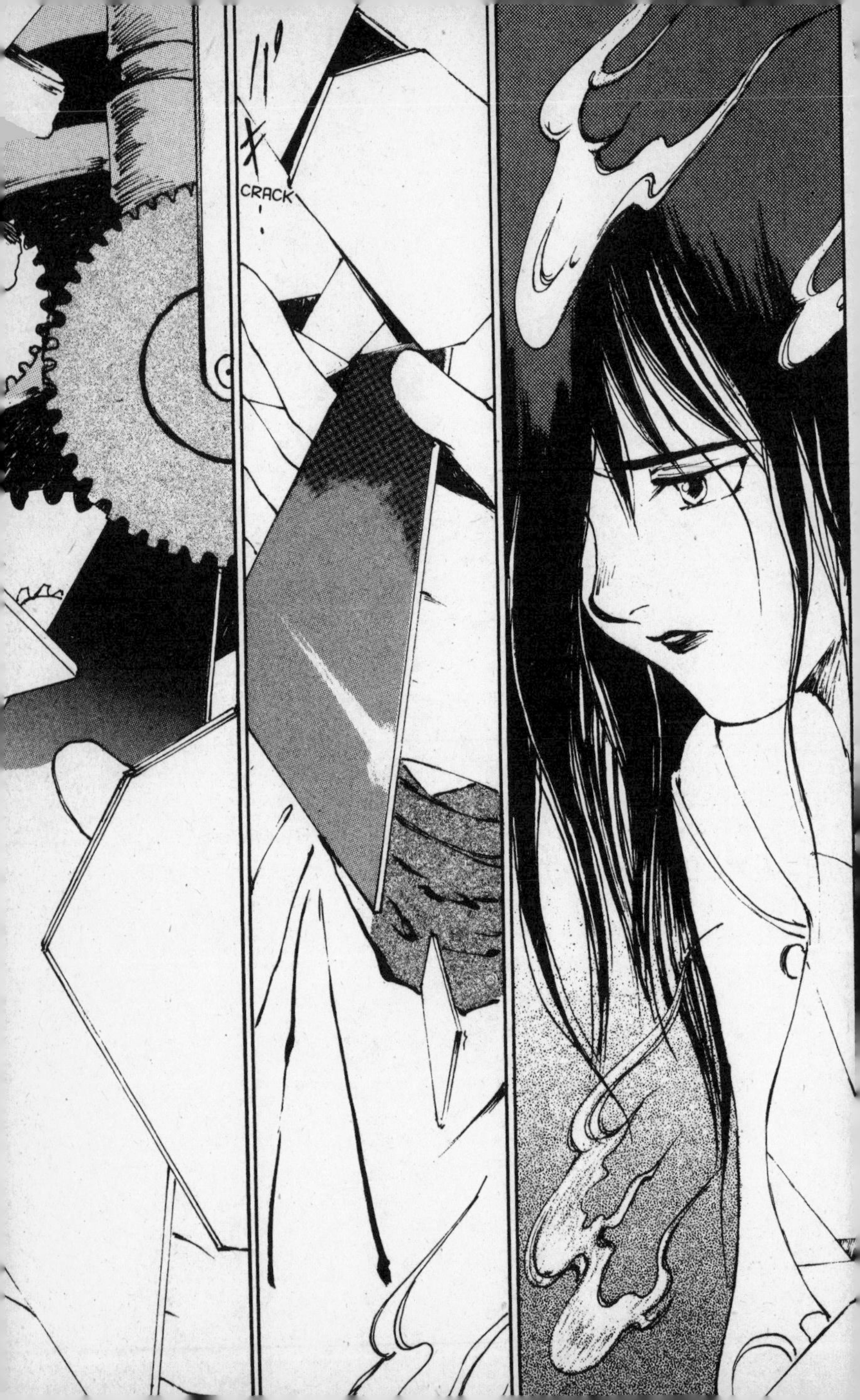
CRACK

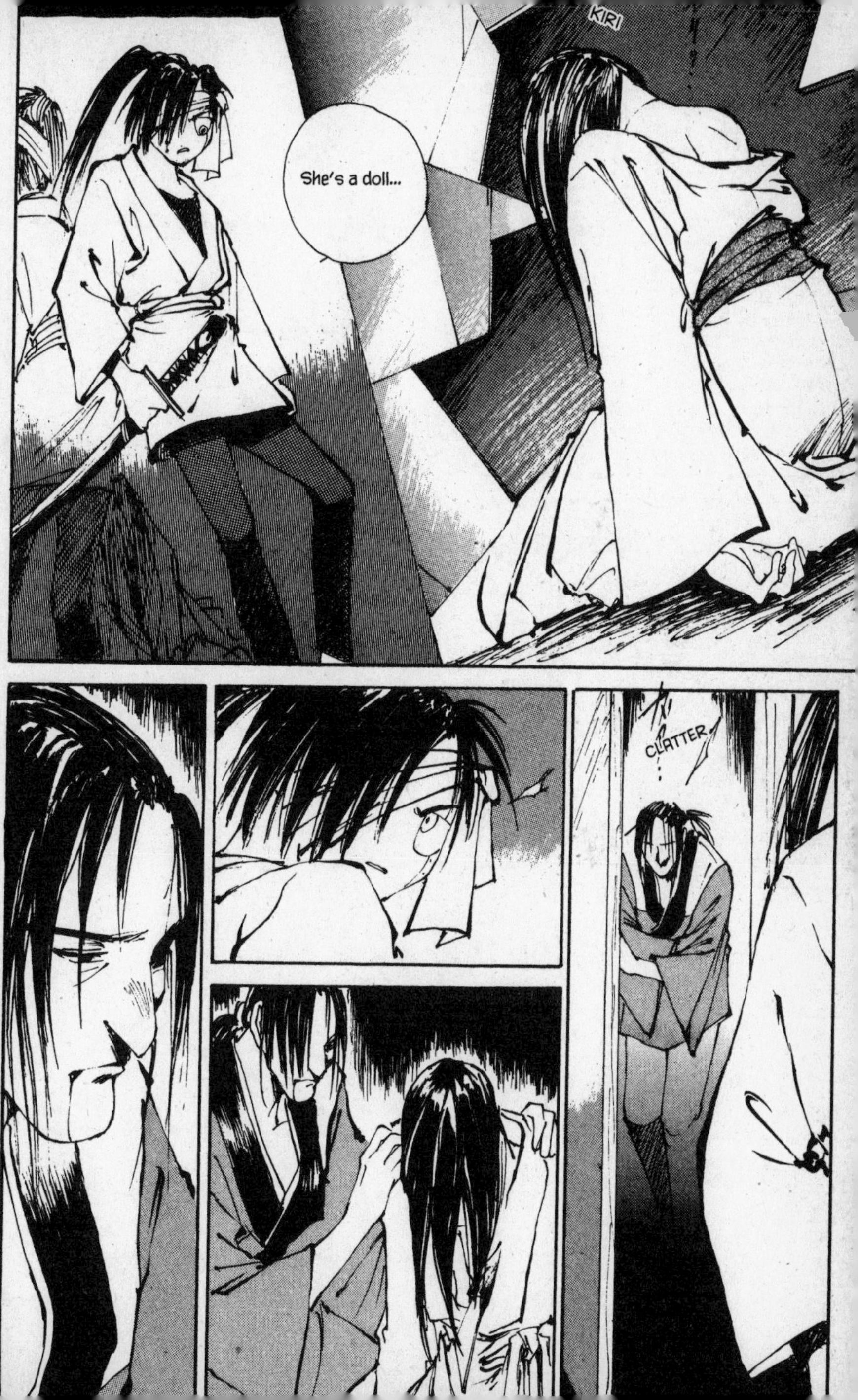
KIRI
She's a doll...
CLATTER

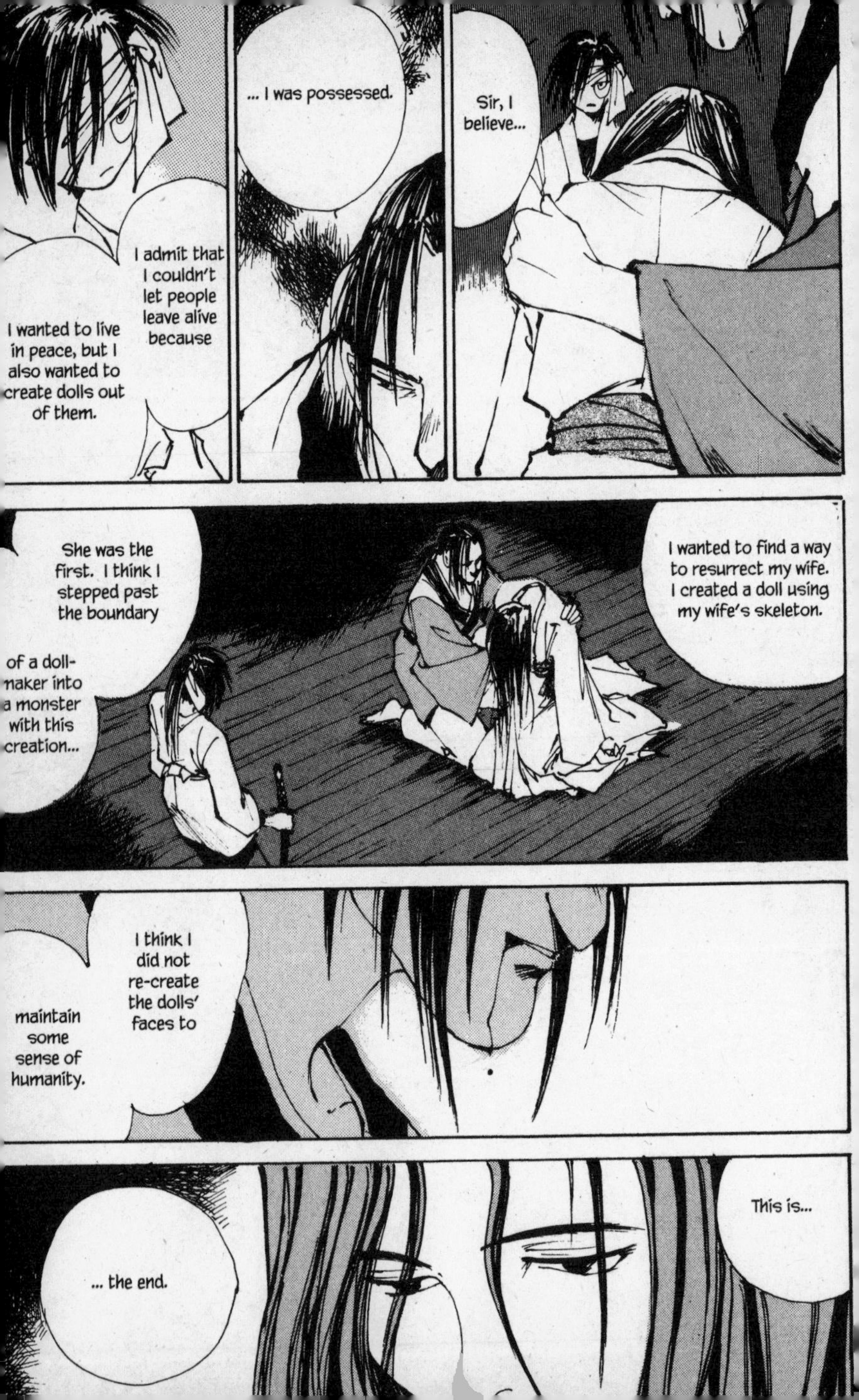
Sir, I believe...
... I was possessed.
I admit that I couldn't let people leave alive because
I wanted to live in peace, but I also wanted to create dolls out of them.
I wanted to find a way to resurrect my wife. I created a doll using my wife's skeleton.
She was the first. I think I stepped past the boundary
of a doll-naker into a monster with this creation...
I think I did not re-create the dolls' faces to
maintain some sense of humanity.
This is...
... the end.

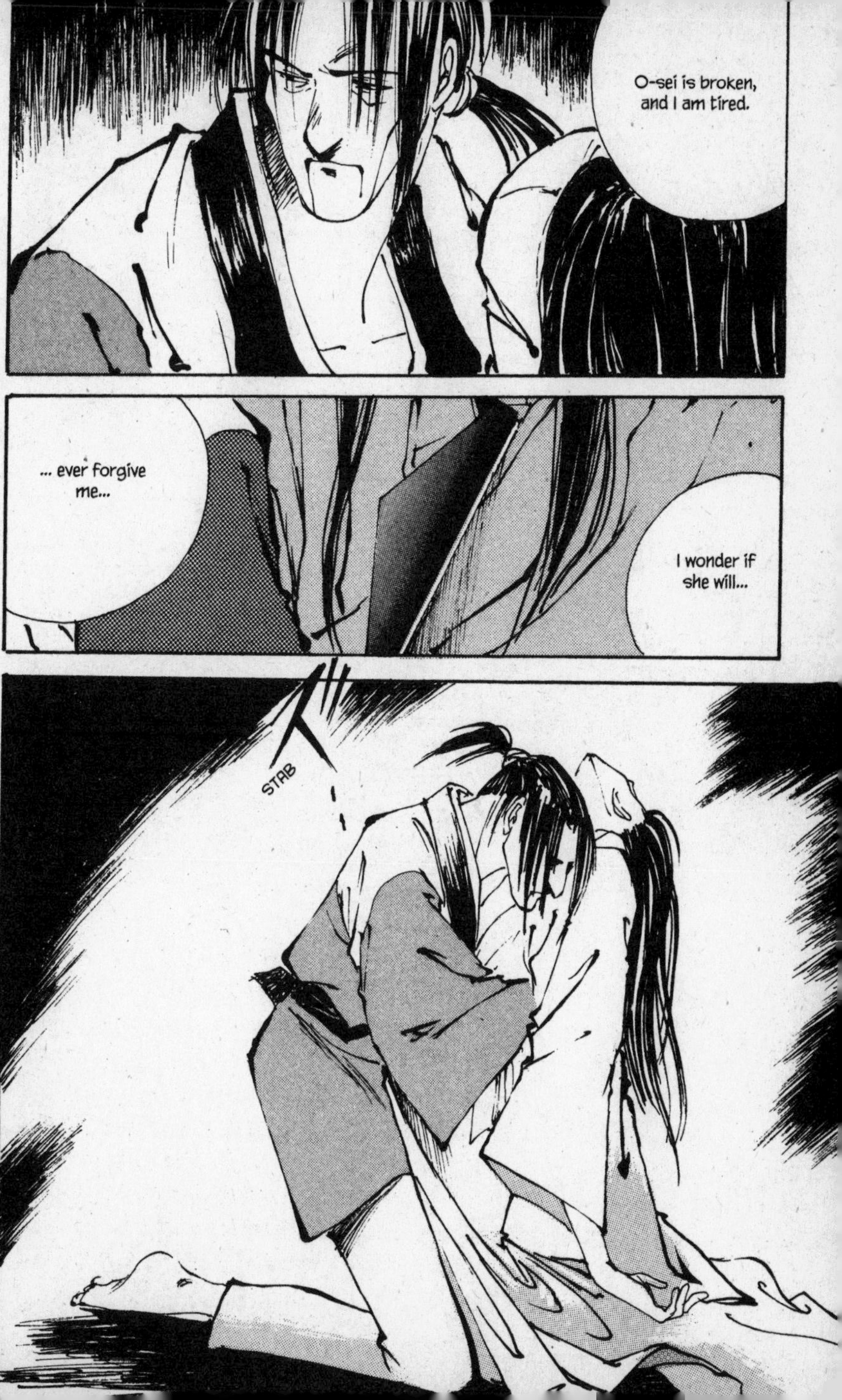
O-sei is broken, and I am tired.
I wonder if she will...
... ever forgive me...
STAB

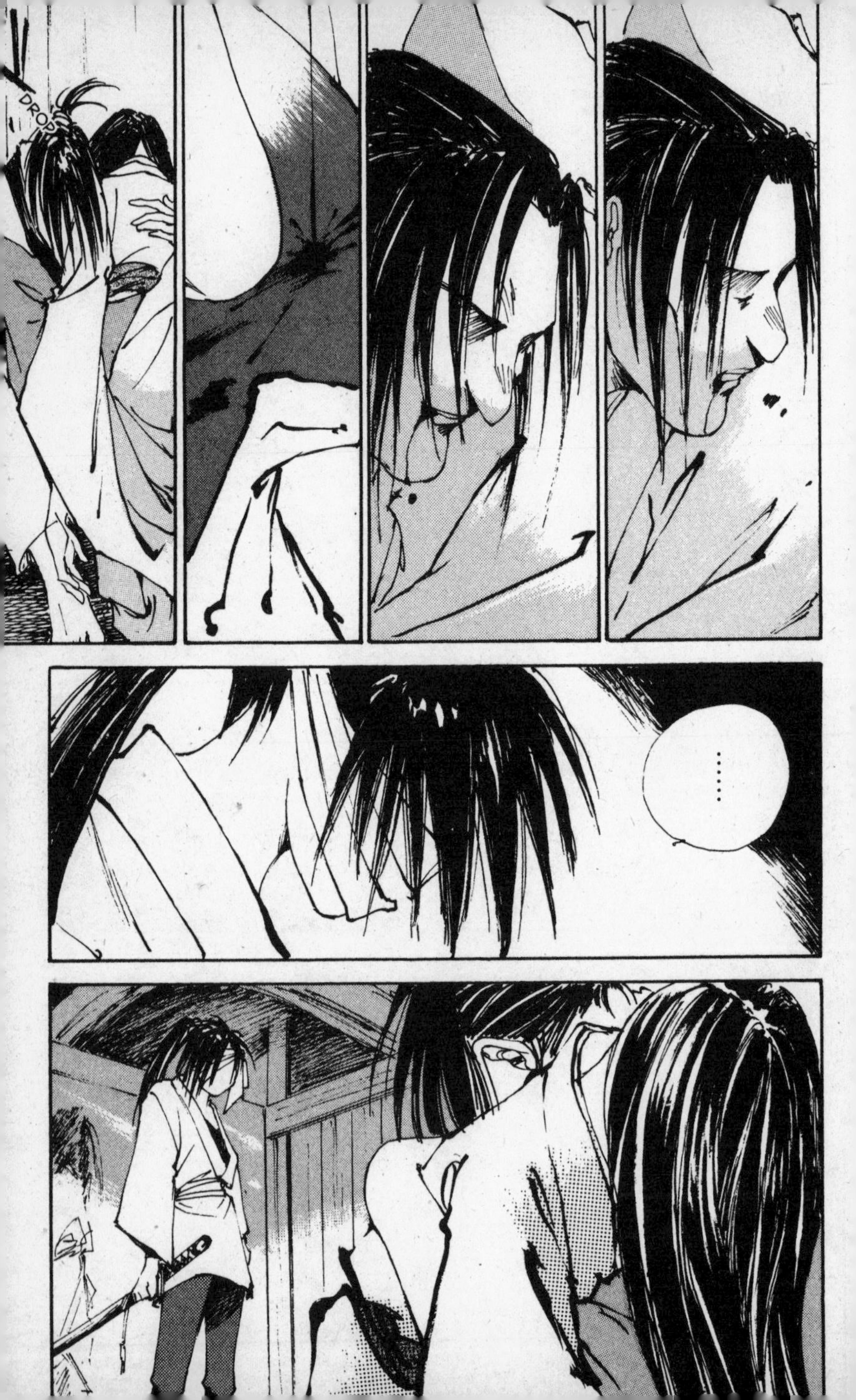
DROP
……

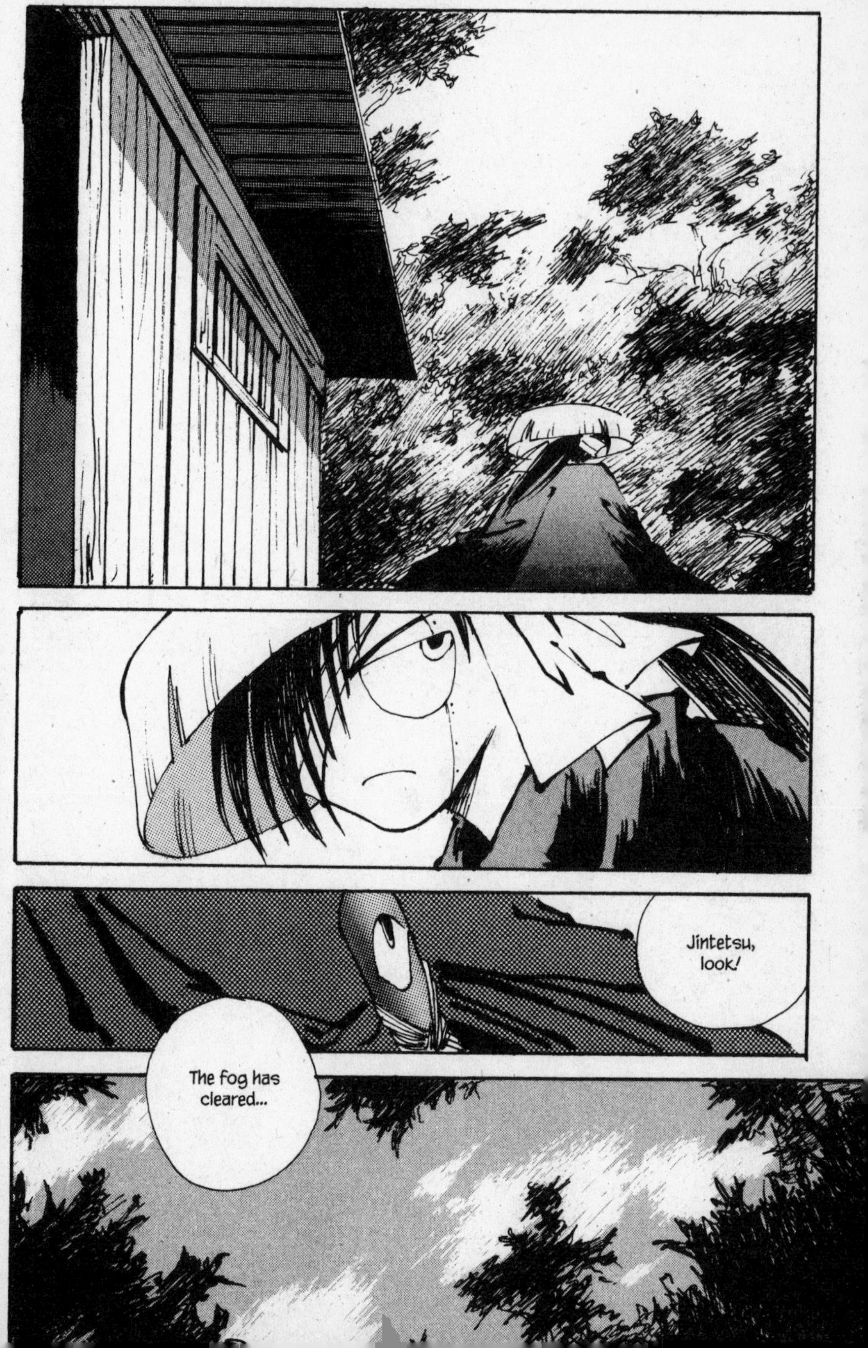
Jintetsu, look!
The fog has cleared...

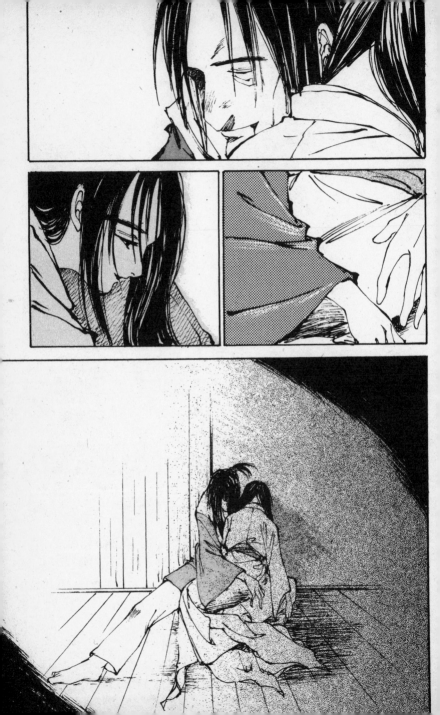

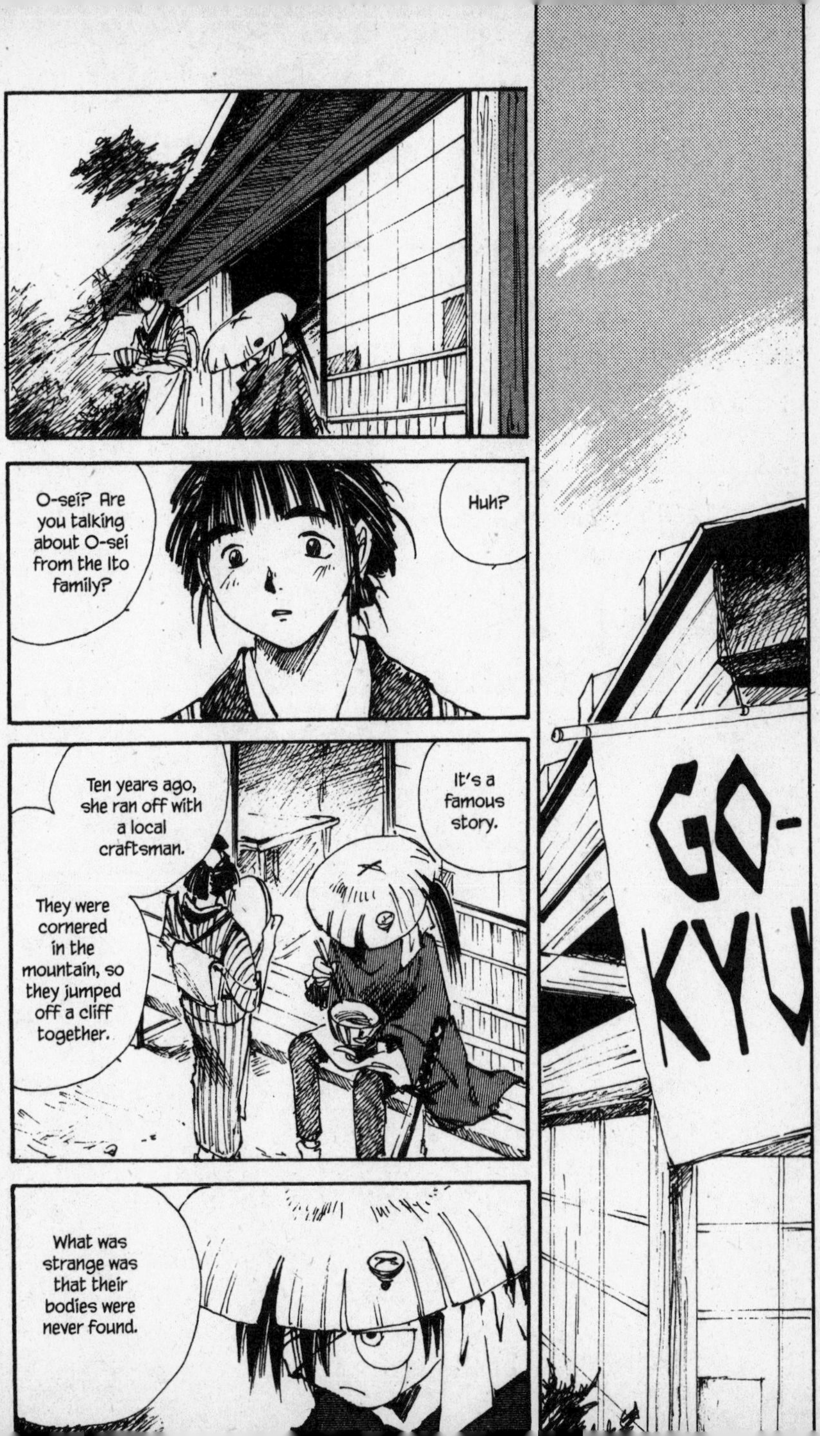
GO-
KYU
Huh?
O-sei? Are you talking about O-sei from the Ito family?
It's a famous story.
Ten years ago, she ran off with a local craftsman.
They were cornered in the mountain, so they jumped off a cliff together.
What was strange was that their bodies were never found.

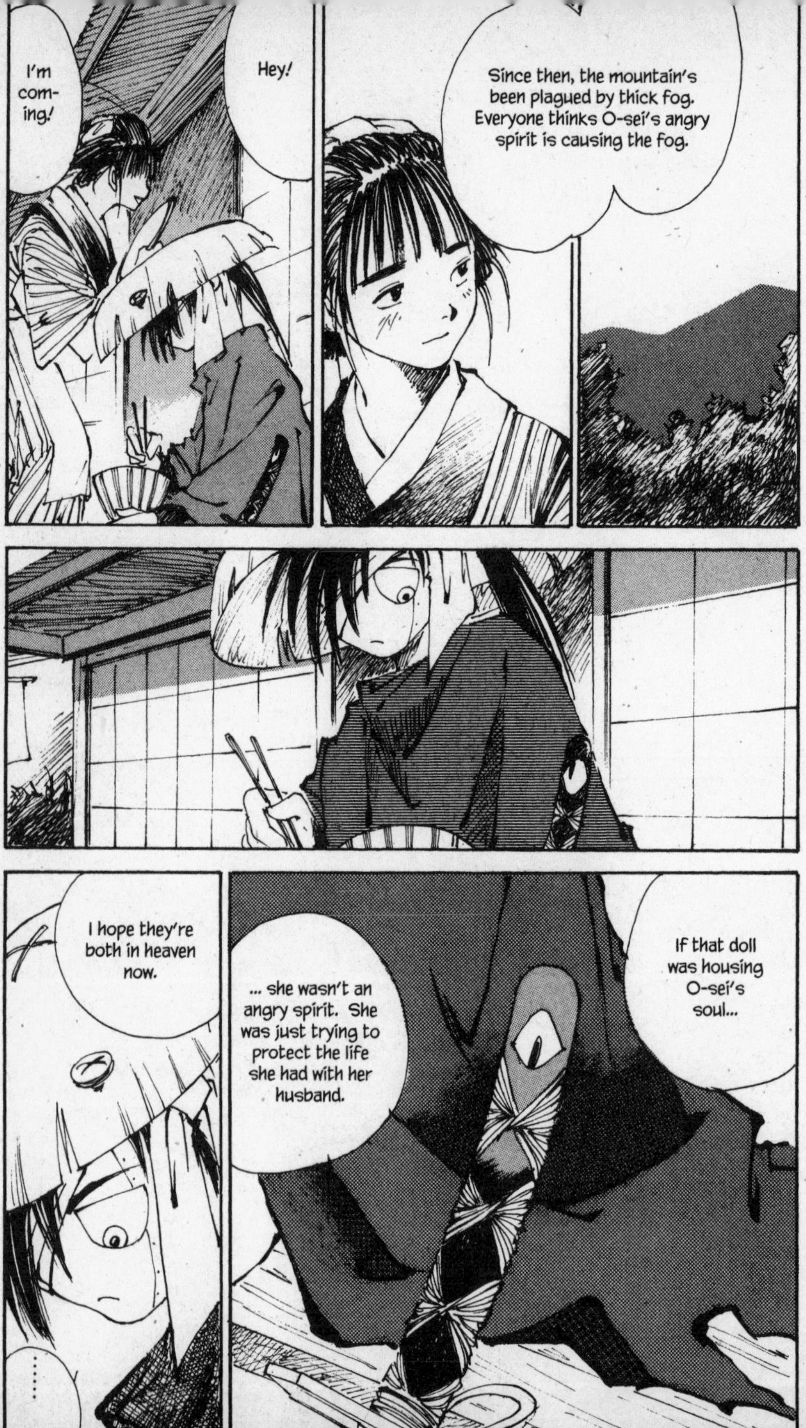
Since then, the mountain's been plagued by thick fog. Everyone thinks O-sei's angry spirit is causing the fog.
Hey!
I'm com-ing!
If that doll was housing O-sei's soul...
... she wasn't an angry spirit. She was just trying to protect the life she had with her husband.
I hope they're both in heaven now.
......

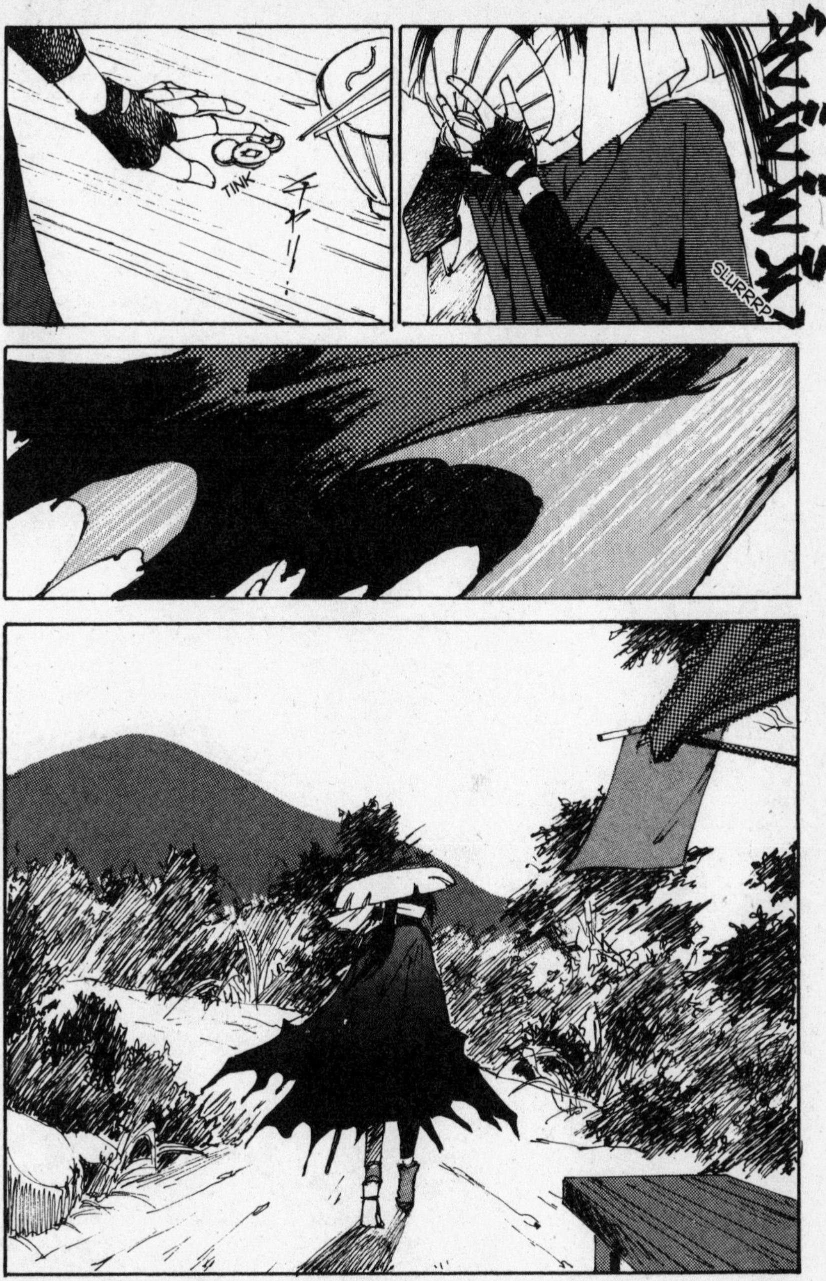
SLURRRP
TINK

THE END OF CHAPTER 7

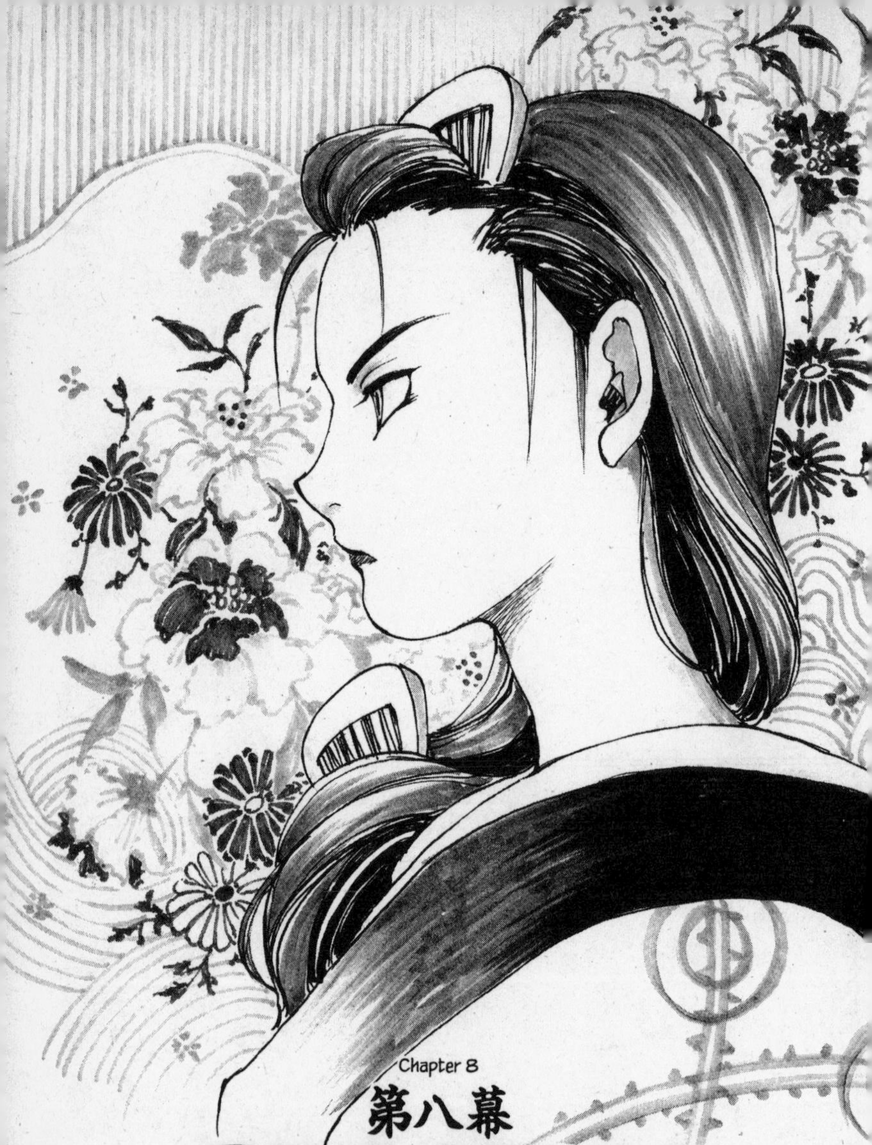

Chapter 8

第八幕

CRIMSON

あざみ　どうじゃ

(薊の道者)

—第一景—

Episode 1

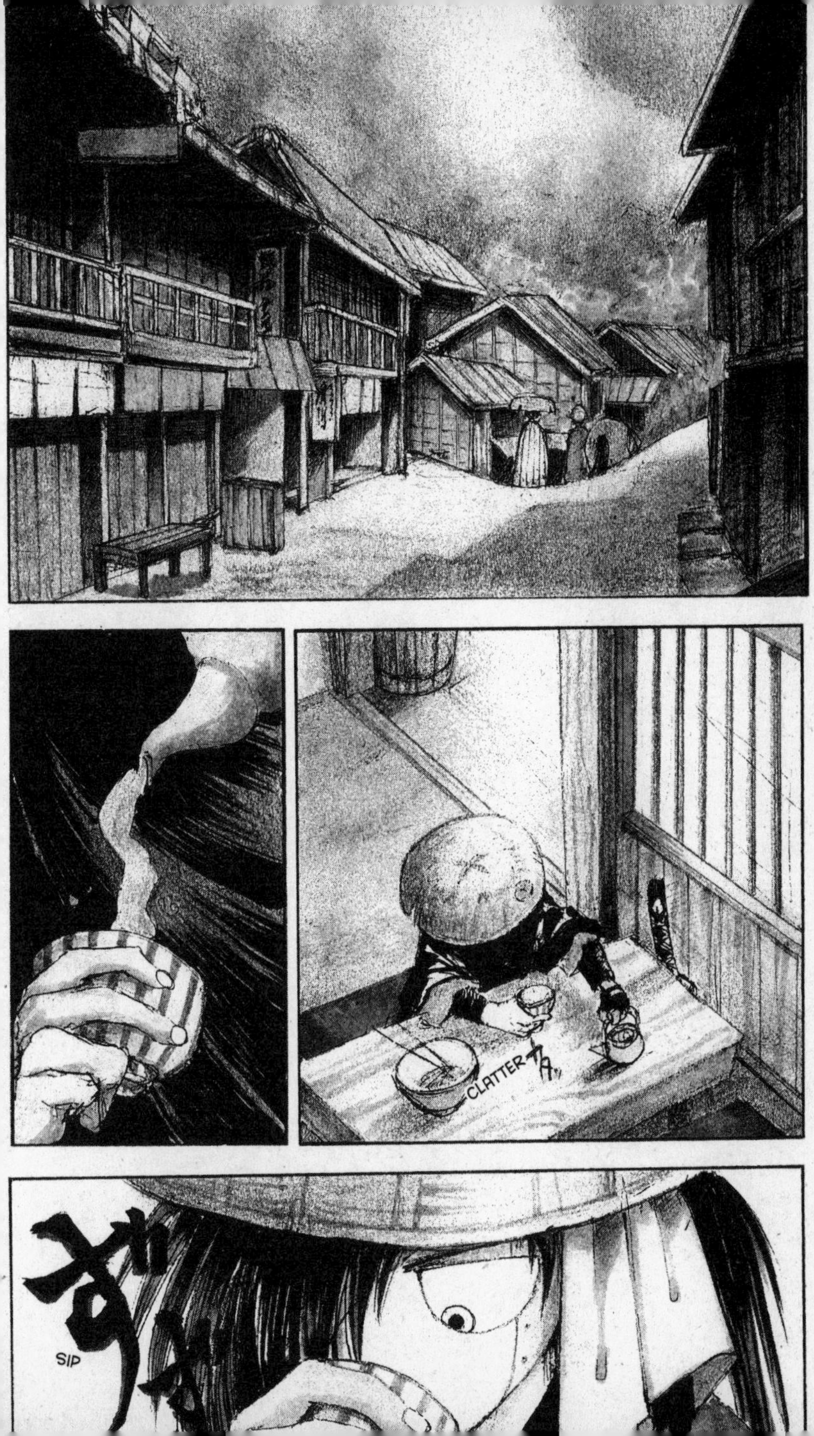
CLATTER
SIP

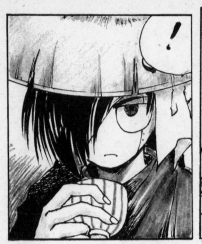

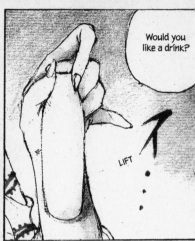

Would you like a drink?

LIFT

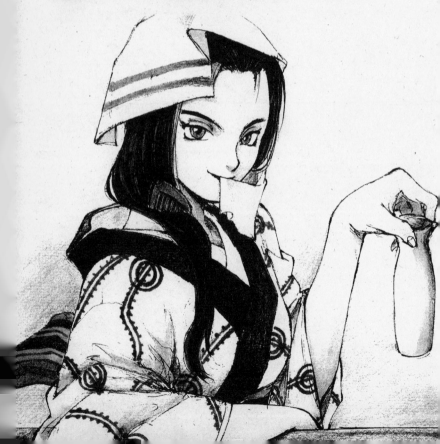

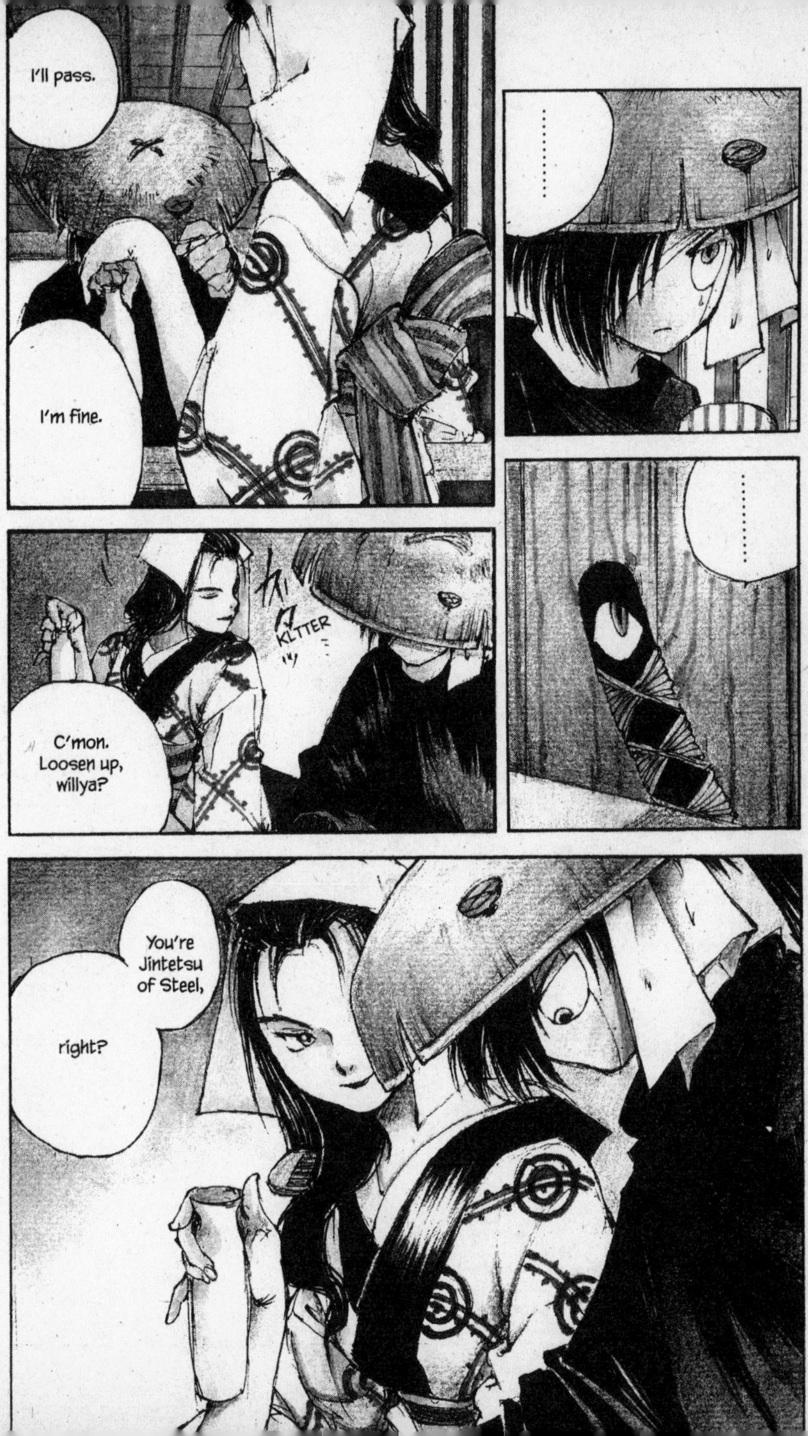
......
I'll pass.
I'm fine.
......
KLTTER
C'mon. Loosen up, willya?
You're Jintetsu of Steel,
right?

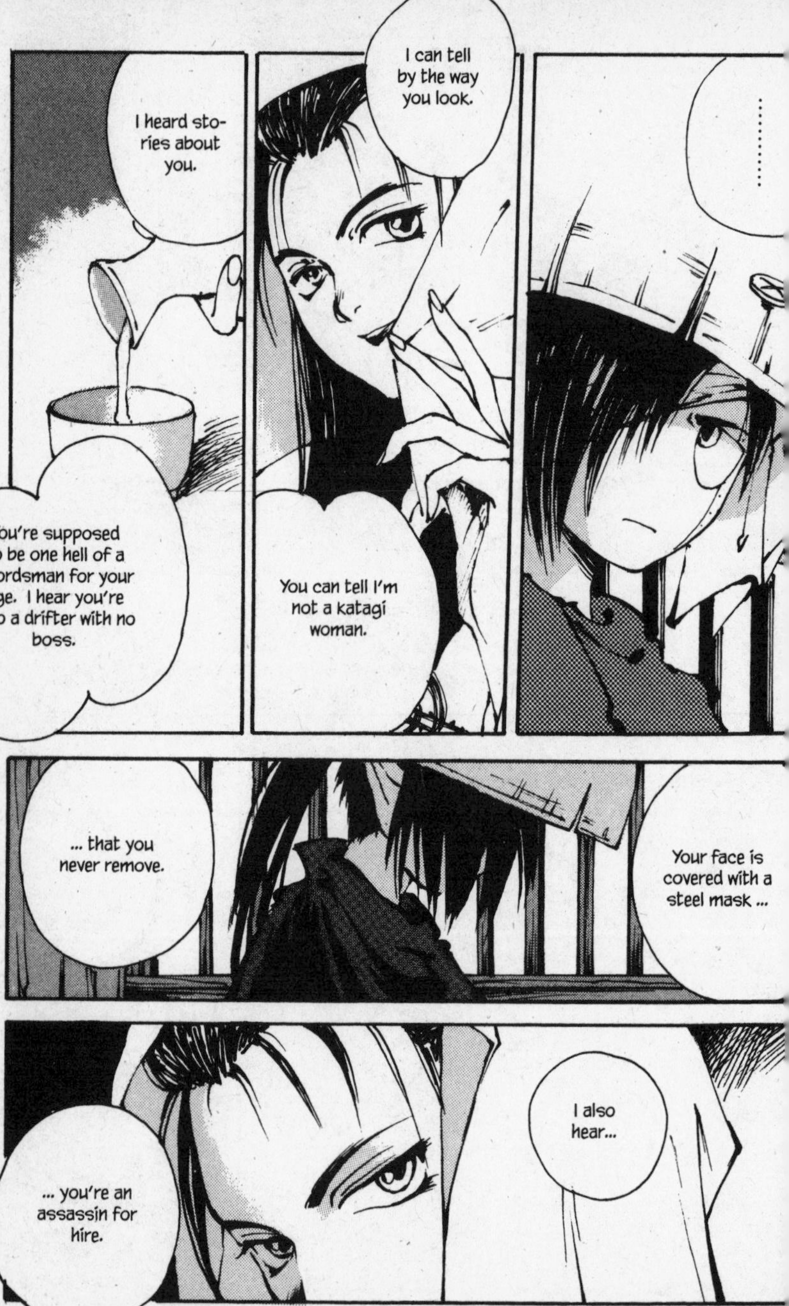
……
I can tell by the way you look.
You can tell I'm not a katagi woman.
I heard stories about you.
You're supposed to be one hell of a swordsman for your age. I hear you're also a drifter with no boss.
Your face is covered with a steel mask ...
... that you never remove.
I also hear...
... you're an assassin for hire.

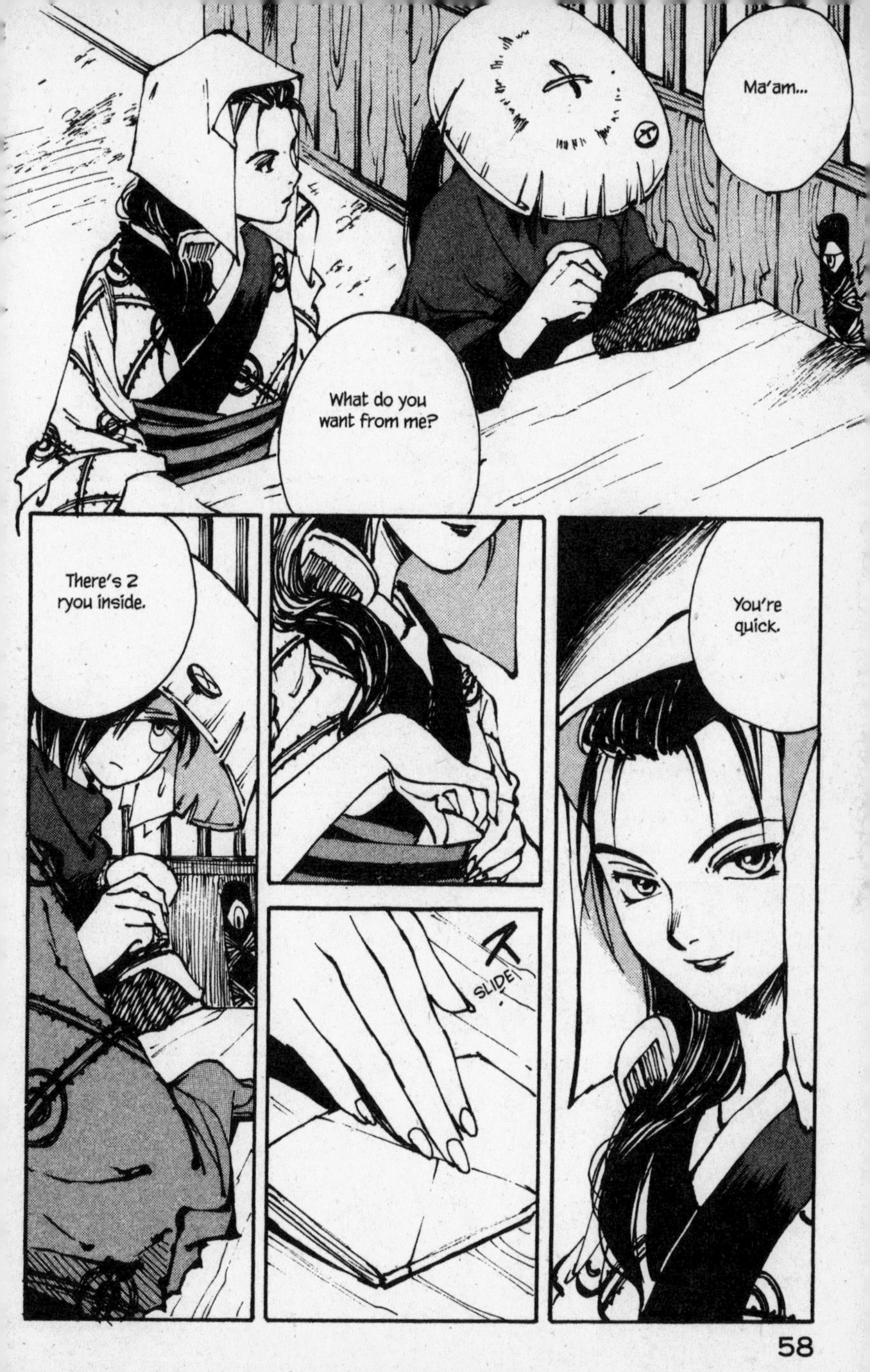
Ma'am...
What do you want from me?
You're quick.
SLIDE
There's 2 ryou inside.

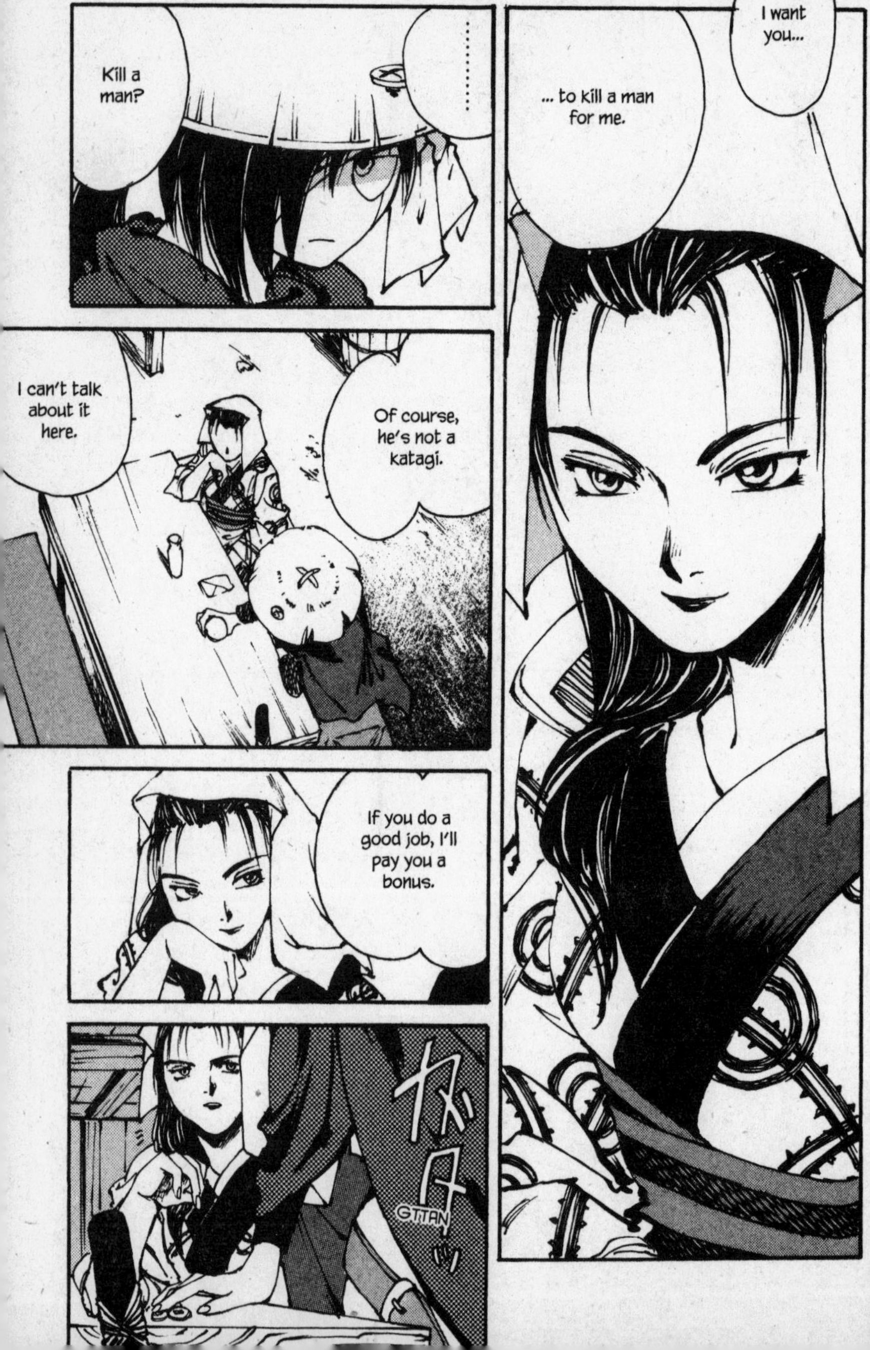
I want you...
... to kill a man for me.
......
Kill a man?
Of course, he's not a katagi.
I can't talk about it here.
If you do a good job, I'll pay you a bonus.
GTTAN

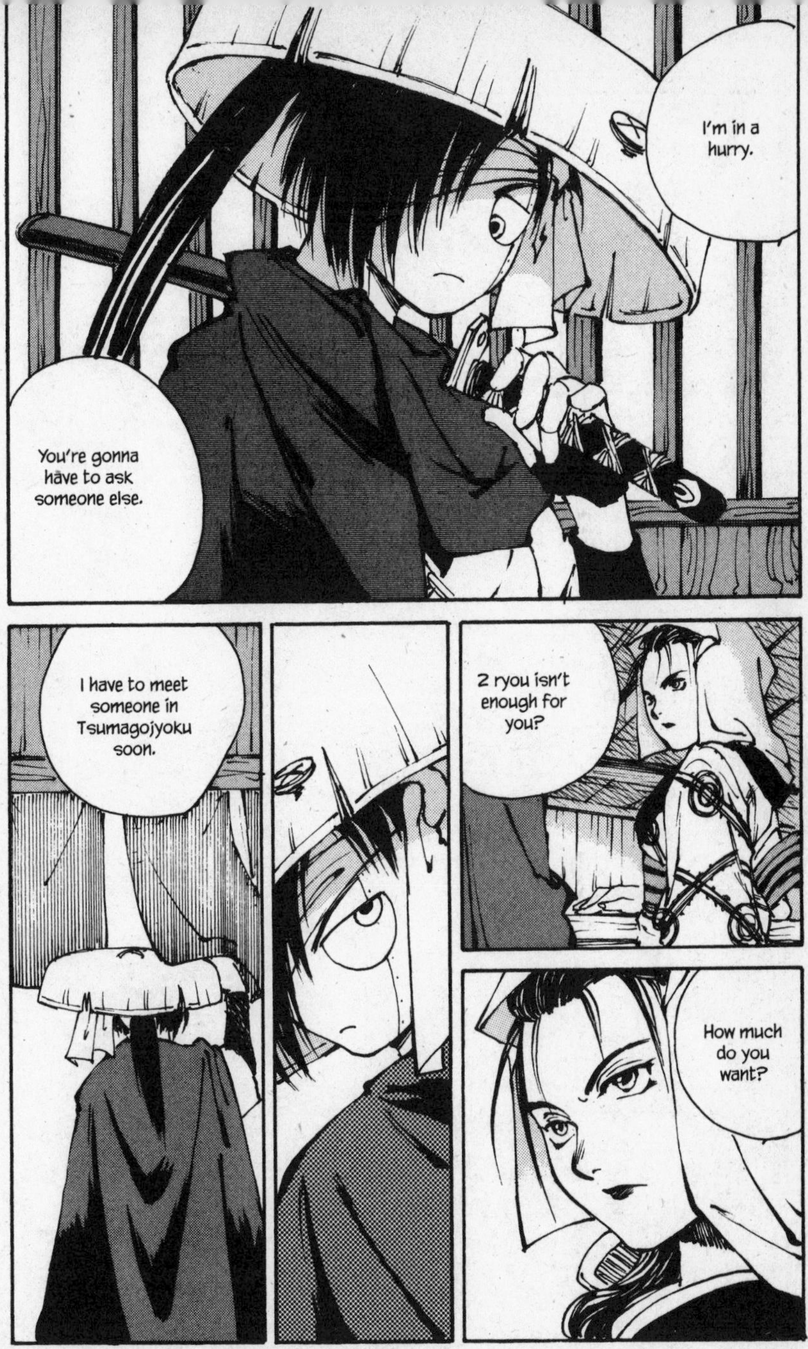
I'm in a hurry.
You're gonna have to ask someone else.
2 ryou isn't enough for you?
How much do you want?
I have to meet someone in Tsumagojyoku soon.

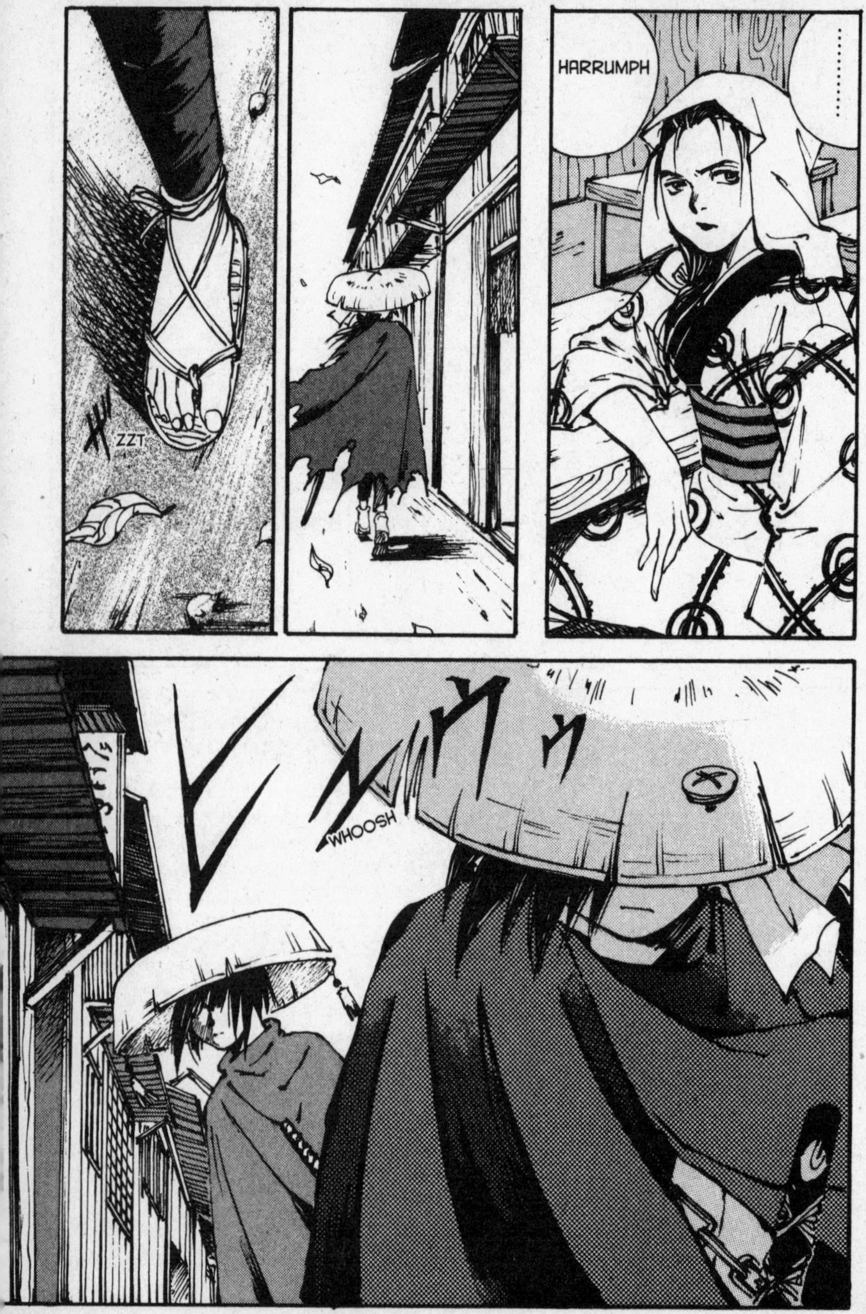
......
HARRUMPH
ZZT
WHOOSH

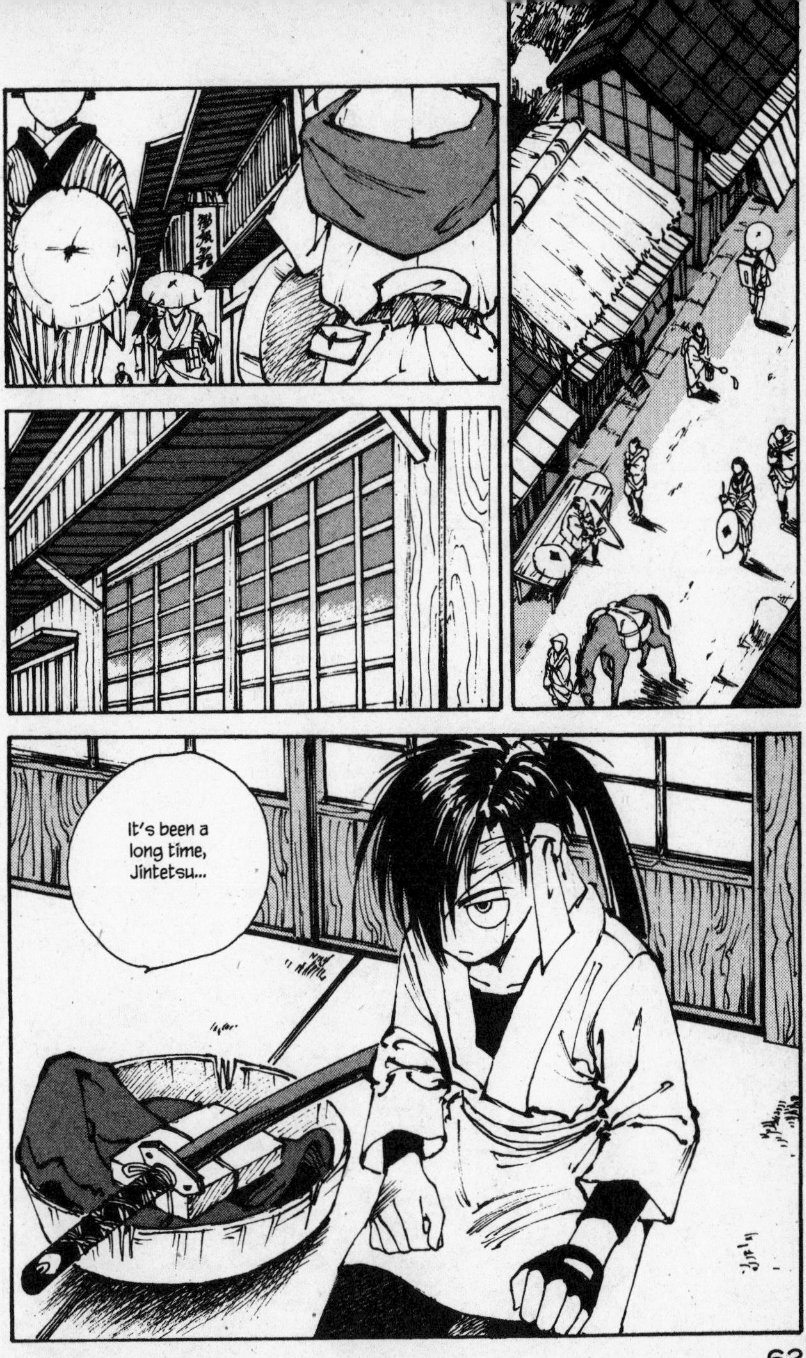
It's been a long time, Jintetsu...

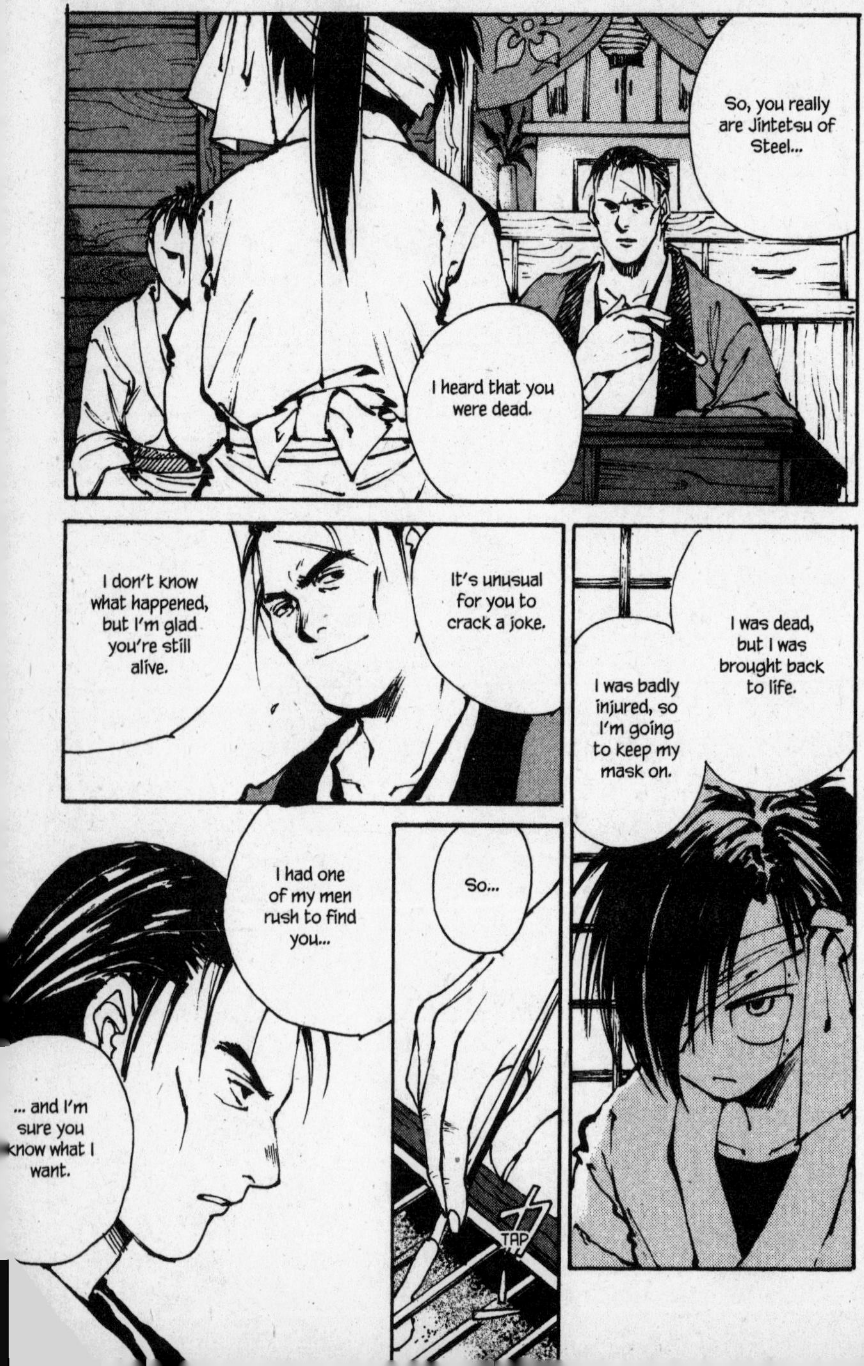
So, you really are Jintetsu of Steel...
I heard that you were dead.
I was dead, but I was brought back to life.
I was badly injured, so I'm going to keep my mask on.
It's unusual for you to crack a joke.
I don't know what happened, but I'm glad you're still alive.
So...
TAP
I had one of my men rush to find you...
... and I'm sure you know what I want.

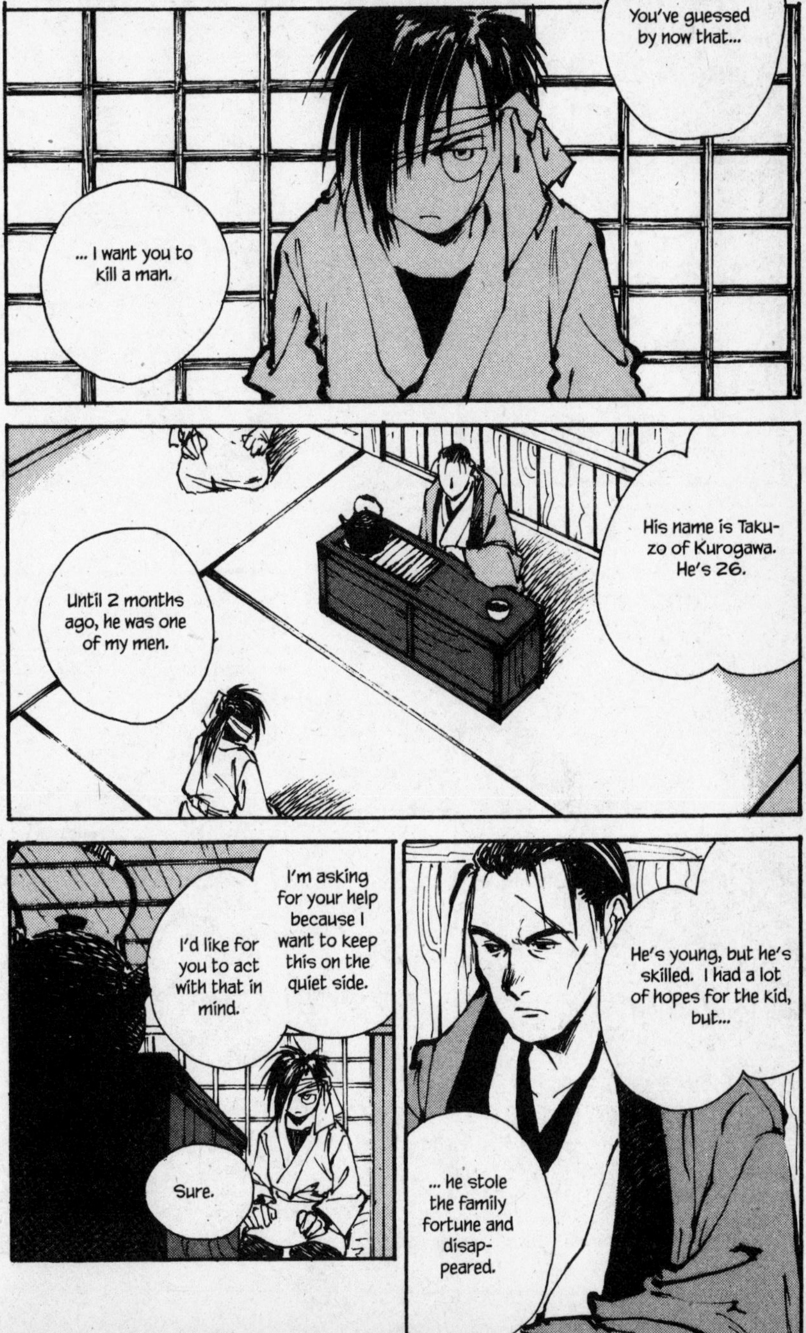
You've guessed by now that...
... I want you to kill a man.
His name is Takuzo of Kurogawa. He's 26.
Until 2 months ago, he was one of my men.
He's young, but he's skilled. I had a lot of hopes for the kid, but...
... he stole the family fortune and disappeared.
I'm asking for your help because I want to keep this on the quiet side.
I'd like for you to act with that in mind.
Sure.

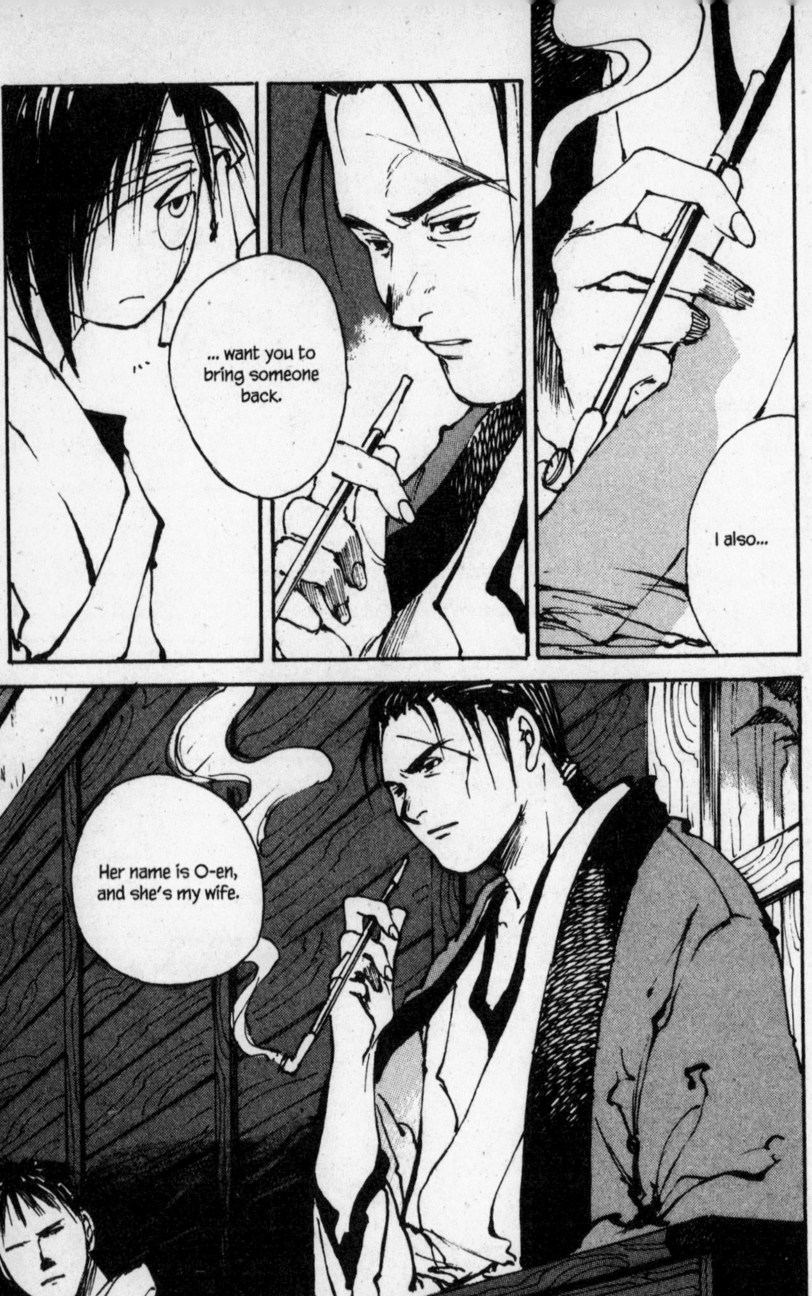
I also...
... want you to bring someone back.
Her name is O-en, and she's my wife.

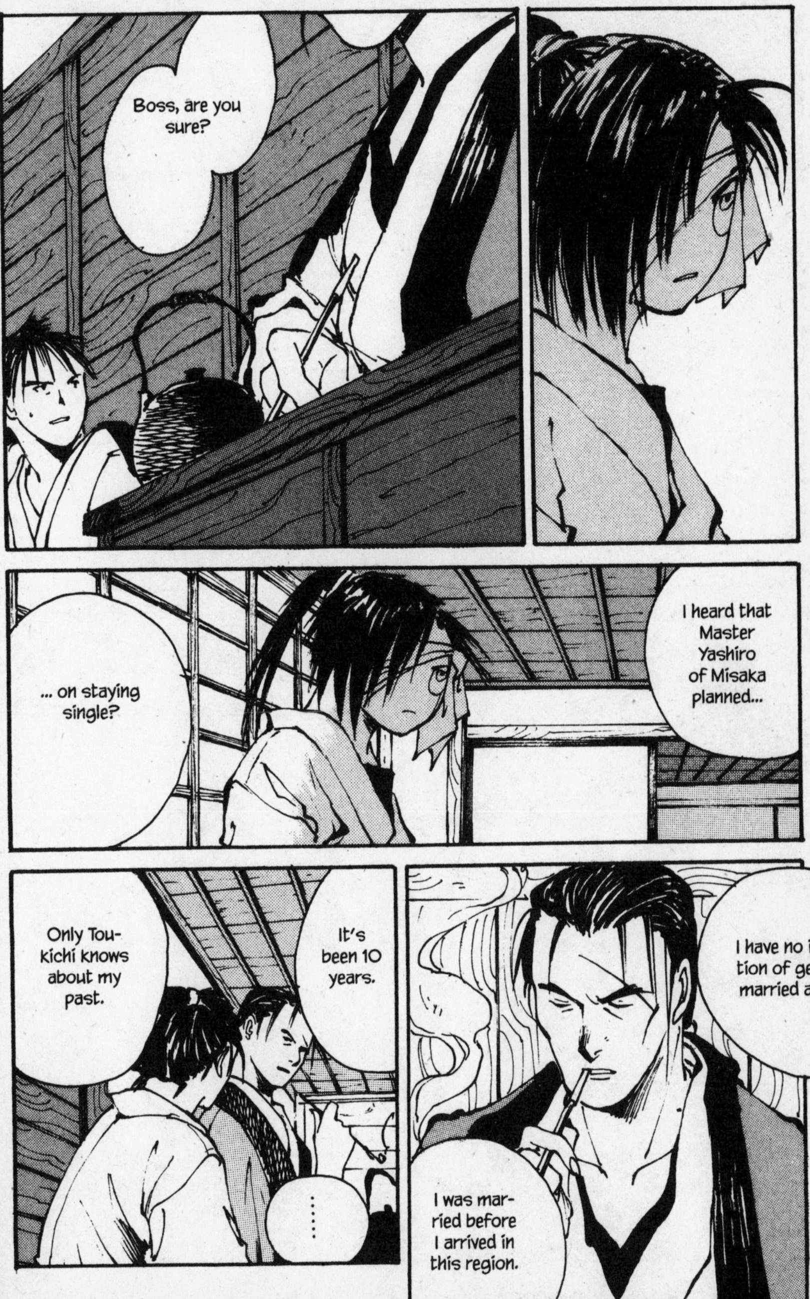
Boss, are you sure?
I heard that Master Yashiro of Misaka planned...
... on staying single?
I have no intention of getting married again.
I was married before I arrived in this region.
It's been 10 years.
Only Tou-kichi knows about my past.
......

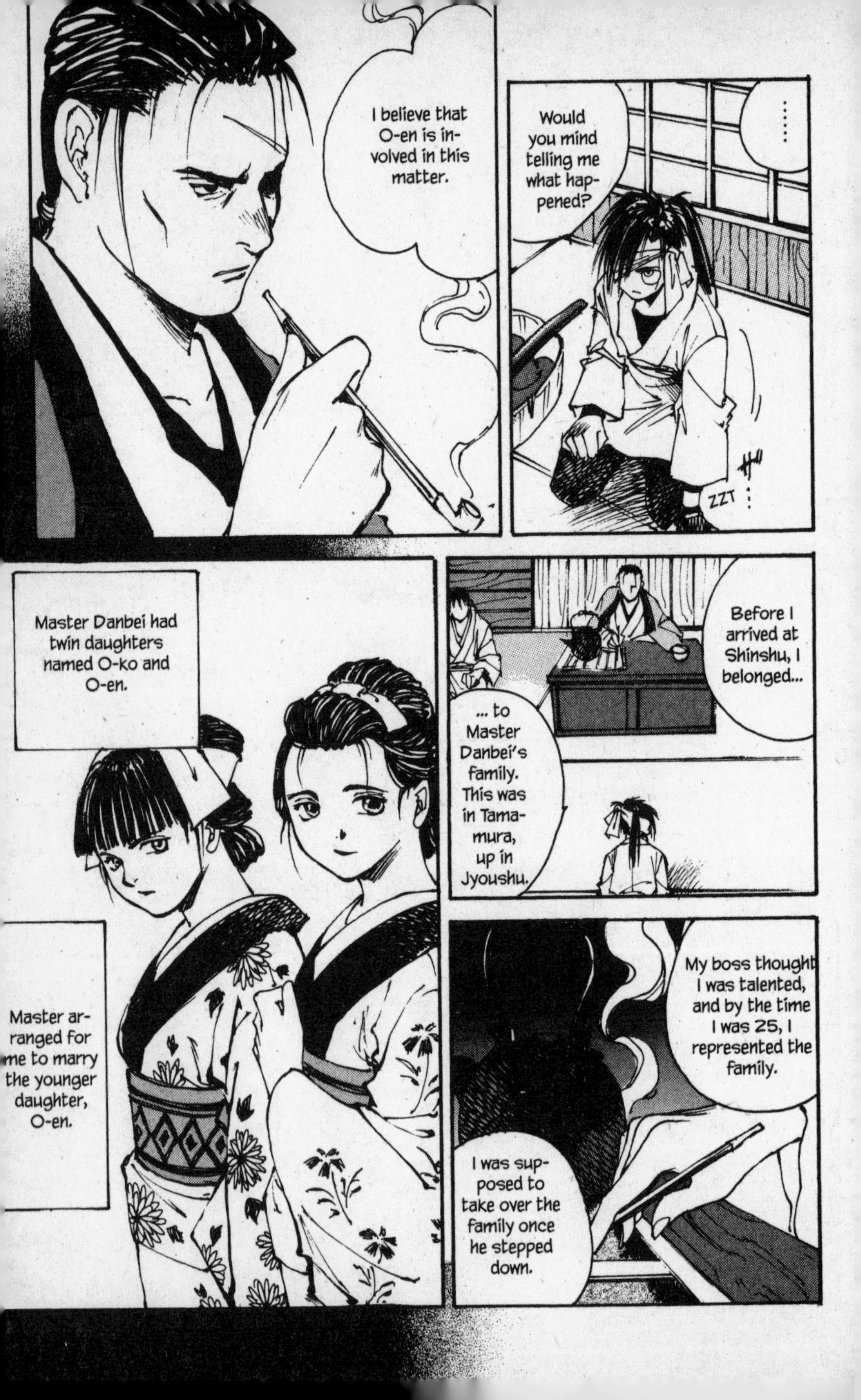
......
Would you mind telling me what happened?
ZZT...
I believe that O-en is involved in this matter.
Before I arrived at Shinshu, I belonged...
... to Master Danbei's family. This was in Tamamura, up in Jyoushu.
My boss thought I was talented, and by the time I was 25, I represented the family.
I was supposed to take over the family once he stepped down.
Master Danbei had twin daughters named O-ko and O-en.
Master arranged for me to marry the younger daughter, O-en.

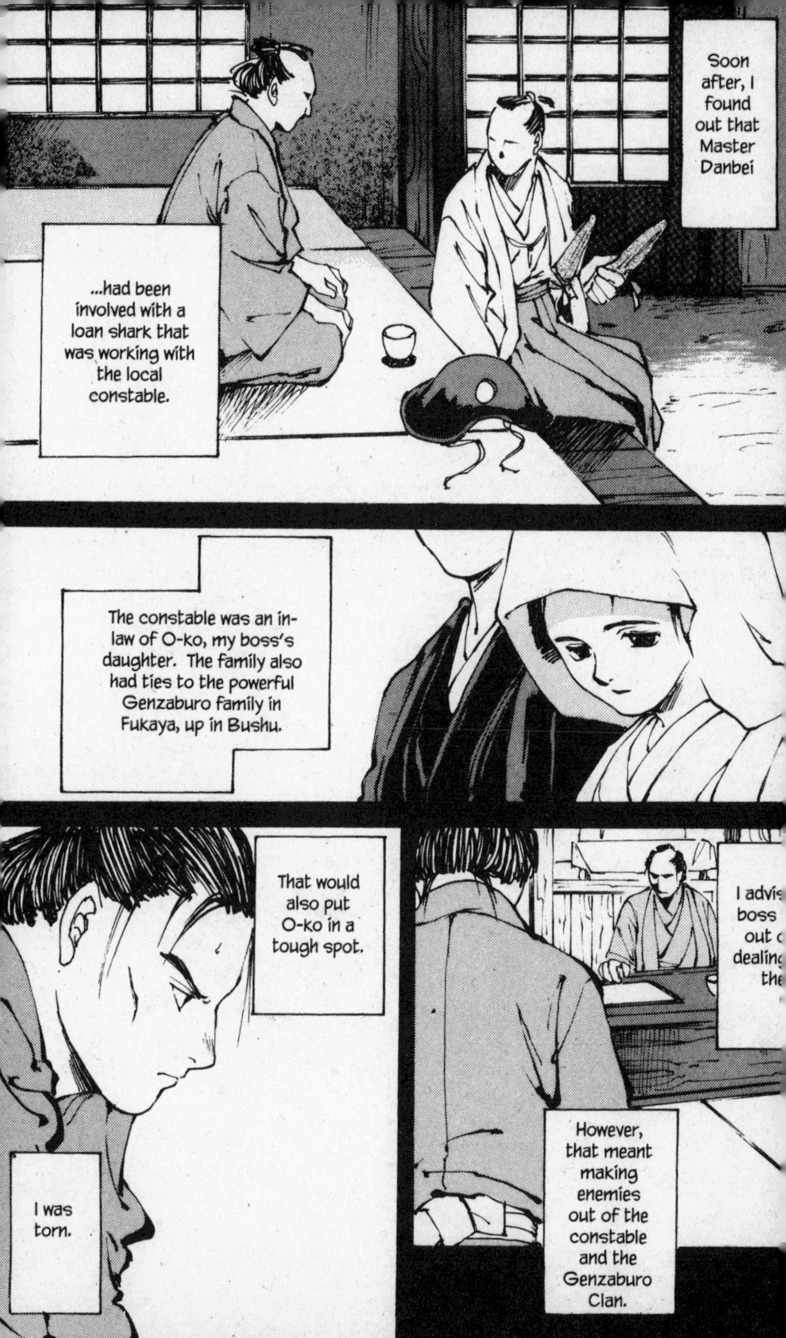
Soon after, I found out that Master Danbei
...had been involved with a loan shark that was working with the local constable.
The constable was an in-law of O-ko, my boss's daughter. The family also had ties to the powerful Genzaburo family in Fukaya, up in Bushu.
However, that meant making enemies out of the constable and the Genzaburo Clan.
That would also put O-ko in a tough spot.
I was torn.

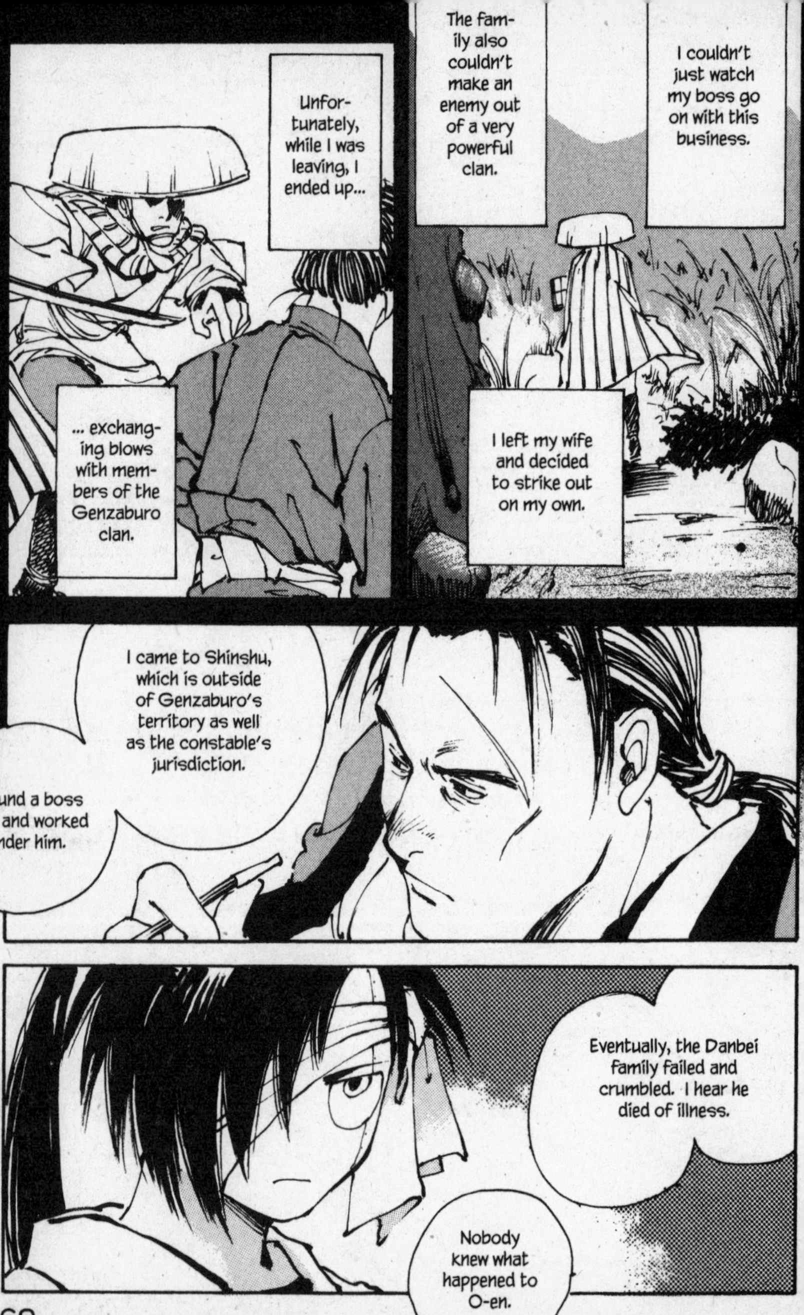
I couldn't just watch my boss go on with this business.
The family also couldn't make an enemy out of a very powerful clan.
I left my wife and decided to strike out on my own.
Unfortunately, while I was leaving, I ended up...
... exchanging blows with members of the Genzaburo clan.
I came to Shinshu, which is outside of Genzaburo's territory as well as the constable's jurisdiction.
I found a boss here and worked under him.
Eventually, the Danbei family failed and crumbled. I hear he died of illness.
Nobody knew what happened to O-en.

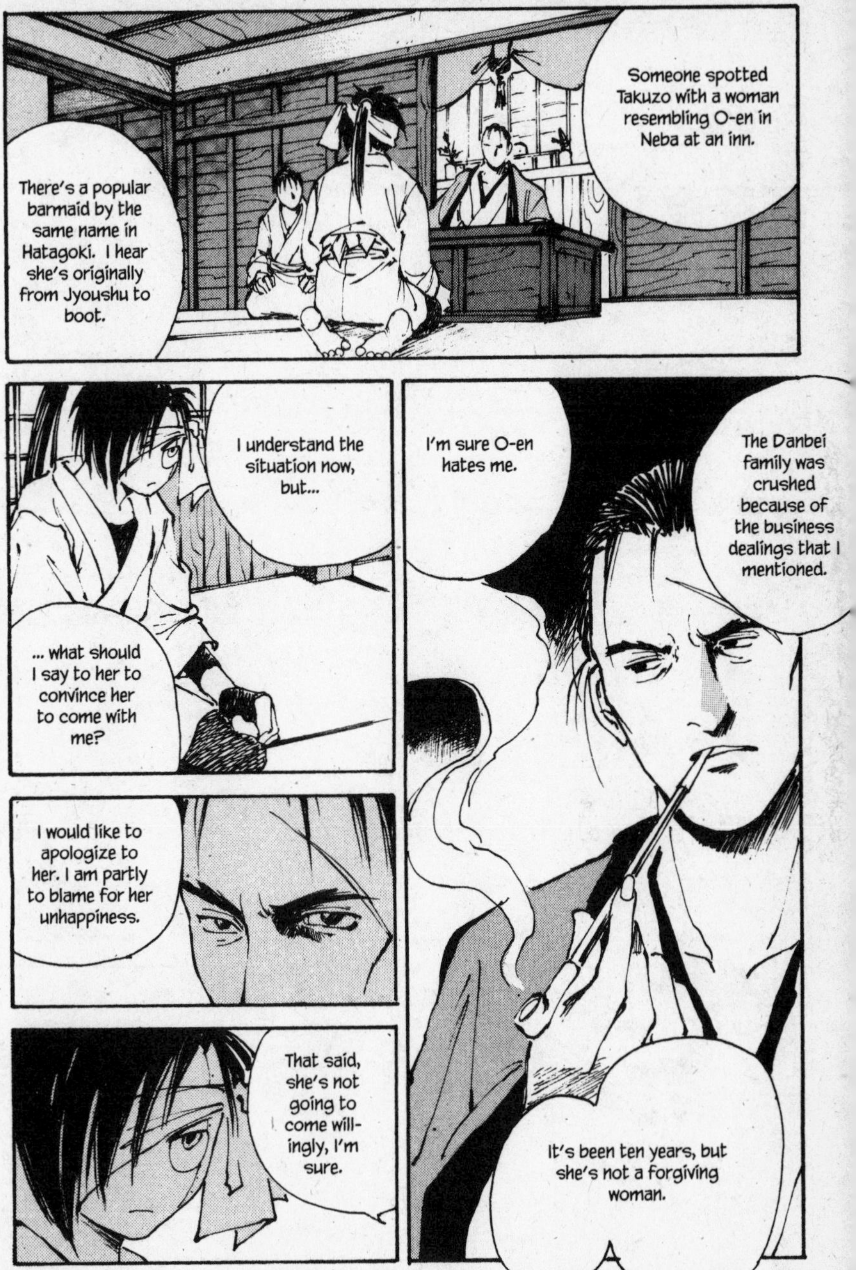

Someone spotted Takuzo with a woman resembling O-en in Neba at an inn.
There's a popular barmaid by the same name in Hatagoki. I hear she's originally from Jyoushu to boot.
The Danbei family was crushed because of the business dealings that I mentioned.
I'm sure O-en hates me.
It's been ten years, but she's not a forgiving woman.
I understand the situation now, but...
... what should I say to her to convince her to come with me?
I would like to apologize to her. I am partly to blame for her unhappiness.
That said, she's not going to come willingly, I'm sure.

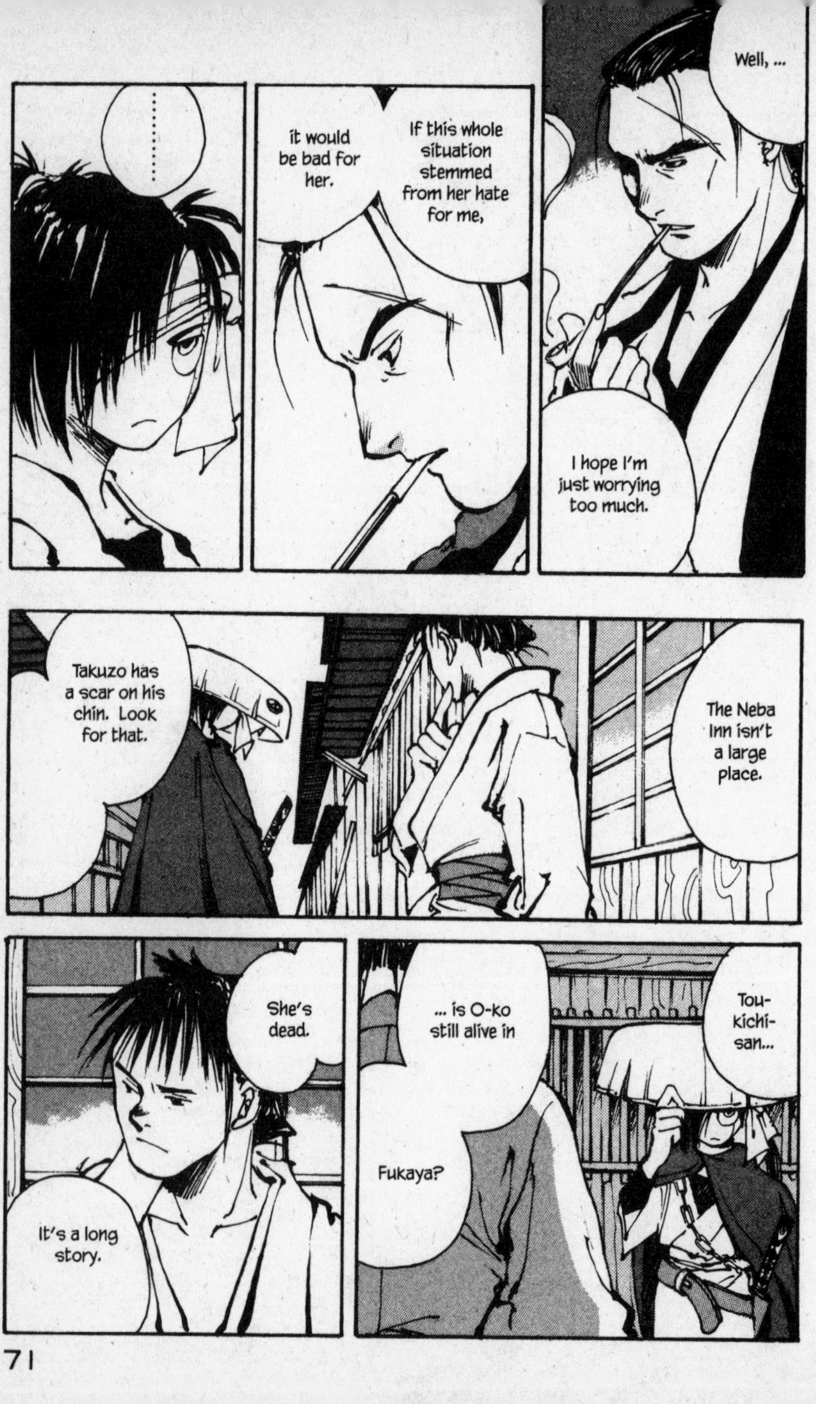
Well, ...
I hope I'm just worrying too much.
If this whole situation stemmed from her hate for me,
it would be bad for her.
......
The Neba Inn isn't a large place.
Takuzo has a scar on his chin. Look for that.
Tou-kichi-san...
... is O-ko still alive in
Fukaya?
She's dead.
It's a long story.

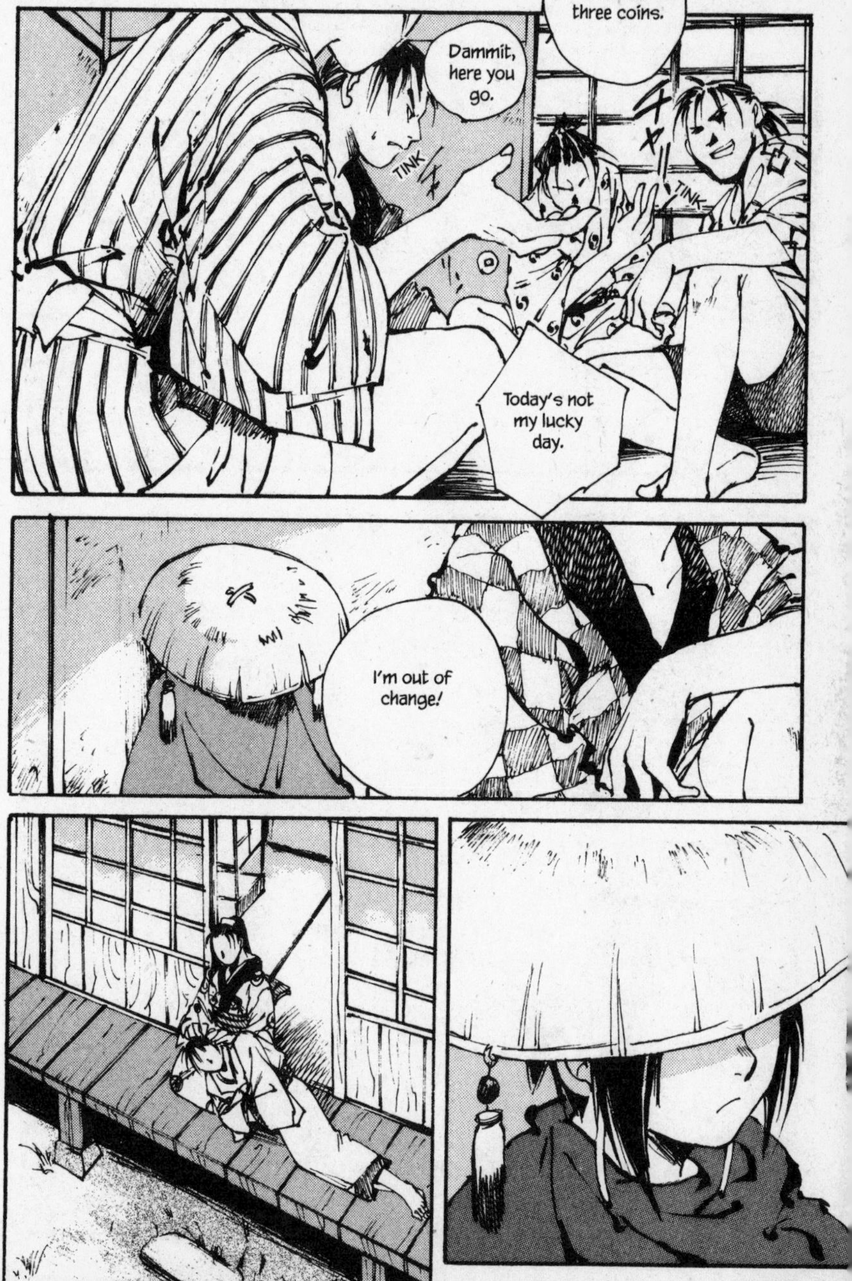
Two and three coins.
TINK
Dammit, here you go.
TINK
Today's not my lucky day.
I'm out of change!

* Nango- a gambling game using spare change. It is played by having your opponent guess the number of coins you hold in your hand.

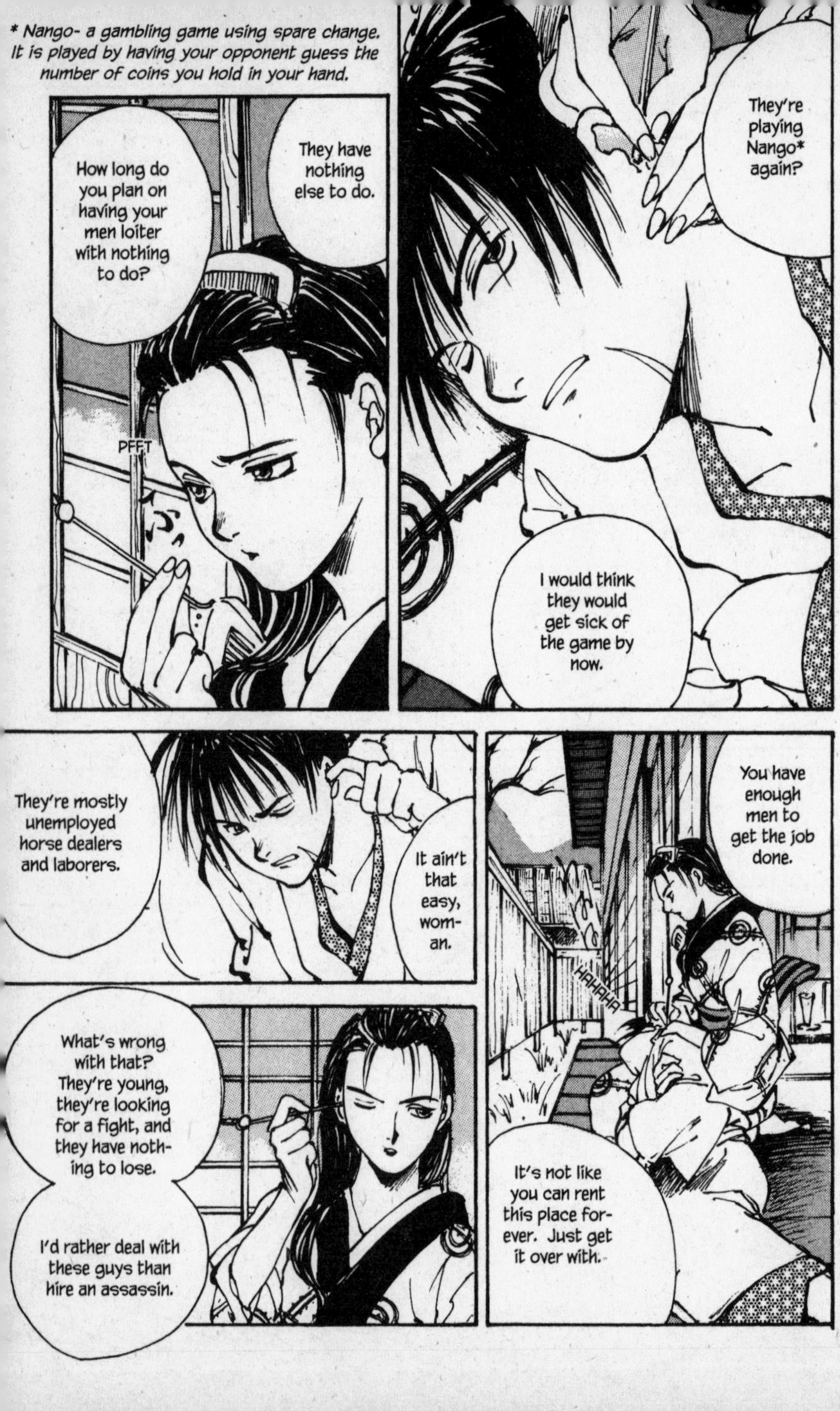
They're playing Nango* again?
I would think they would get sick of the game by now.
They have nothing else to do.
How long do you plan on having your men loiter with nothing to do?
PFFT
You have enough men to get the job done.
HAHAHA
It's not like you can rent this place forever. Just get it over with.
It ain't that easy, woman.
They're mostly unemployed horse dealers and laborers.
What's wrong with that? They're young, they're looking for a fight, and they have nothing to lose.
I'd rather deal with these guys than hire an assassin.

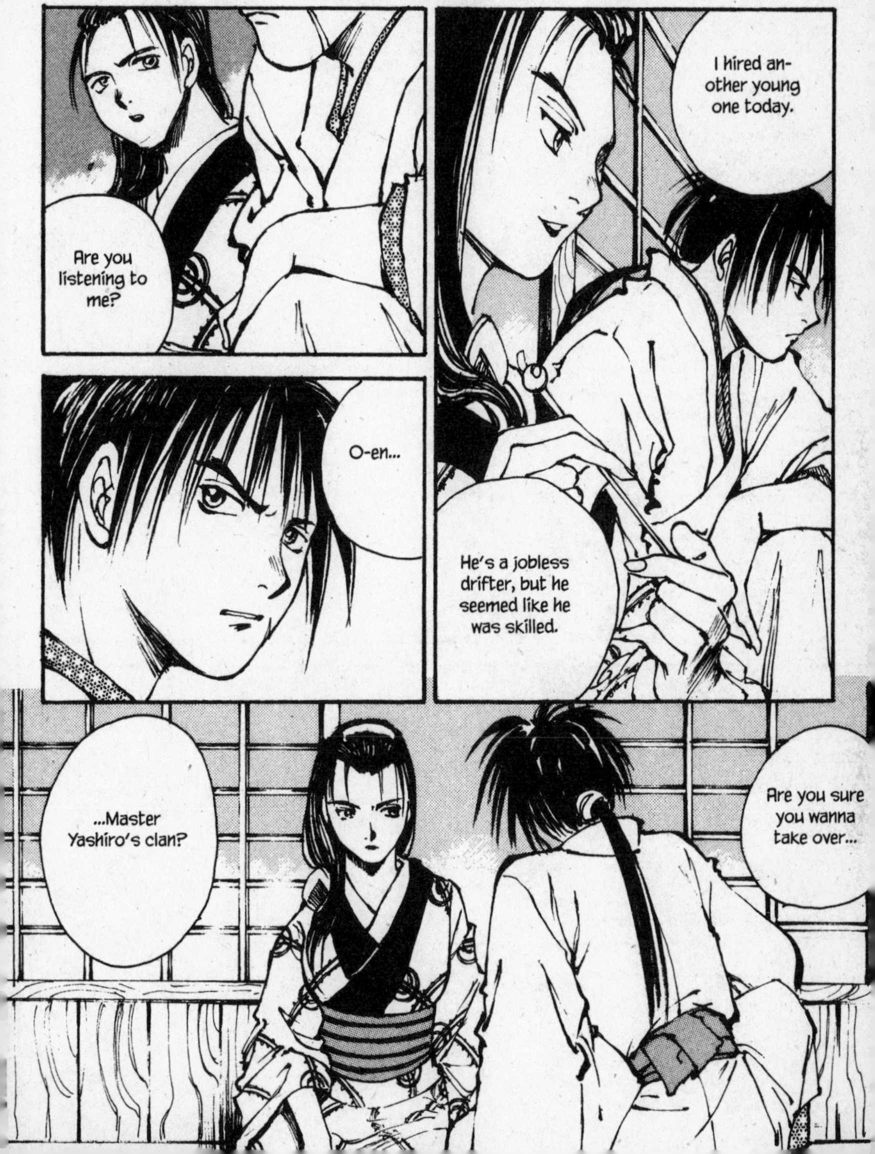
I hired an-other young one today.
He's a jobless drifter, but he seemed like he was skilled.
Are you listening to me?
O-en...
Are you sure you wanna take over...
...Master Yashiro's clan?

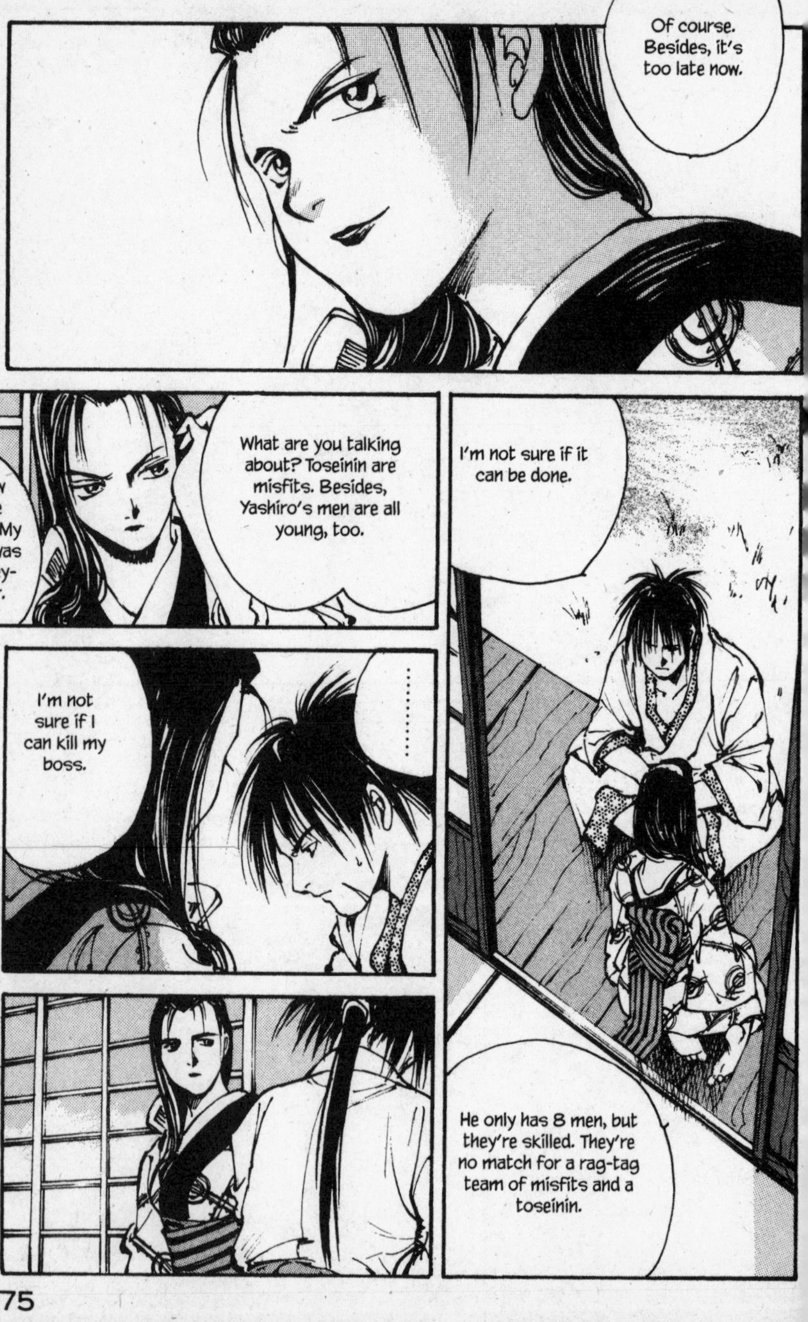
Of course. Besides, it's too late now.
I'm not sure if it can be done.
He only has 8 men, but they're skilled. They're no match for a rag-tag team of misfits and a toseinin.
What are you talking about? Toseinin are misfits. Besides, Yashiro's men are all young, too.
I know these things. My father was a money-lender.
......
I'm not sure if I can kill my boss.

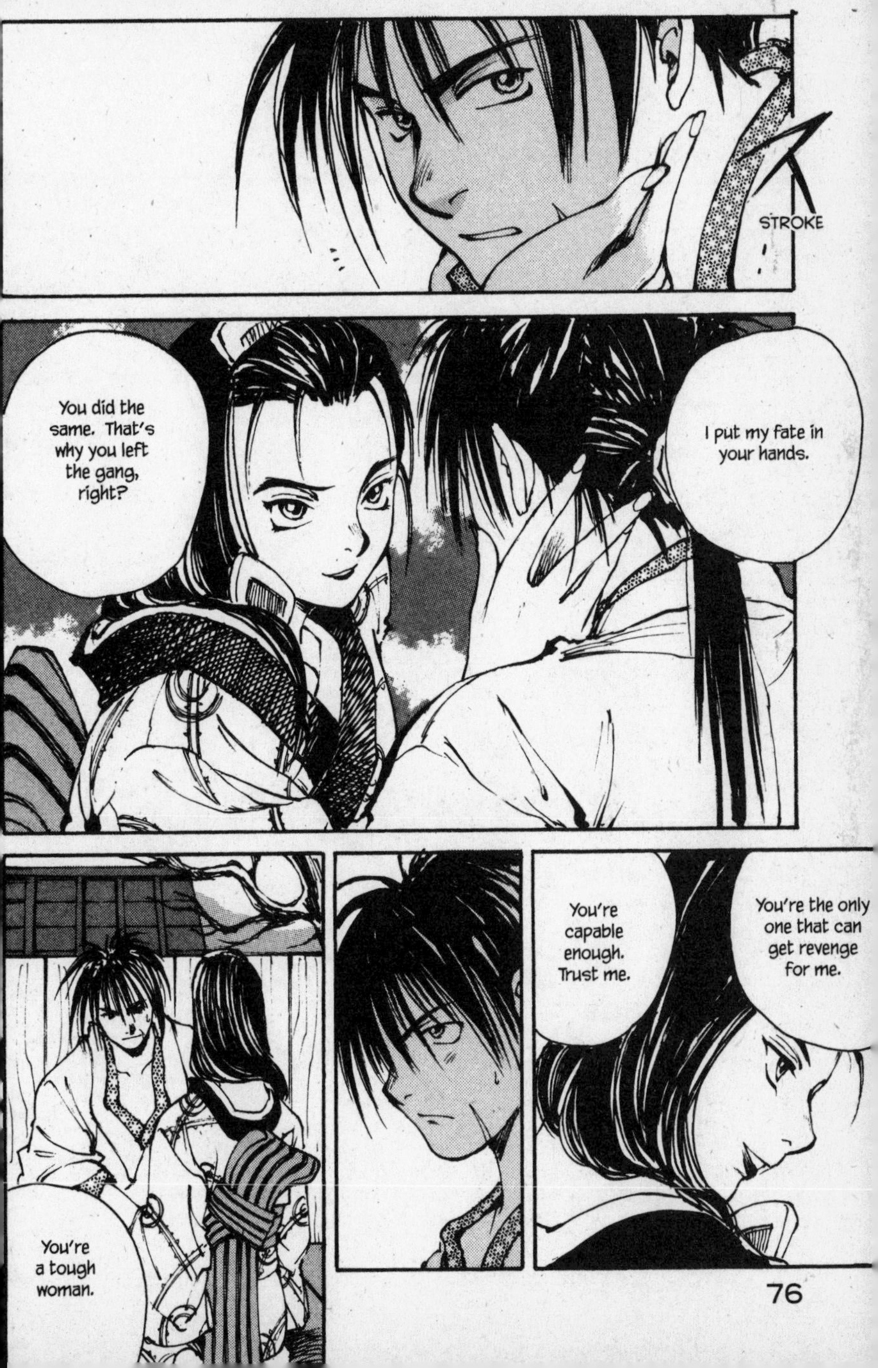
STROKE
I put my fate in your hands.
You did the same. That's why you left the gang, right?
You're the only one that can get revenge for me.
You're capable enough. Trust me.
You're a tough woman.

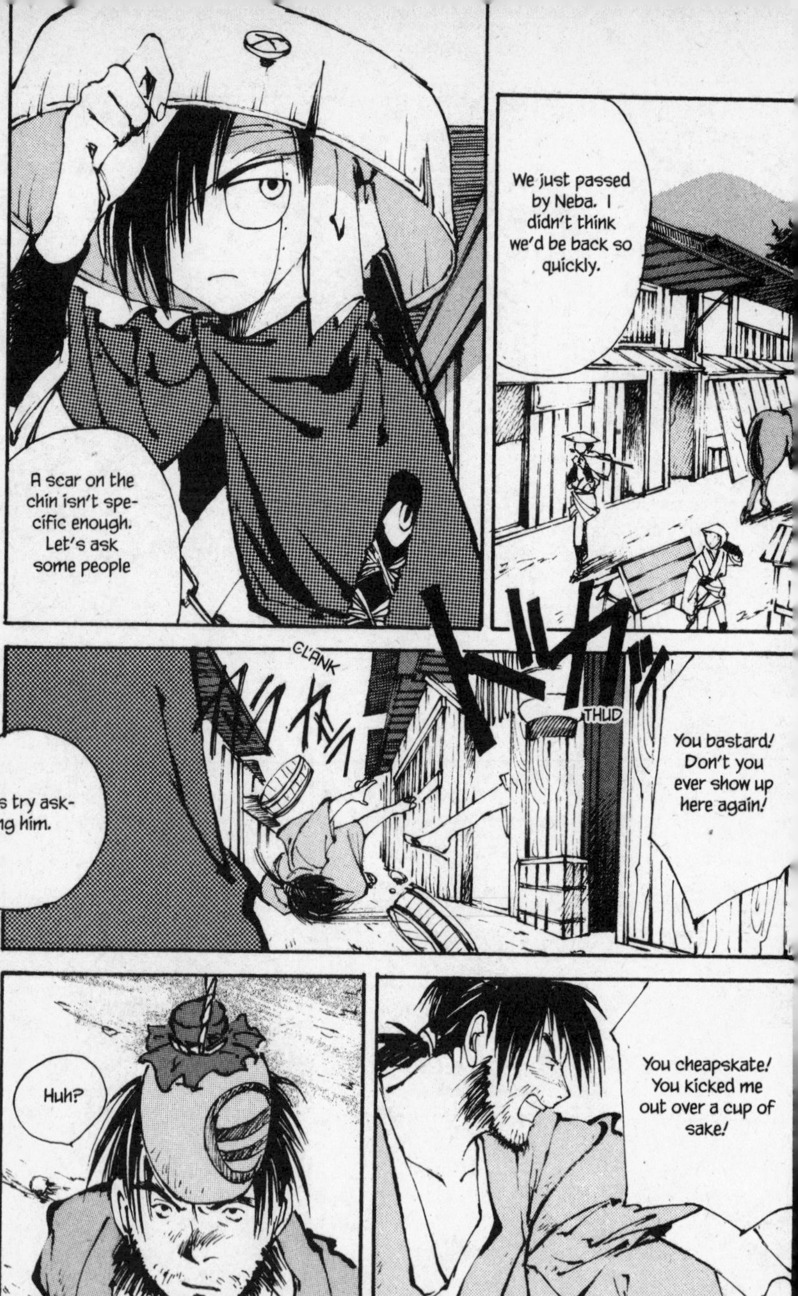
We just passed by Neba. I didn't think we'd be back so quickly.
A scar on the chin isn't specific enough. Let's ask some people
THUD
You bastard! Don't you ever show up here again!
CLANK
Let's try asking him.
You cheapskate! You kicked me out over a cup of sake!
Huh?

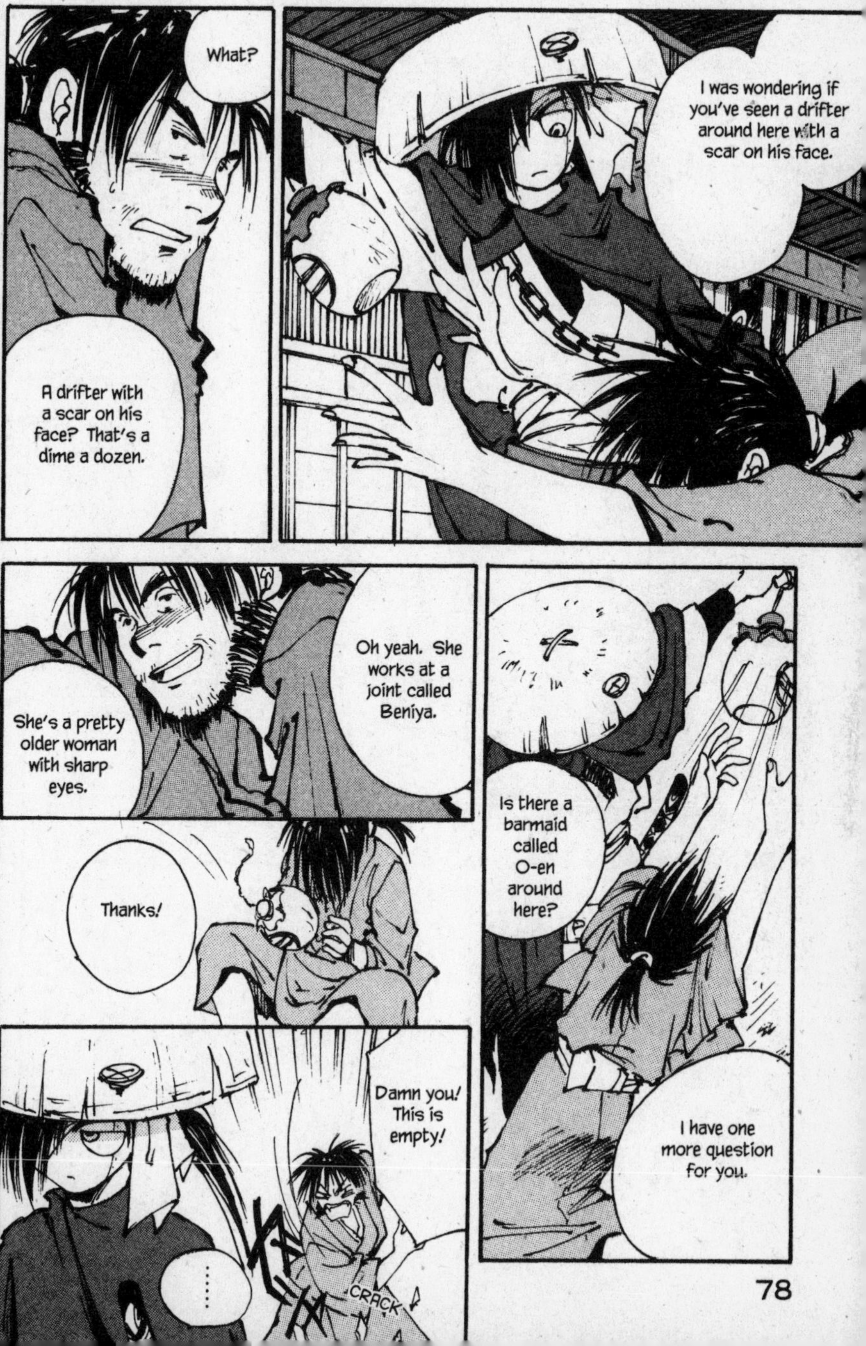
I was wondering if you've seen a drifter around here with a scar on his face.
What?
A drifter with a scar on his face? That's a dime a dozen.
I have one more question for you.
Is there a barmaid called O-en around here?
Oh yeah. She works at a joint called Beniya.
She's a pretty older woman with sharp eyes.
Thanks!
Damn you! This is empty!
CRACK
......

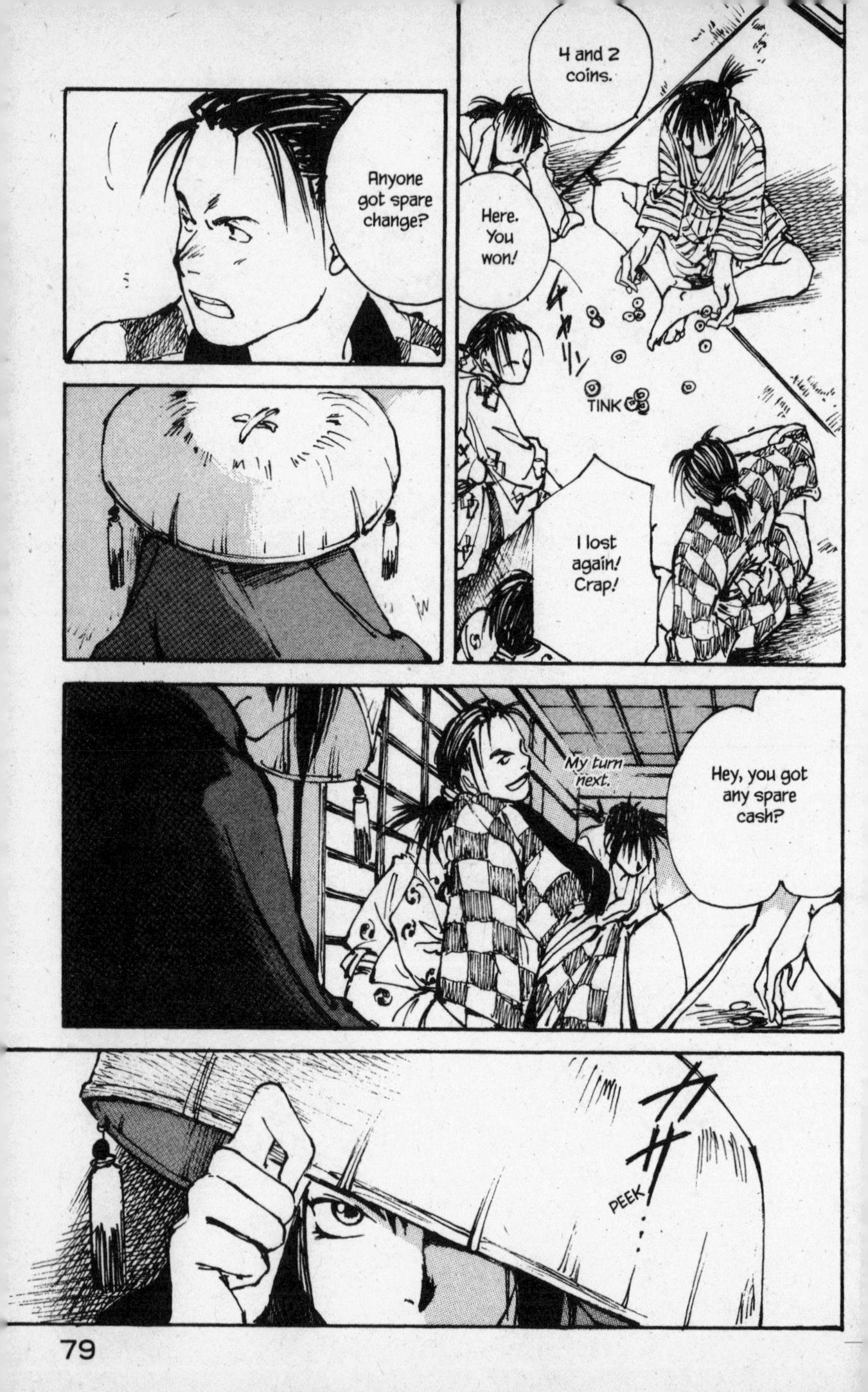
4 and 2 coins.
Here. You won!
TINK
I lost again! Crap!
Anyone got spare change?
Hey, you got any spare cash?
My turn next.
PEEK

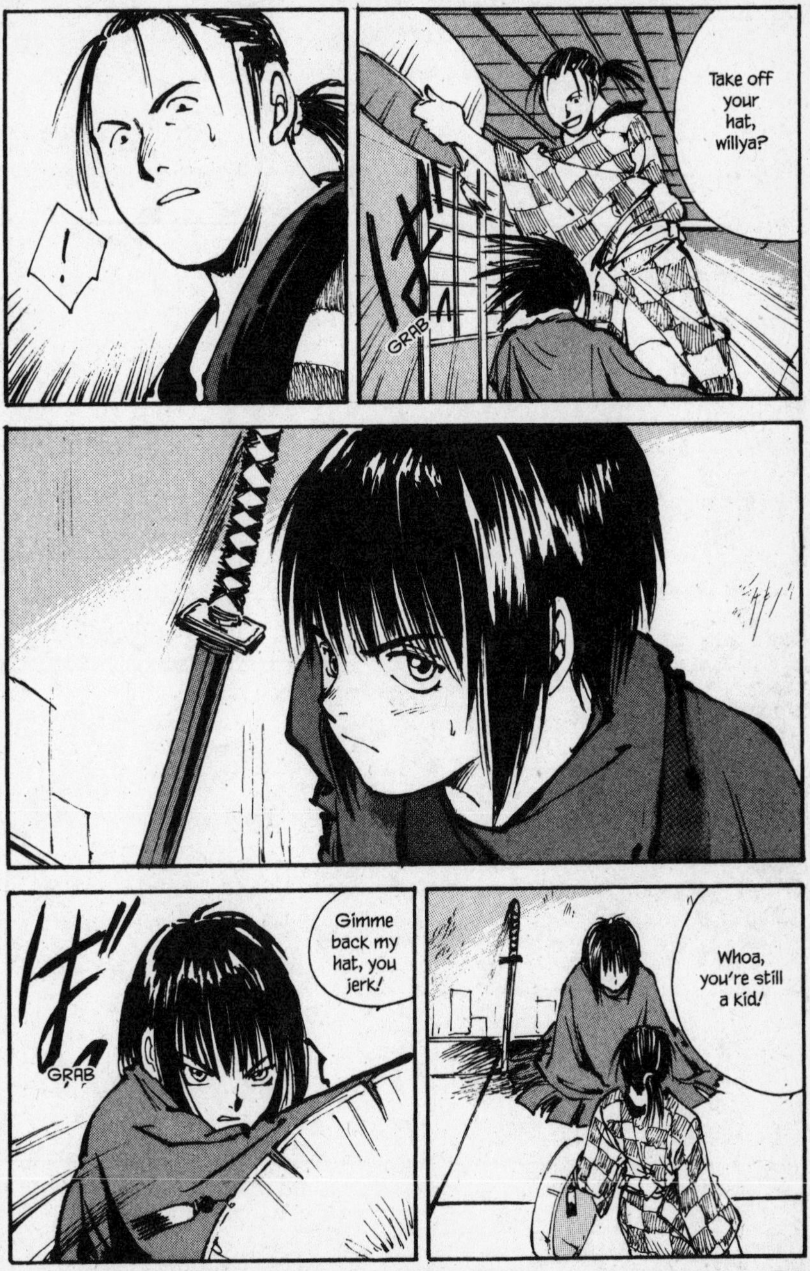
Take off your hat, willya?
GRAB
!
Whoa, you're still a kid!
Gimme back my hat, you jerk!
GRAB

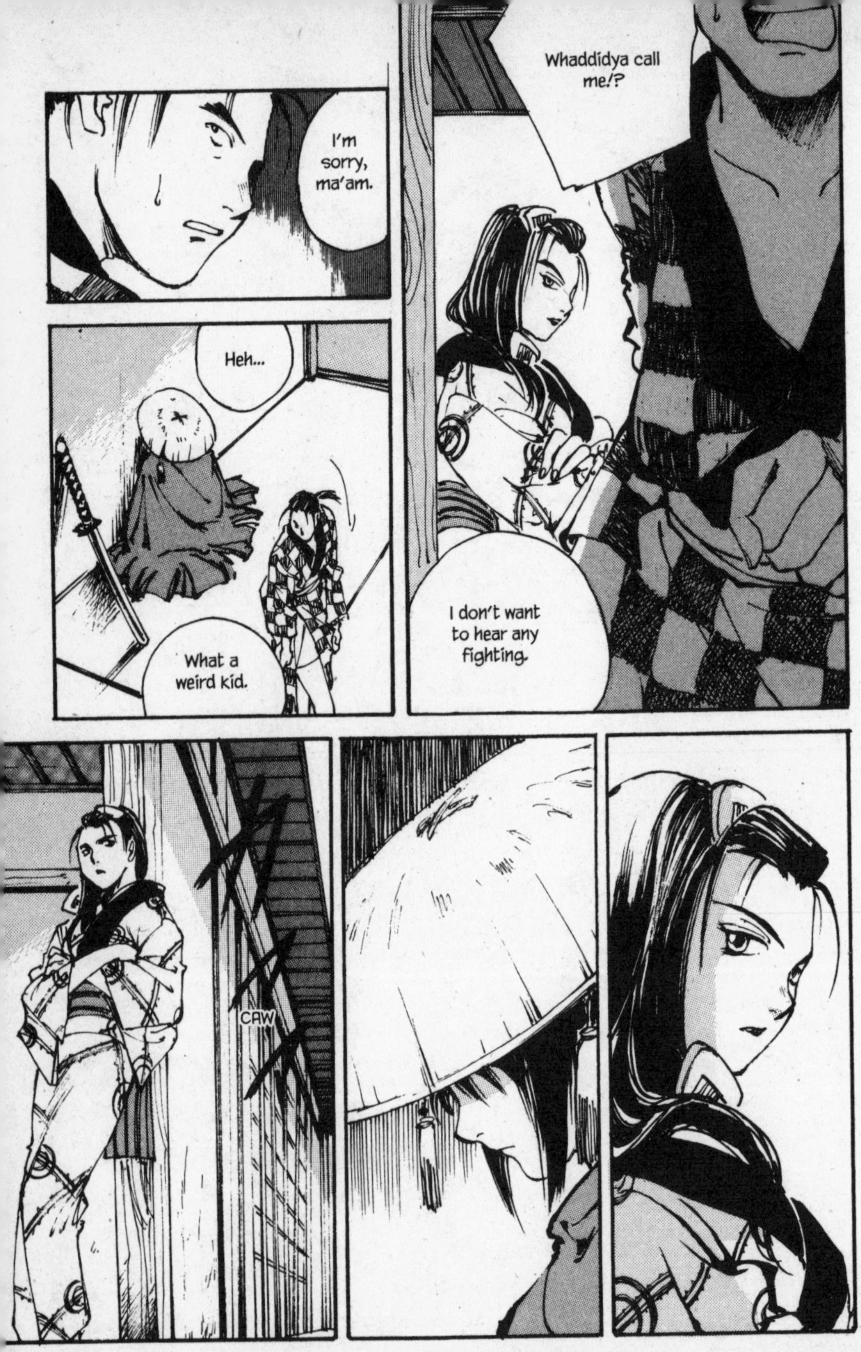
Whaddidya call me!?
I don't want to hear any fighting.
I'm sorry, ma'am.
Heh...
What a weird kid.
CAW

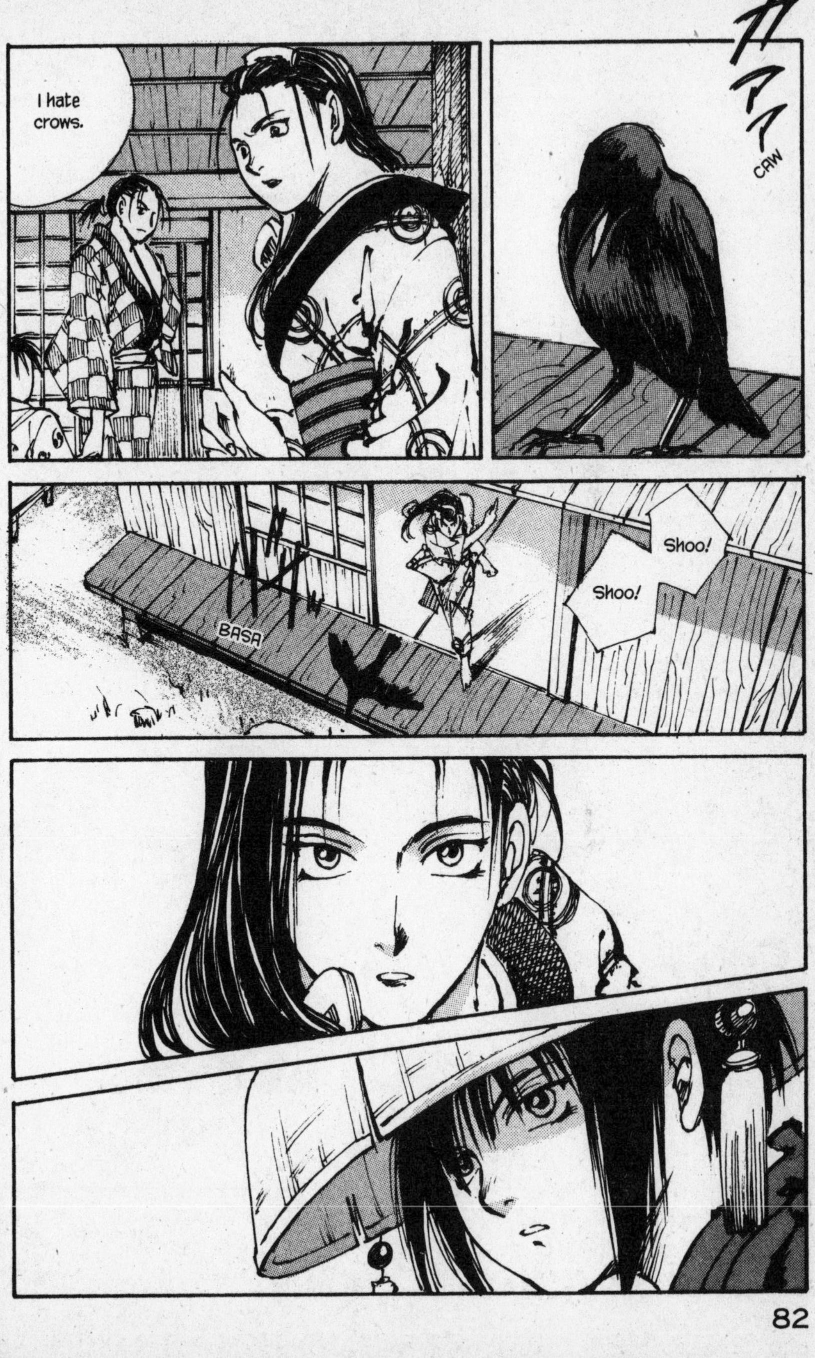
カアア
CAW
I hate crows.
Shoo!
Shoo!
BASA

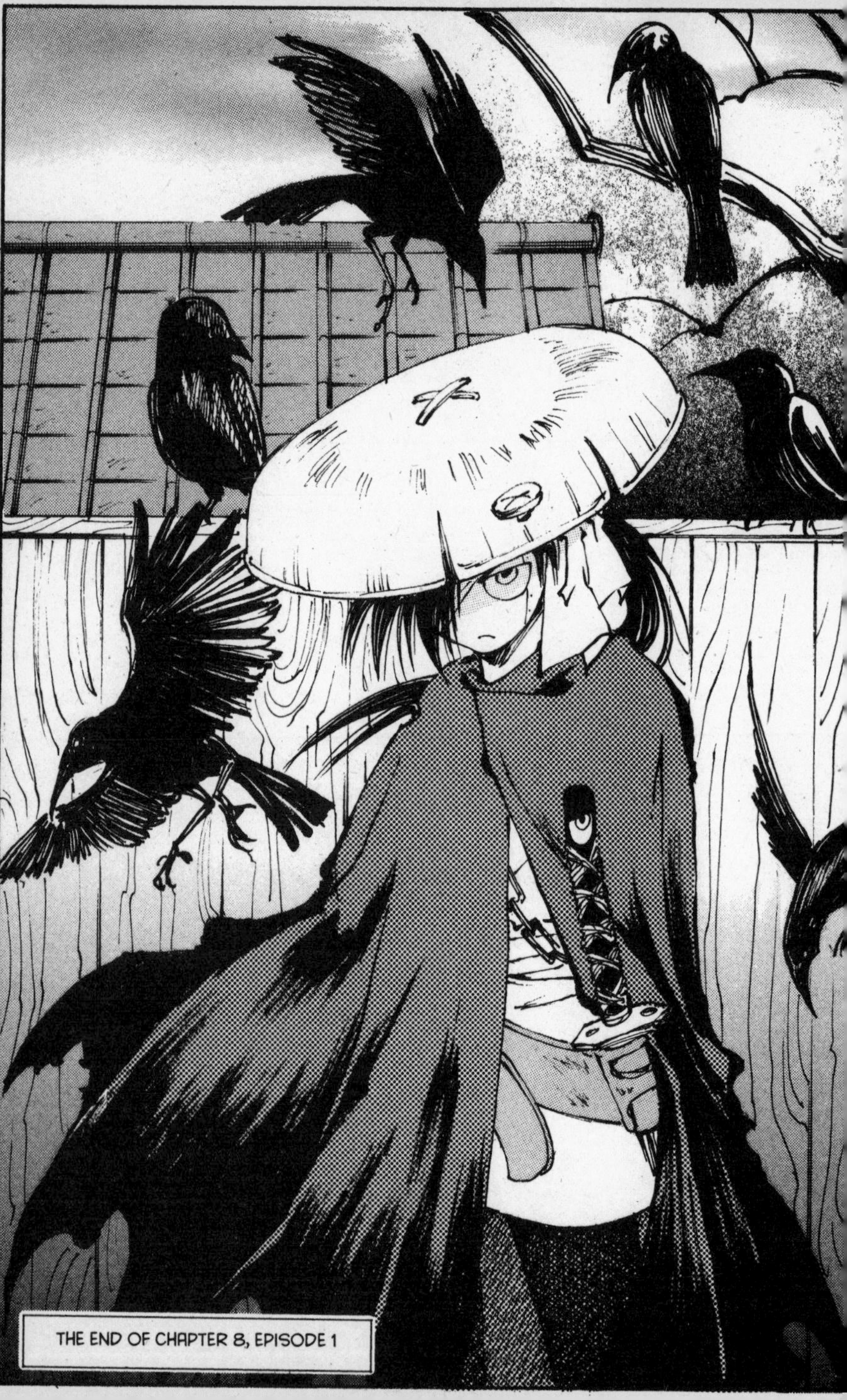
THE END OF CHAPTER 8, EPISODE 1

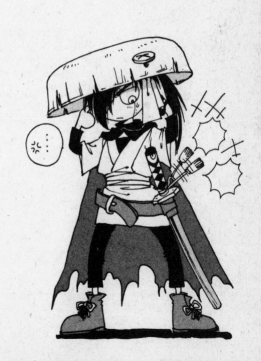

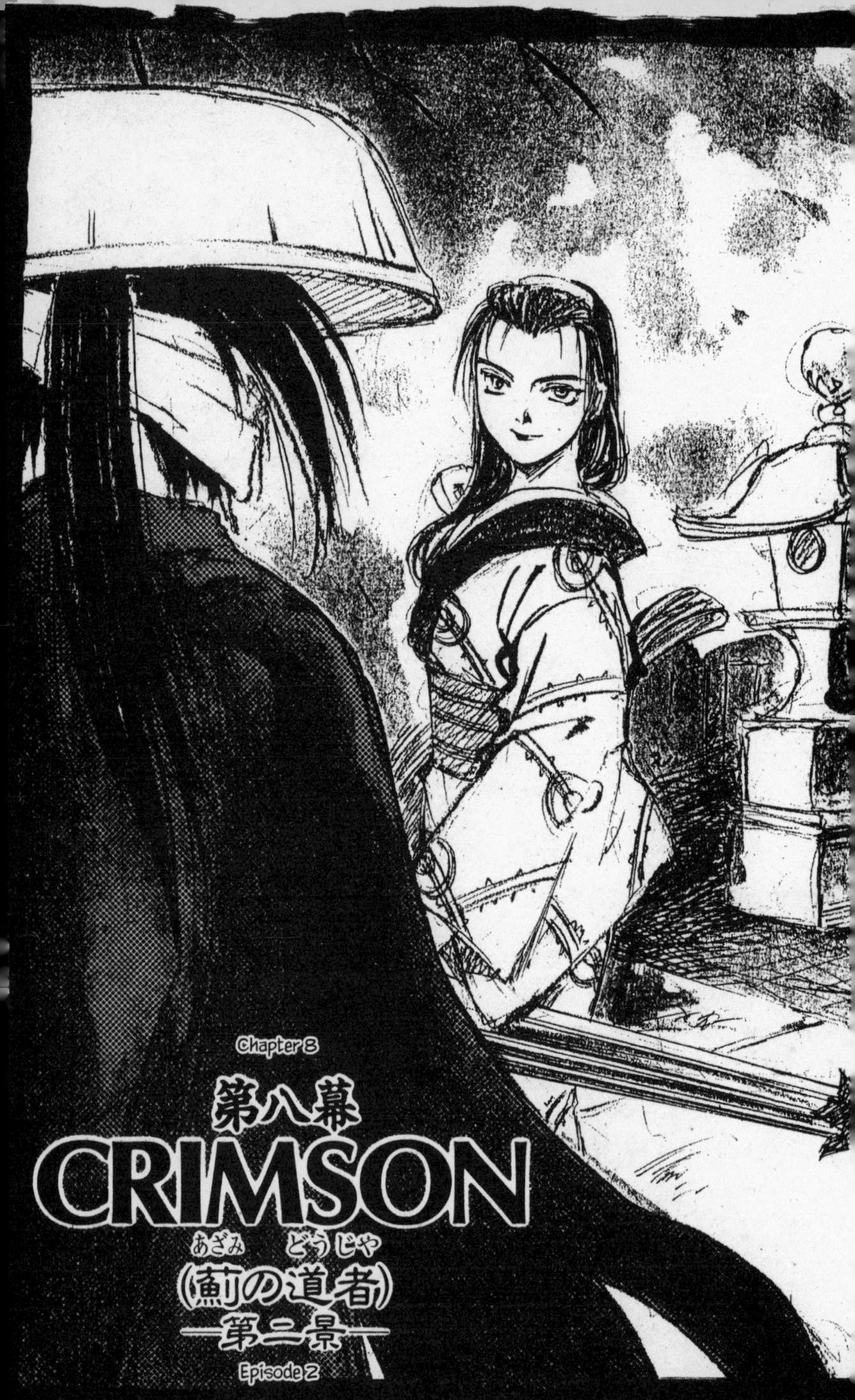
Chapter 8
第八幕
CRIMSON
あざみ　どうじゃ
(薊の道者)
—第二景—
Episode 2

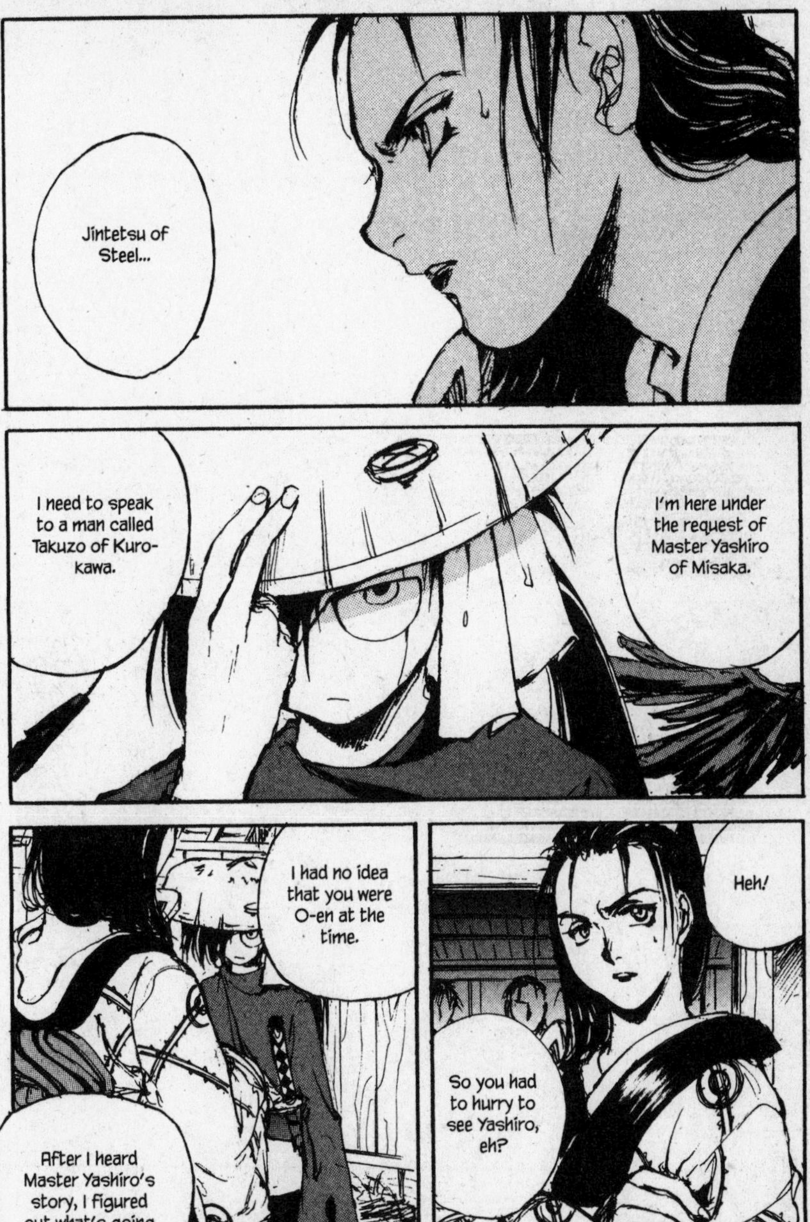
Jintetsu of Steel...
I'm here under the request of Master Yashiro of Misaka.
I need to speak to a man called Takuzo of Kuro-kawa.
Heh!
So you had to hurry to see Yashiro, eh?
I had no idea that you were O-en at the time.
After I heard Master Yashiro's story, I figured out what's going on.

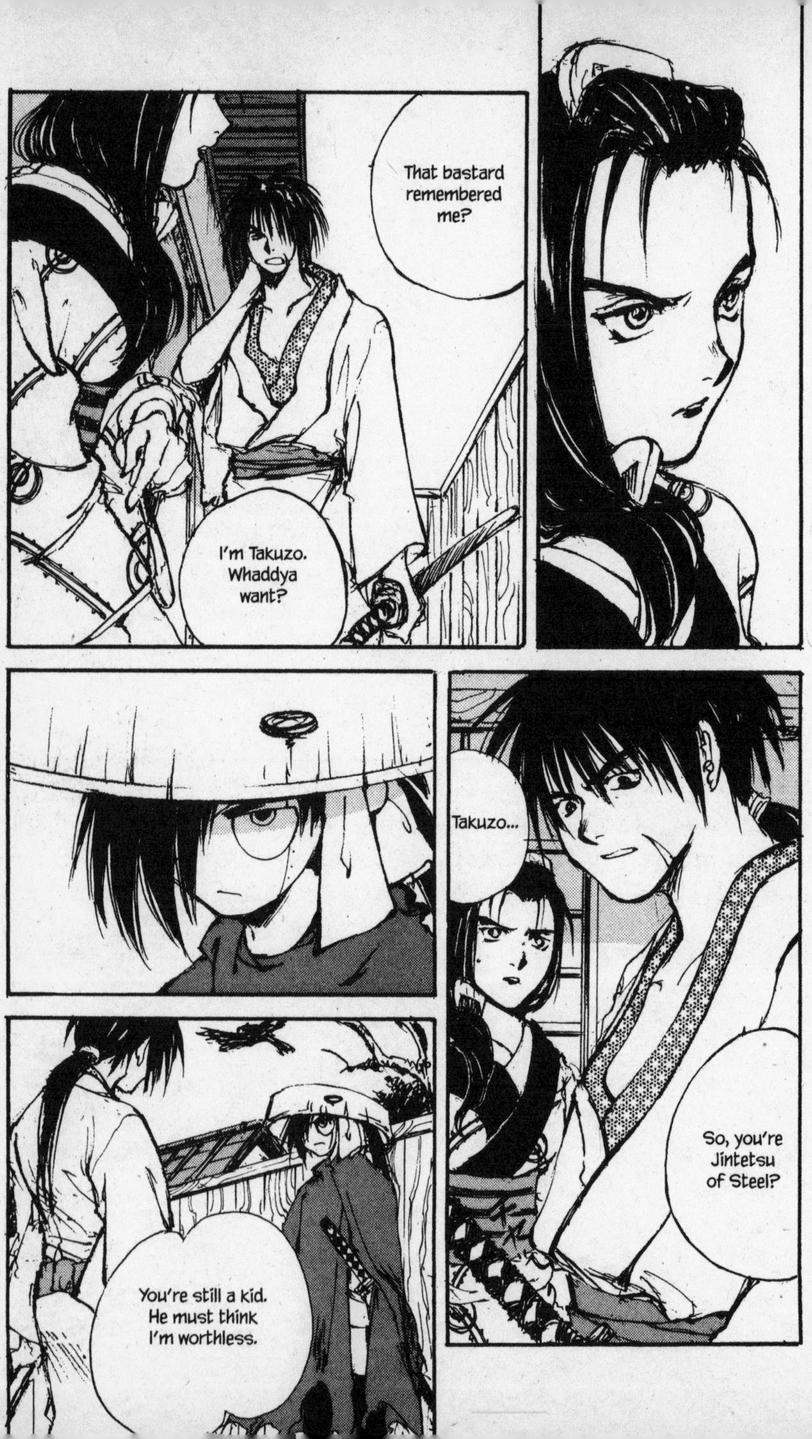
That bastard remembered me?
I'm Takuzo. Whaddya want?
Takuzo...
So, you're Jintetsu of Steel?
You're still a kid. He must think I'm worthless.

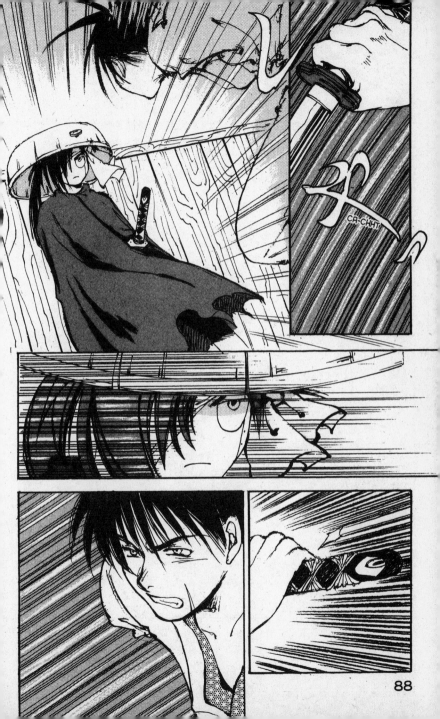

CA-CHHT

88

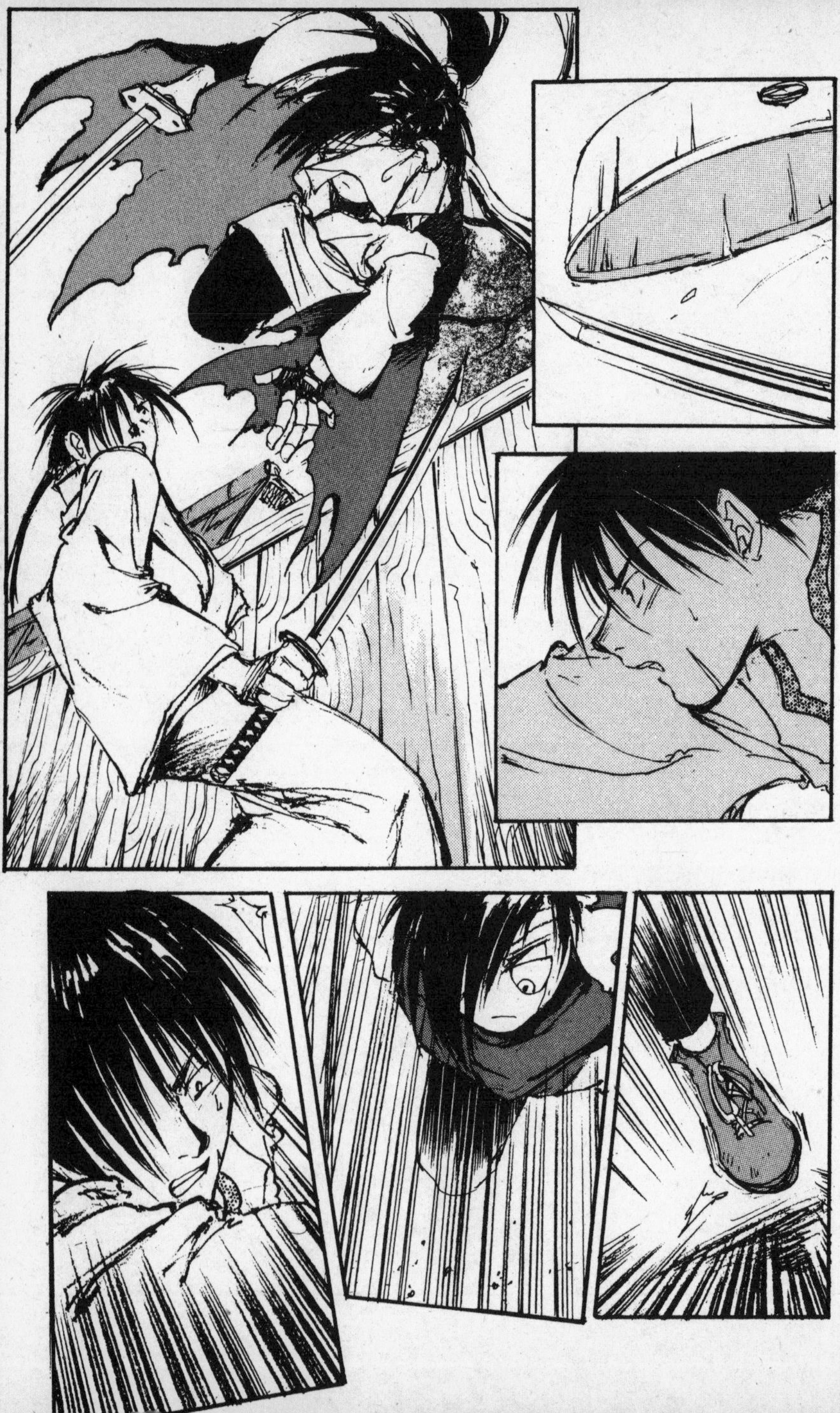

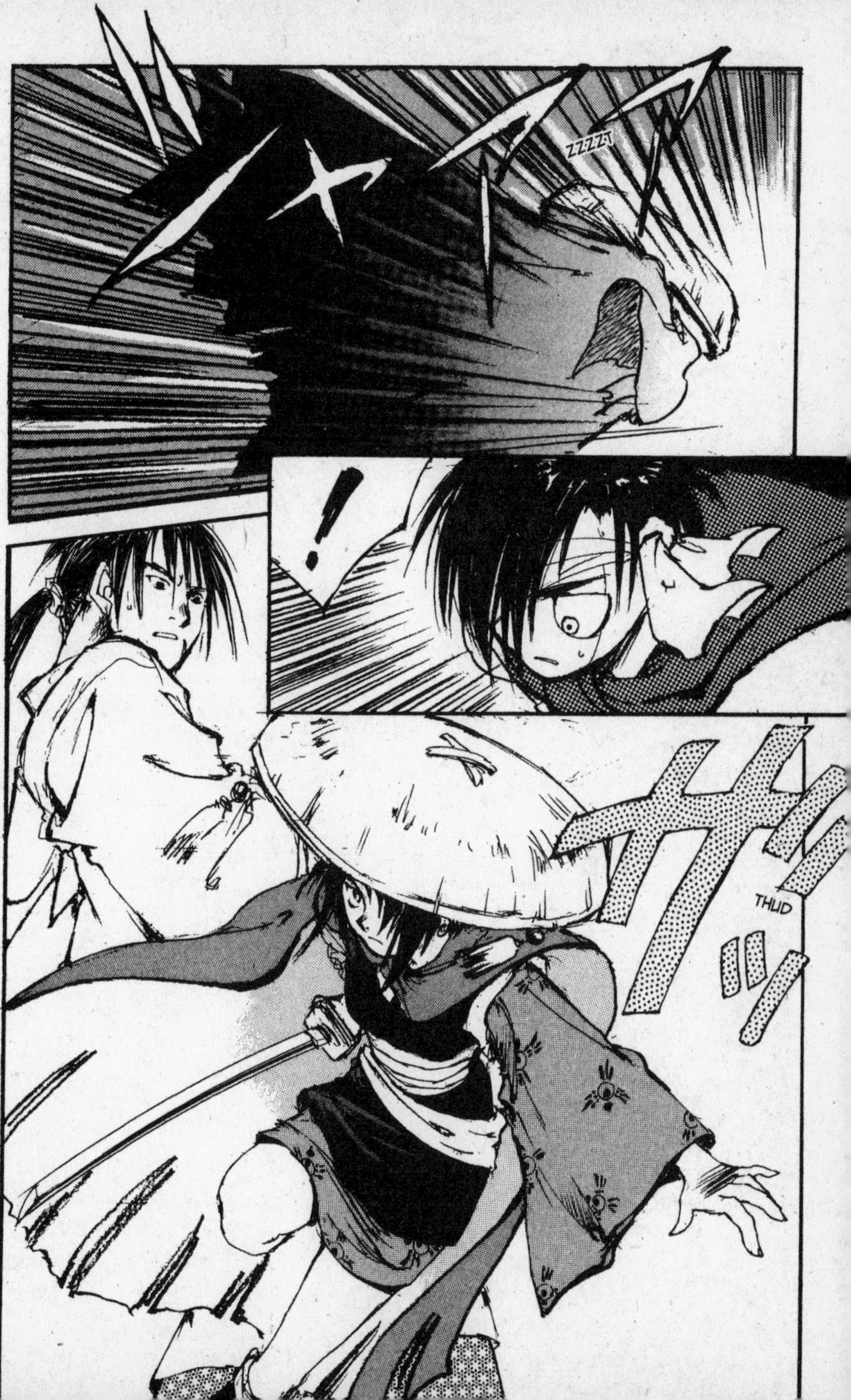
ZZZZZT
!
THUD

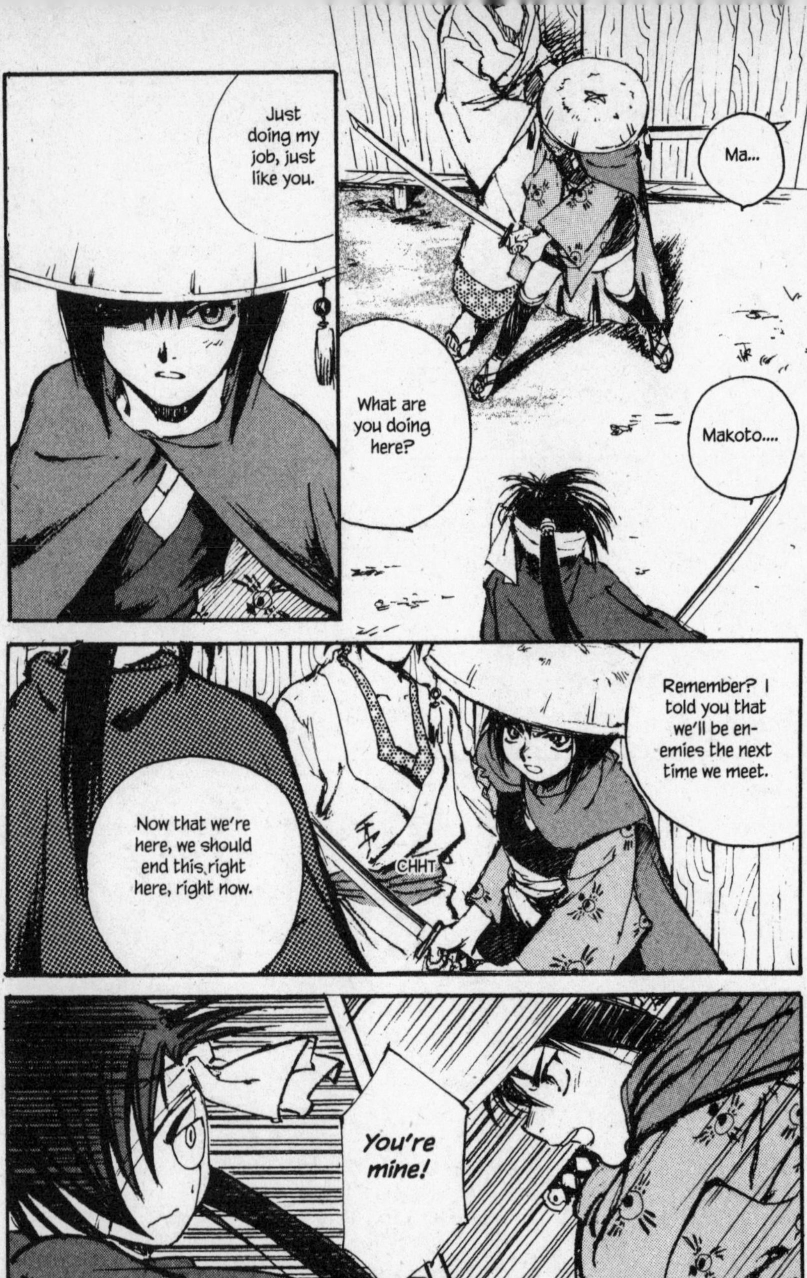
Ma...
Makoto....
What are you doing here?
Just doing my job, just like you.
Remember? I told you that we'll be enemies the next time we meet.
CHHT
Now that we're here, we should end this right here, right now.
You're mine!

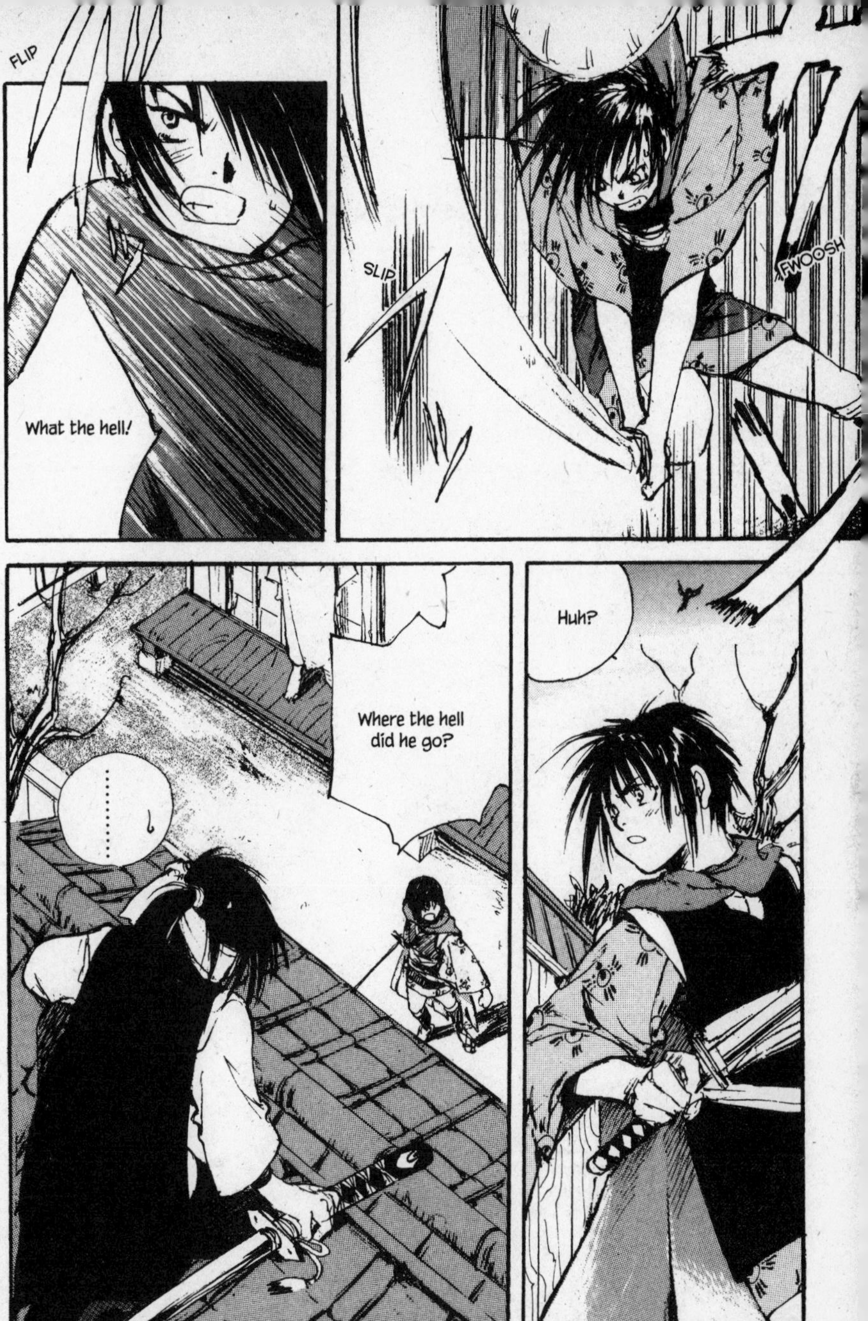
FWOOSH
SLIP
FLIP
What the hell!
Huh?
Where the hell did he go?
......

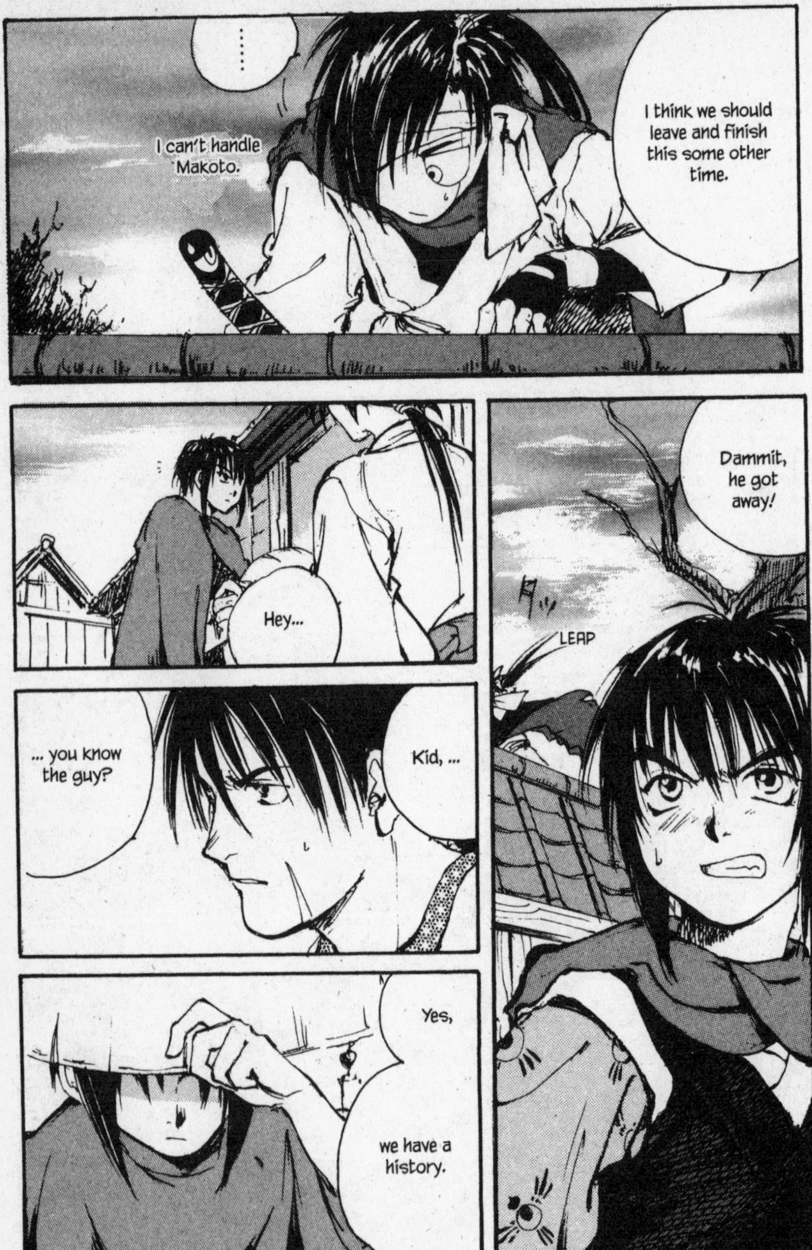
I think we should leave and finish this some other time.
......
I can't handle Makoto.
Dammit, he got away!
LEAP
Hey...
Kid, ...
... you know the guy?
Yes,
we have a history.

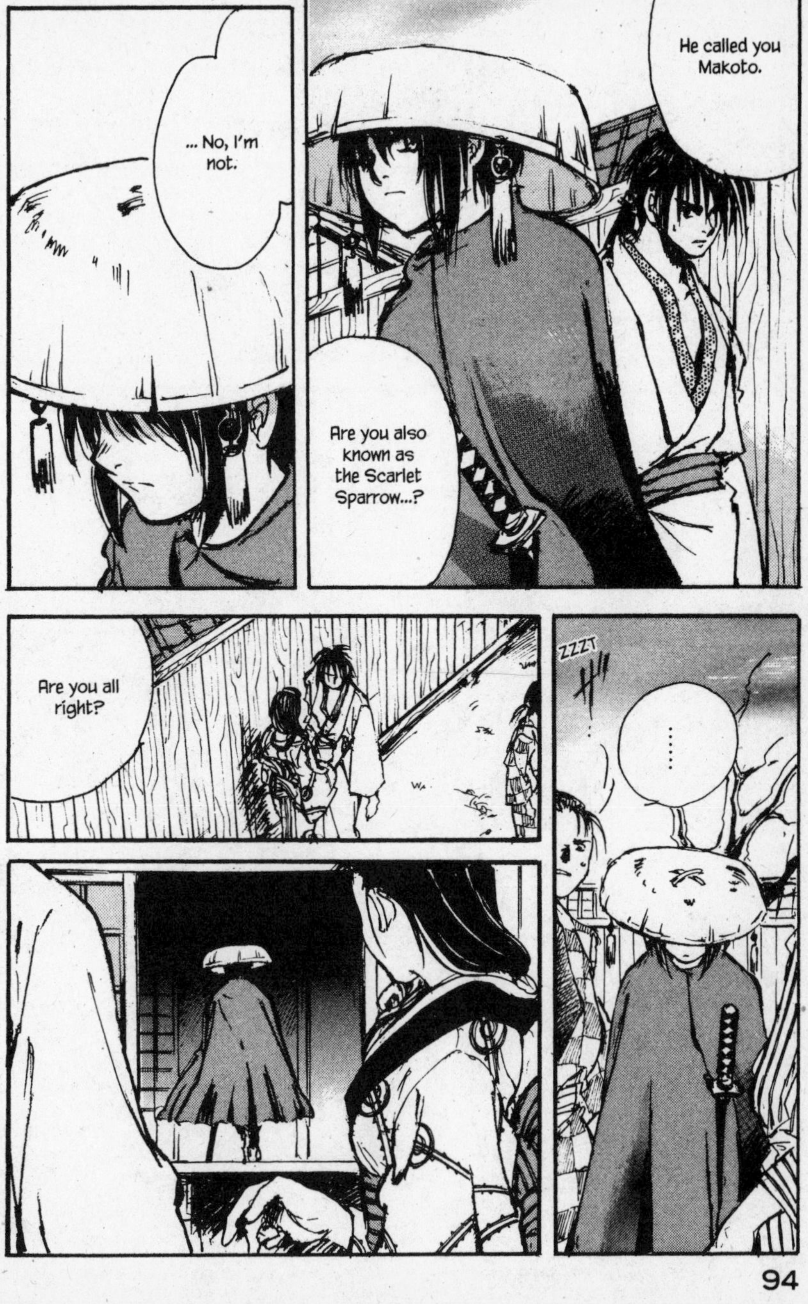
He called you Makoto.
Are you also known as the Scarlet Sparrow...?
... No, I'm not.
ZZZT
......
Are you all right?

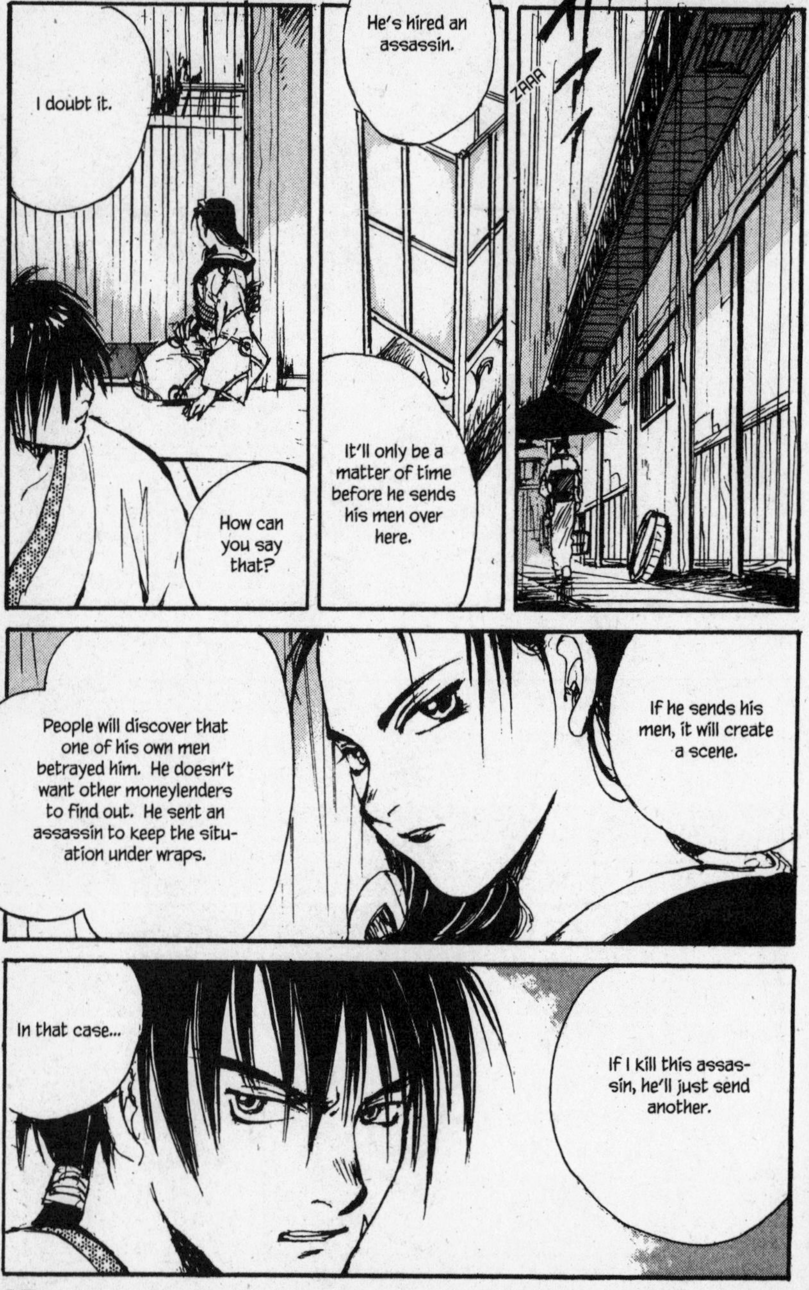
ZAAA
He's hired an assassin.
It'll only be a matter of time before he sends his men over here.
I doubt it.
How can you say that?
If he sends his men, it will create a scene.
People will discover that one of his own men betrayed him. He doesn't want other moneylenders to find out. He sent an assassin to keep the situation under wraps.
If I kill this assassin, he'll just send another.
In that case...

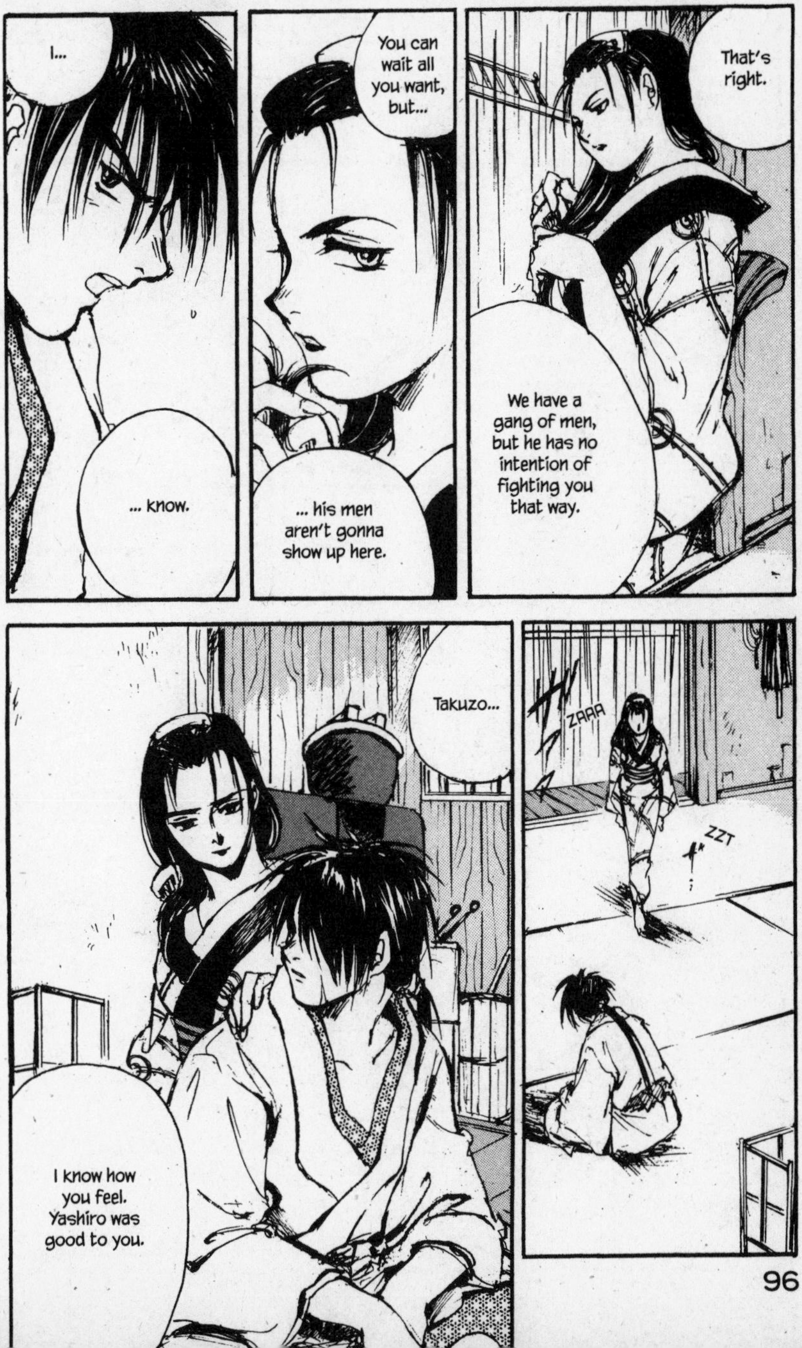
That's right.
We have a gang of men, but he has no intention of fighting you that way.
You can wait all you want, but...
... his men aren't gonna show up here.
I...
... know.
ZAAA
ZZT
Takuzo...
I know how you feel. Yashiro was good to you.

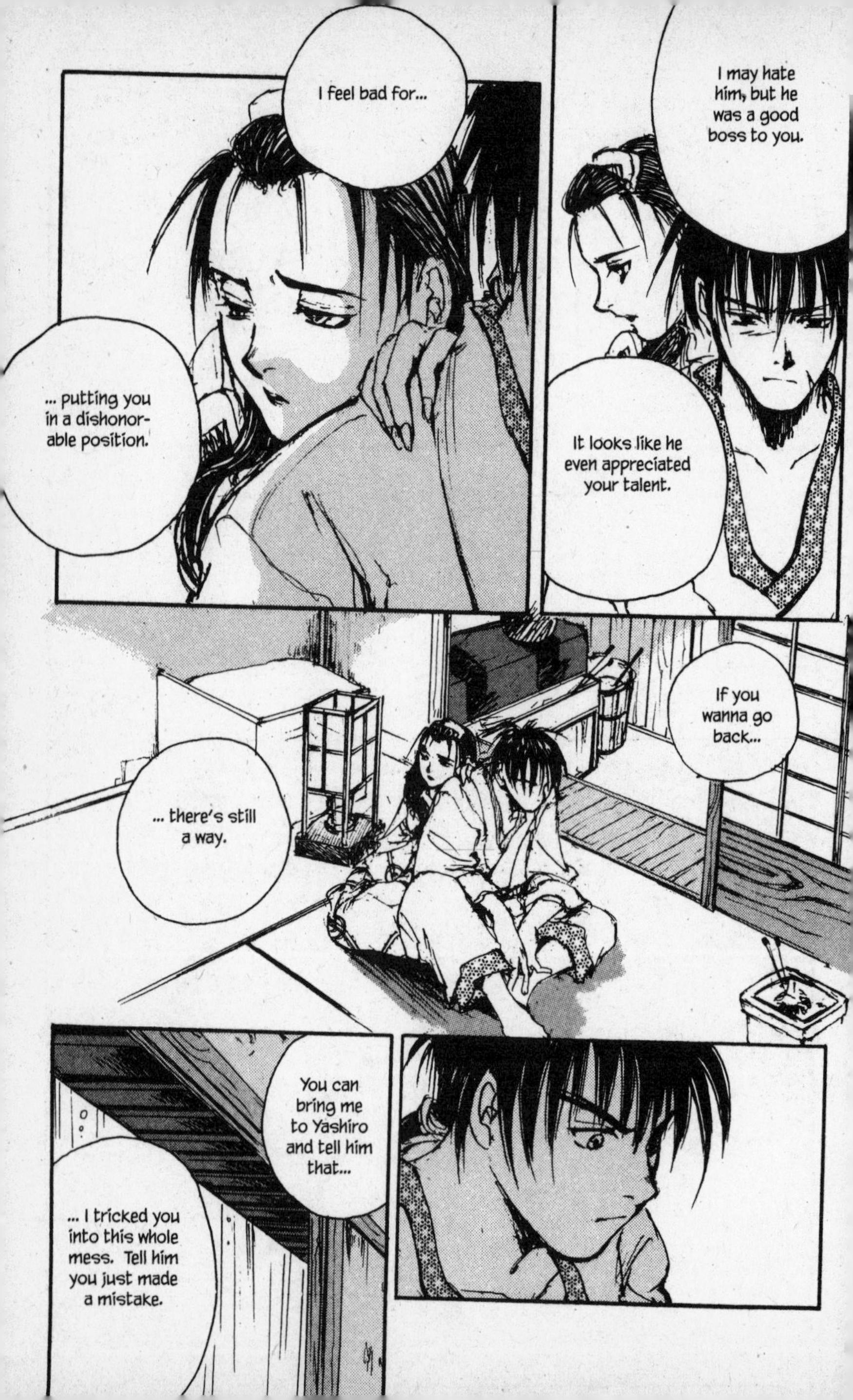
I may hate him, but he was a good boss to you.
It looks like he even appreciated your talent.
I feel bad for...
... putting you in a dishonorable position.
If you wanna go back...
... there's still a way.
You can bring me to Yashiro and tell him that...
... I tricked you into this whole mess. Tell him you just made a mistake.

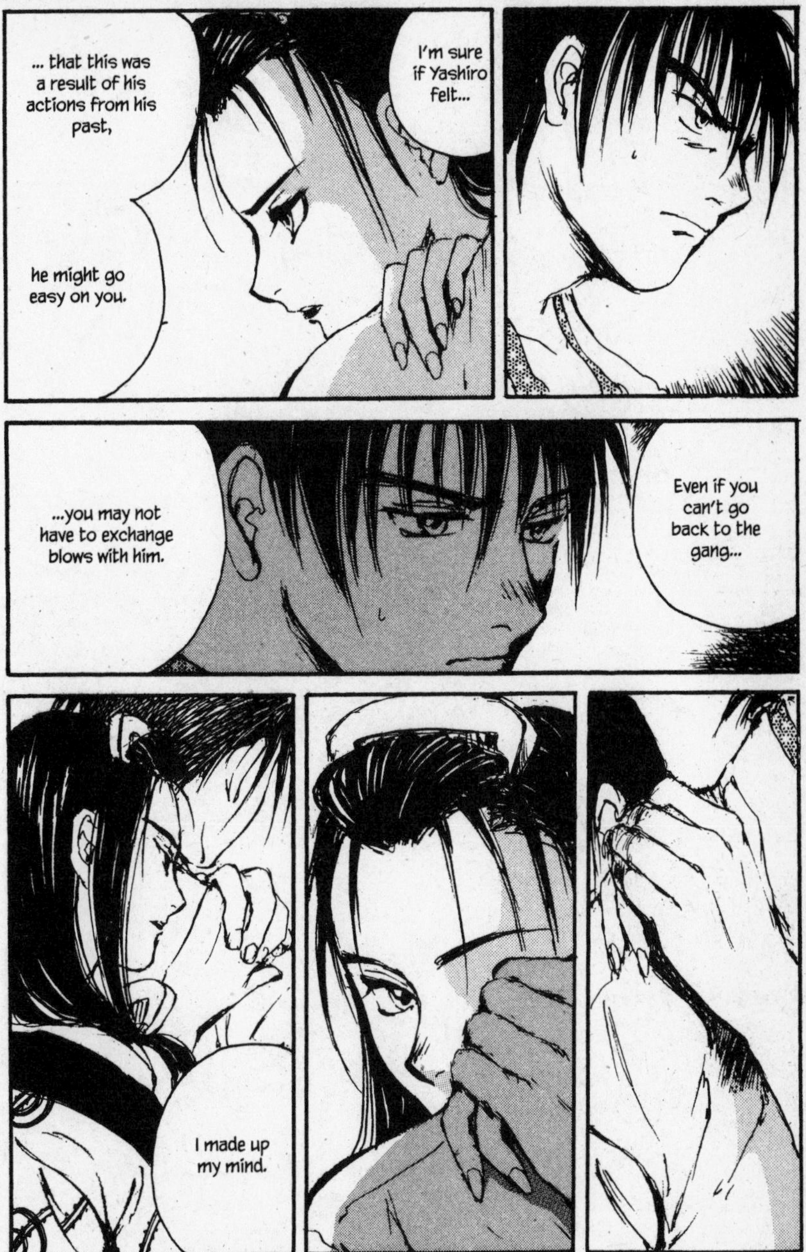
I'm sure if Yashiro felt...
... that this was a result of his actions from his past,
he might go easy on you.
Even if you can't go back to the gang...
...you may not have to exchange blows with him.
I made up my mind.

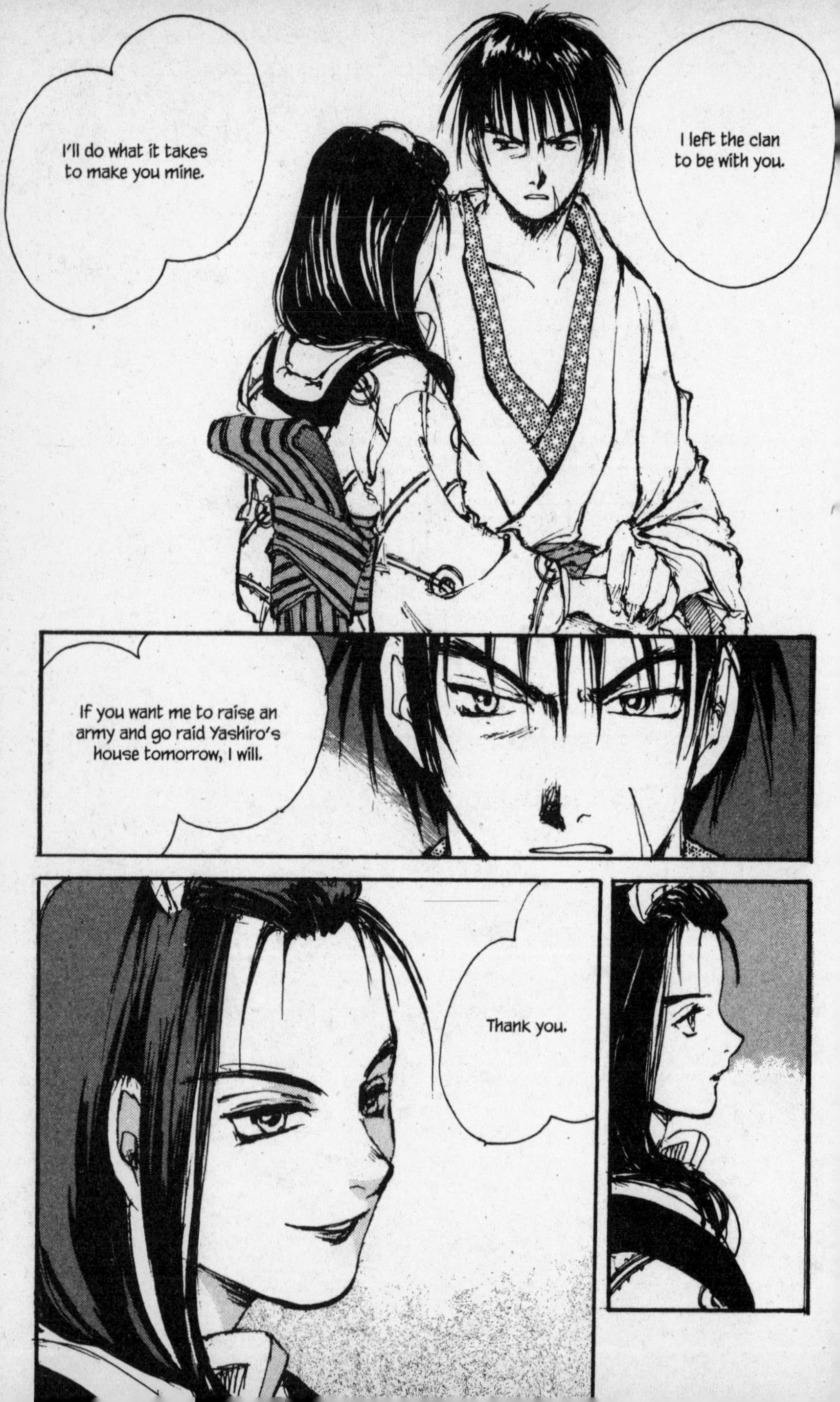
I left the clan to be with you.
I'll do what it takes to make you mine.
If you want me to raise an army and go raid Yashiro's house tomorrow, I will.
Thank you.

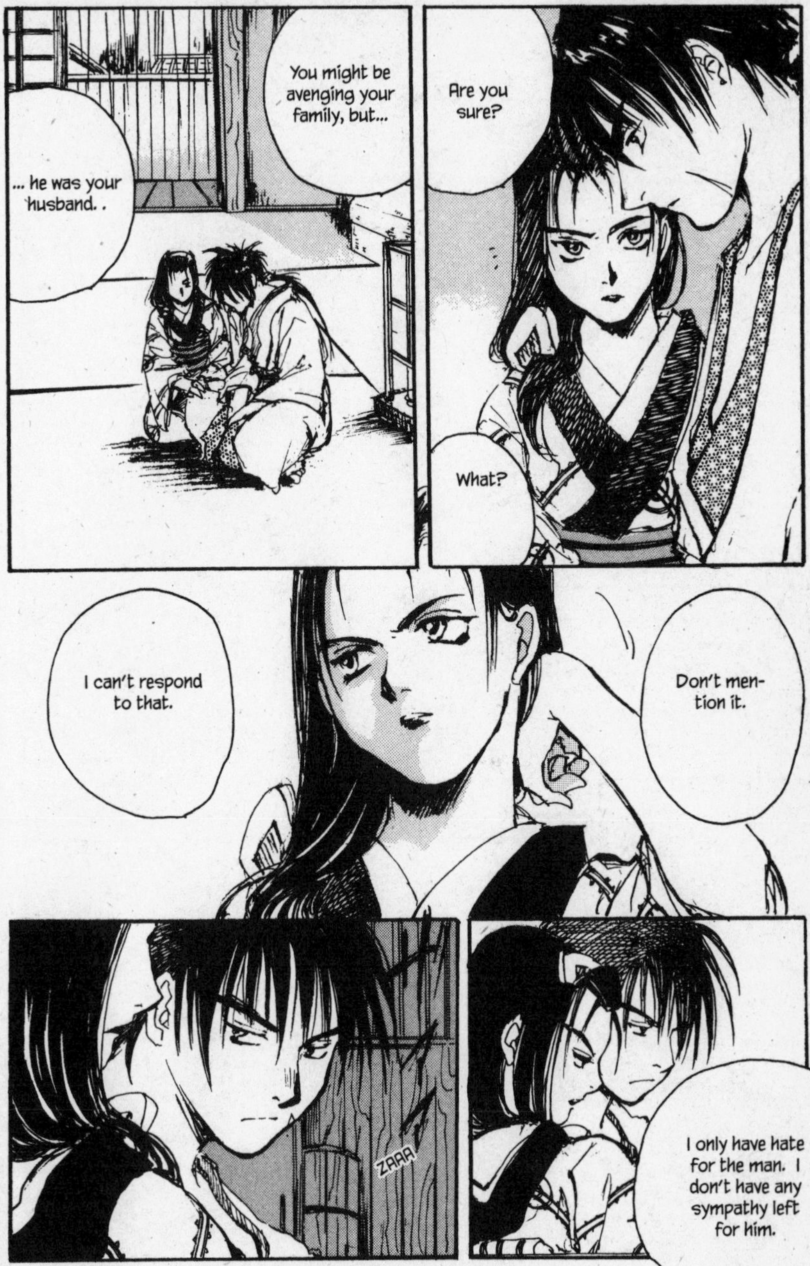
Are you sure?
What?
You might be avenging your family, but...
... he was your husband. .
Don't mention it.
I can't respond to that.
I only have hate for the man. I don't have any sympathy left for him.
ZAAA

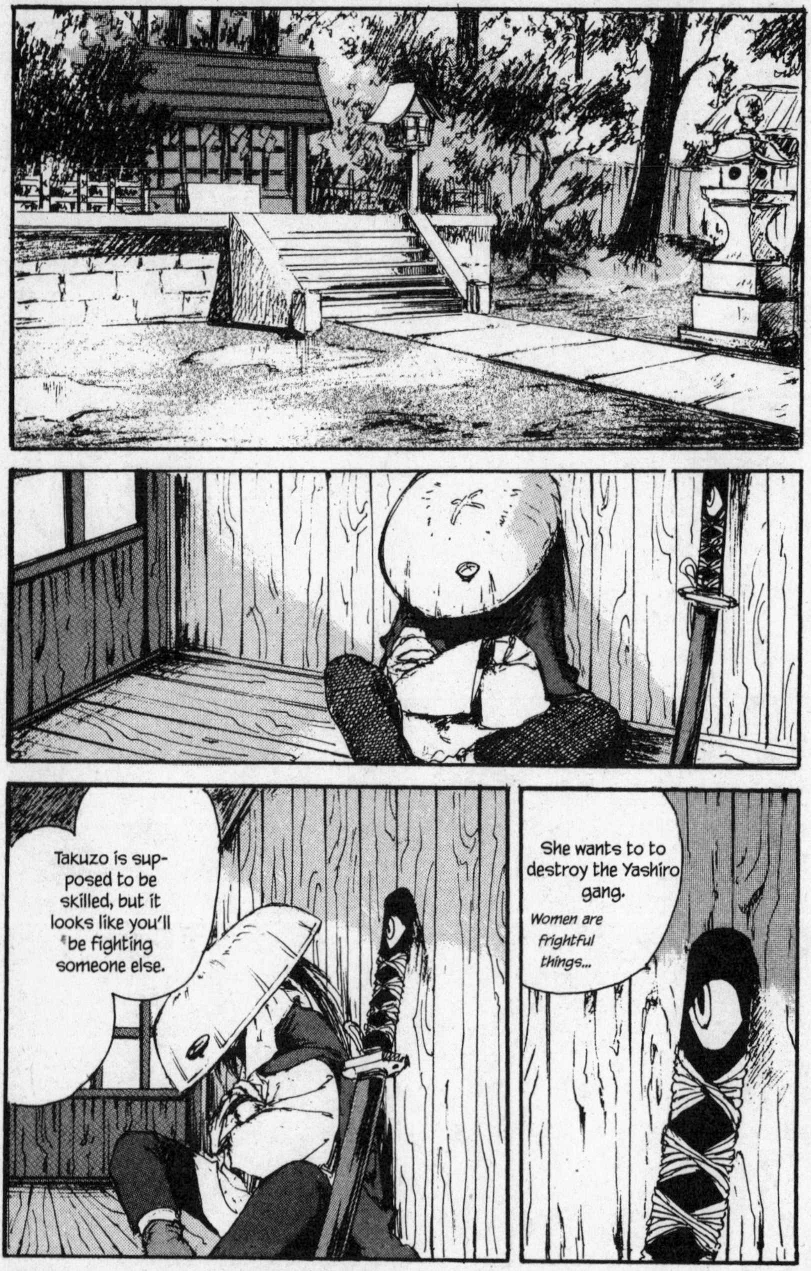
She wants to to destroy the Yashiro gang.
Women are frightful things...
Takuzo is sup-posed to be skilled, but it looks like you'll be fighting someone else.

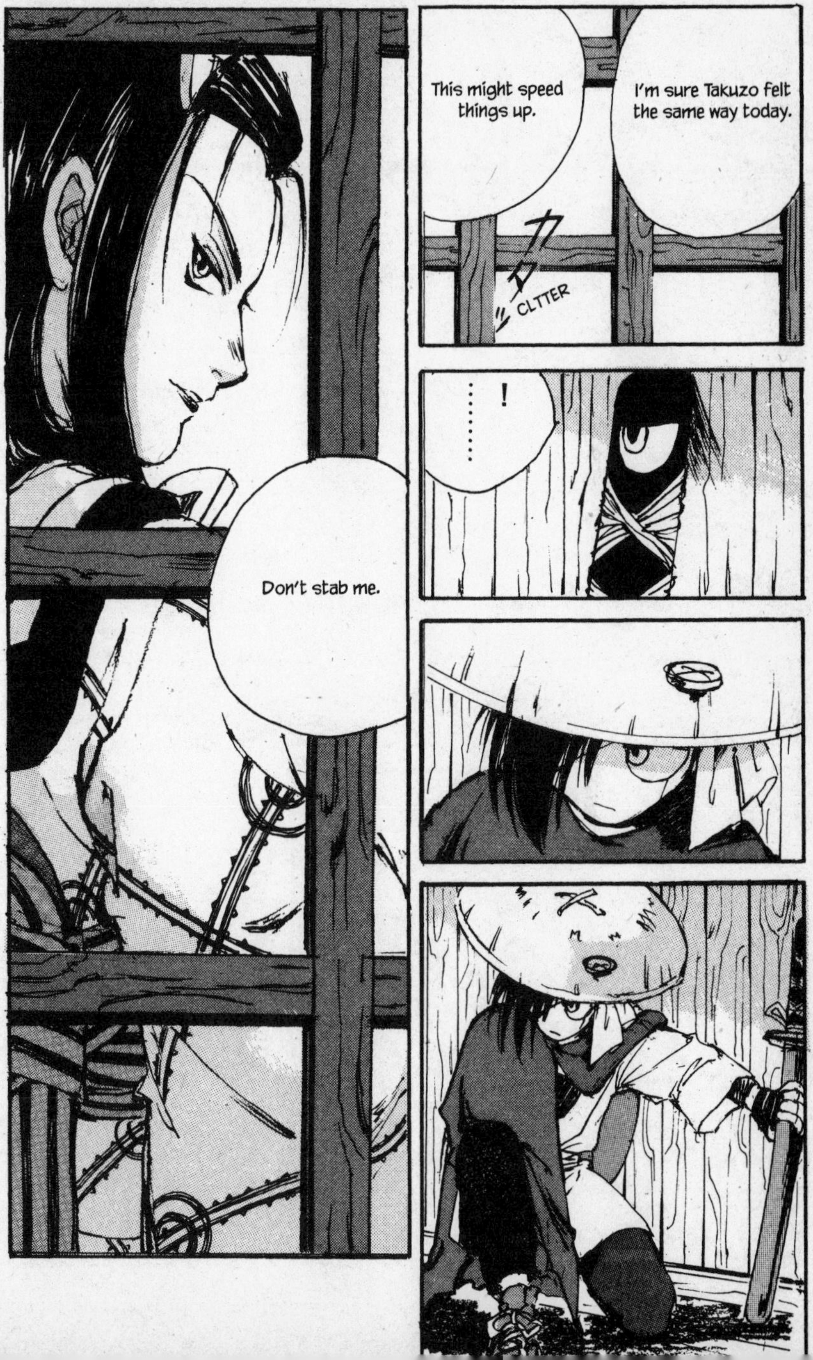
I'm sure Takuzo felt the same way today.
This might speed things up.
CLTTER
......!
Don't stab me.

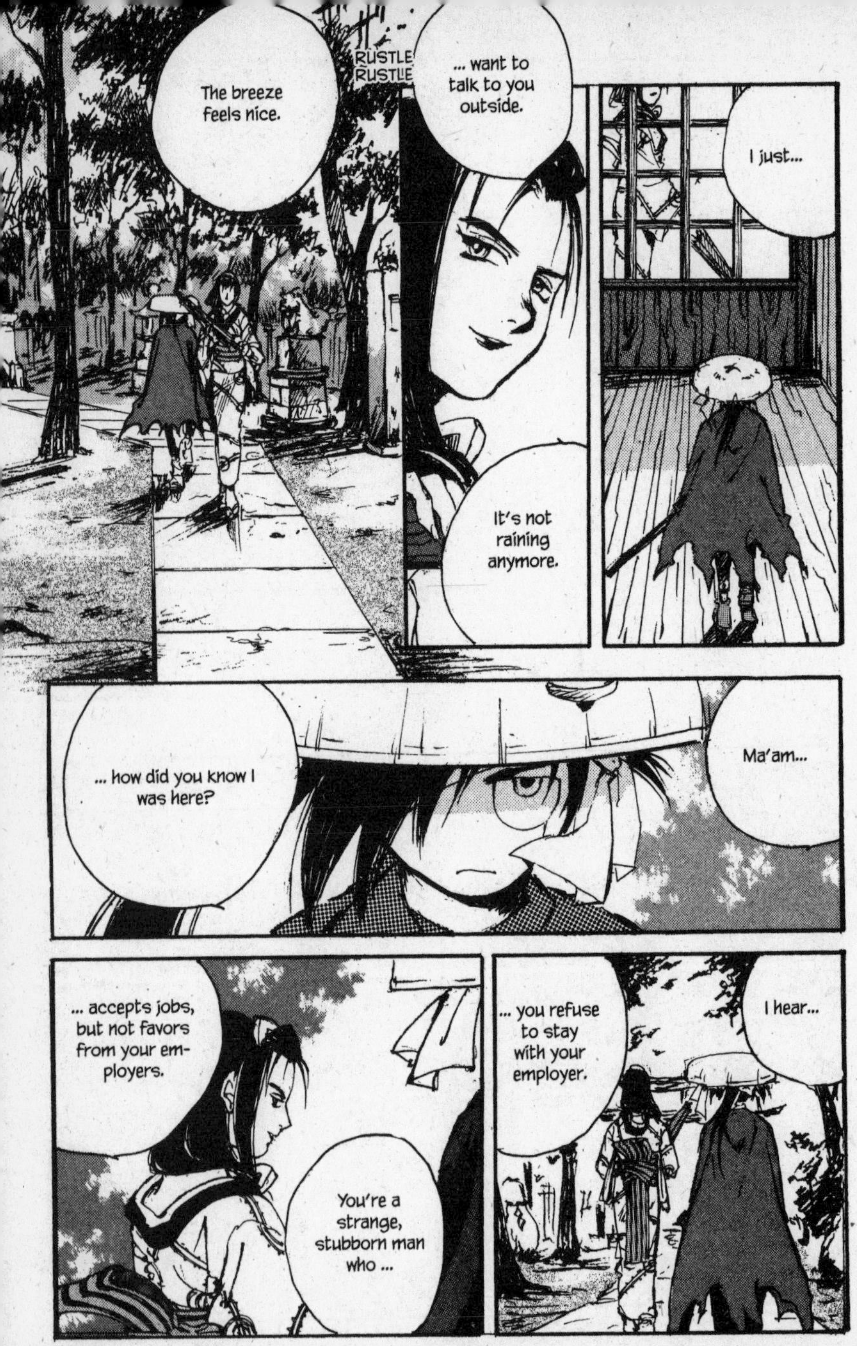
I just...
... want to talk to you outside.
It's not raining anymore.
RUSTLE
RUSTLE
The breeze feels nice.
Ma'am...
... how did you know I was here?
I hear...
... you refuse to stay with your employer.
You're a strange, stubborn man who ...
... accepts jobs, but not favors from your employers.

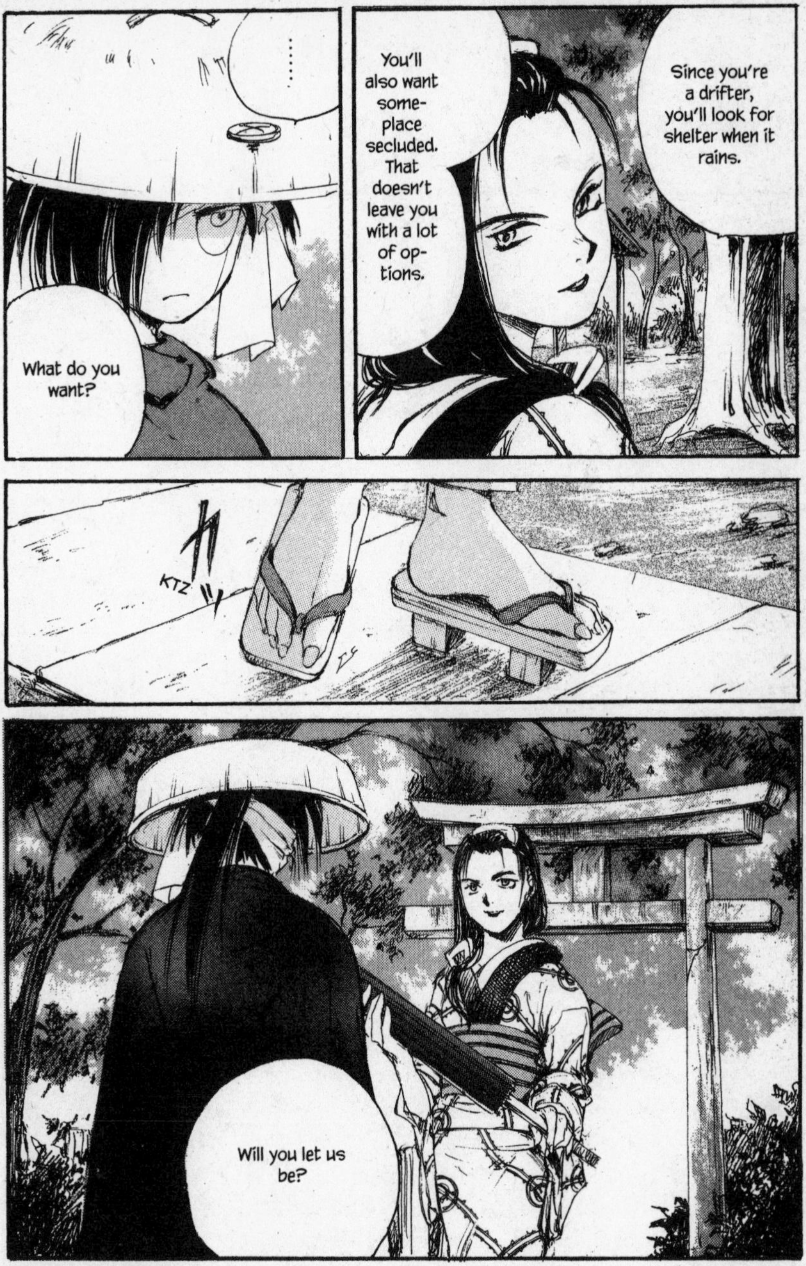
Since you're a drifter, you'll look for shelter when it rains.
You'll also want some-place secluded. That doesn't leave you with a lot of op-tions.
......
What do you want?
KTZ
Will you let us be?

THE END OF CHAPTER 8, EPISODE 2

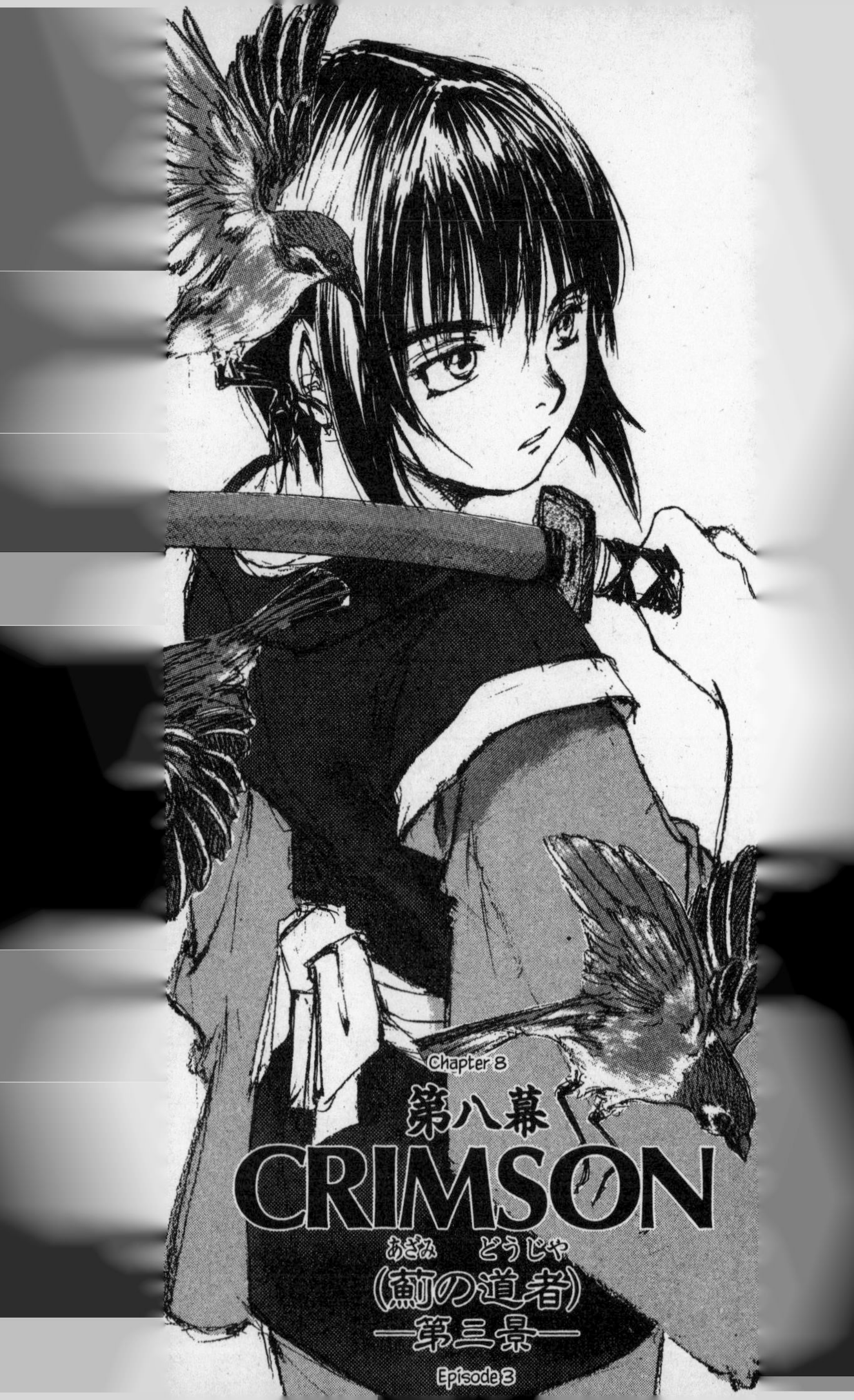
Chapter 8
第八幕
CRIMSON
あざみ　どうじゃ
(薊の道者)
—第三景—
Episode 3

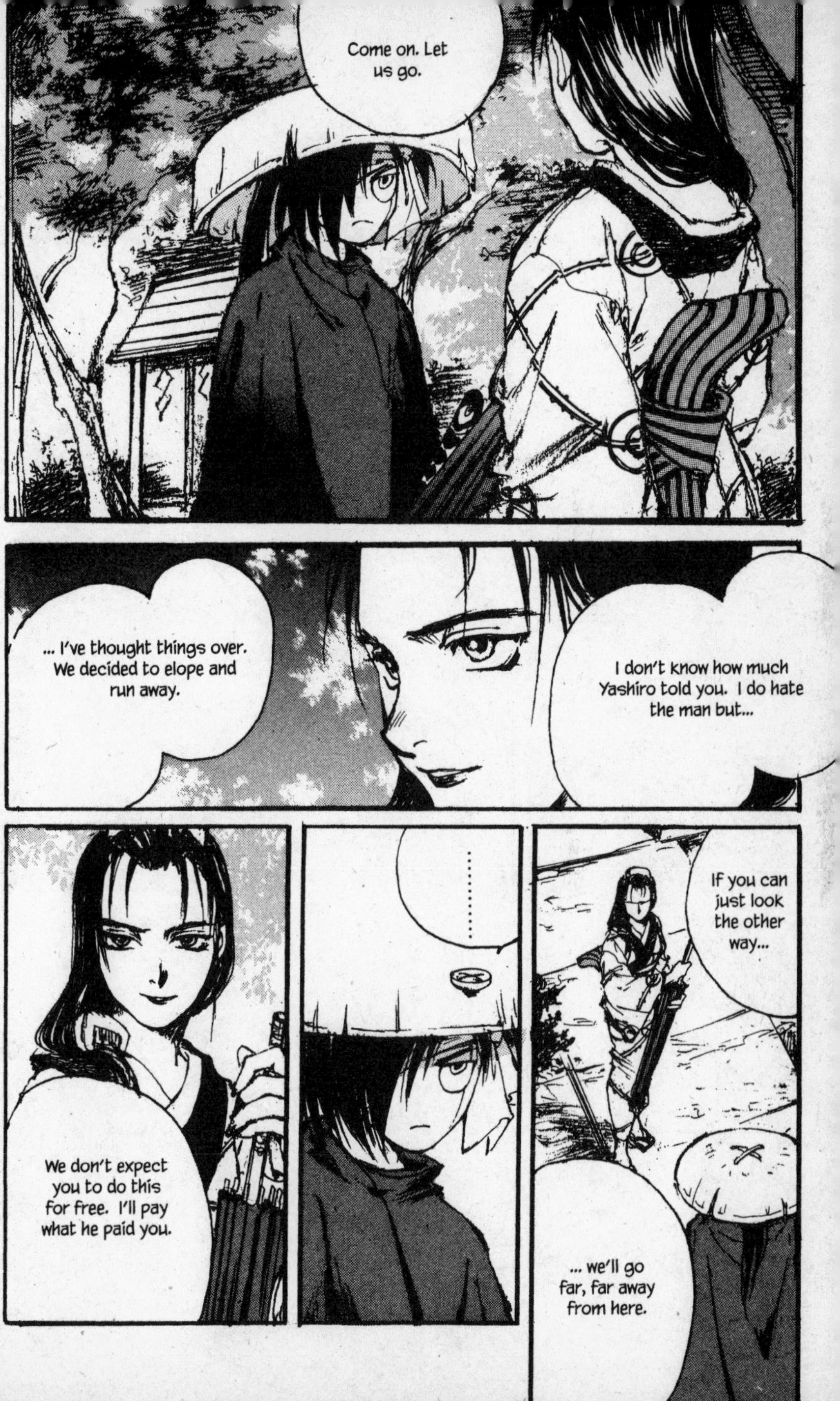
Come on. Let us go.
I don't know how much Yashiro told you. I do hate the man but...
... I've thought things over. We decided to elope and run away.
If you can just look the other way...
... we'll go far, far away from here.
......
We don't expect you to do this for free. I'll pay what he paid you.

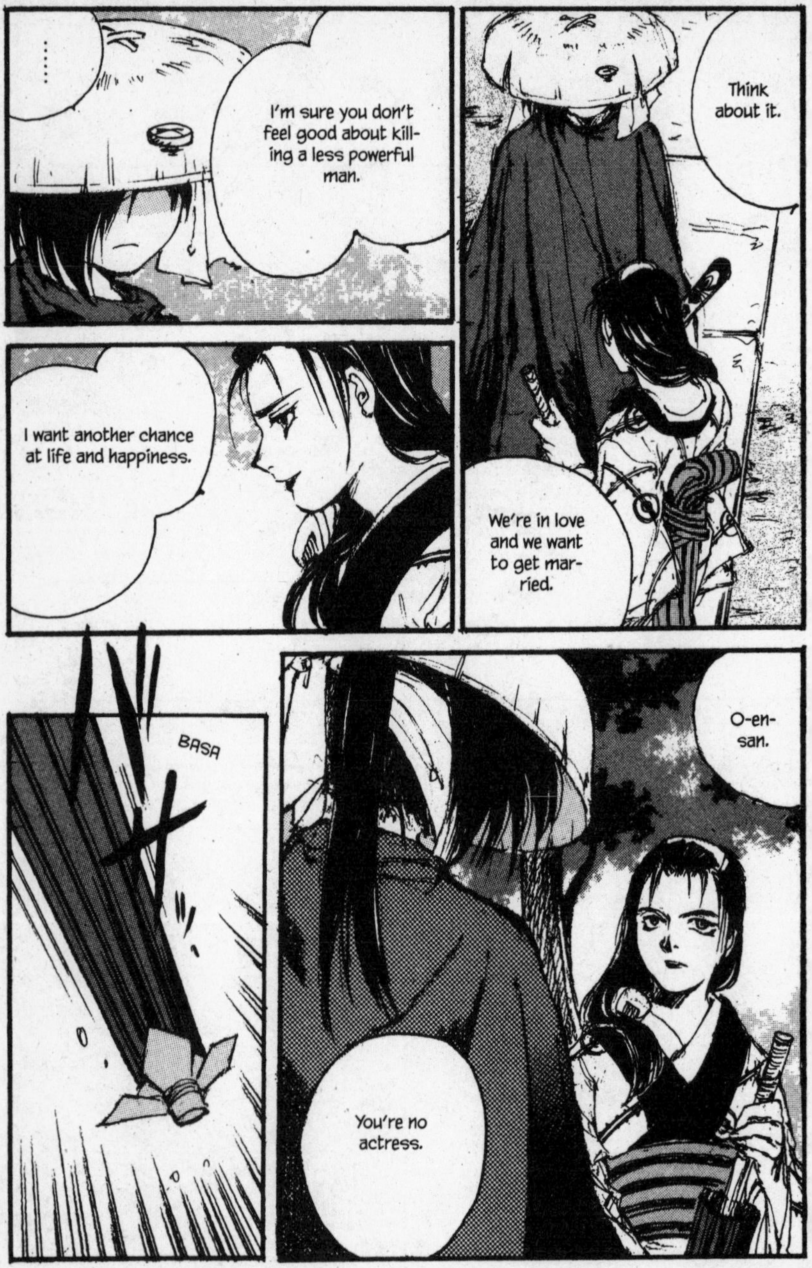
Think about it.
We're in love and we want to get mar-ried.
......
I'm sure you don't feel good about kill-ing a less powerful man.
I want another chance at life and happiness.
O-en-san.
You're no actress.
BASA

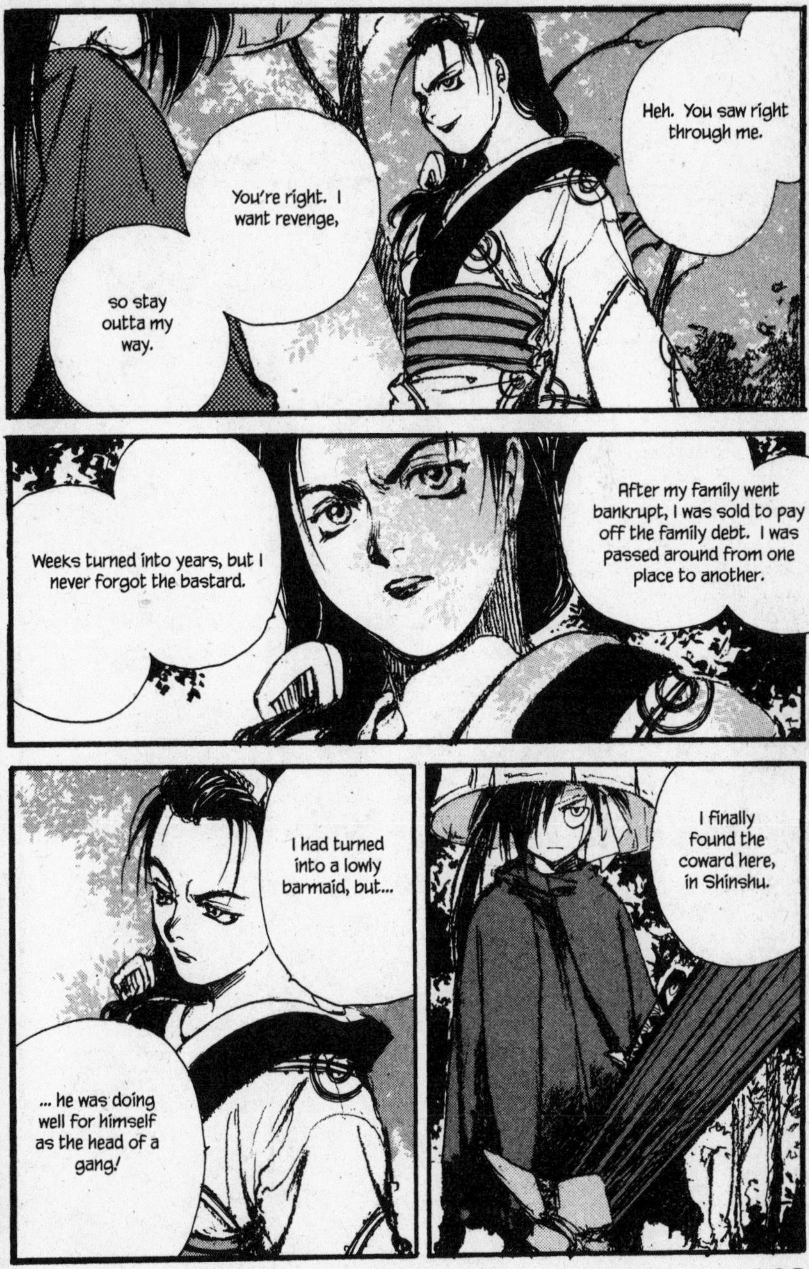
Heh. You saw right through me.
You're right. I want revenge,
so stay outta my way.
After my family went bankrupt, I was sold to pay off the family debt. I was passed around from one place to another.
Weeks turned into years, but I never forgot the bastard.
I finally found the coward here, in Shinshu.
I had turned into a lowly barmaid, but...
... he was doing well for himself as the head of a gang!

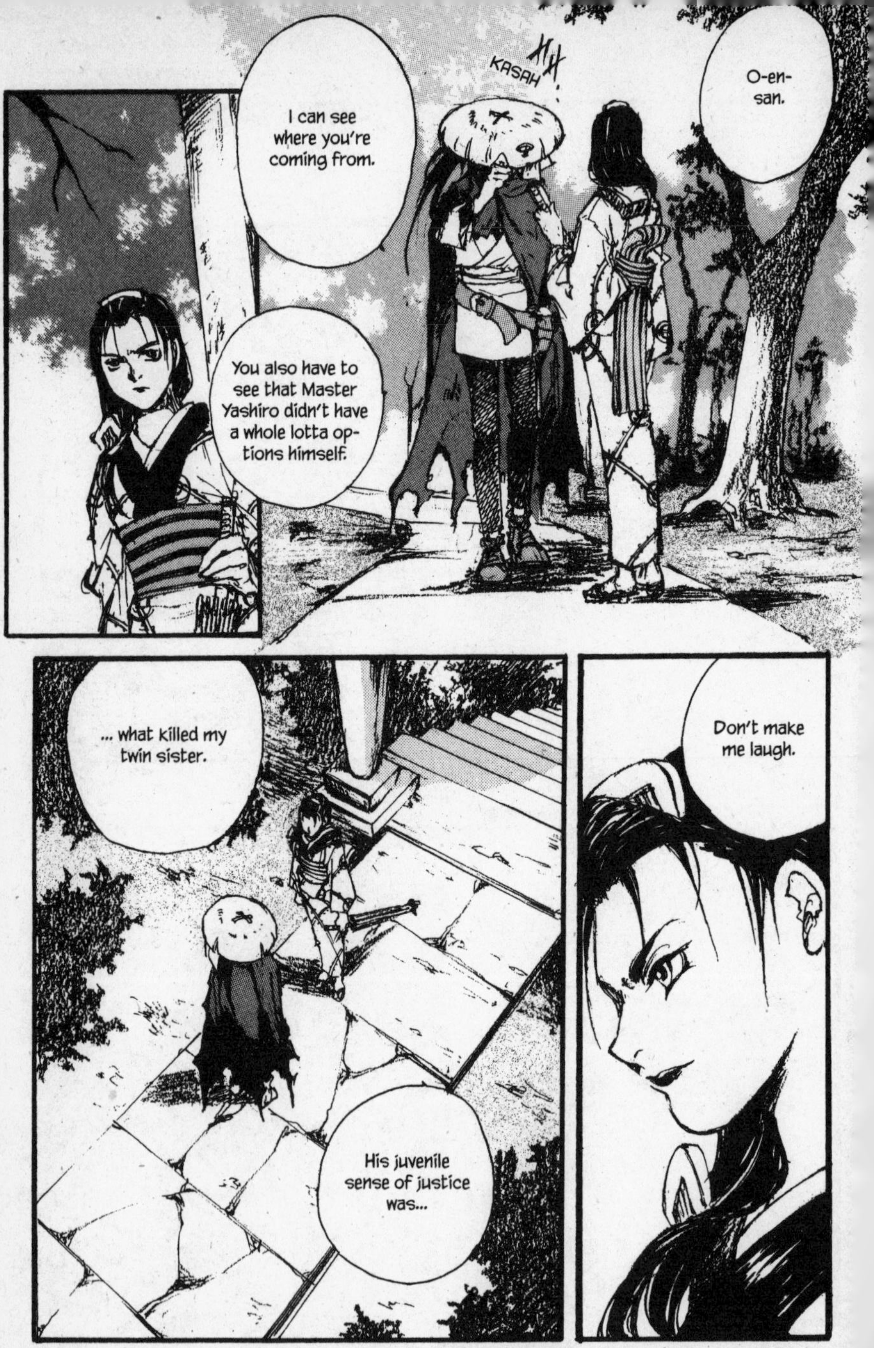
O-en-san.
KASAH
I can see where you're coming from.
You also have to see that Master Yashiro didn't have a whole lotta options himself.
Don't make me laugh.
His juvenile sense of justice was...
... what killed my twin sister.

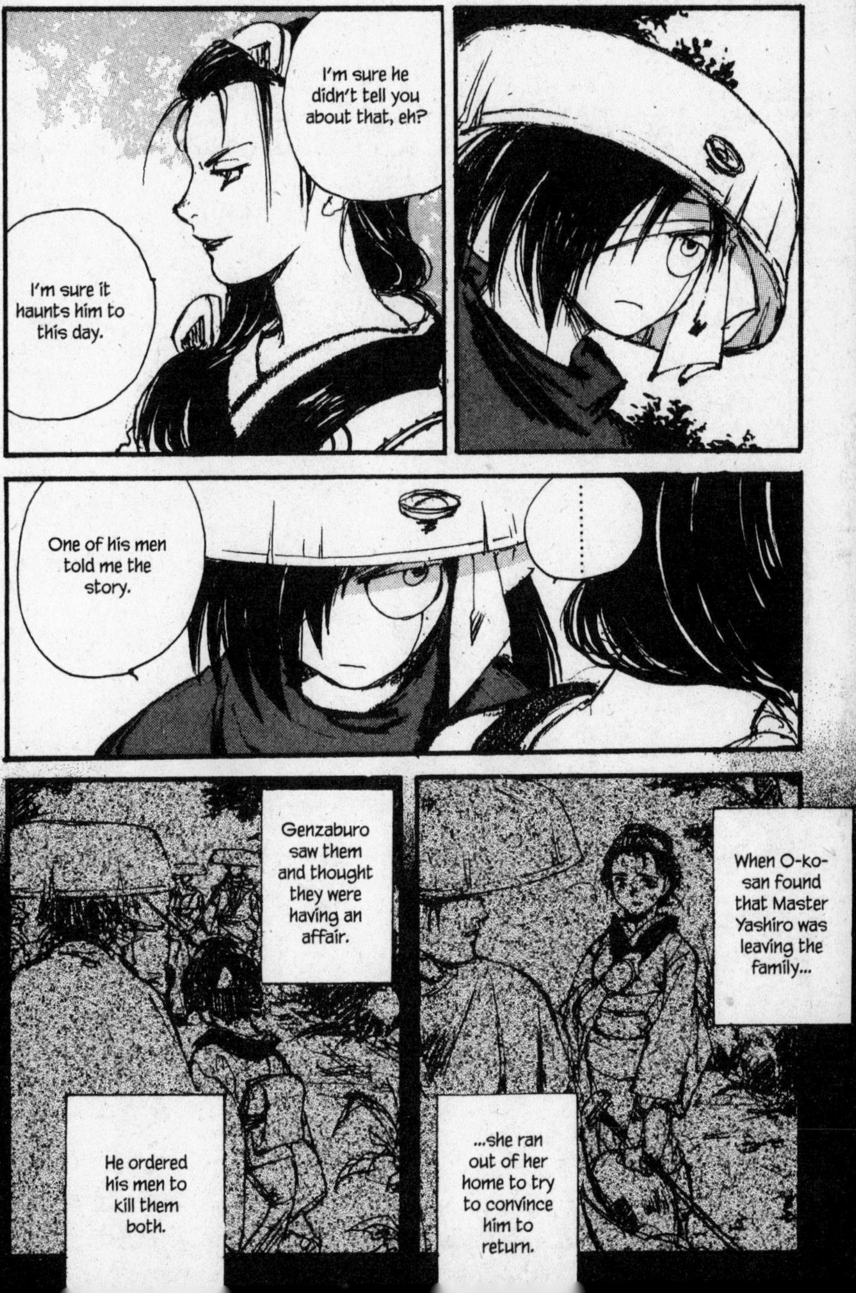
I'm sure he didn't tell you about that, eh?
I'm sure it haunts him to this day.
One of his men told me the story.
When O-ko-san found that Master Yashiro was leaving the family...
...she ran out of her home to try to convince him to return.
Genzaburo saw them and thought they were having an affair.
He ordered his men to kill them both.

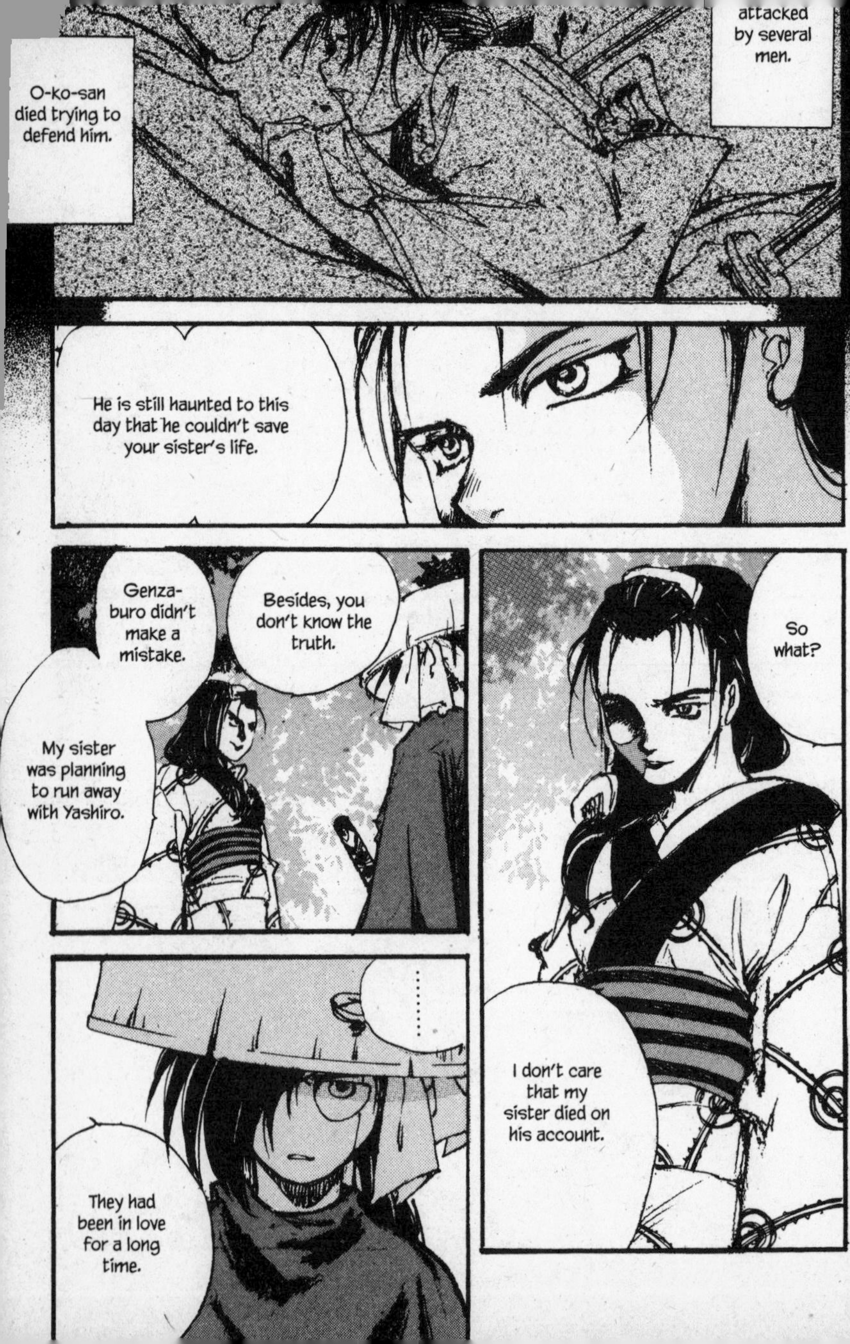
attacked by several men.
O-ko-san died trying to defend him.
He is still haunted to this day that he couldn't save your sister's life.
So what?
I don't care that my sister died on his account.
Besides, you don't know the truth.
Genza-buro didn't make a mistake.
My sister was planning to run away with Yashiro.
......
They had been in love for a long time.

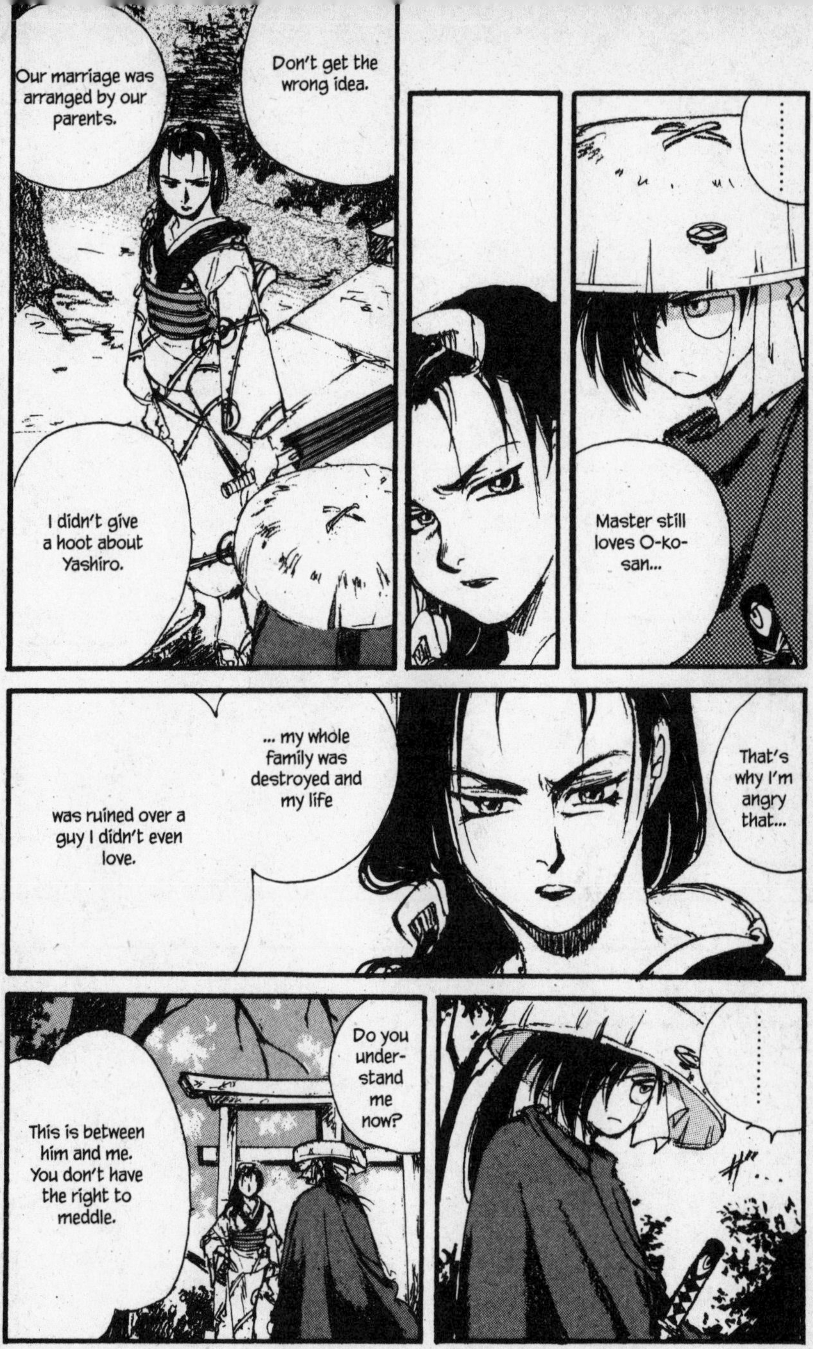
......
Master still loves O-ko-san...
Don't get the wrong idea.
Our marriage was arranged by our parents.
I didn't give a hoot about Yashiro.
That's why I'm angry that...
... my whole family was destroyed and my life
was ruined over a guy I didn't even love.
......
Do you understand me now?
This is between him and me. You don't have the right to meddle.

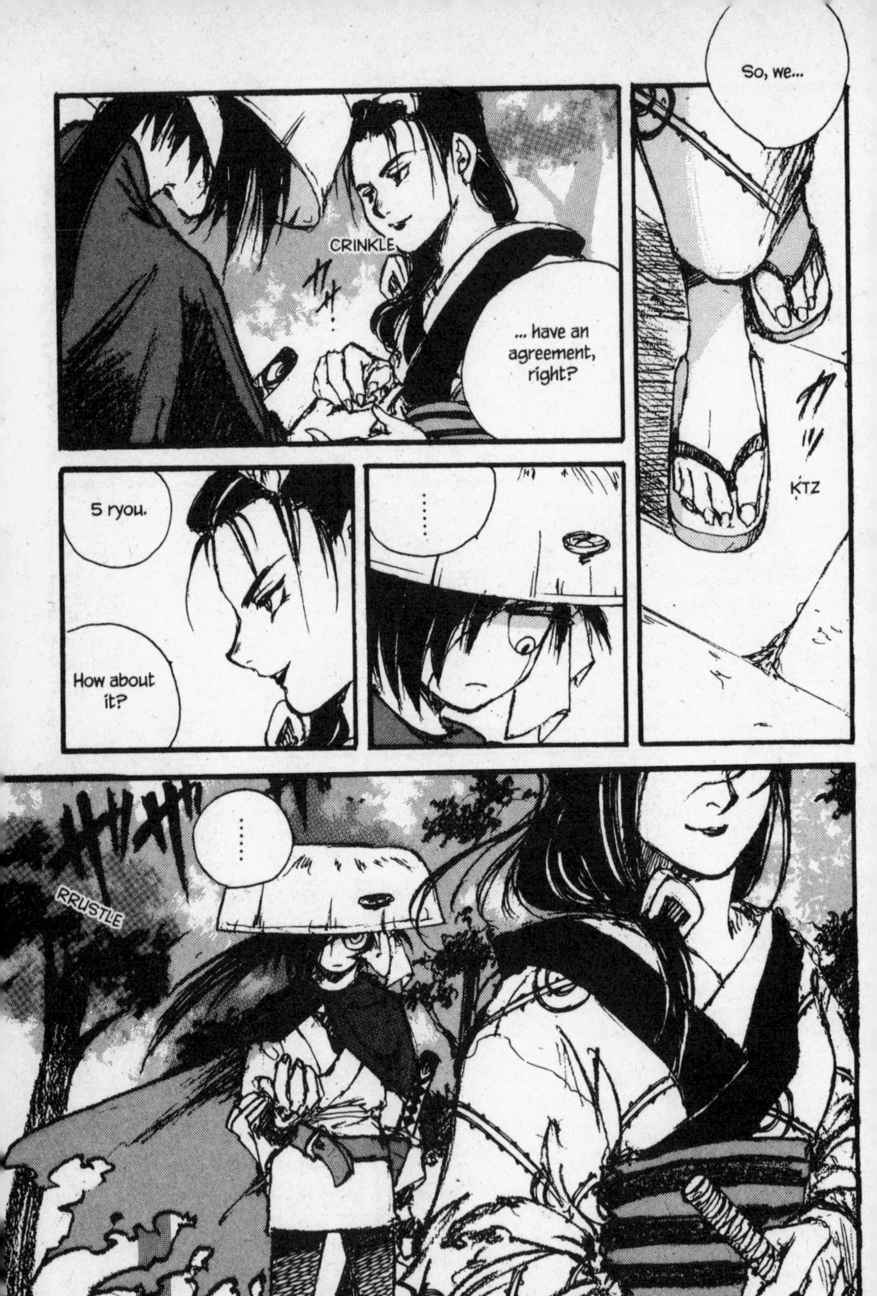
So, we...
KTZ
CRINKLE
... have an agreement, right?
......
5 ryou.
How about it?
......
RRUSTLE

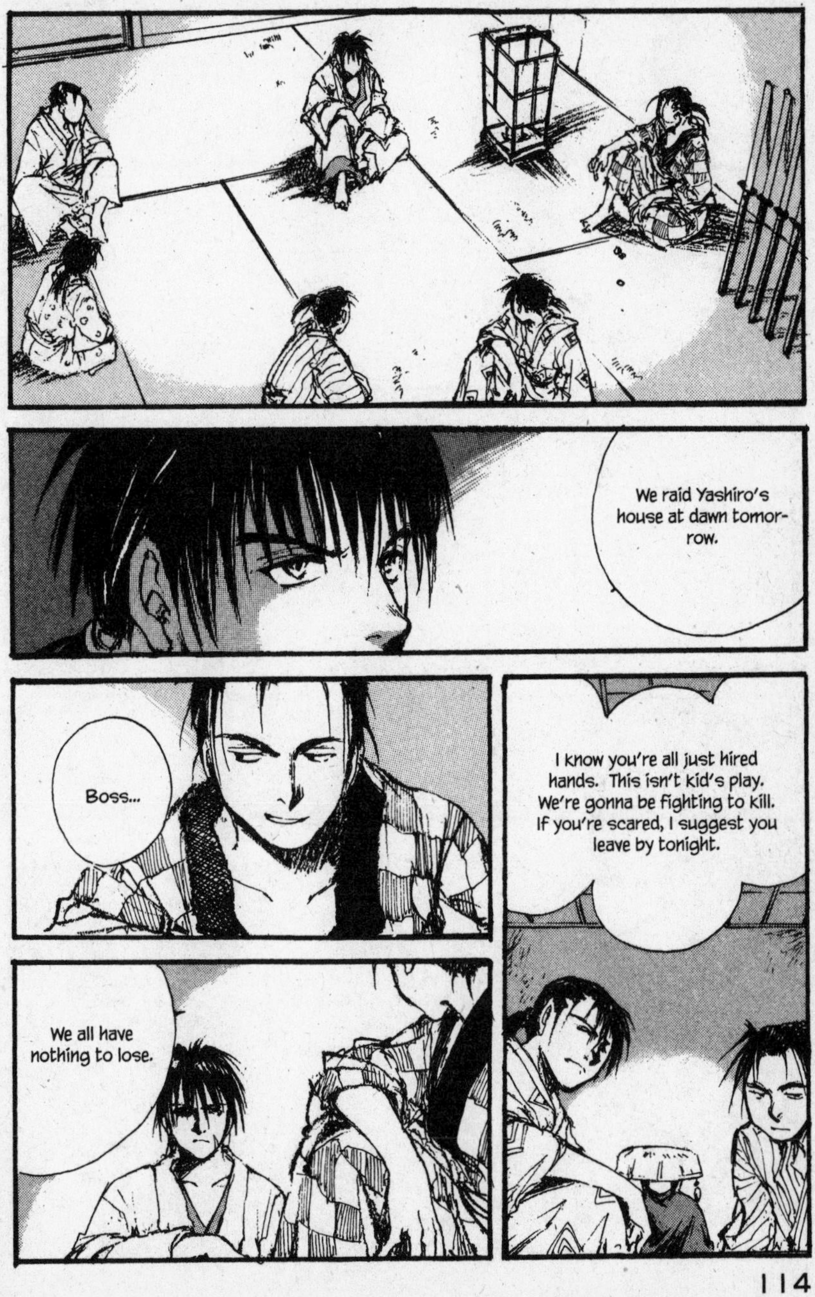
We raid Yashiro's house at dawn tomor-row.
I know you're all just hired hands. This isn't kid's play. We're gonna be fighting to kill. If you're scared, I suggest you leave by tonight.
Boss...
We all have nothing to lose.

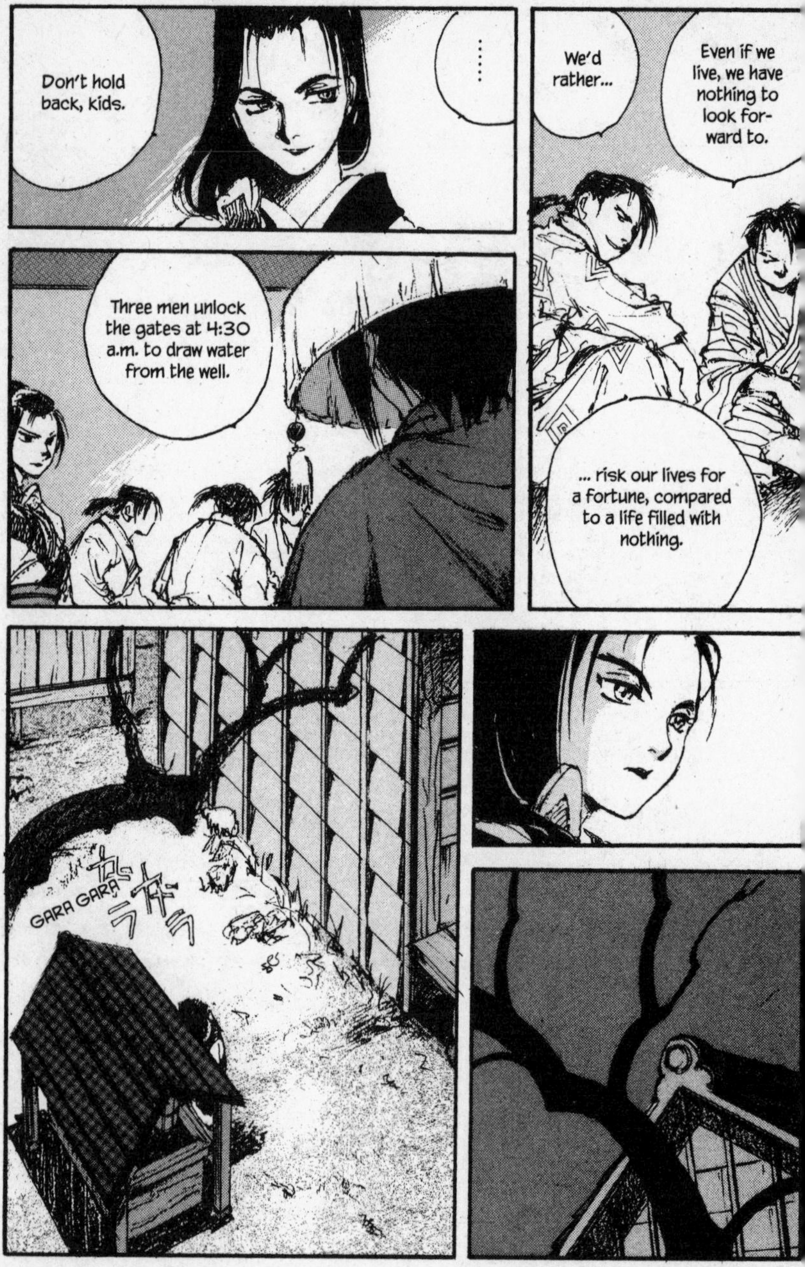
Even if we live, we have nothing to look forward to.
We'd rather...
... risk our lives for a fortune, compared to a life filled with nothing.
......
Don't hold back, kids.
Three men unlock the gates at 4:30 a.m. to draw water from the well.
GARA GARA

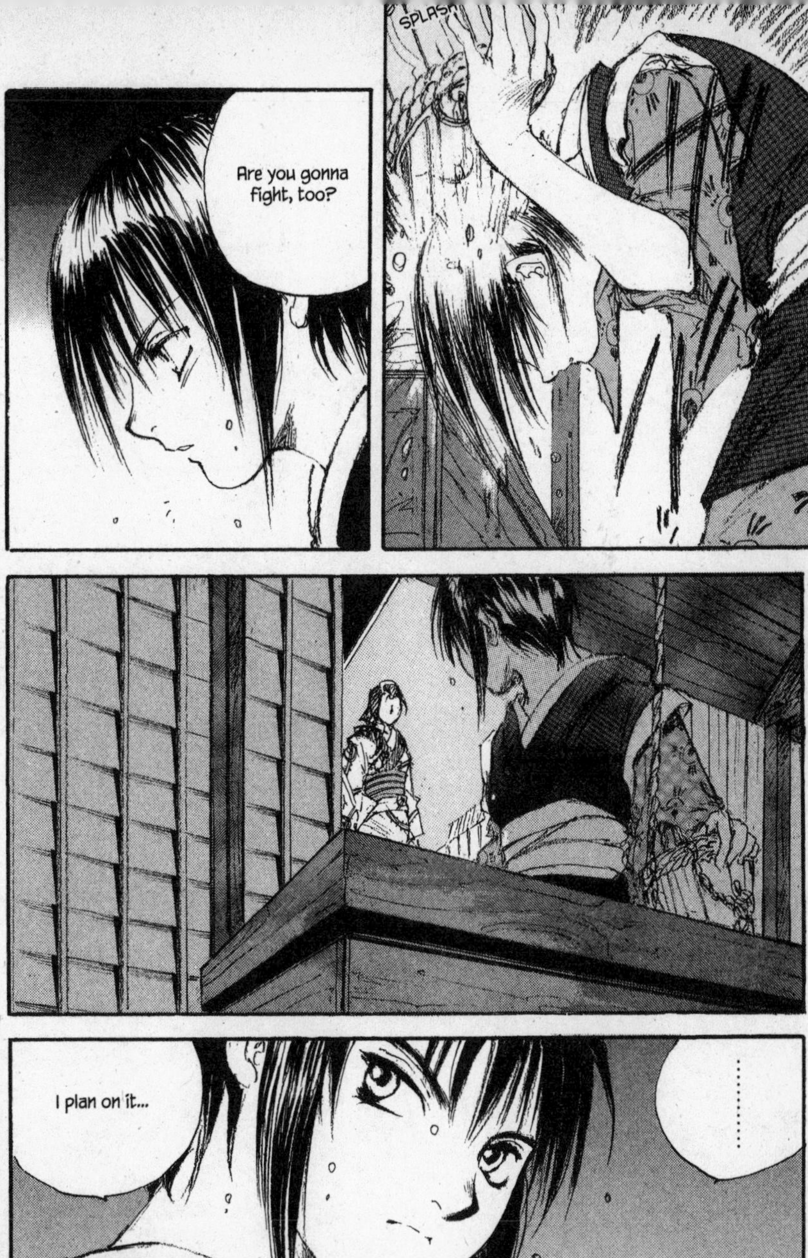

SPLASH
Are you gonna fight, too?
……
I plan on it...

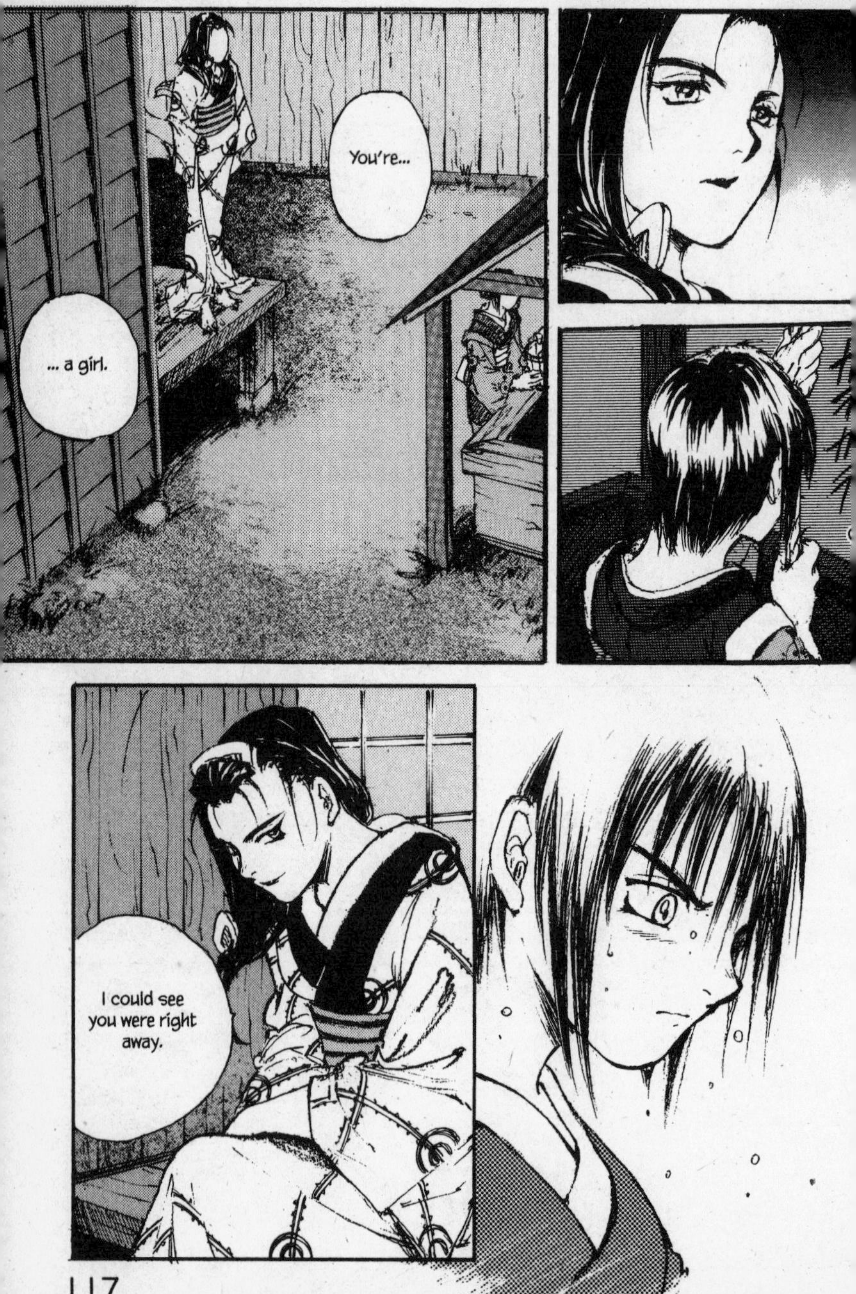
You're...
... a girl.
I could see you were right away.

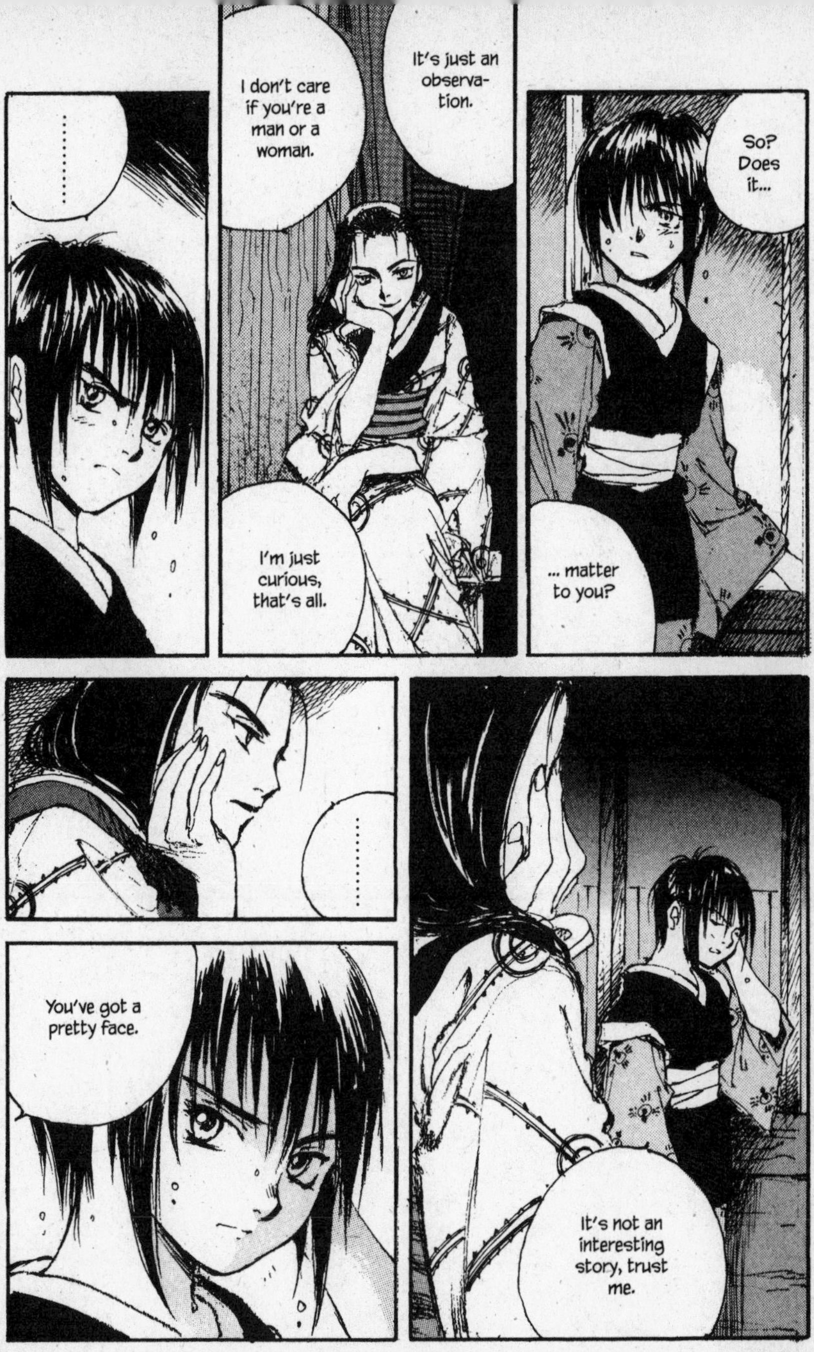
So? Does it...
... matter to you?
It's just an observation.
I don't care if you're a man or a woman.
I'm just curious, that's all.
......
It's not an interesting story, trust me.
......
You've got a pretty face.

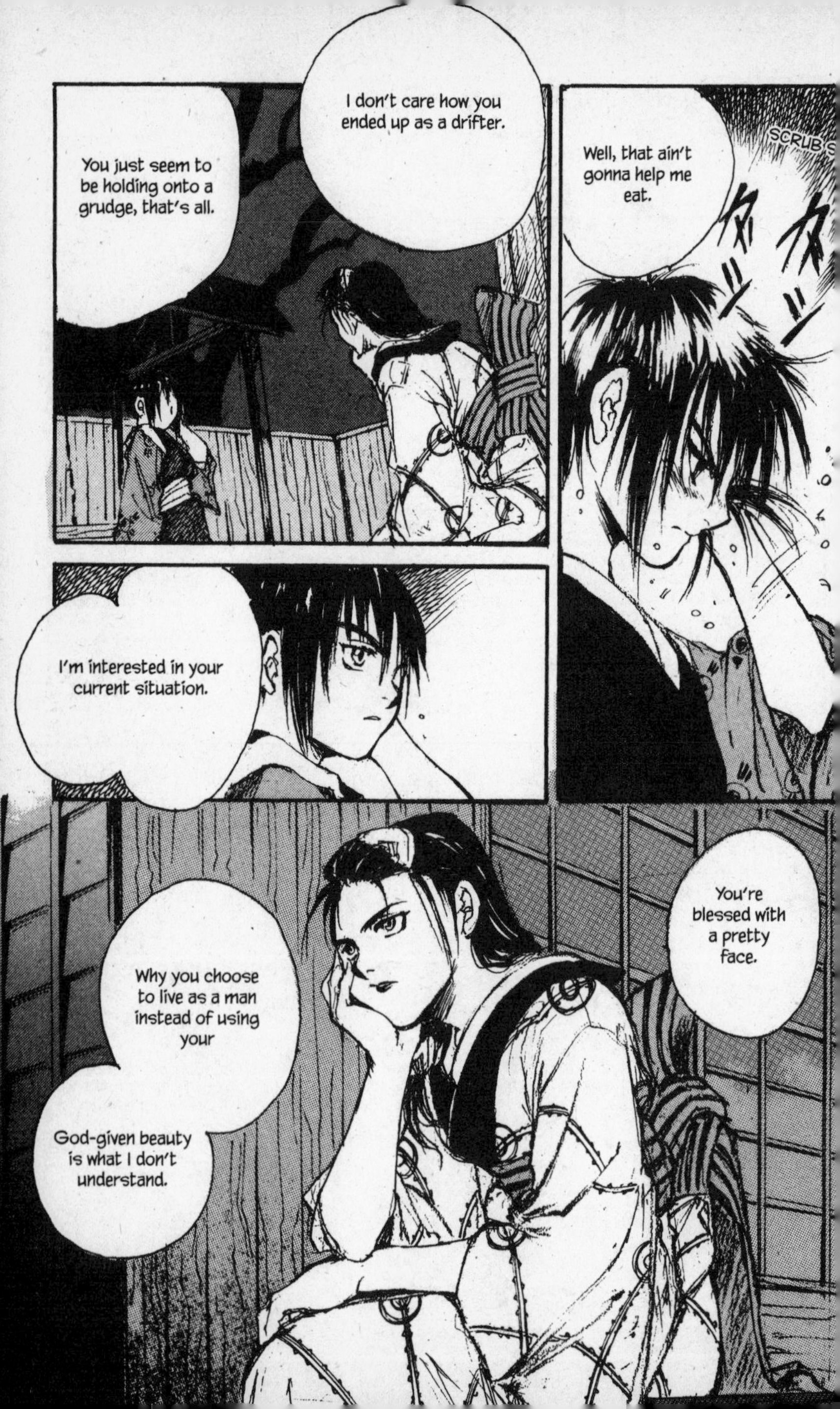
SCRUB S
Well, that ain't gonna help me eat.
I don't care how you ended up as a drifter.
You just seem to be holding onto a grudge, that's all.
I'm interested in your current situation.
You're blessed with a pretty face.
Why you choose to live as a man instead of using your
God-given beauty is what I don't understand.

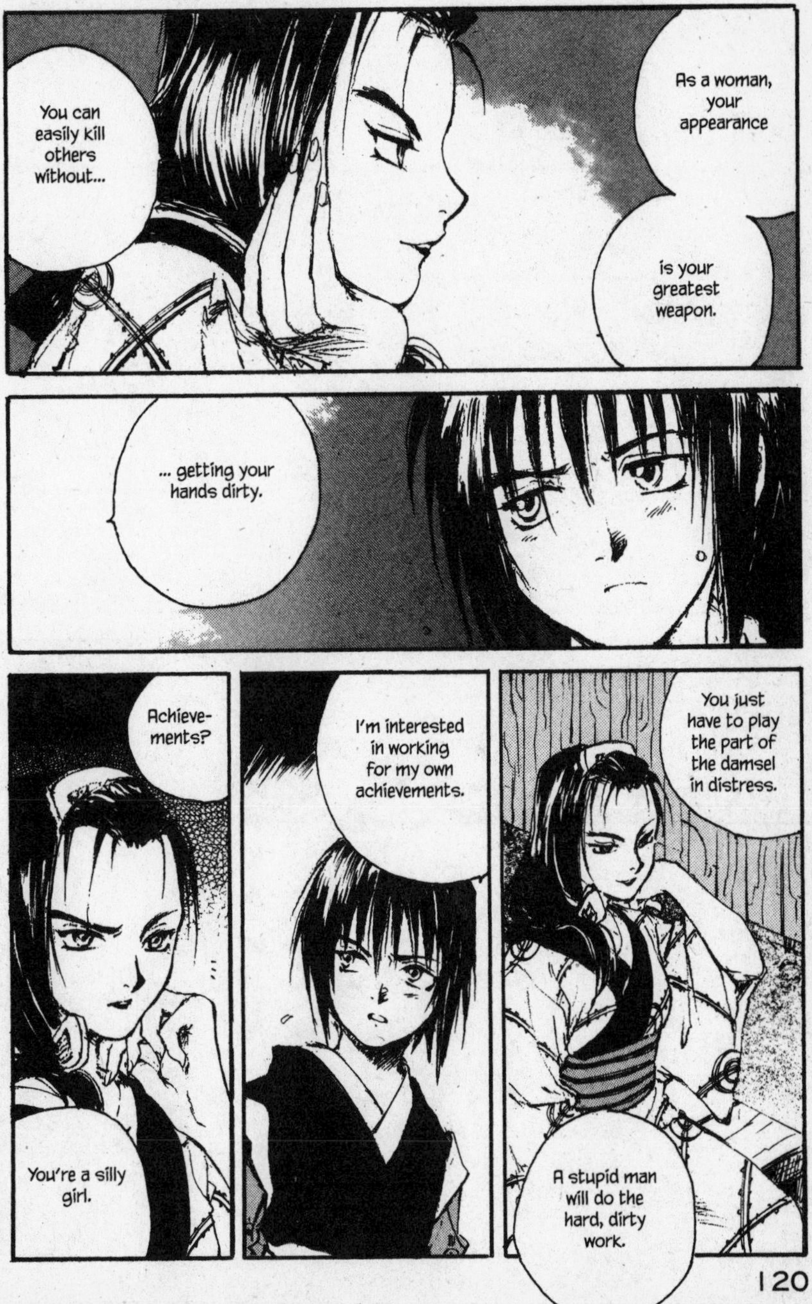
As a woman, your appearance
is your greatest weapon.
You can easily kill others without...
... getting your hands dirty.
You just have to play the part of the damsel in distress.
A stupid man will do the hard, dirty work.
I'm interested in working for my own achievements.
Achievements?
You're a silly girl.

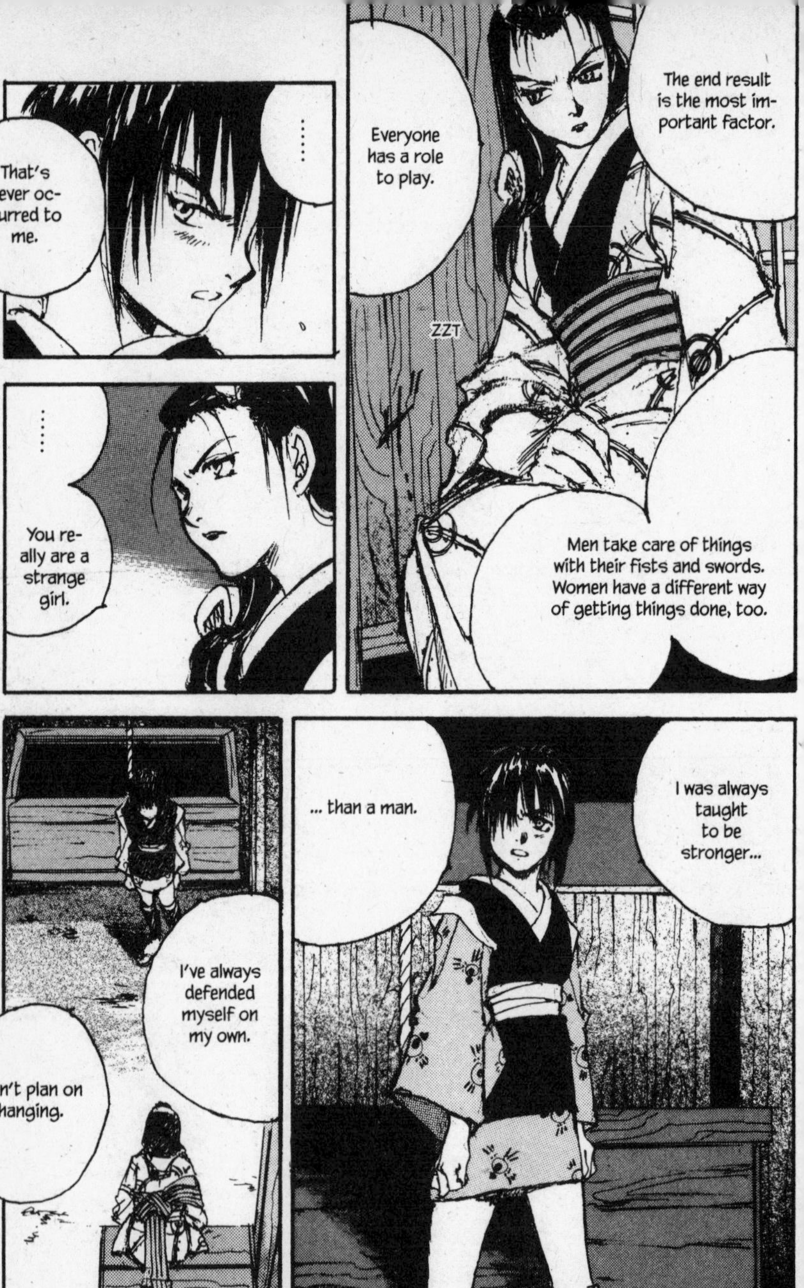
The end result is the most important factor.
Everyone has a role to play.
ZZT
Men take care of things with their fists and swords. Women have a different way of getting things done, too.
......
That's never occurred to me.
......
You really are a strange girl.
I was always taught to be stronger...
... than a man.
I've always defended myself on my own.
I don't plan on changing.

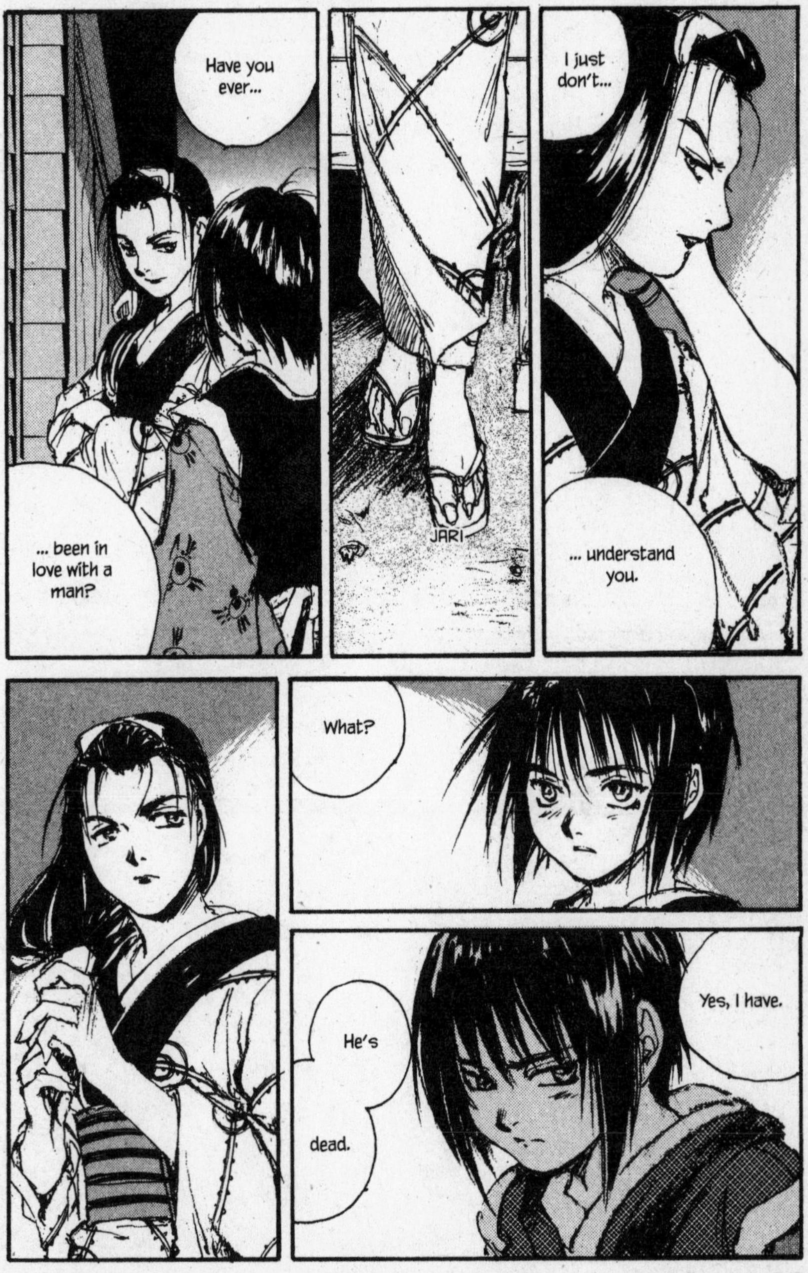
I just don't...
... understand you.
JARI
Have you ever...
... been in love with a man?
What?
Yes, I have.
He's
dead.

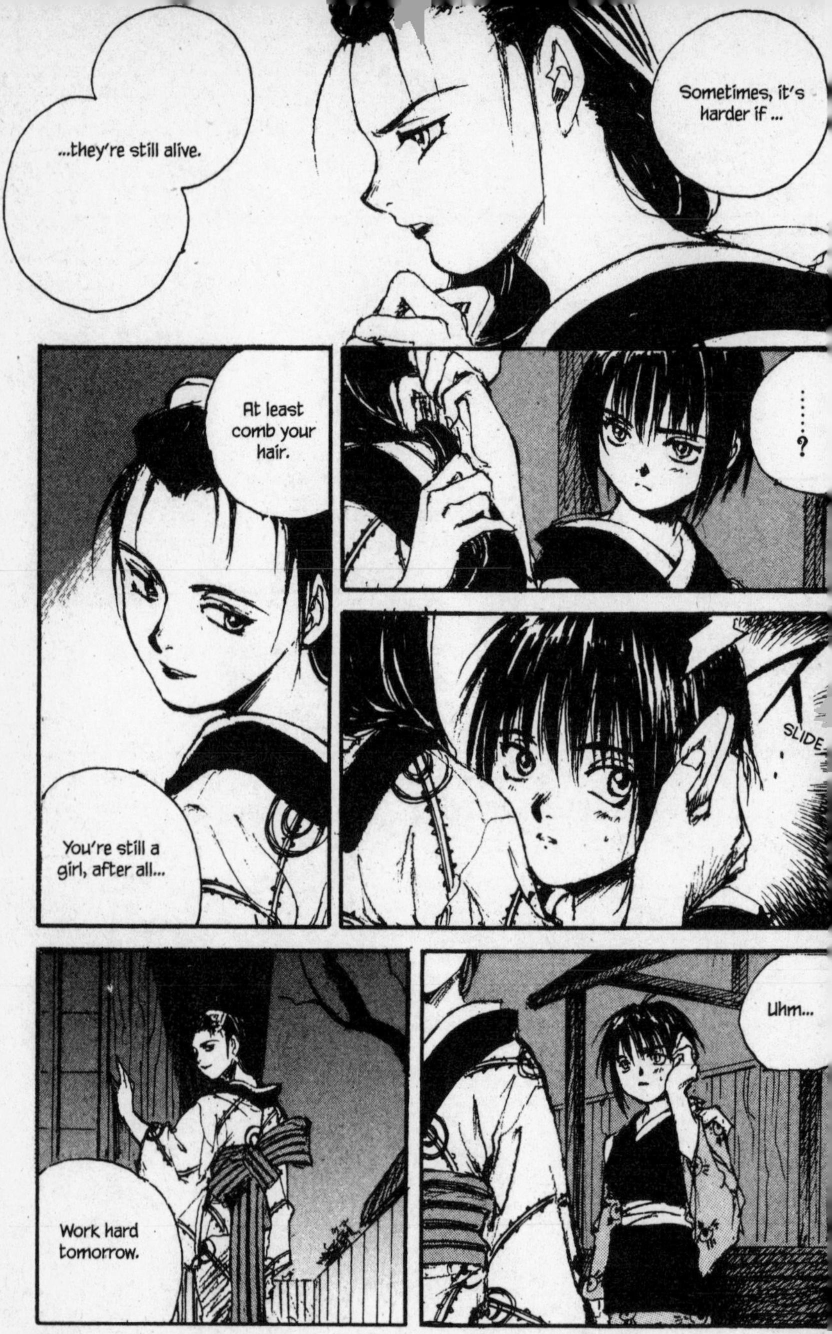
Sometimes, it's harder if ...
...they're still alive.
......?
SLIDE
At least comb your hair.
You're still a girl, after all...
Uhm...
Work hard tomorrow.

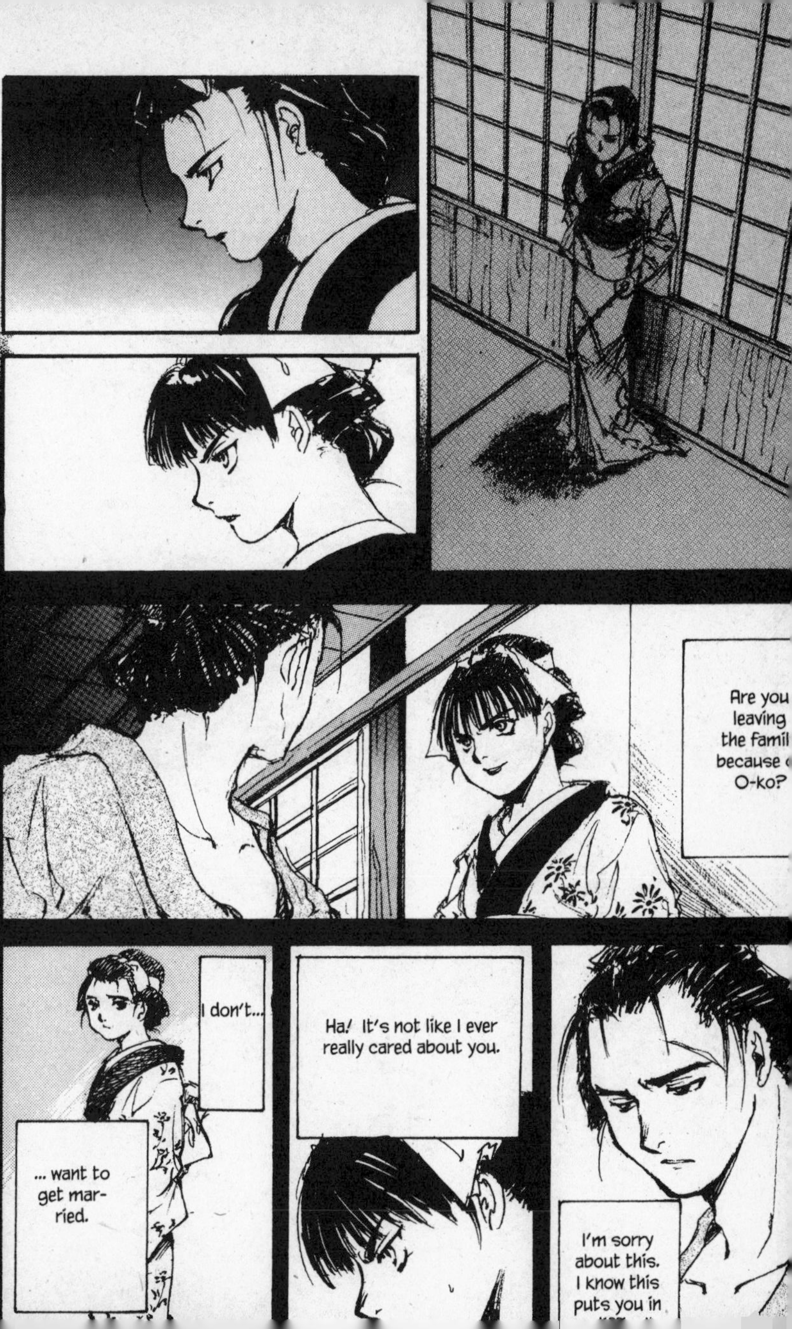
Are you leaving the famil because o O-ko?
I'm sorry about this. I know this puts you in
Ha! It's not like I ever really cared about you.
I don't...
... want to get mar-ried.

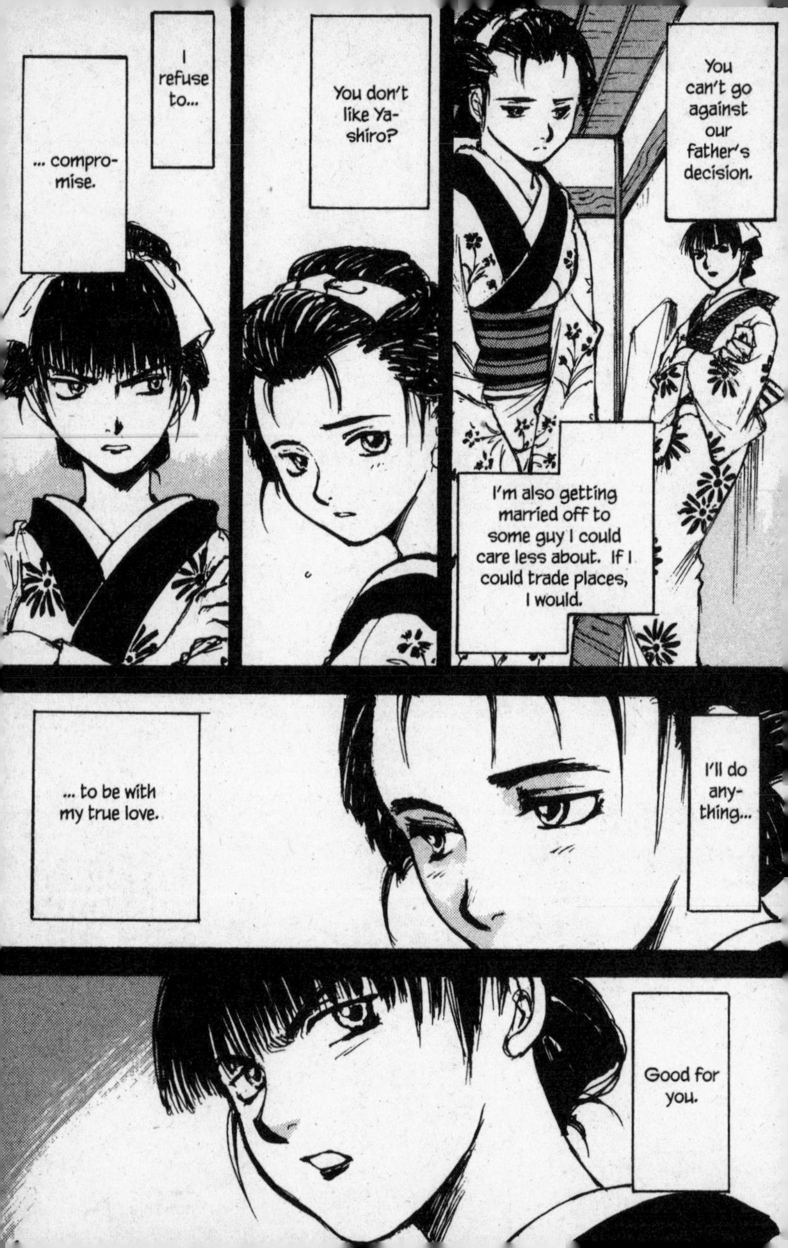
You can't go against our father's decision.
I'm also getting married off to some guy I could care less about. If I could trade places, I would.
You don't like Ya-shiro?
I refuse to...
... compro-mise.
I'll do any-thing...
... to be with my true love.
Good for you.

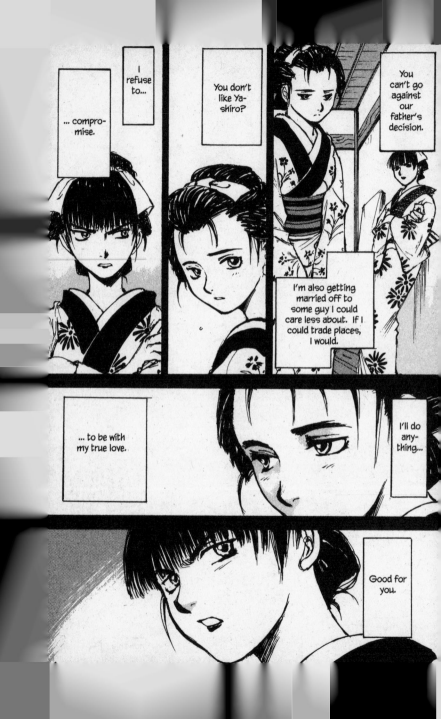

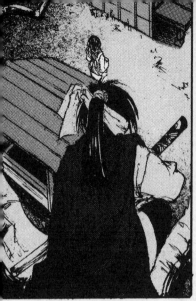
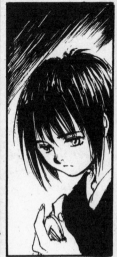
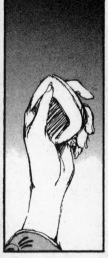

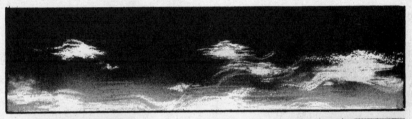

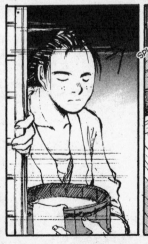

SPLISH SPLASH

IGA-RAN

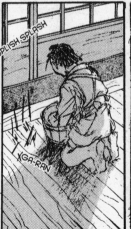

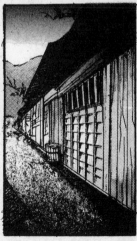

126

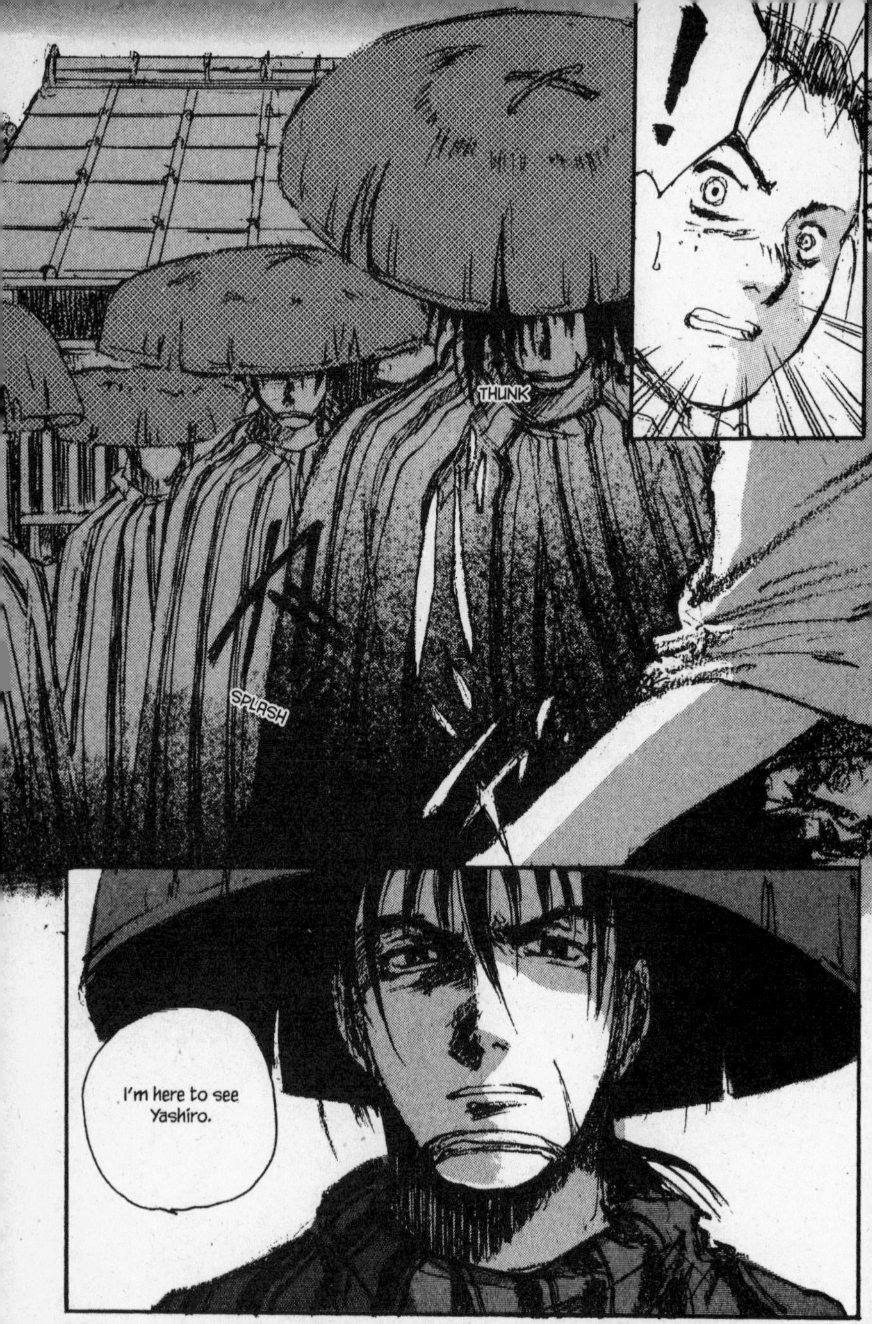
!
THUNK
SPLASH
I'm here to see Yashiro.

THE END OF CHAPTER 8, EPISODE 3

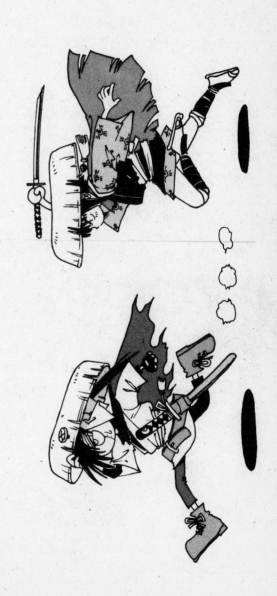

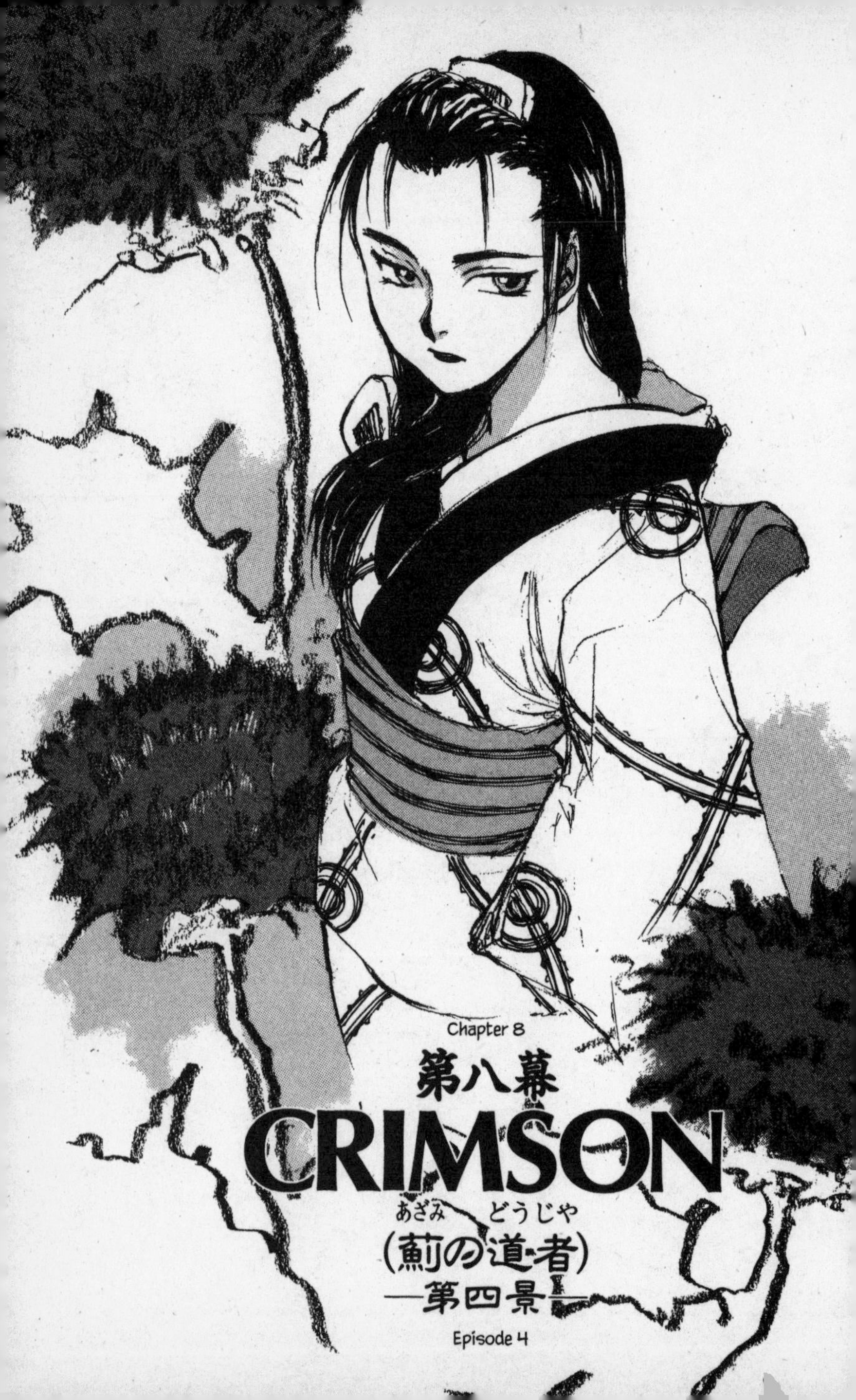
Chapter 8
第八幕
CRIMSON
あざみ どうじゃ
(薊の道者)
—第四景—
Episode 4

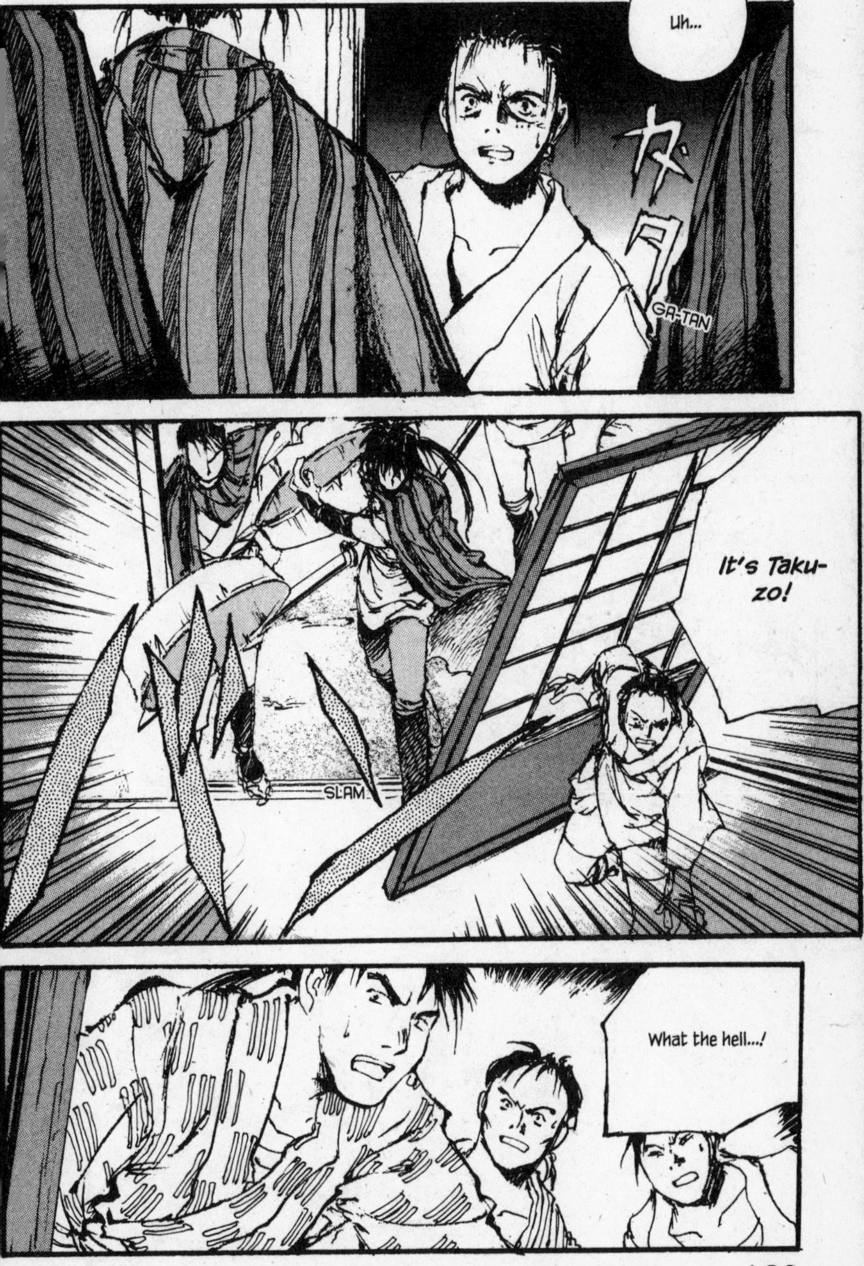
Uh...
GA-TAN
It's Taku-zo!
SLAM
What the hell...!

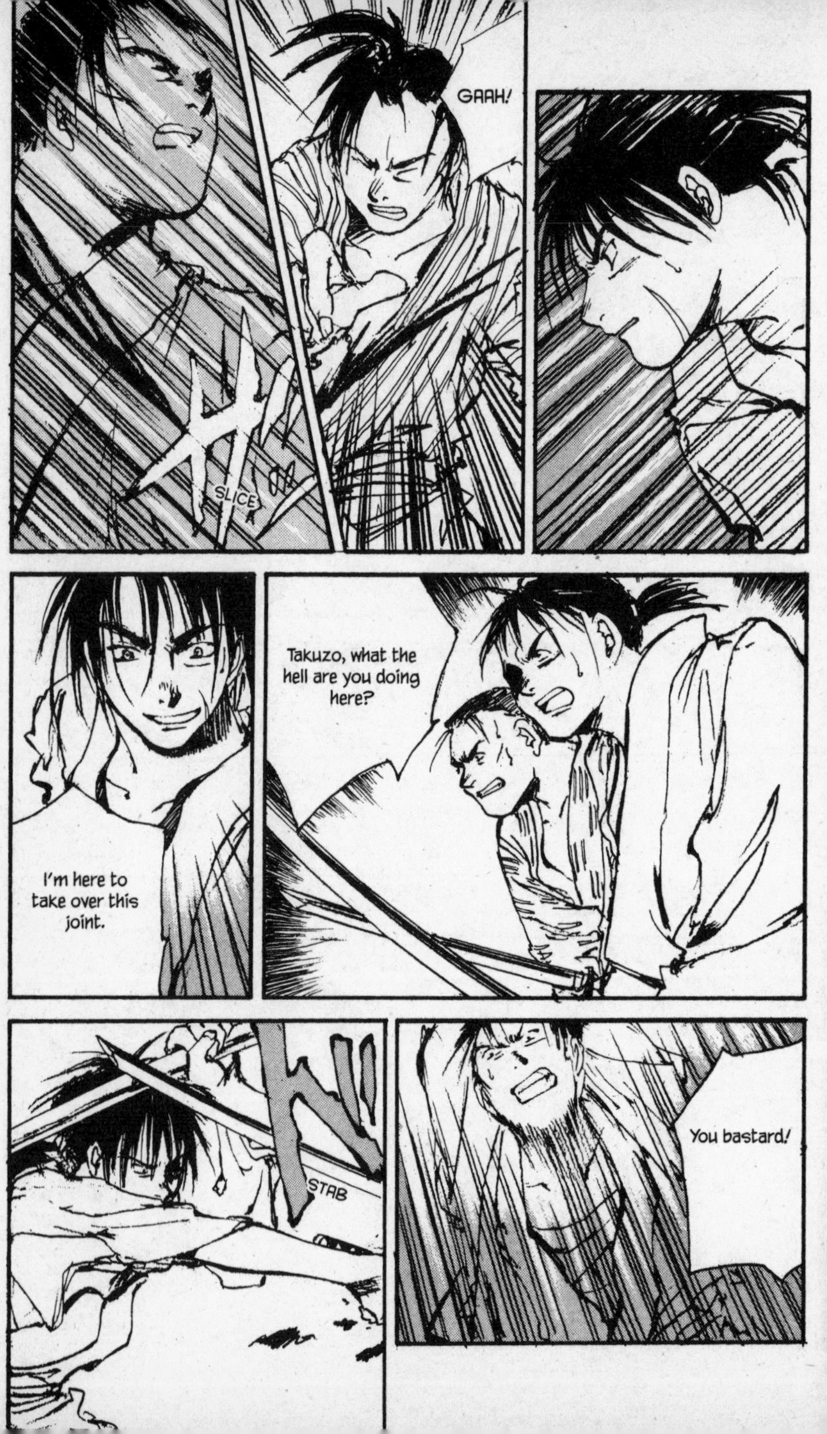
GAAH!
SLICE
Takuzo, what the hell are you doing here?
I'm here to take over this joint.
You bastard!
STAB

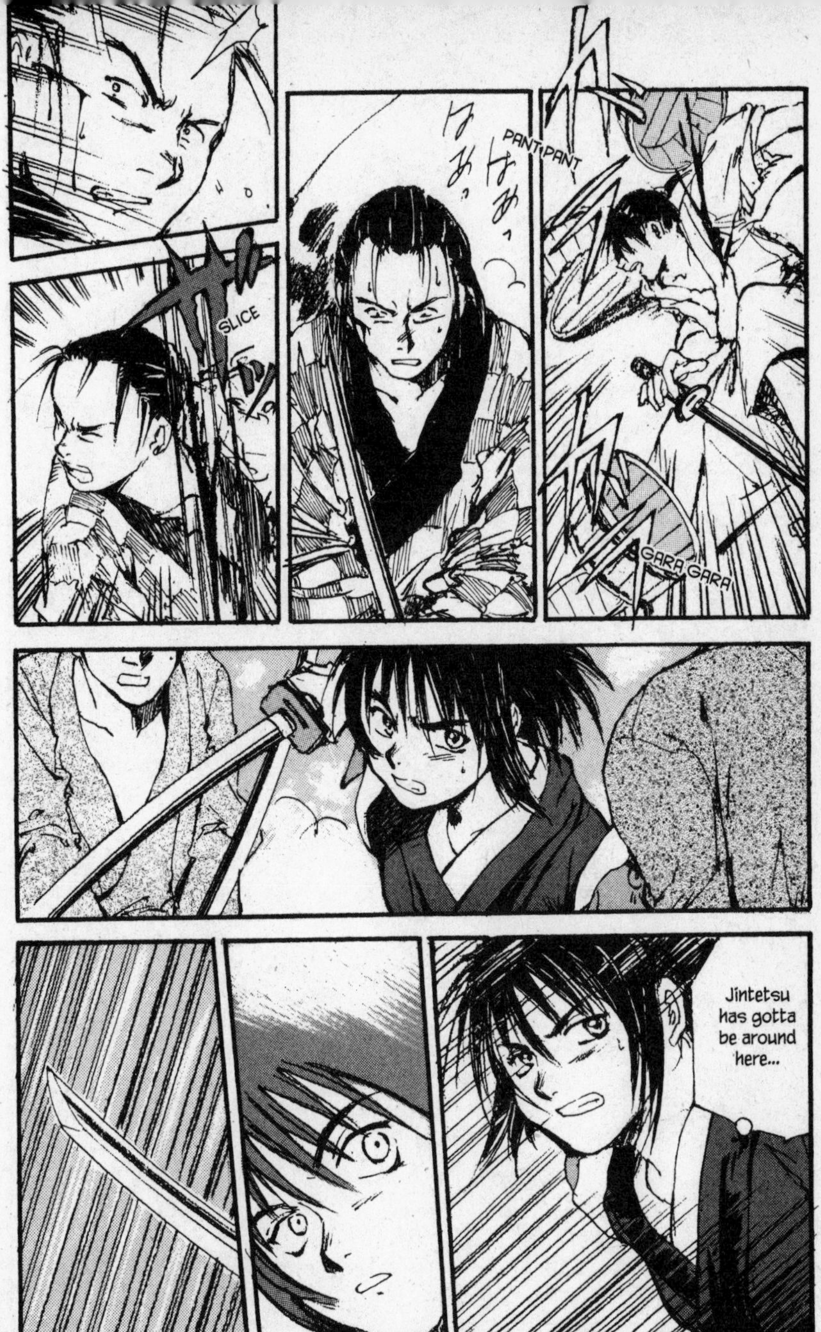
GARA GARA
はぁっ はぁっ
PANT PANT
SLICE
Jintetsu has gotta be around here...

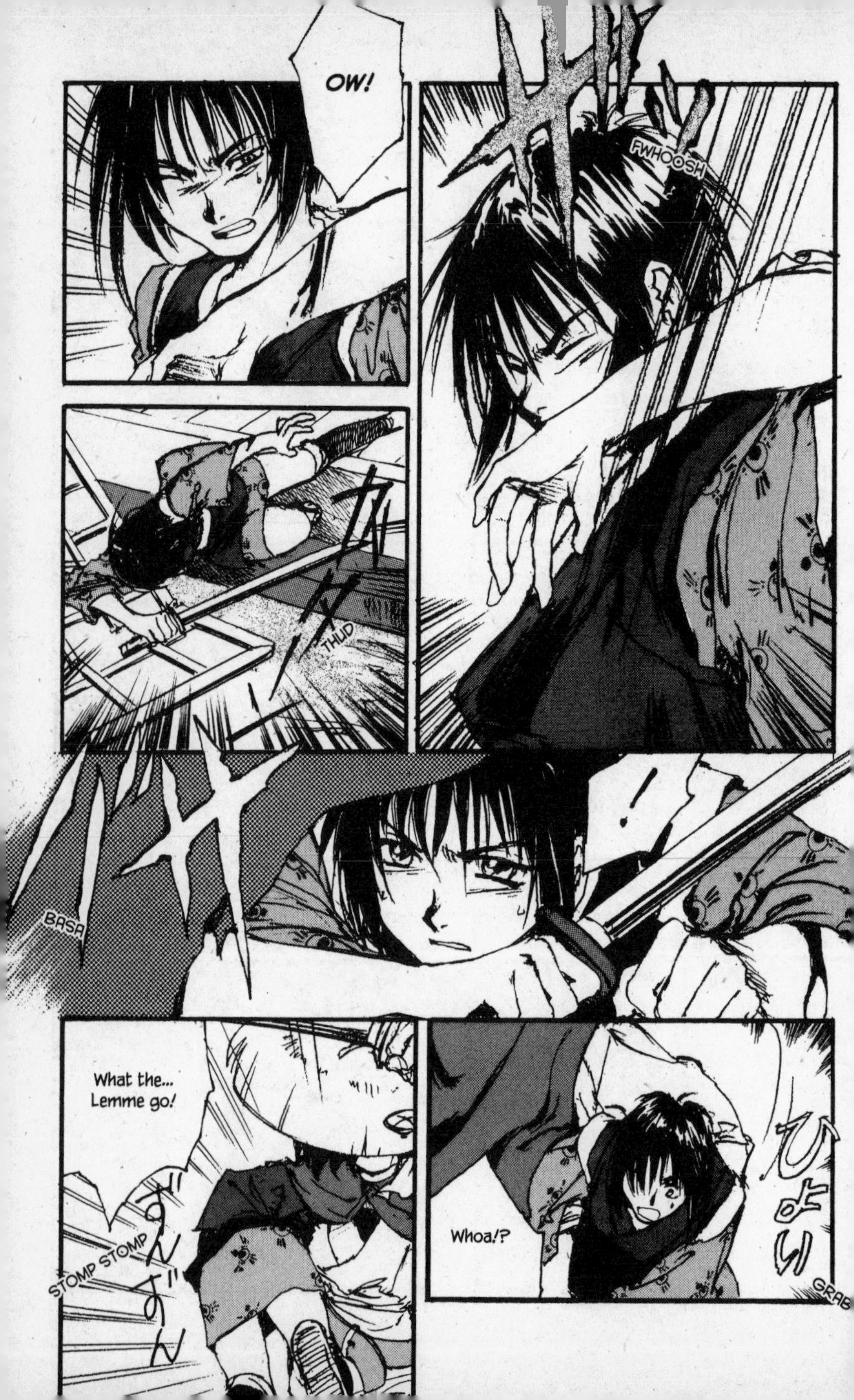
FWHOOSH
OW!
THUD
!
BASA
Whoa!?
GRAB
What the...
Lemme go!
STOMP STOMP

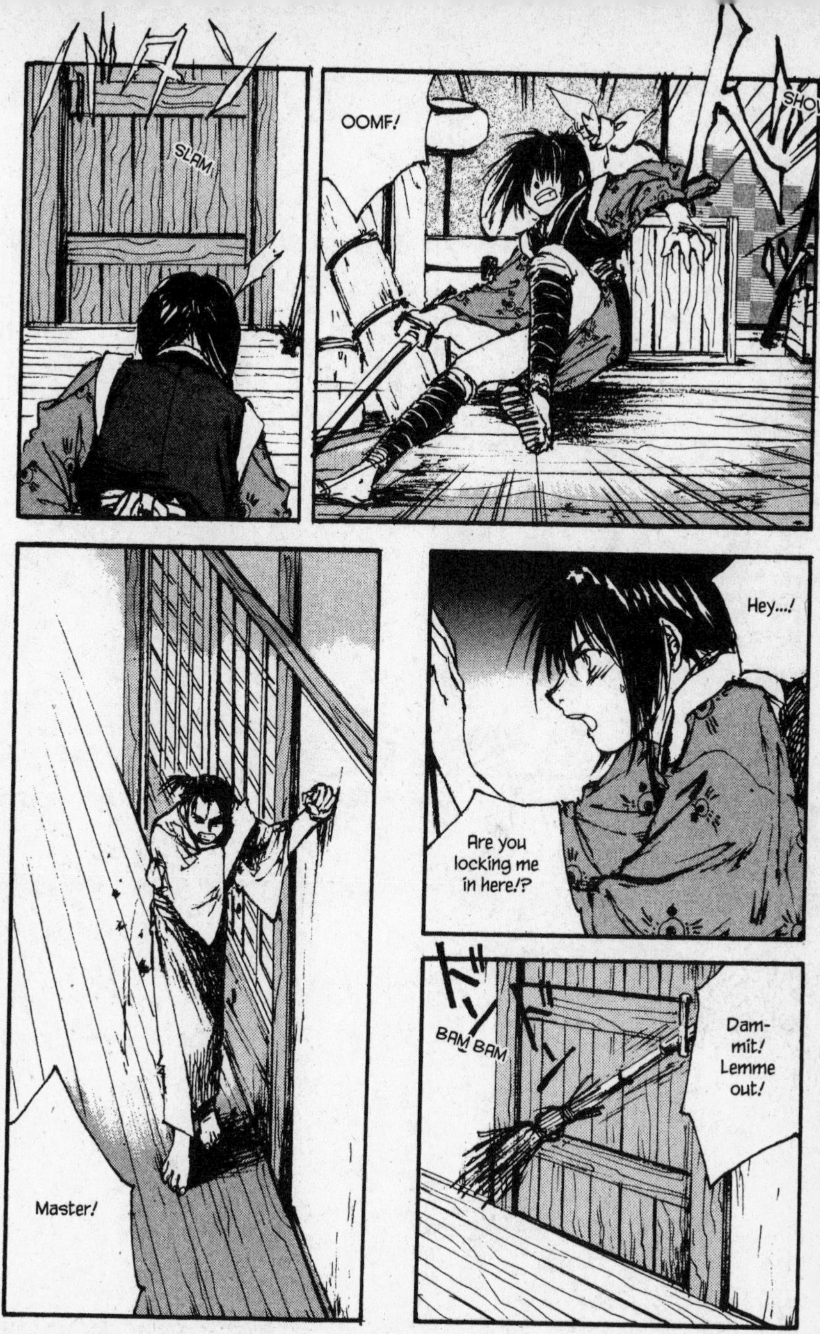
SHOVE
OOMF!
SLAM
Hey...!
Are you locking me in here!?
BAM BAM
Dam-mit! Lemme out!
Master!

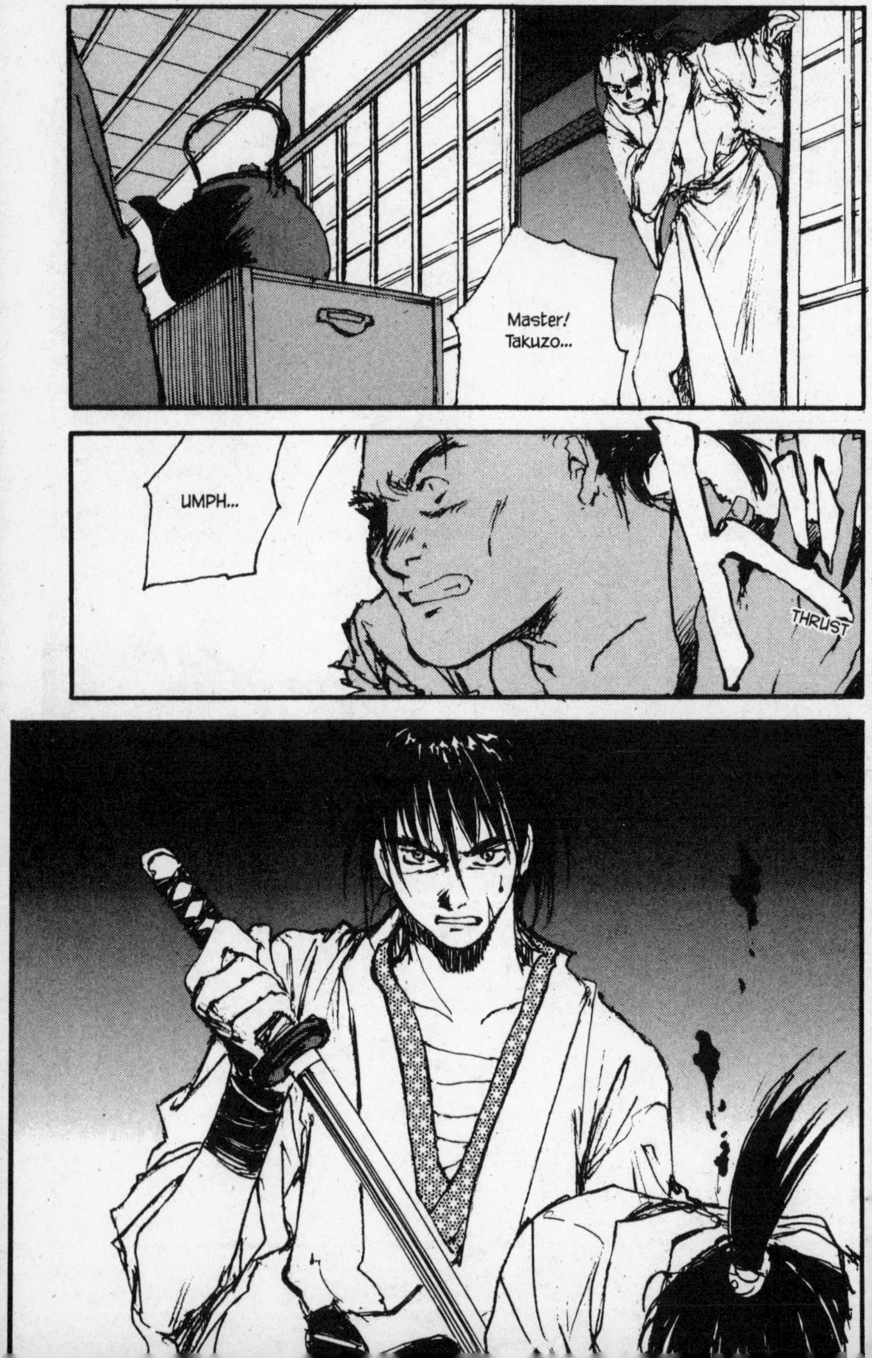
Master! Takuzo...
THRUST
UMPH...

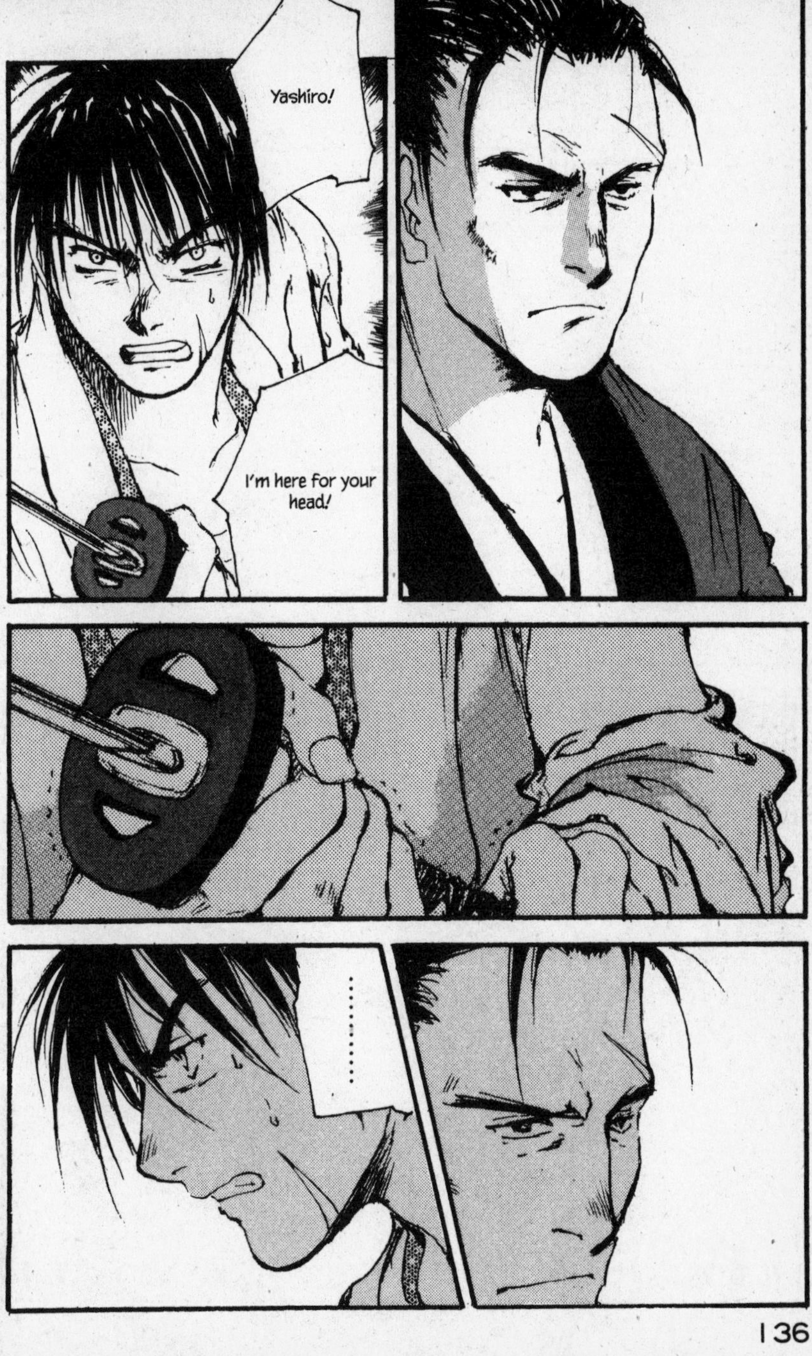
Yashiro!
I'm here for your head!
......

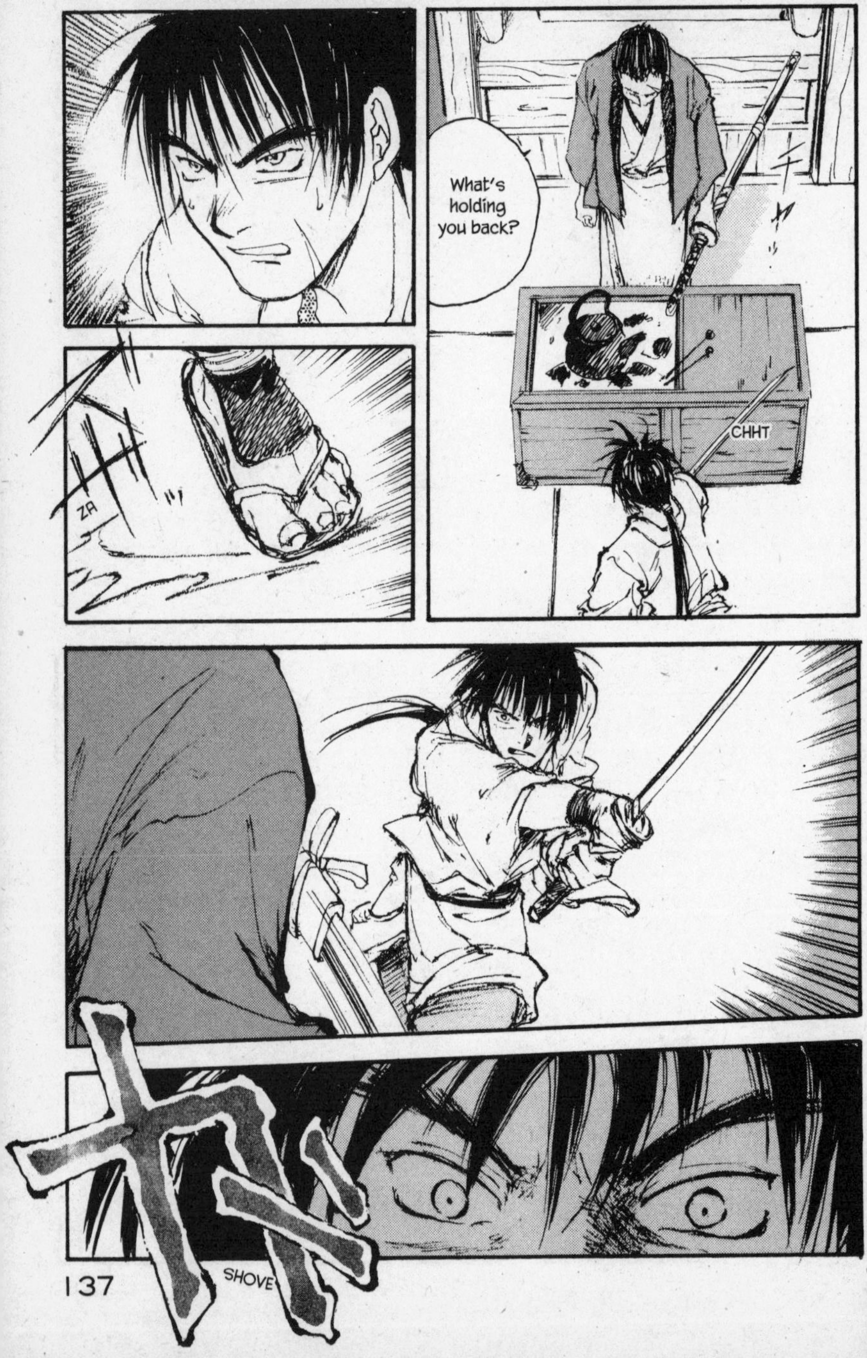
What's holding you back?
CHHT
ZA
SHOVE

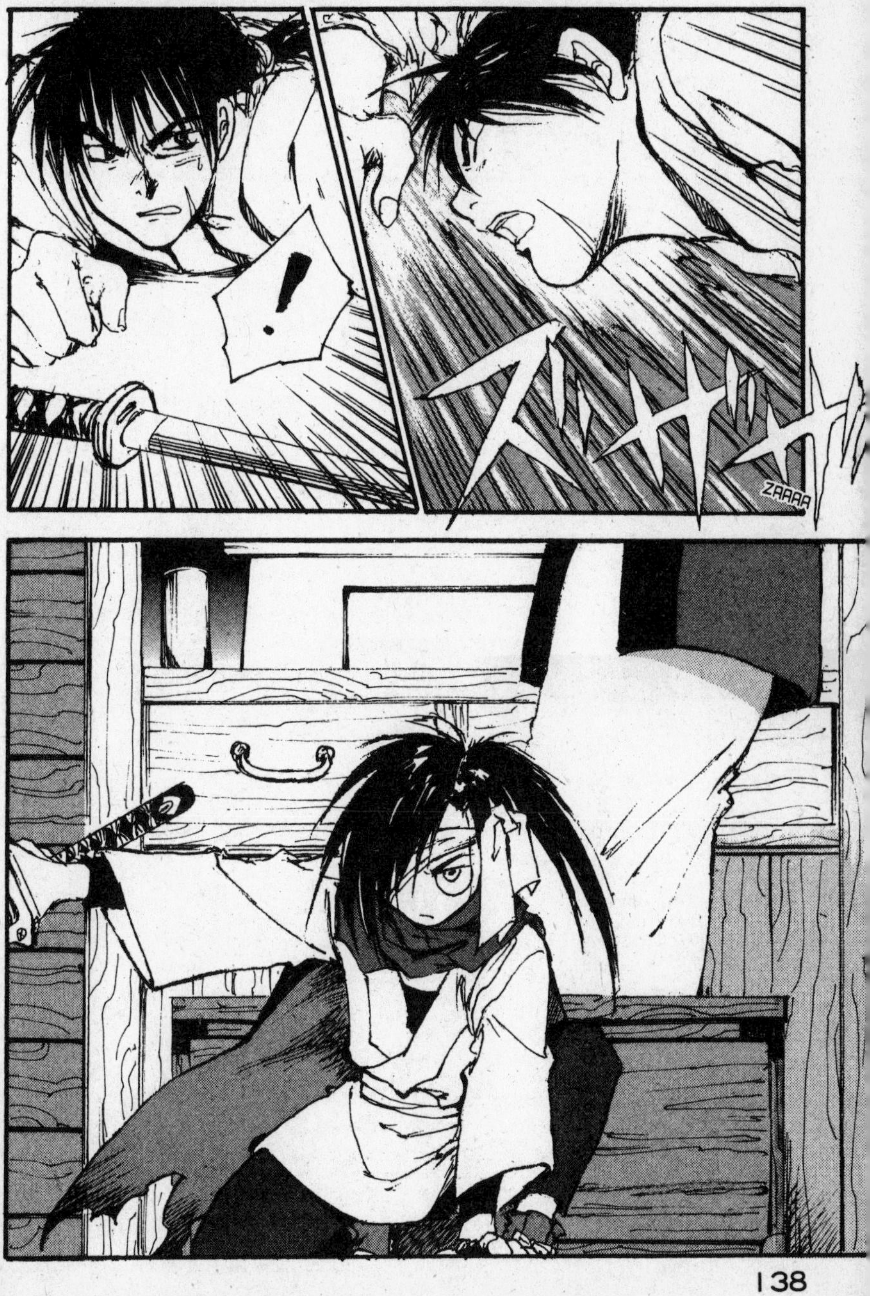
ZAAAA
!

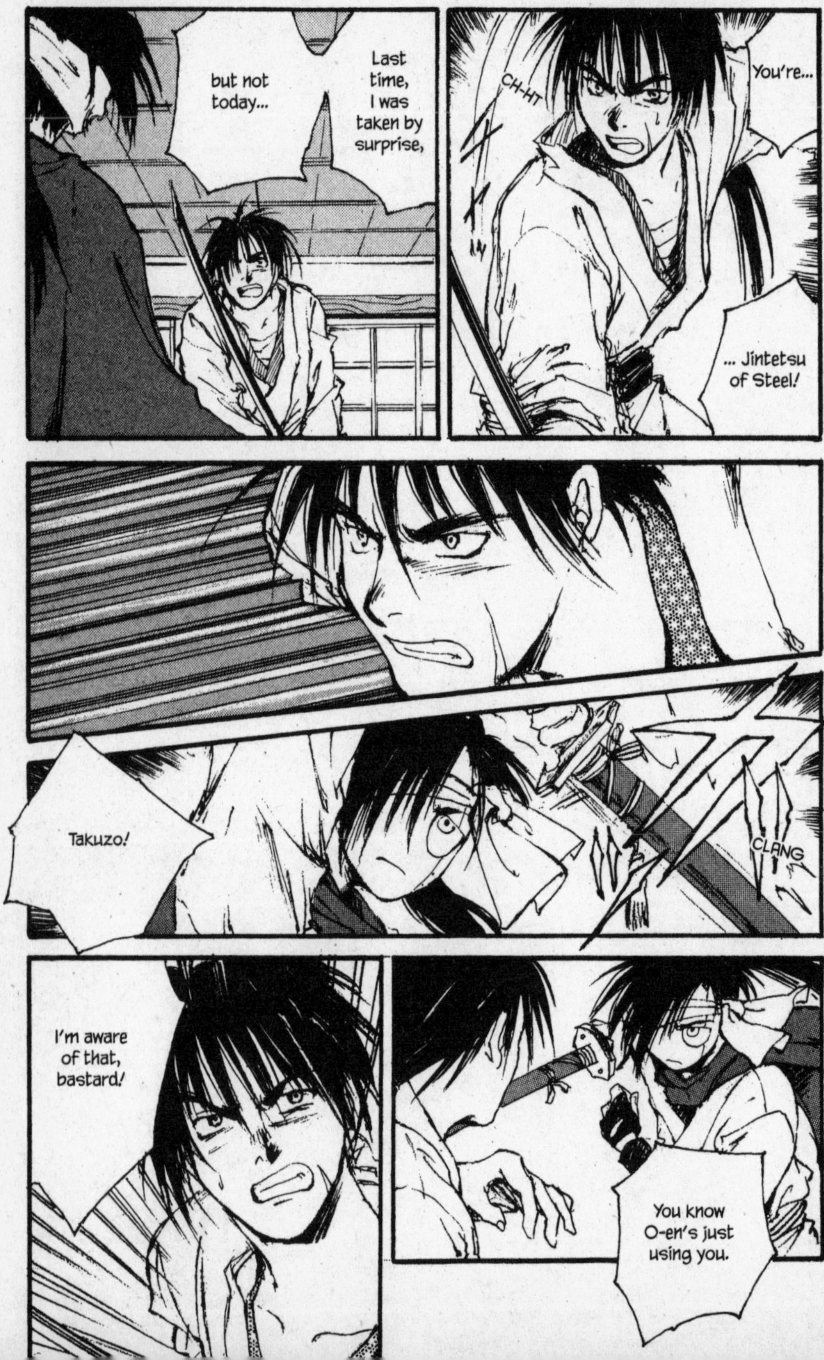
CH-HT
You're...
... Jintetsu of Steel!
Last time, I was taken by surprise,
but not today...
Takuzo!
CLANG
You know O-en's just using you.
I'm aware of that, bastard!

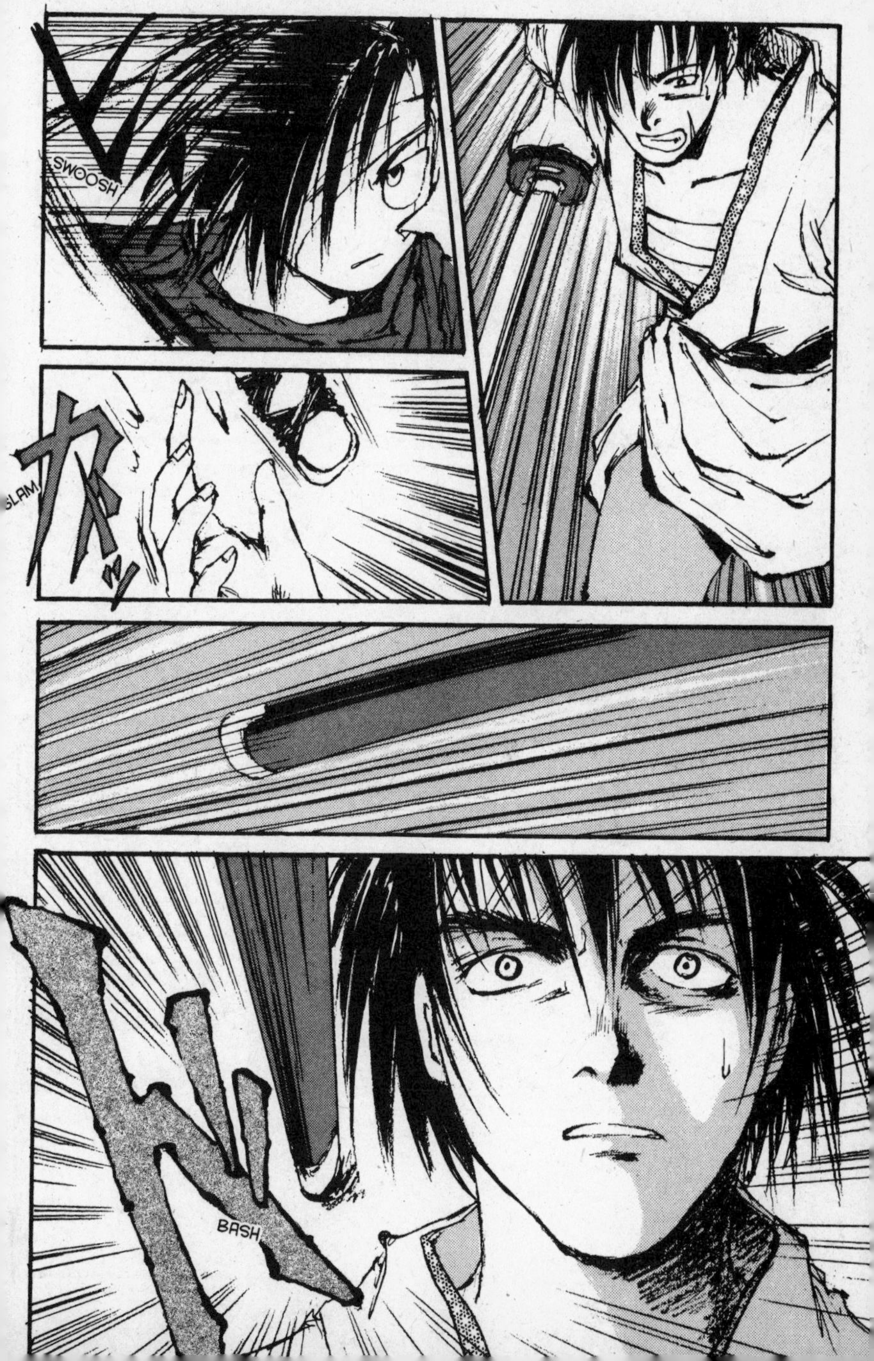
SWOOSH
SLAM
BASH

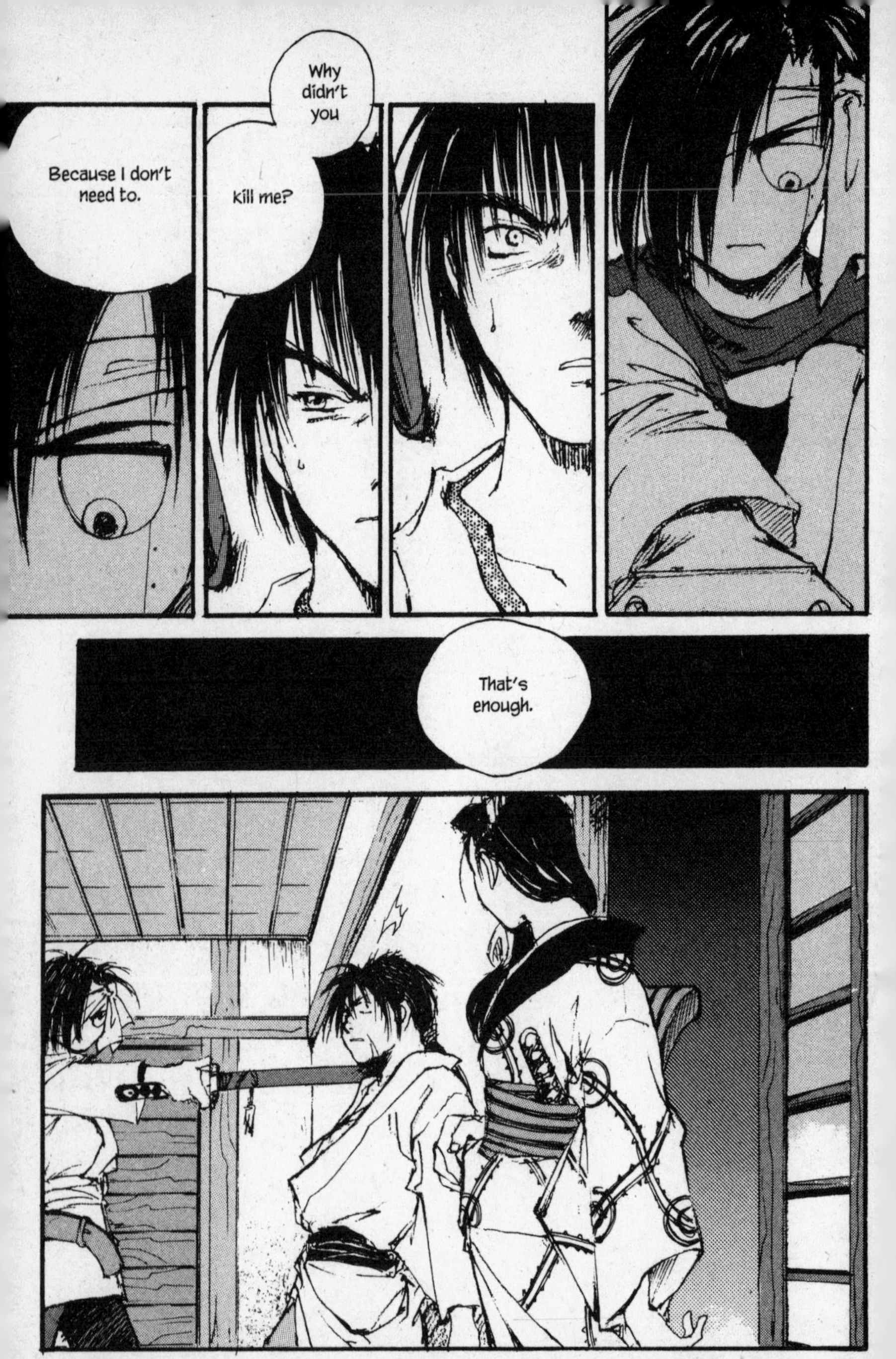
Why didn't you kill me?
Because I don't need to.
That's enough.

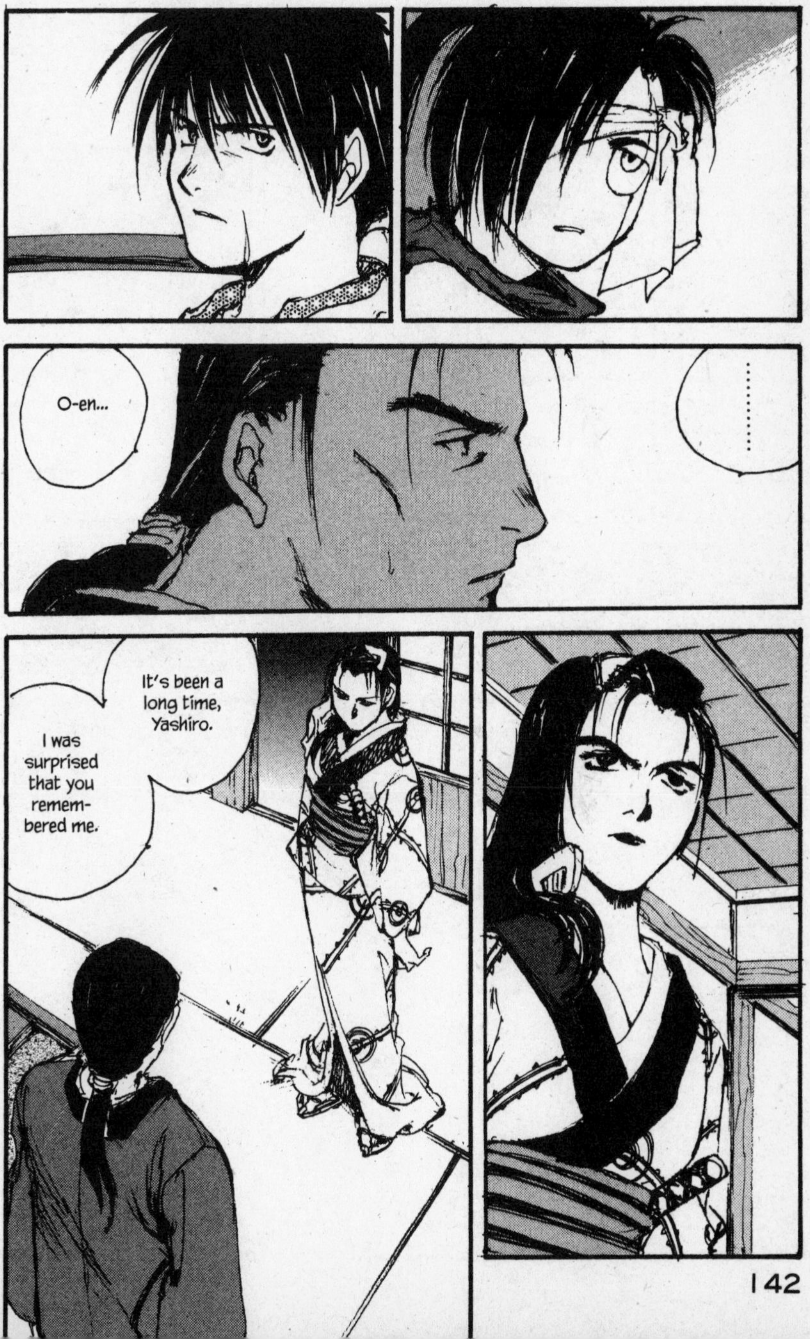

……
O-en...
It's been a long time, Yashiro.
I was surprised that you remem-bered me.

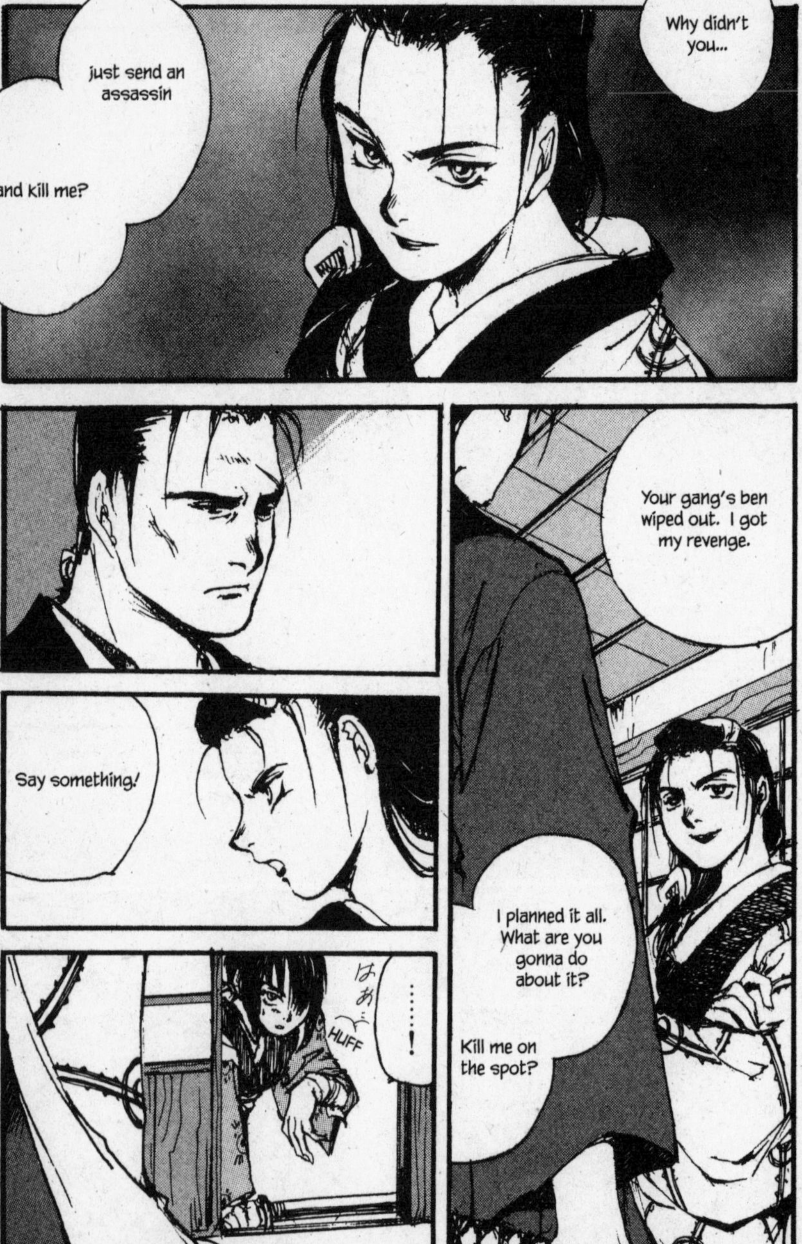
Why didn't you...
just send an assassin
and kill me?
Your gang's ben wiped out. I got my revenge.
I planned it all. What are you gonna do about it?
Kill me on the spot?
Say something!
......!
はあ
HUFF

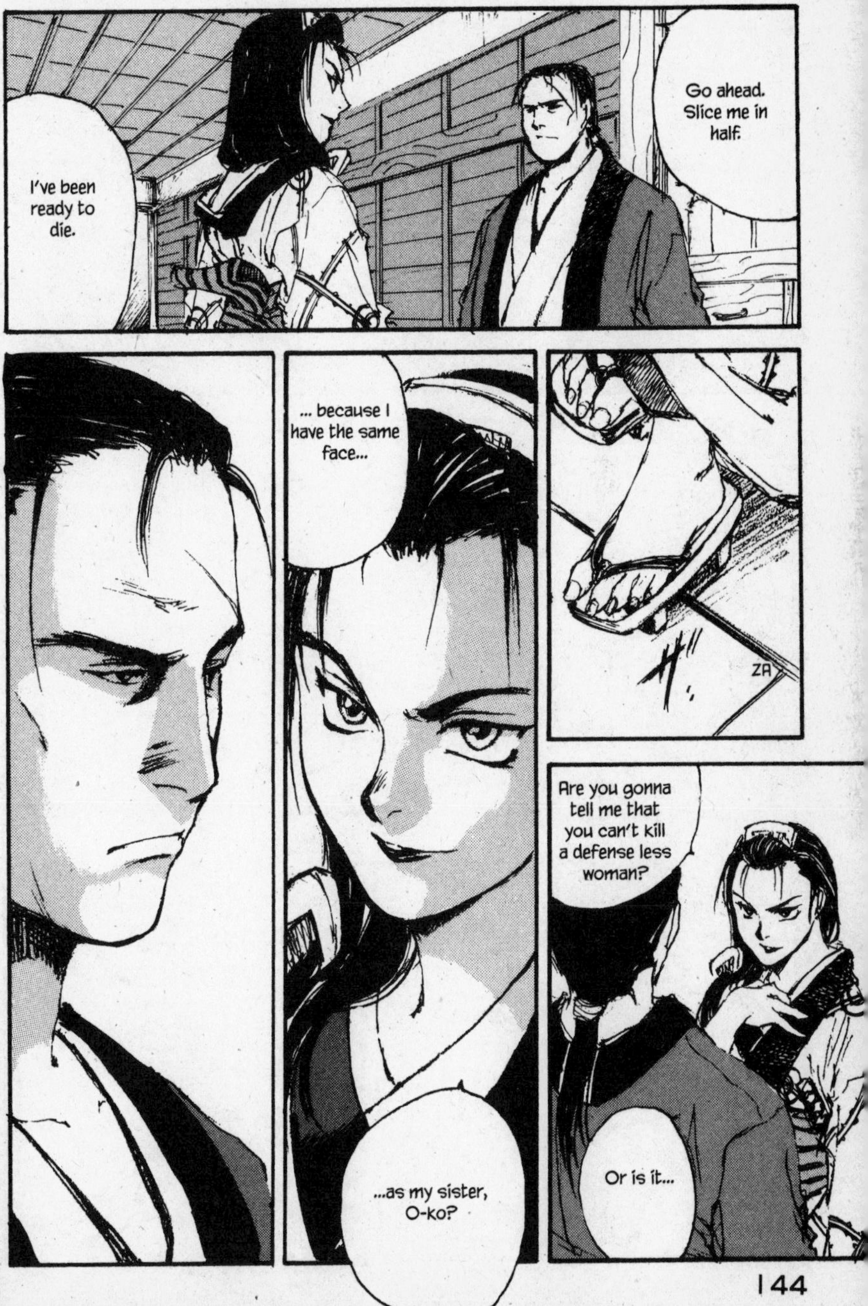
Go ahead. Slice me in half.
I've been ready to die.
ZA
Are you gonna tell me that you can't kill a defense less woman?
Or is it...
... because I have the same face...
...as my sister, O-ko?

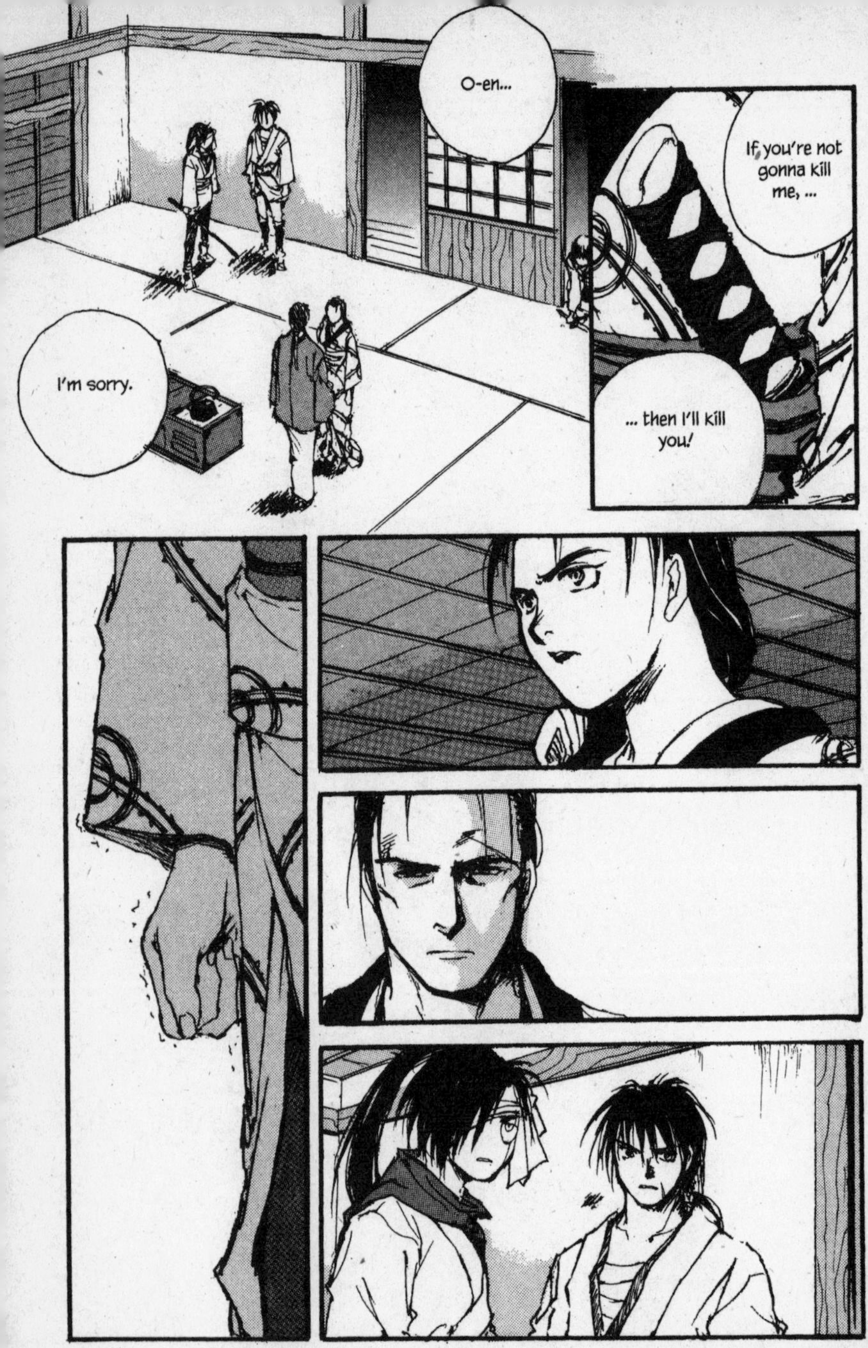
O-en...
If you're not gonna kill me, ...
... then I'll kill you!
I'm sorry.

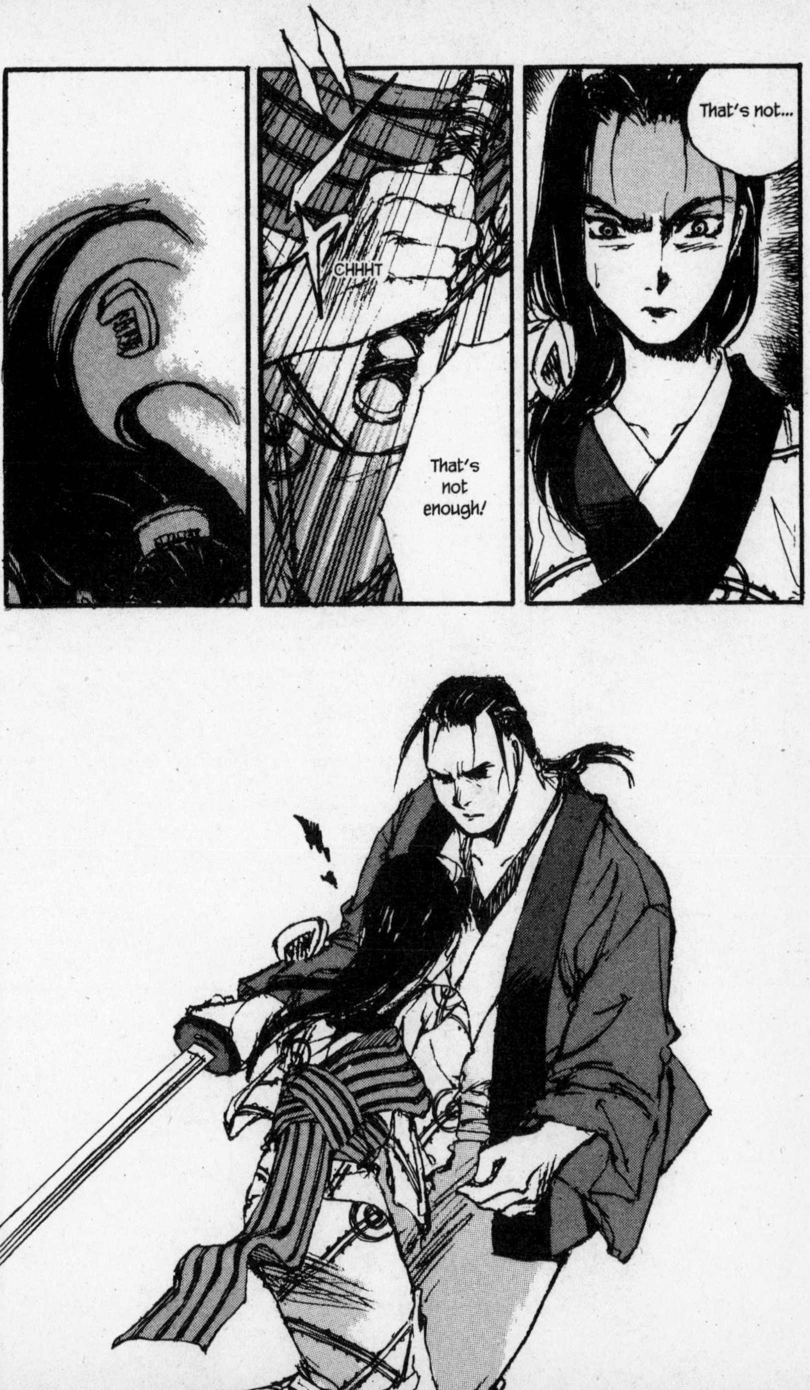
That's not...
CHHHT
That's not enough!

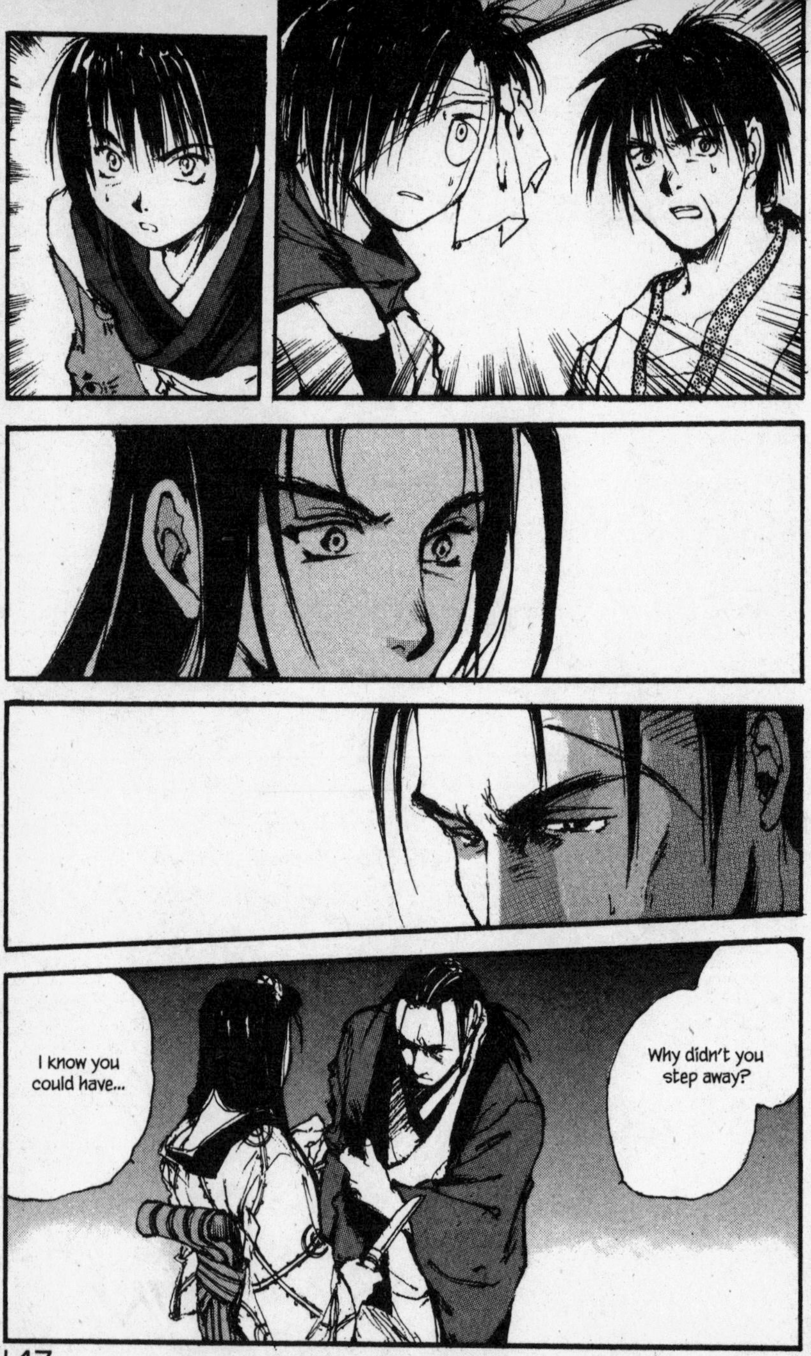
Why didn't you step away?
I know you could have...

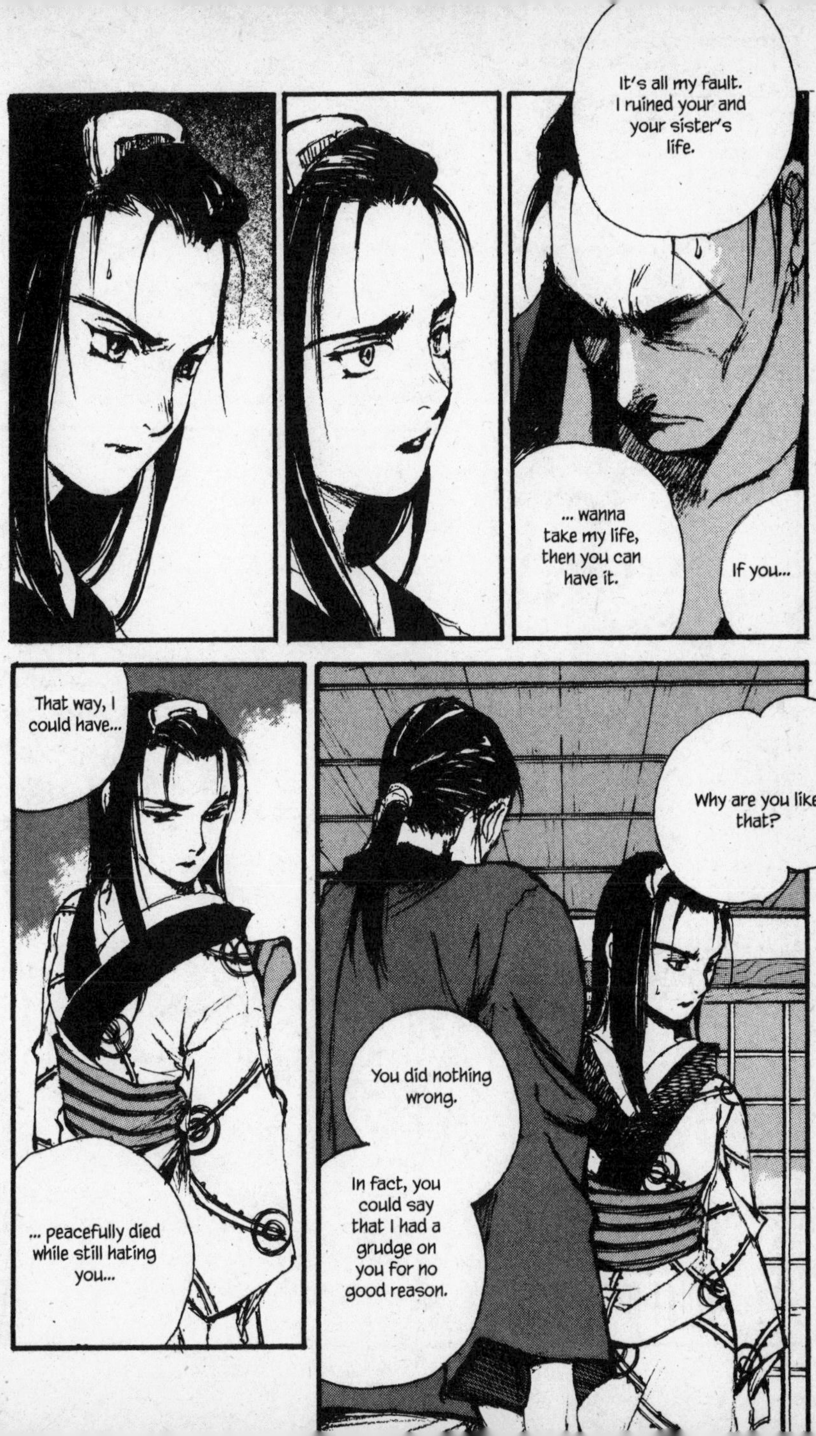
It's all my fault. I ruined your and your sister's life.
If you...
... wanna take my life, then you can have it.
Why are you like that?
You did nothing wrong.
In fact, you could say that I had a grudge on you for no good reason.
That way, I could have...
... peacefully died while still hating you...

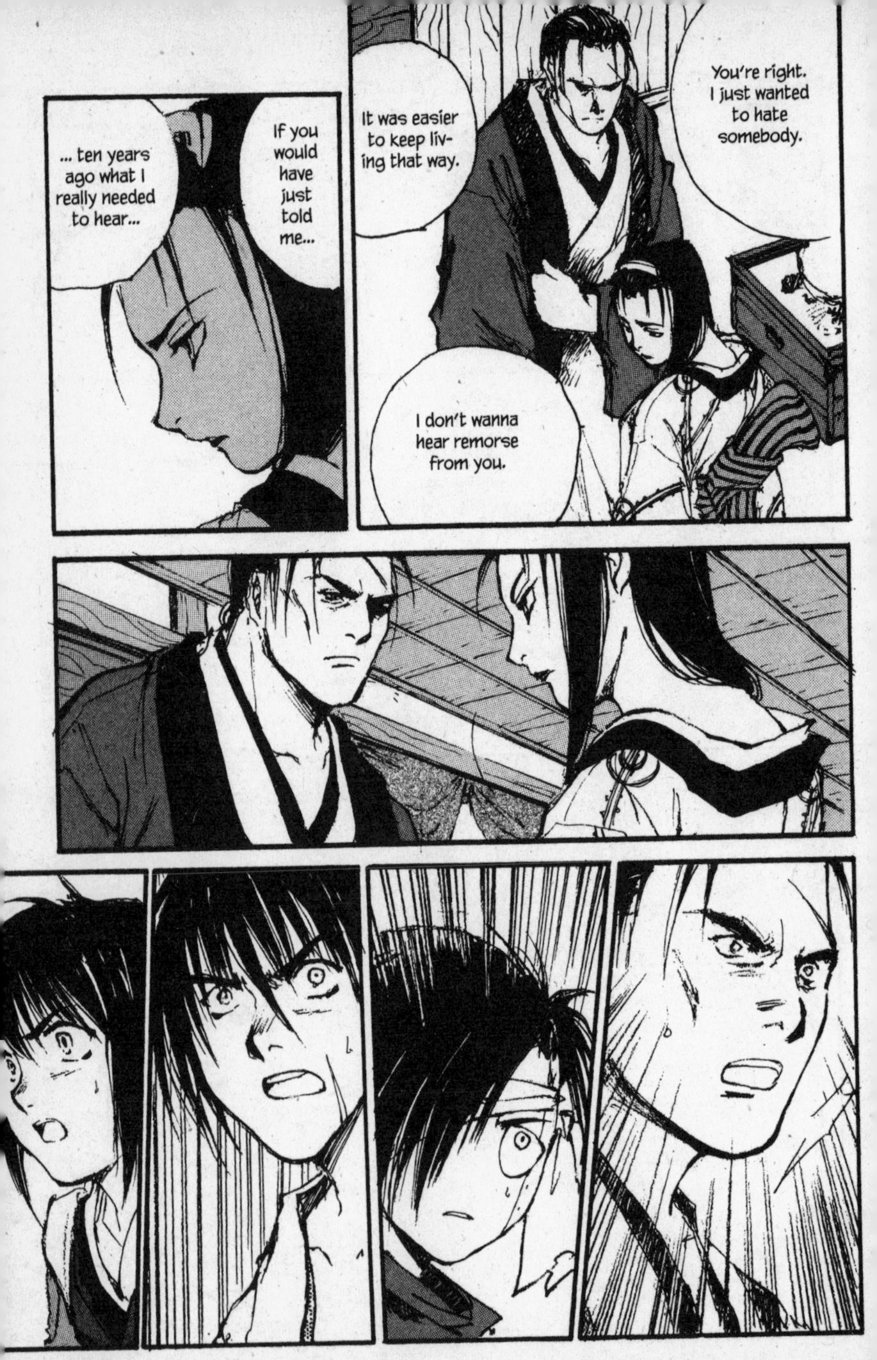
You're right. I just wanted to hate somebody.
It was easier to keep living that way.
I don't wanna hear remorse from you.
If you would have just told me...
... ten years ago what I really needed to hear...

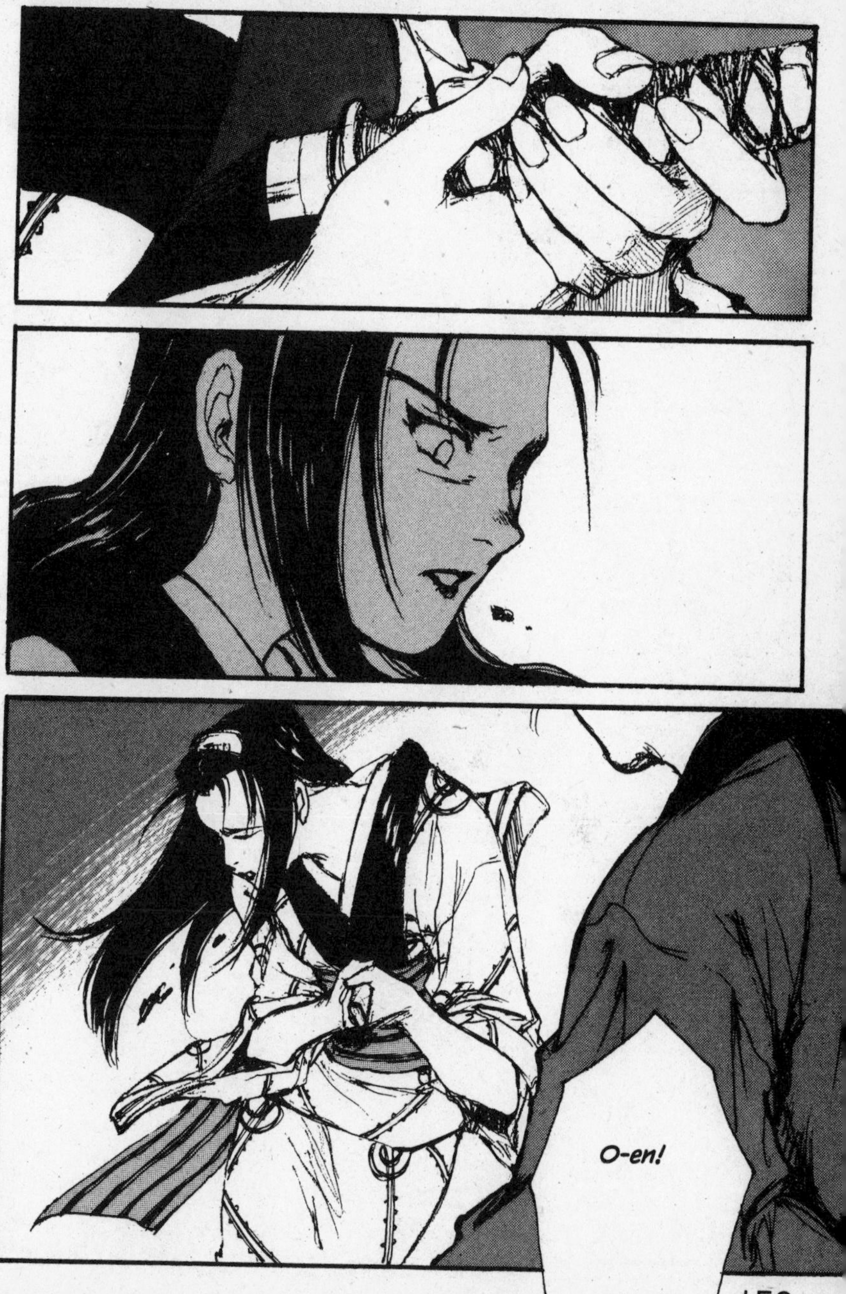
O-en!

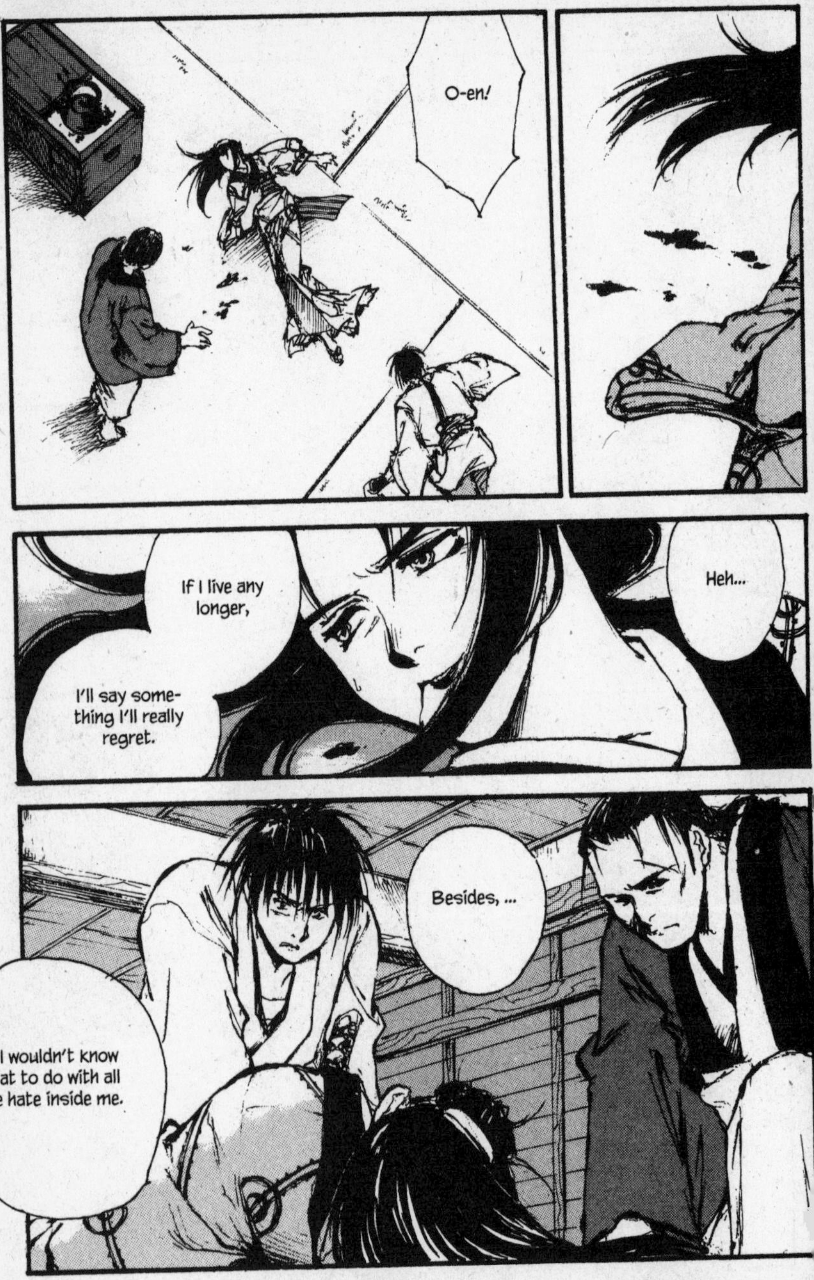
O-en!
Heh...
If I live any longer,
I'll say some-thing I'll really regret.
Besides, ...
... I wouldn't know what to do with all the hate inside me.

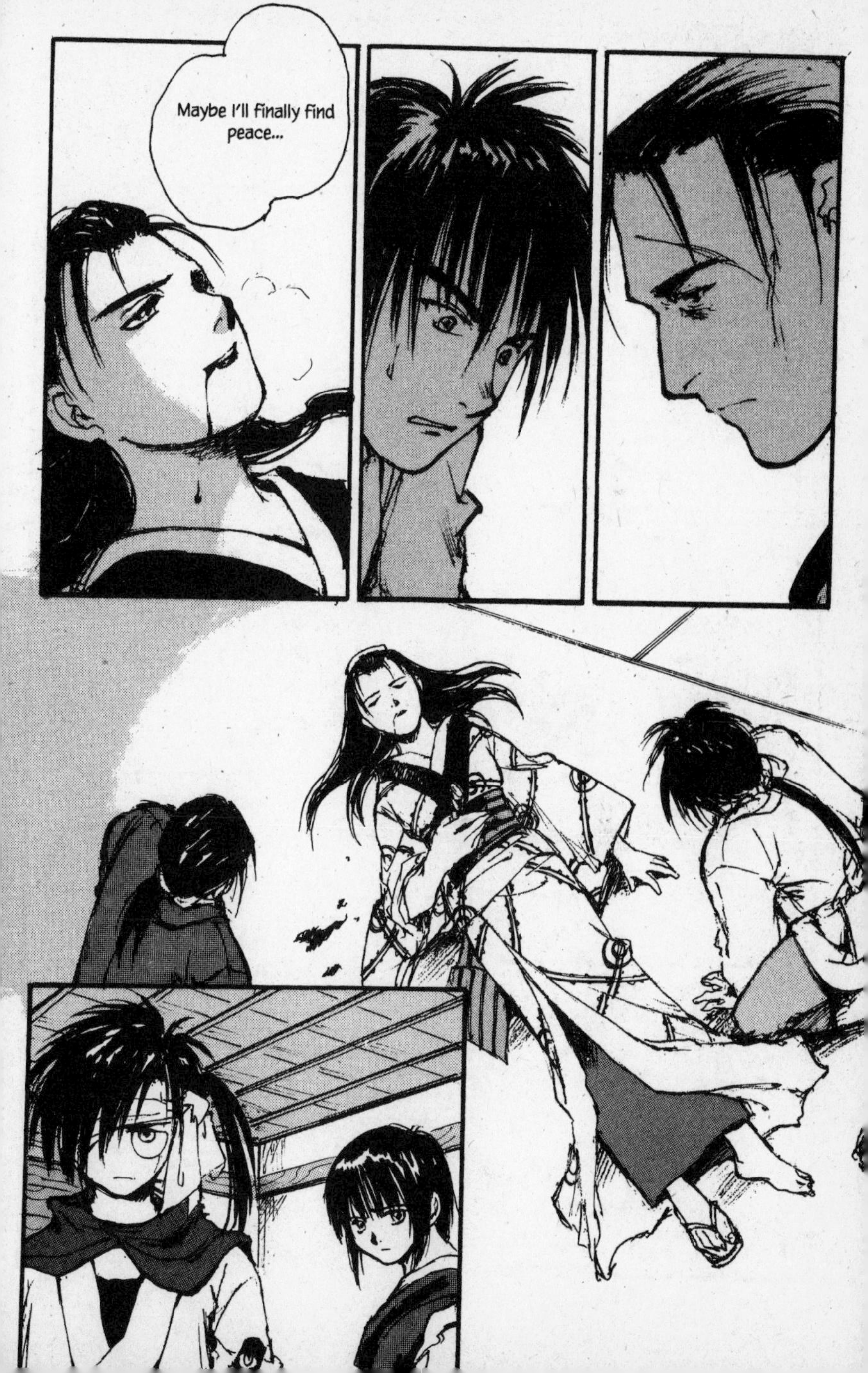
Maybe I'll finally find peace...

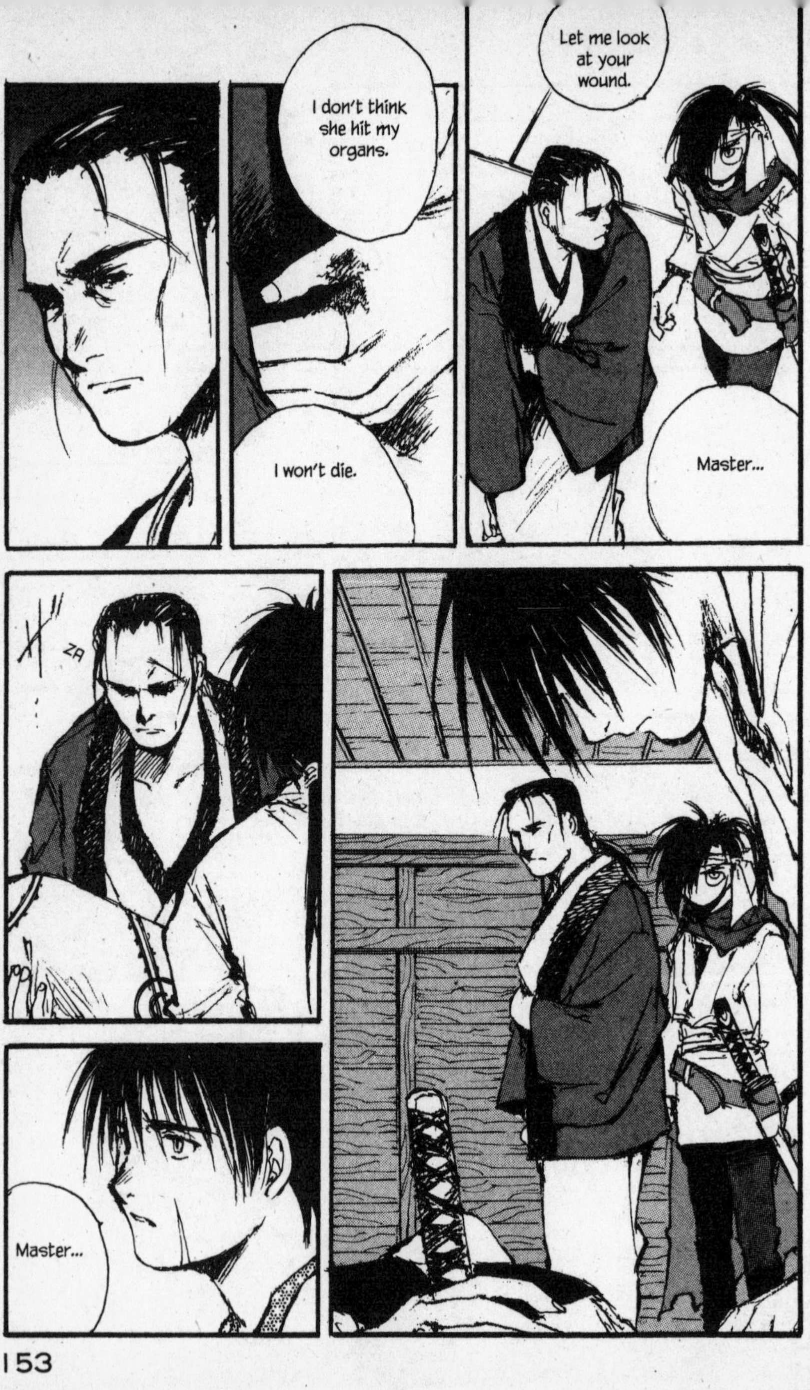
Let me look at your wound.
Master...
I don't think she hit my organs.
I won't die.
ZA
Master...

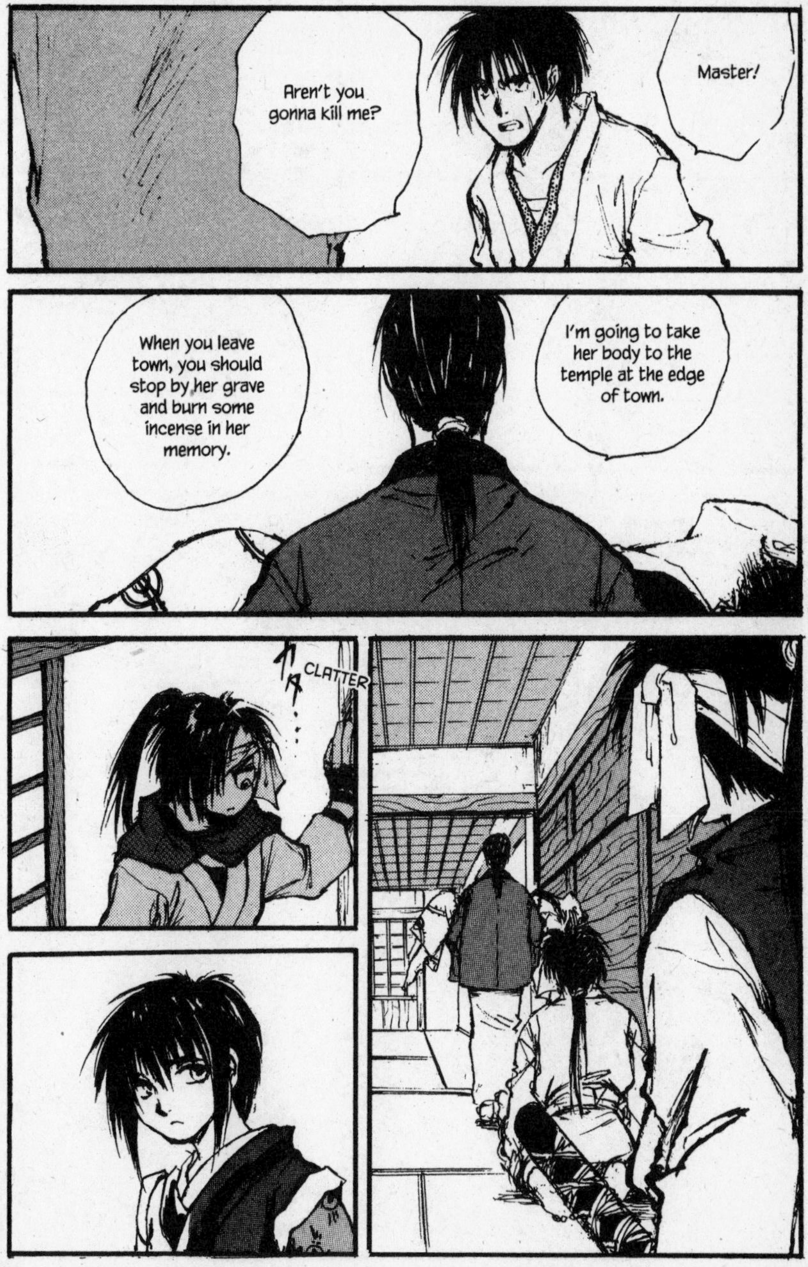
Master!
Aren't you gonna kill me?
I'm going to take her body to the temple at the edge of town.
When you leave town, you should stop by her grave and burn some incense in her memory.
CLATTER

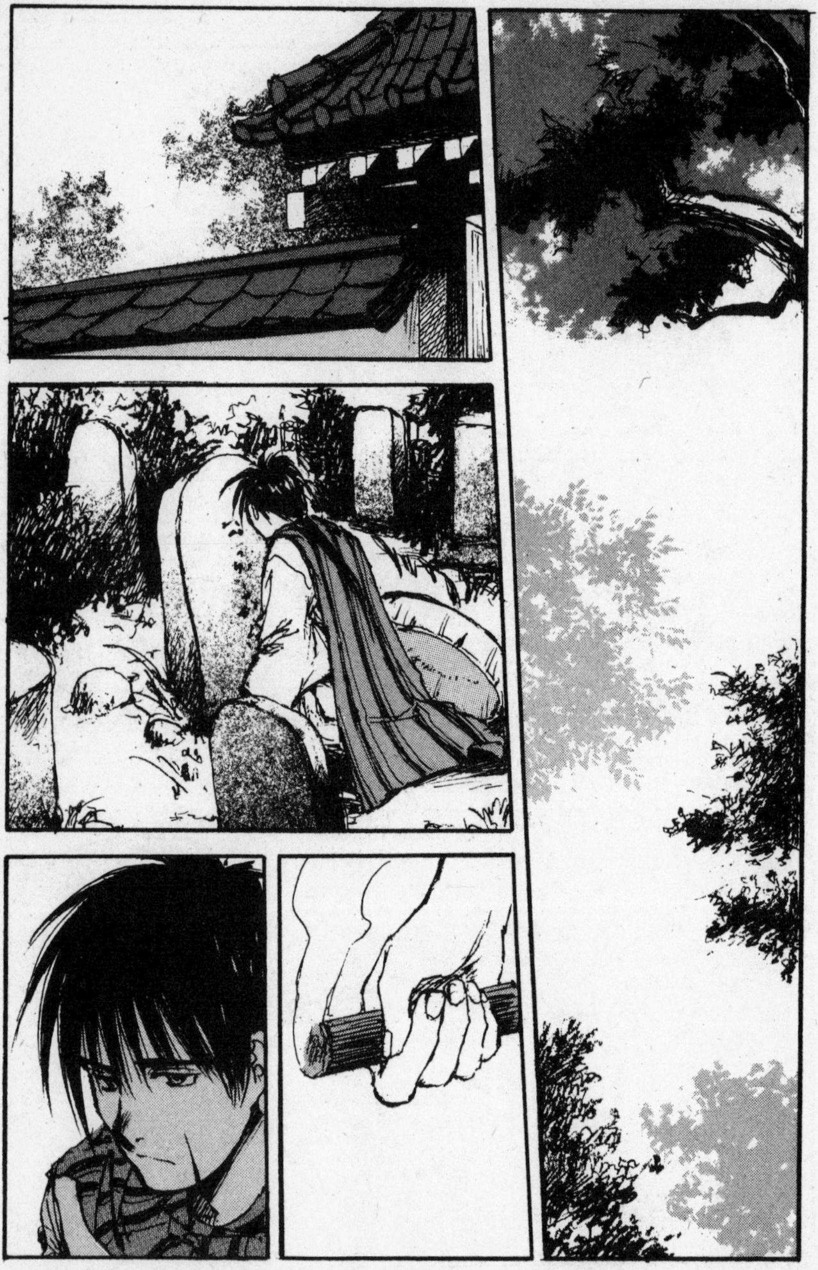

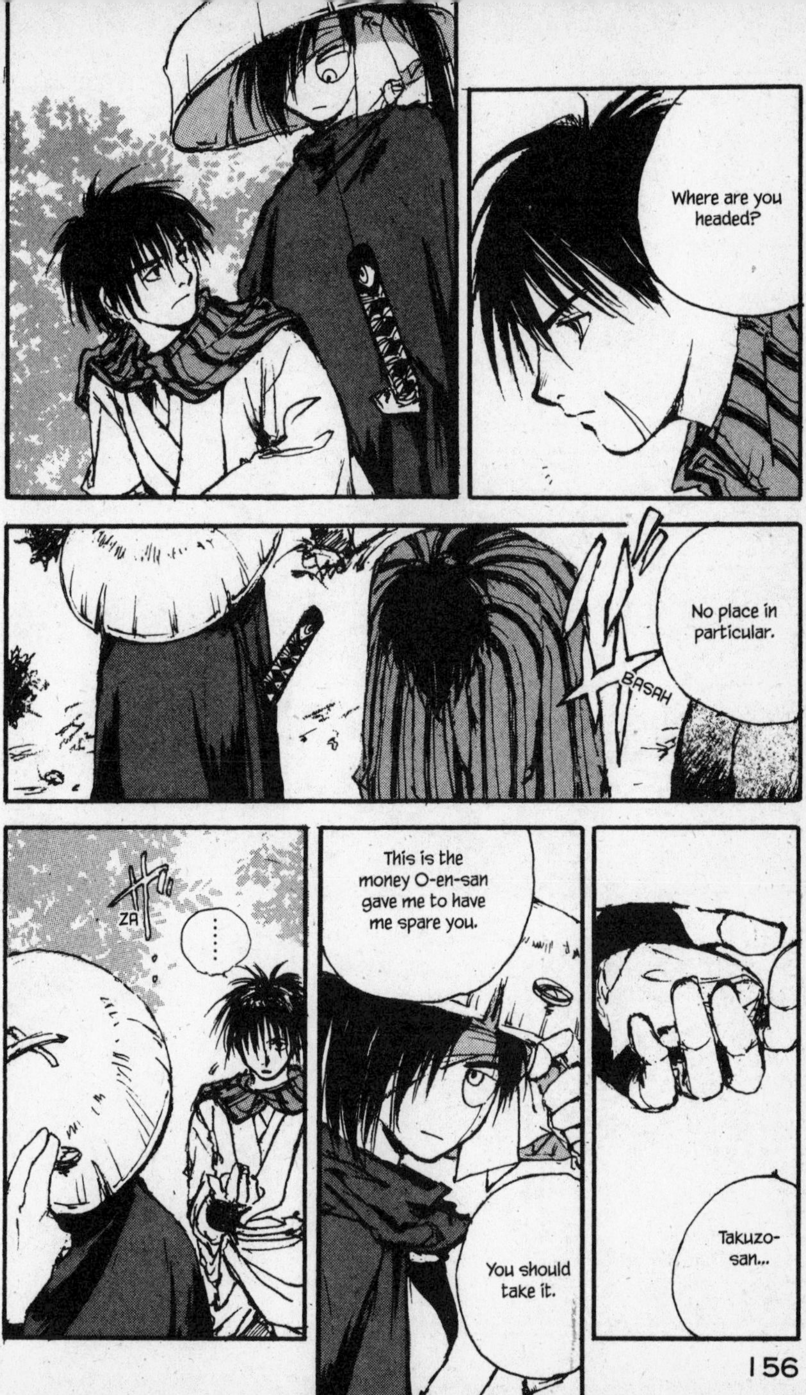
Where are you headed?
No place in particular.
BASAH
Takuzo-san...
This is the money O-en-san gave me to have me spare you.
You should take it.
ZA
......

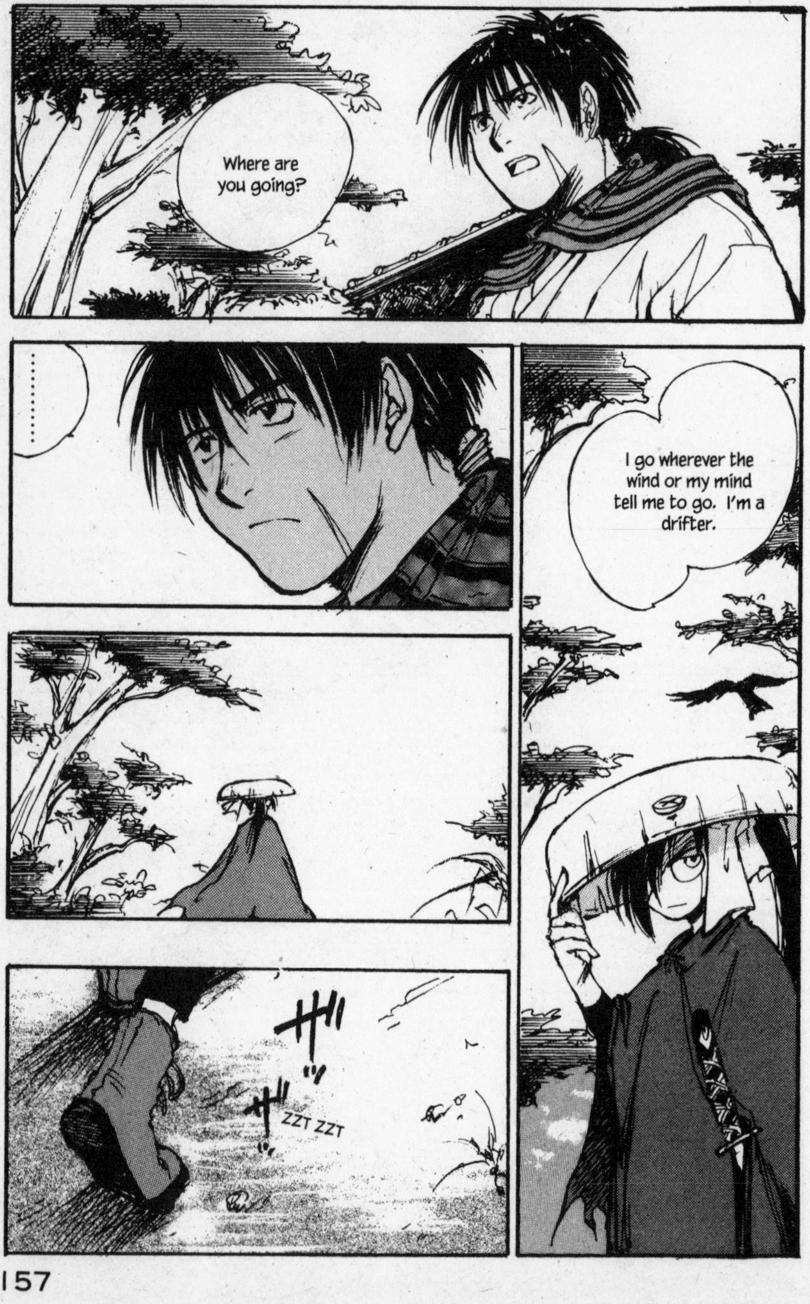
Where are you going?
I go wherever the wind or my mind tell me to go. I'm a drifter.
......
ZZT ZZT

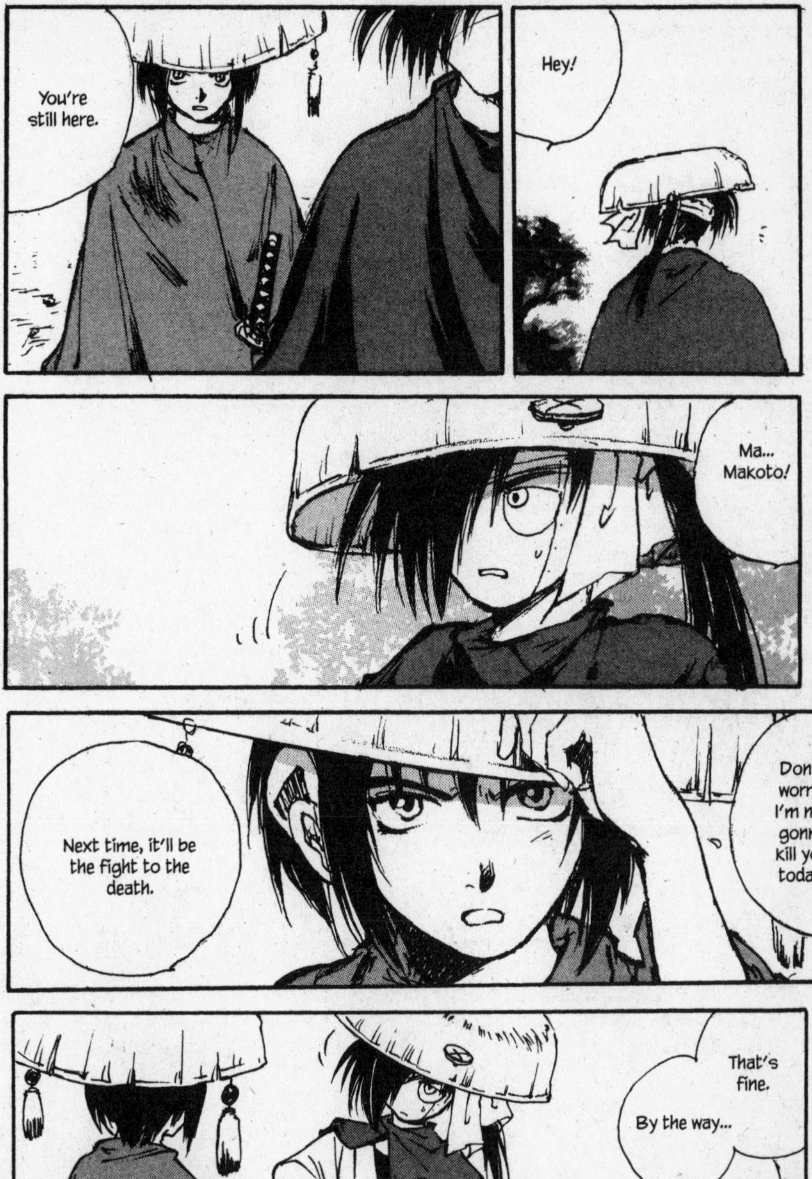
Hey!
You're still here.
Ma... Makoto!
Don't worry. I'm not gonna kill you today.
Next time, it'll be the fight to the death.
That's fine.
By the way...

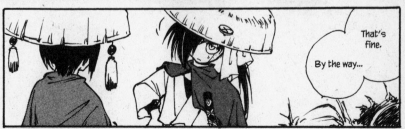

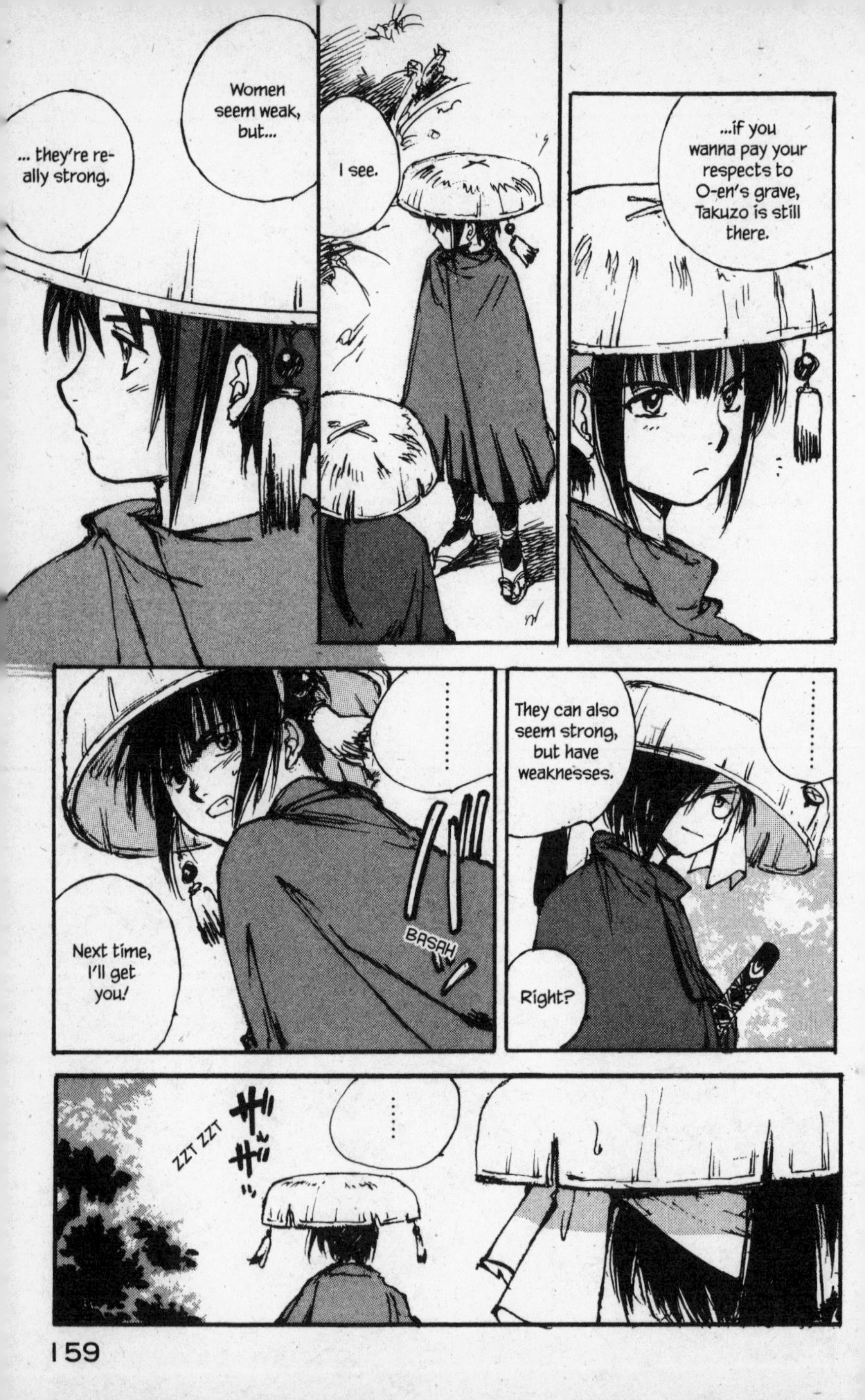
...if you wanna pay your respects to O-en's grave, Takuzo is still there.
I see.
Women seem weak, but...
... they're really strong.
......
They can also seem strong, but have weaknesses.
Right?
......
BASAH
Next time, I'll get you!
......
ZZT ZZT

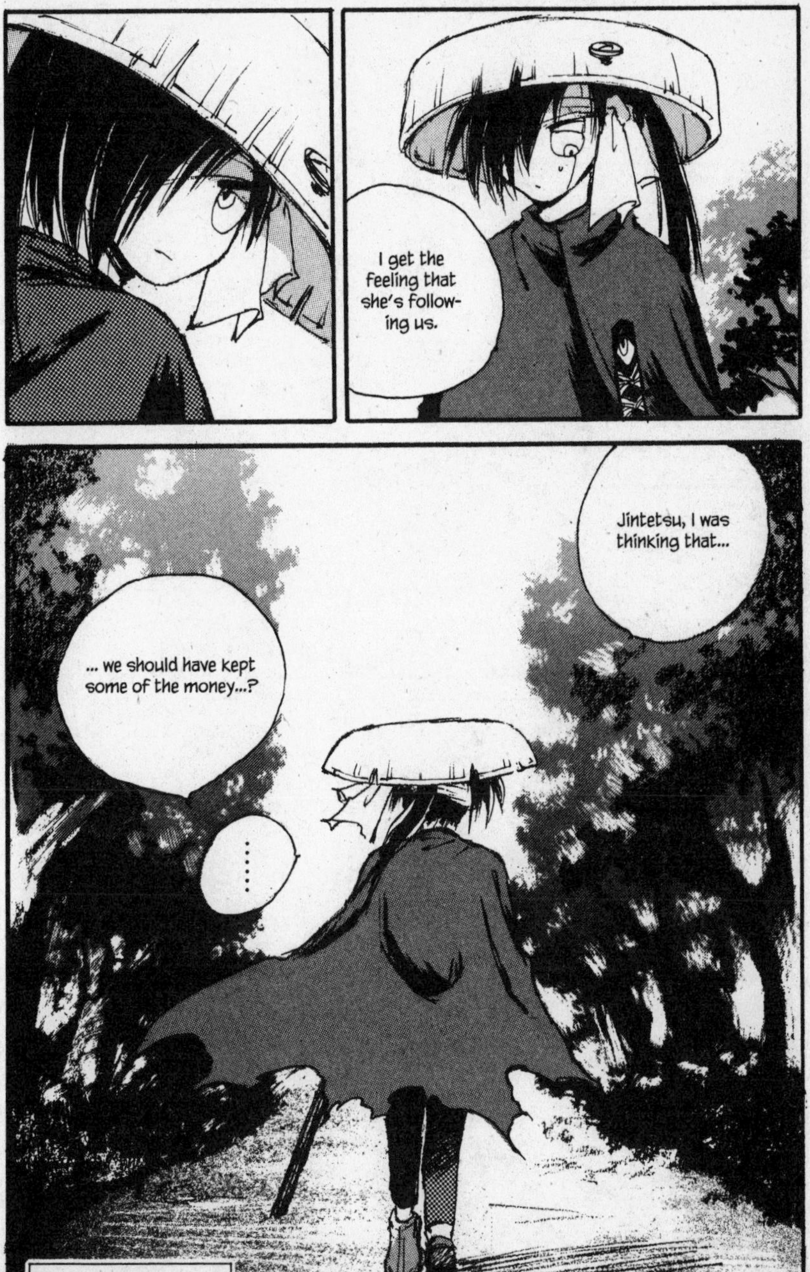
I get the feeling that she's follow-ing us.
Jintetsu, I was thinking that...
... we should have kept some of the money...?
......
THE END OF CHAPTER 8

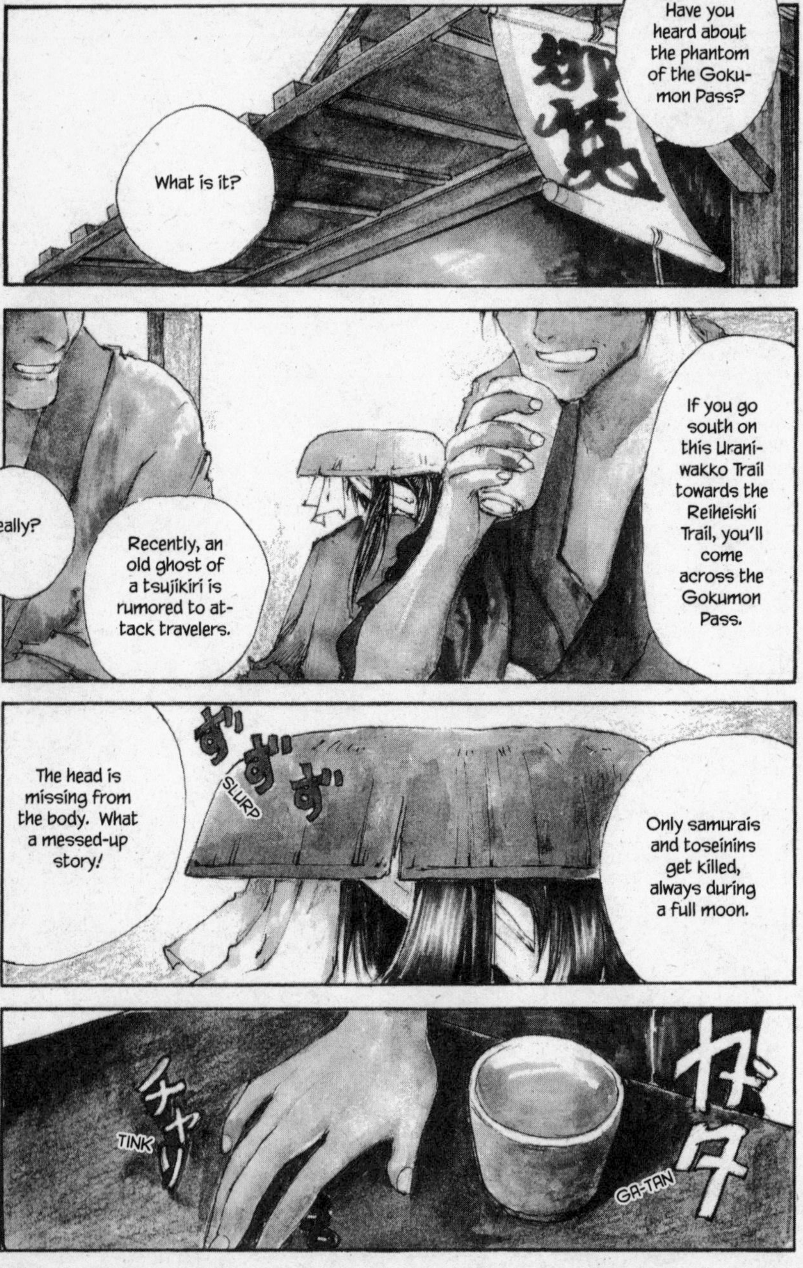

Have you heard about the phantom of the Goku-mon Pass?
What is it?
If you go south on this Urani-wakko Trail towards the Reiheishi Trail, you'll come across the Gokumon Pass.
Recently, an old ghost of a tsujikiri is rumored to at-tack travelers.
Really?
Only samurais and toseinins get killed, always during a full moon.
SLURP
The head is missing from the body. What a messed-up story!
GA-TAN
TINK

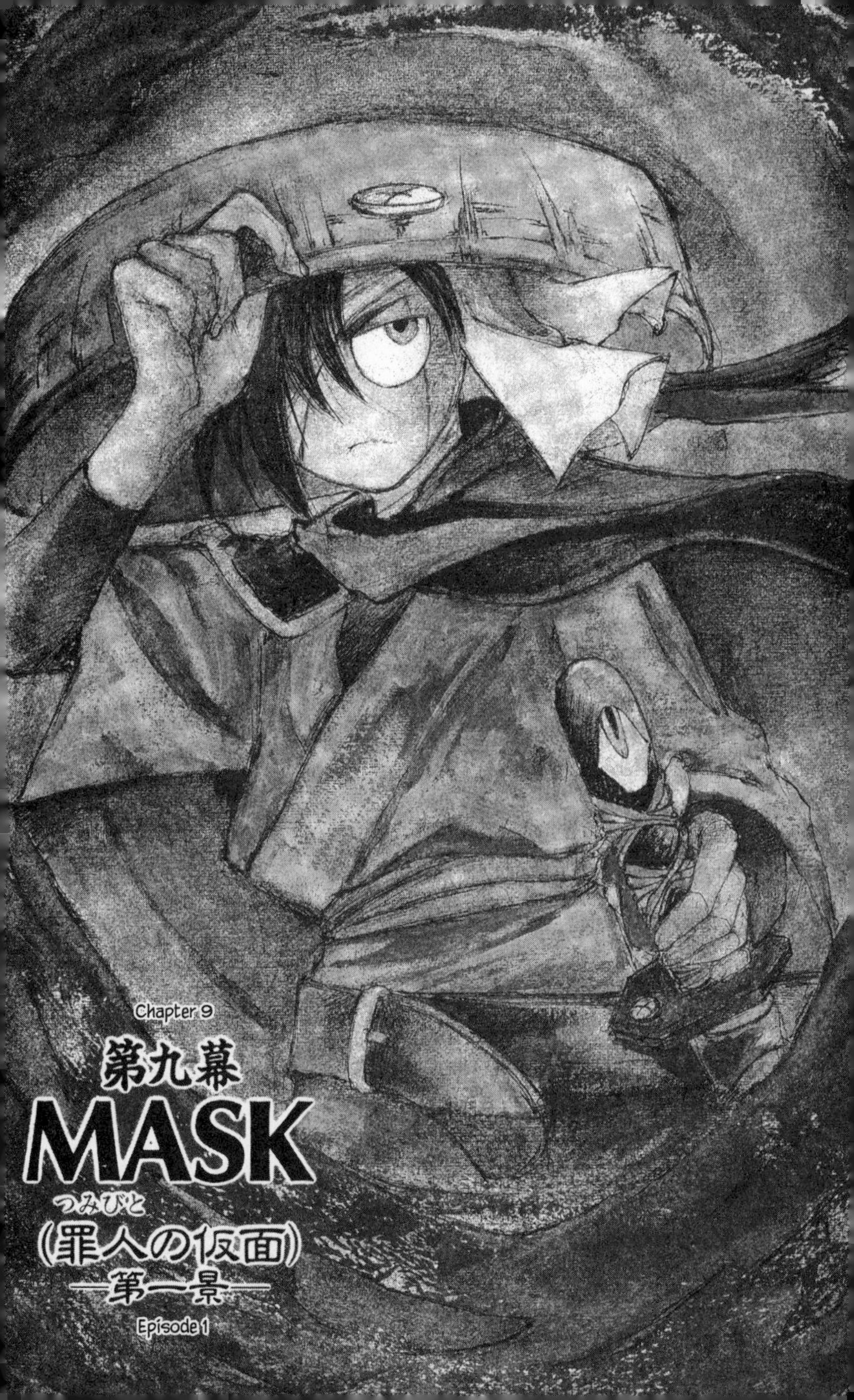
Chapter 9
第九幕
MASK
つみびと
(罪人の仮面)
—第一景—
Episode 1

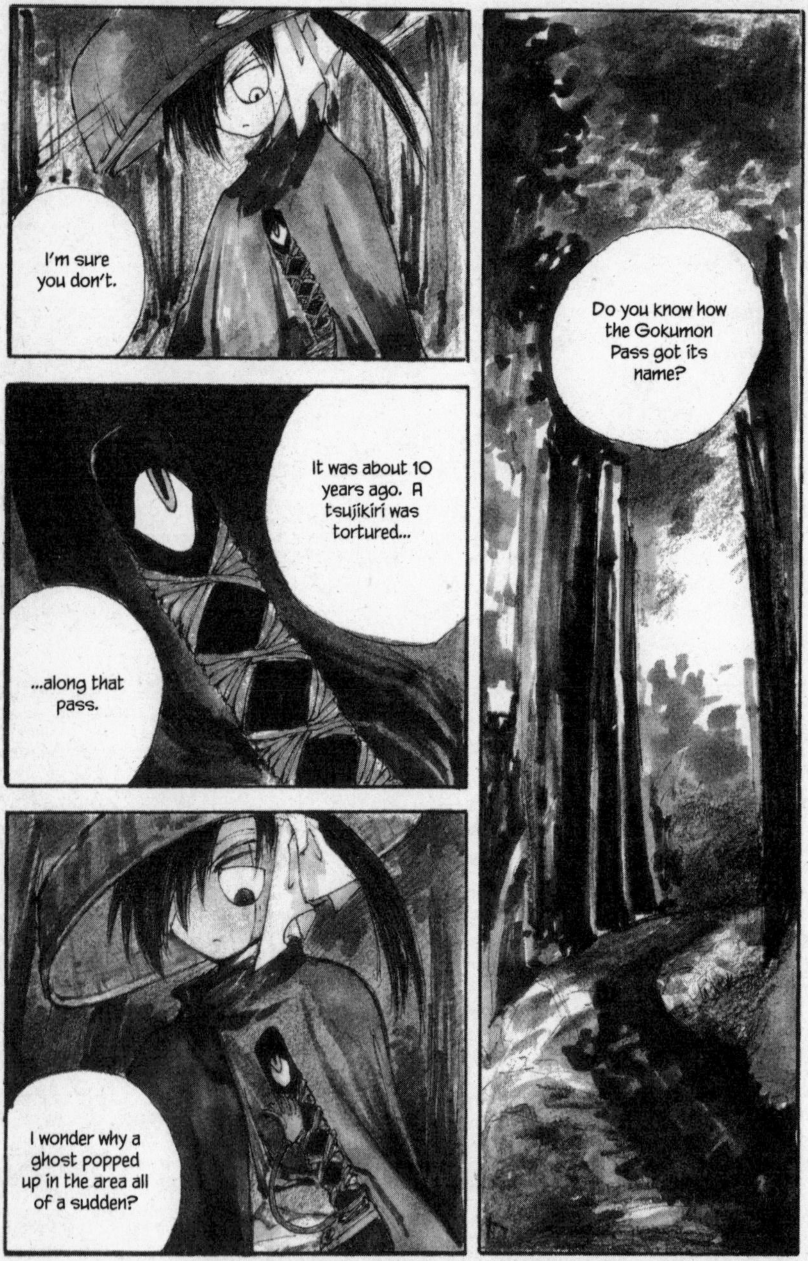
Do you know how the Gokumon Pass got its name?
I'm sure you don't.
It was about 10 years ago. A tsujikiri was tortured...
...along that pass.
I wonder why a ghost popped up in the area all of a sudden?

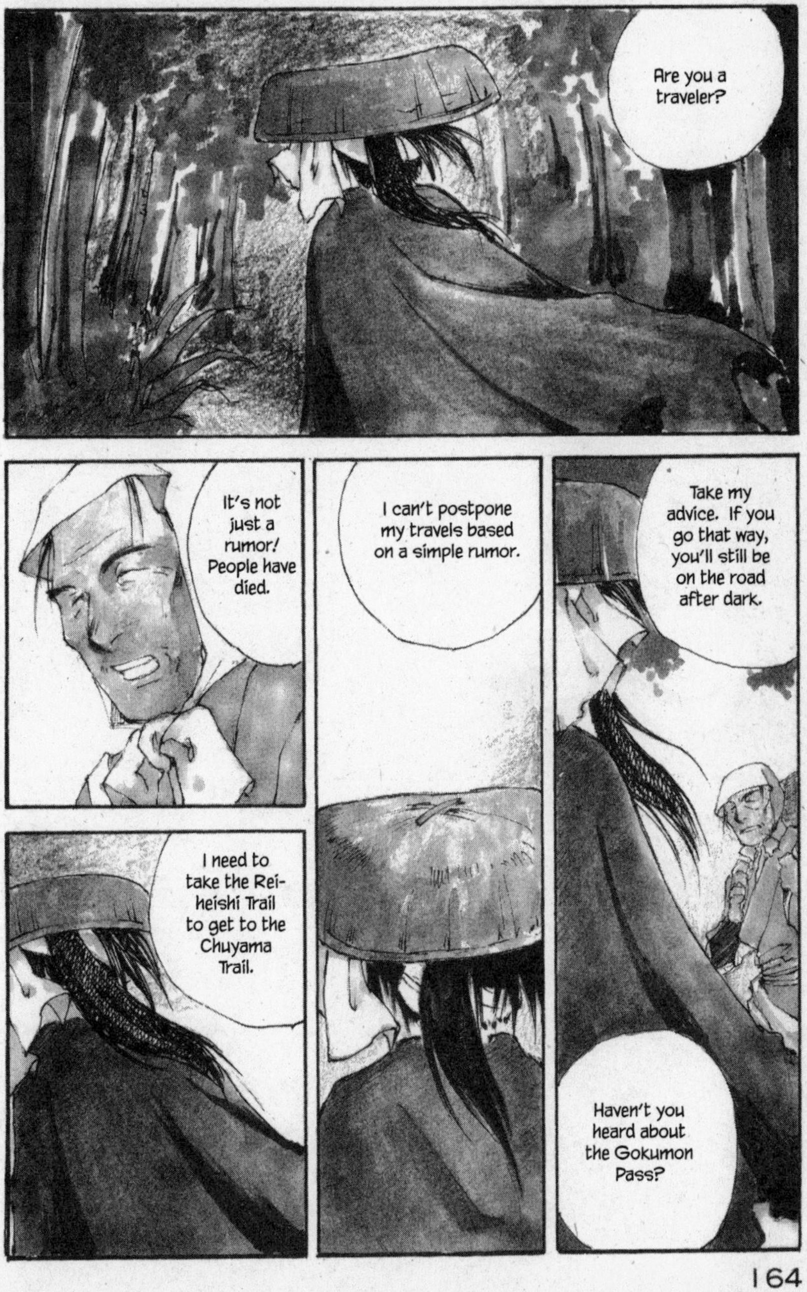
Are you a traveler?
Take my advice. If you go that way, you'll still be on the road after dark.
Haven't you heard about the Gokumon Pass?
I can't postpone my travels based on a simple rumor.
It's not just a rumor! People have died.
I need to take the Rei-heishi Trail to get to the Chuyama Trail.

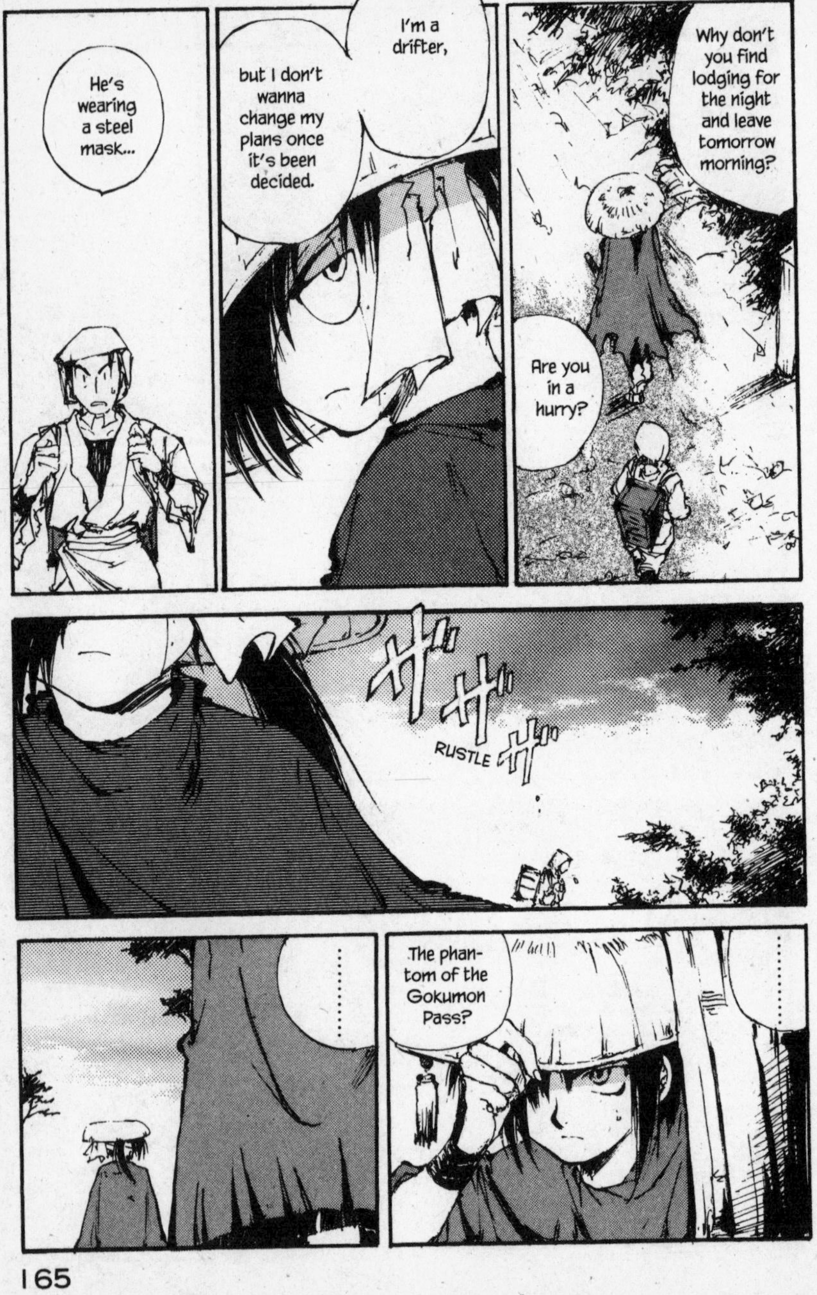
Why don't you find lodging for the night and leave tomorrow morning?
Are you in a hurry?
I'm a drifter,
but I don't wanna change my plans once it's been decided.
He's wearing a steel mask...
RUSTLE
......
The phan-tom of the Gokumon Pass?
......

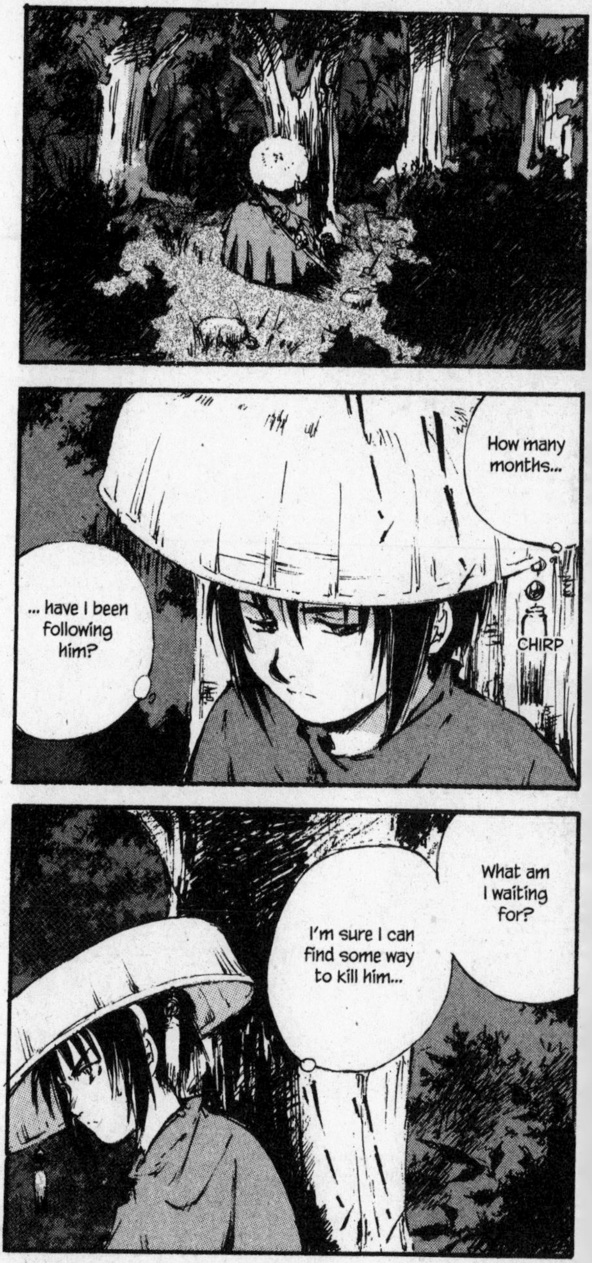
How many months...
... have I been following him?
CHIRP
What am I waiting for?
I'm sure I can find some way to kill him...

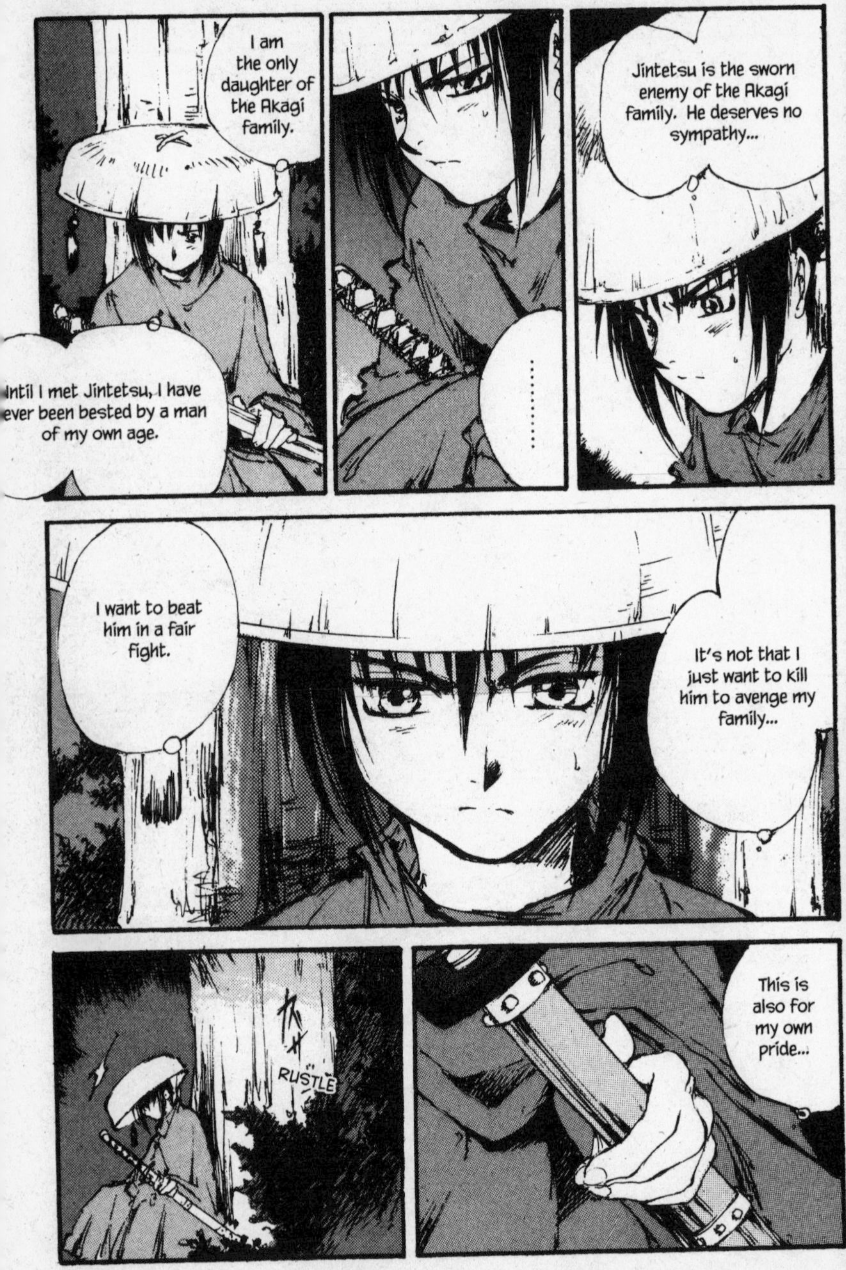
Jintetsu is the sworn enemy of the Akagi family. He deserves no sympathy...
....
I am the only daughter of the Akagi family.
ntil I met Jintetsu, I have ever been bested by a man of my own age.
It's not that I just want to kill him to avenge my family...
I want to beat him in a fair fight.
This is also for my own pride...
RUSTLE

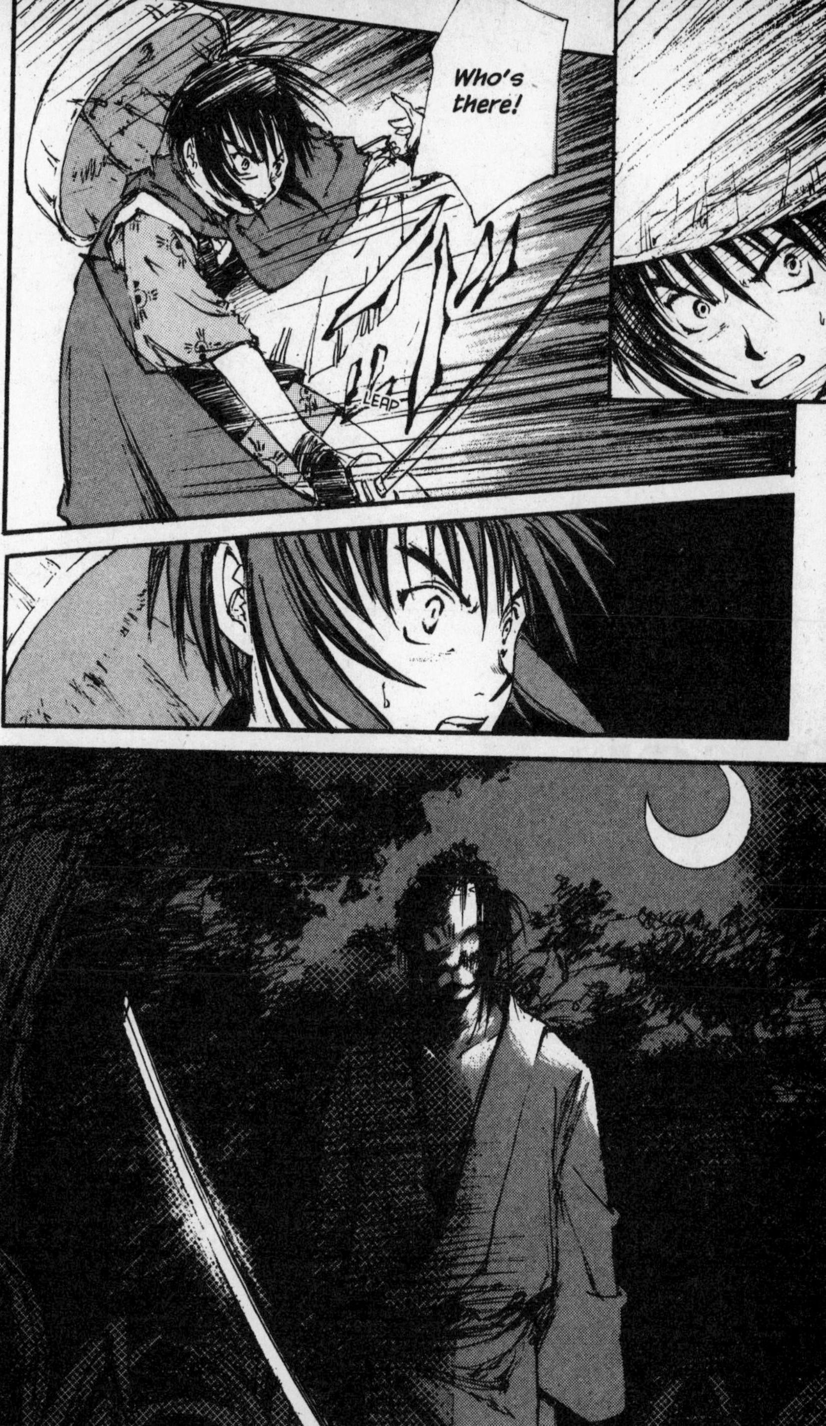
Who's there!
LEAP

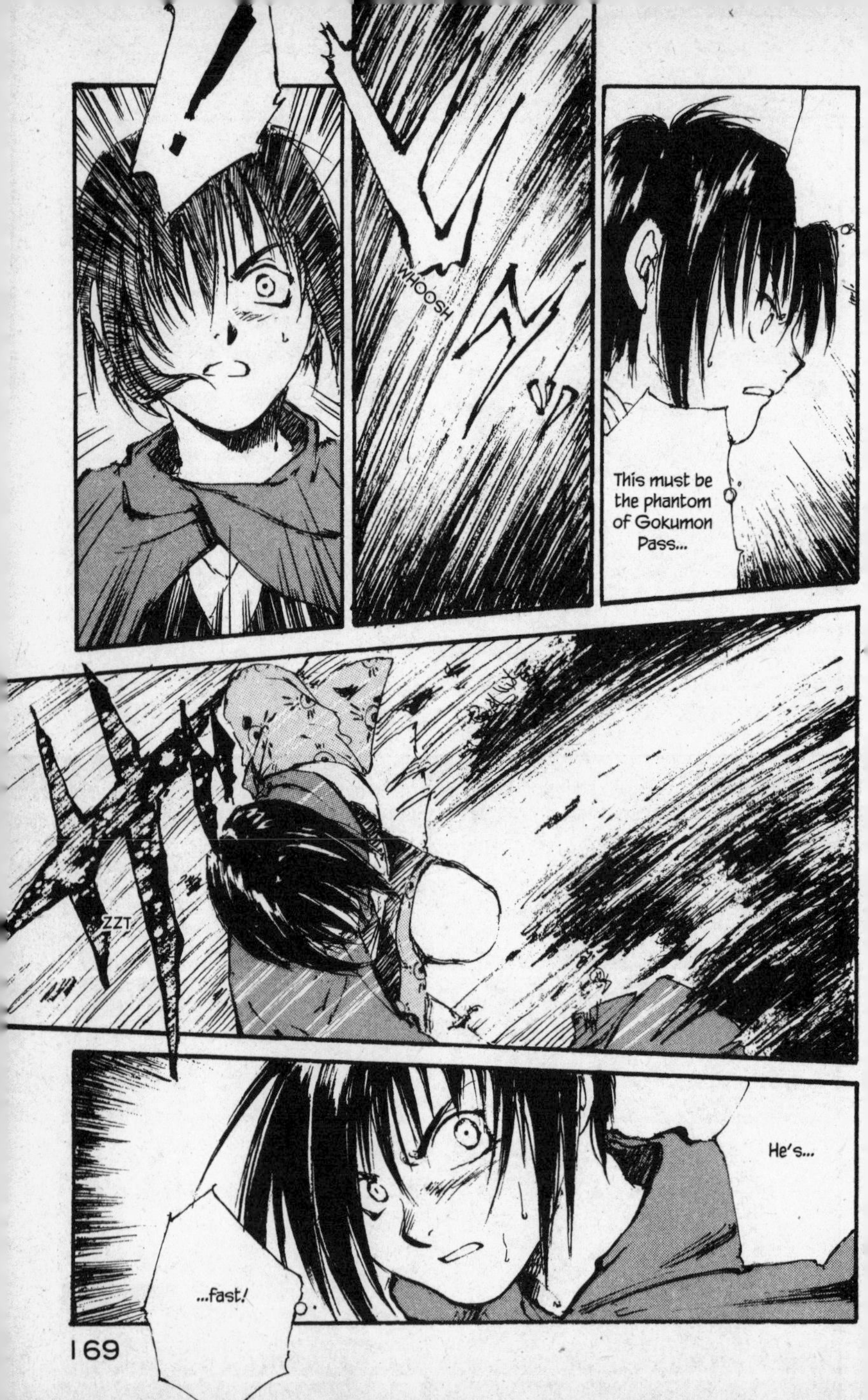
This must be the phantom of Gokumon Pass...
WHOOSH
!
ZZT
He's...
...fast!

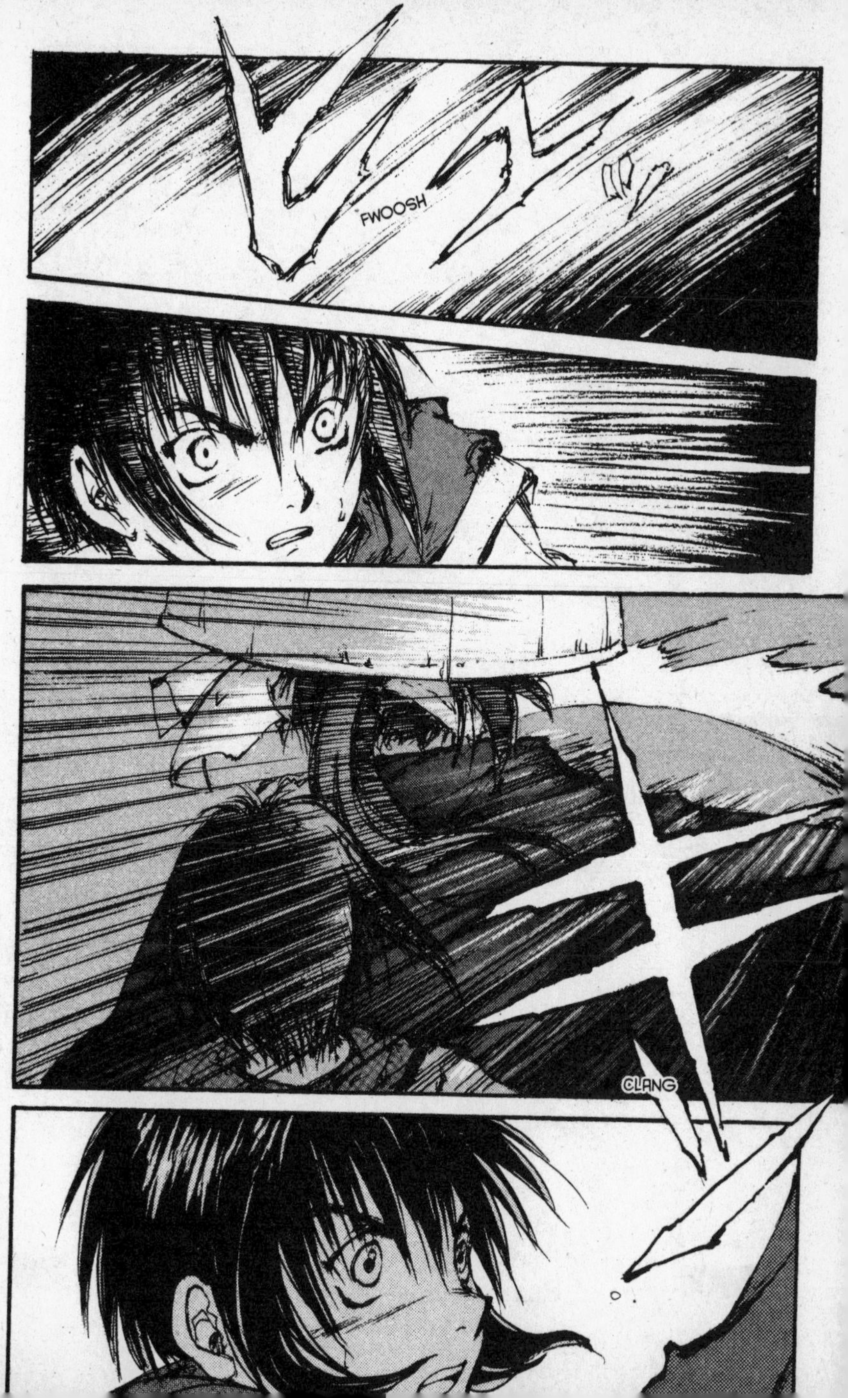
FWOOSH
CLANG

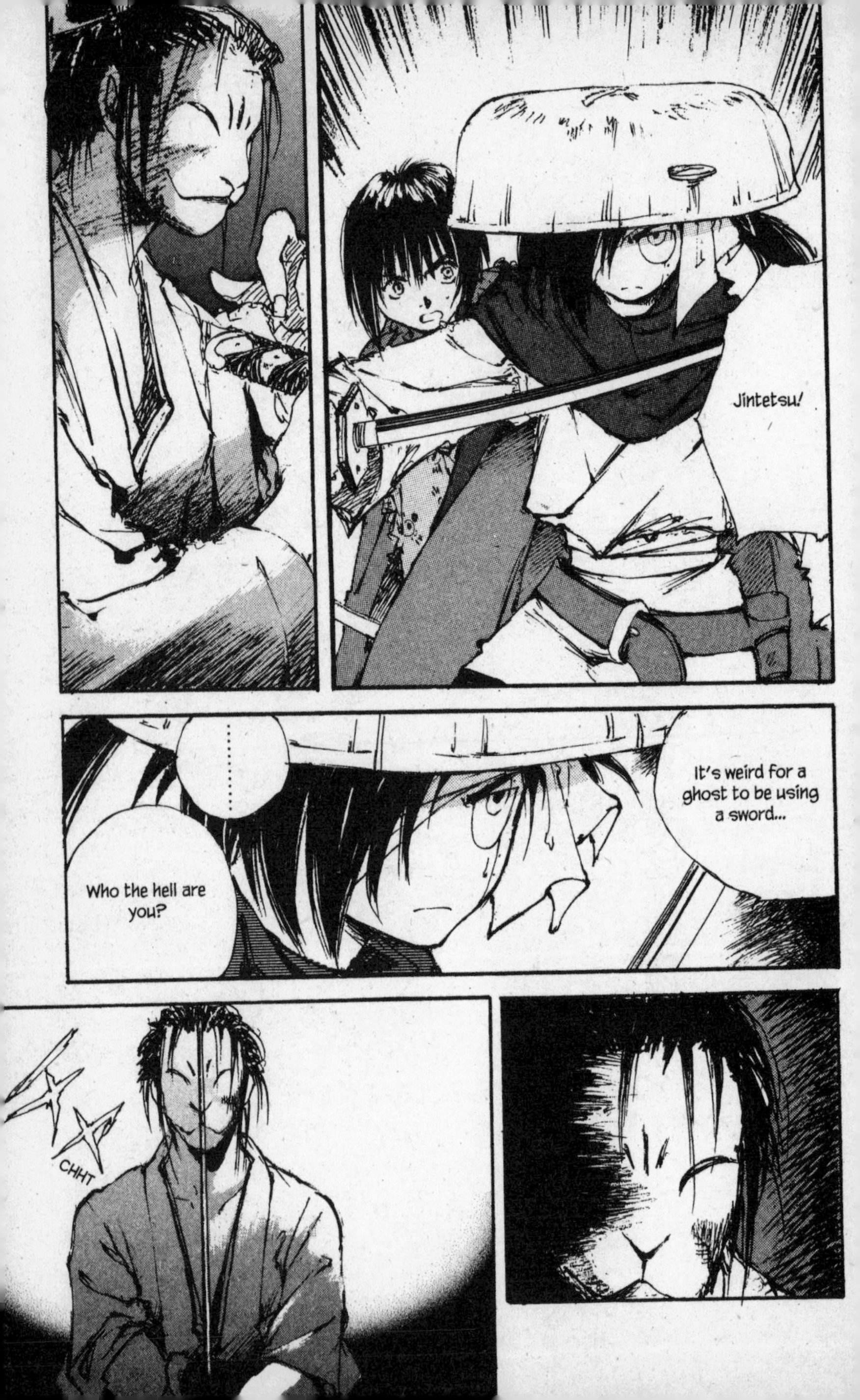
Jintetsu!
It's weird for a ghost to be using a sword...
......
Who the hell are you?
CHHT

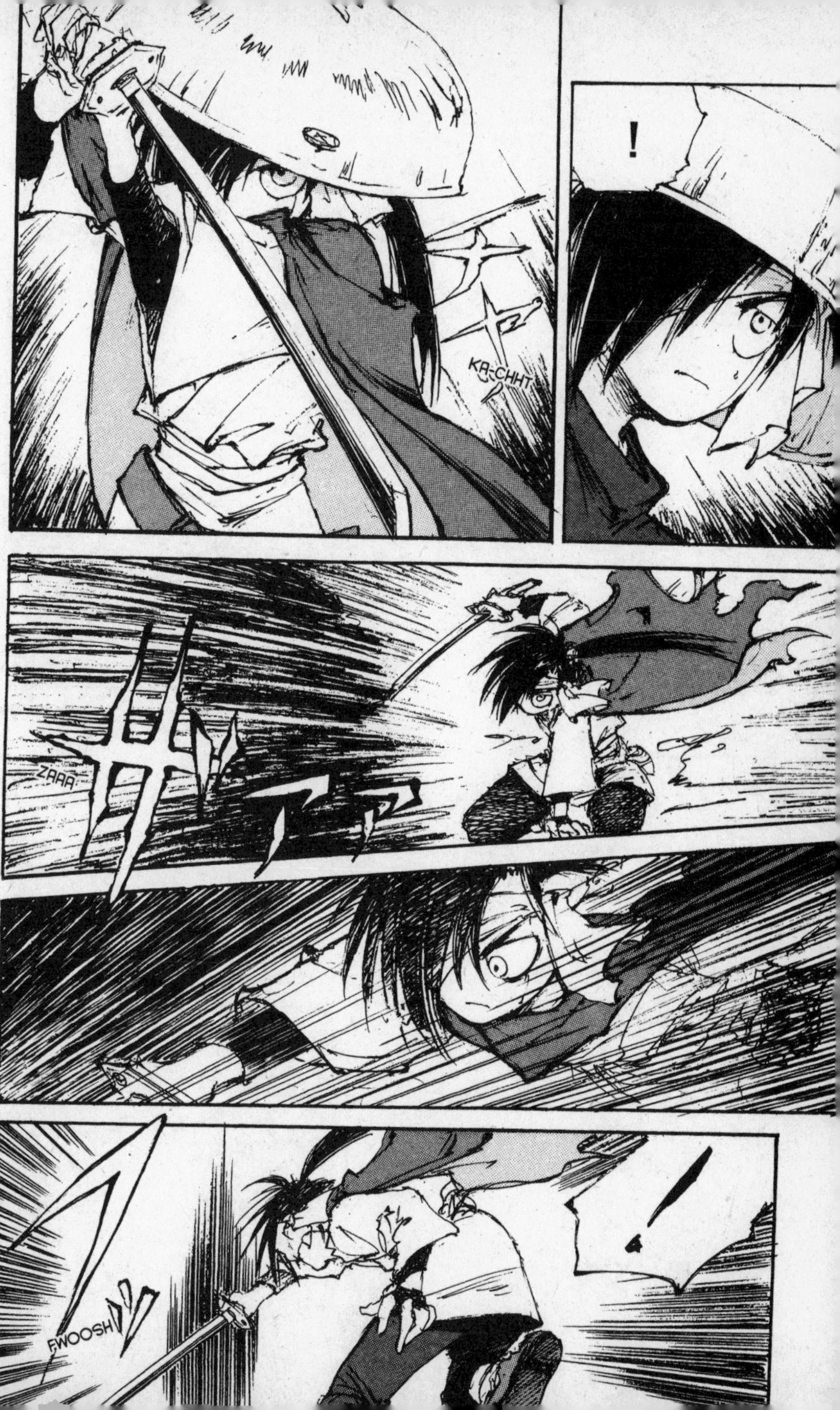
!
KA-CHHT
ZAAA
!
FWOOSH

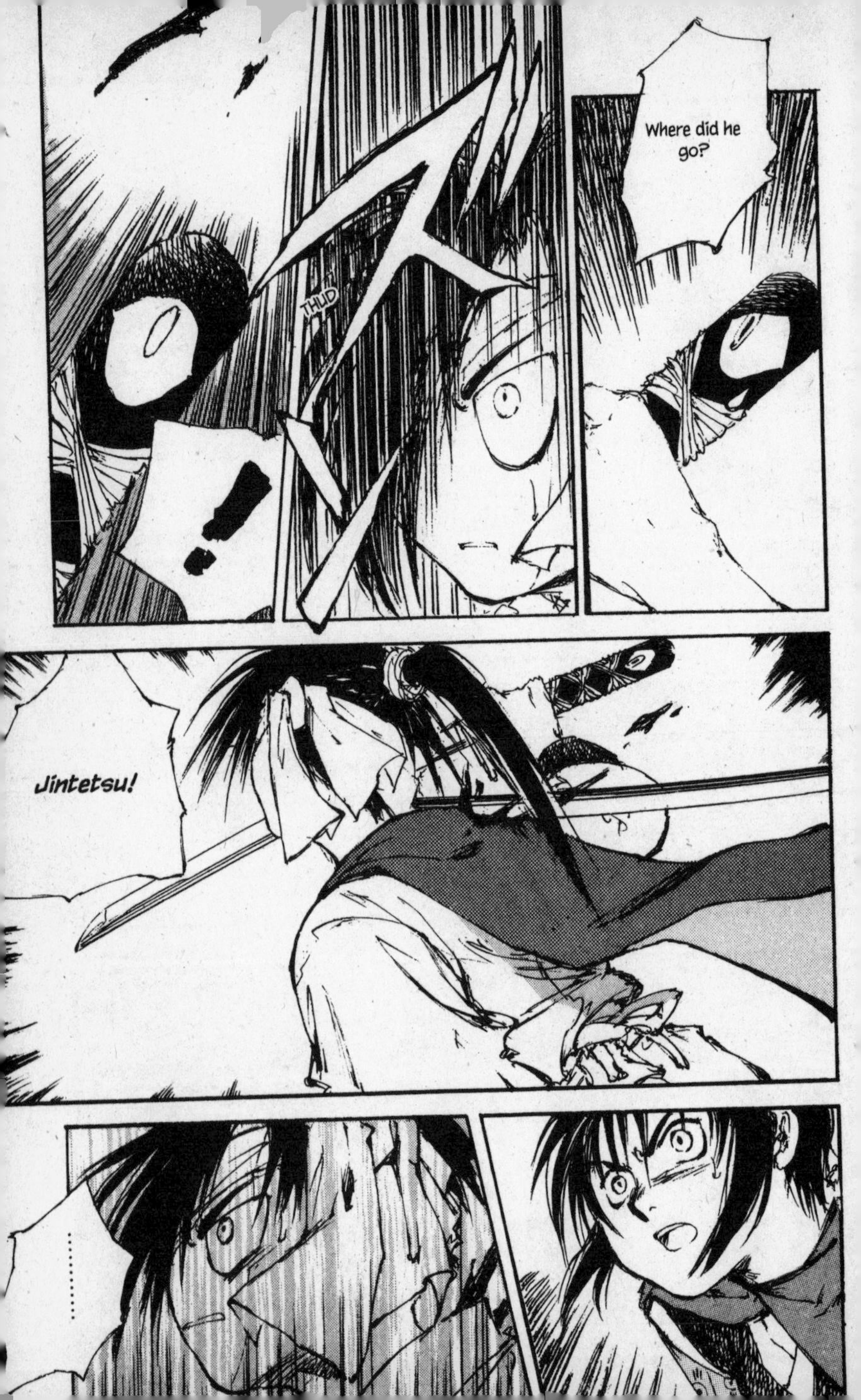
Where did he go?
THUD
!!
Jintetsu!
......

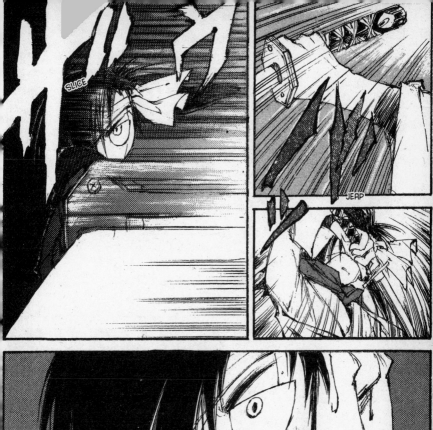

SLICE

JEAP

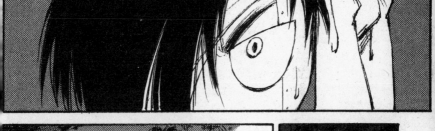

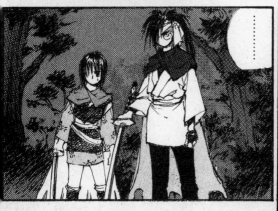

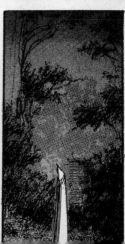

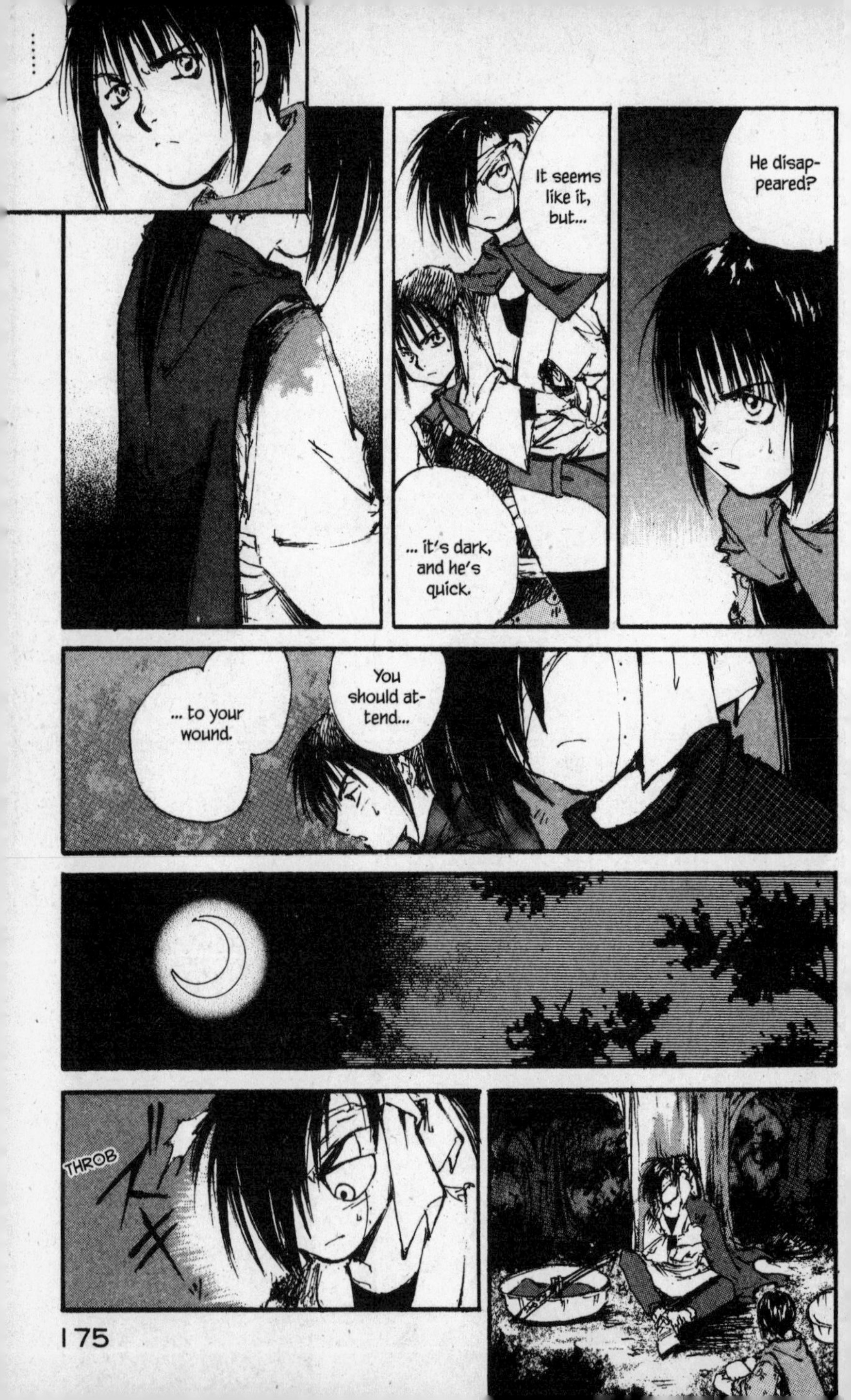
He disap-
peared?
It seems
like it,
but...
... it's dark,
and he's
quick.
......
You
should at-
tend...
... to your
wound.
THROB

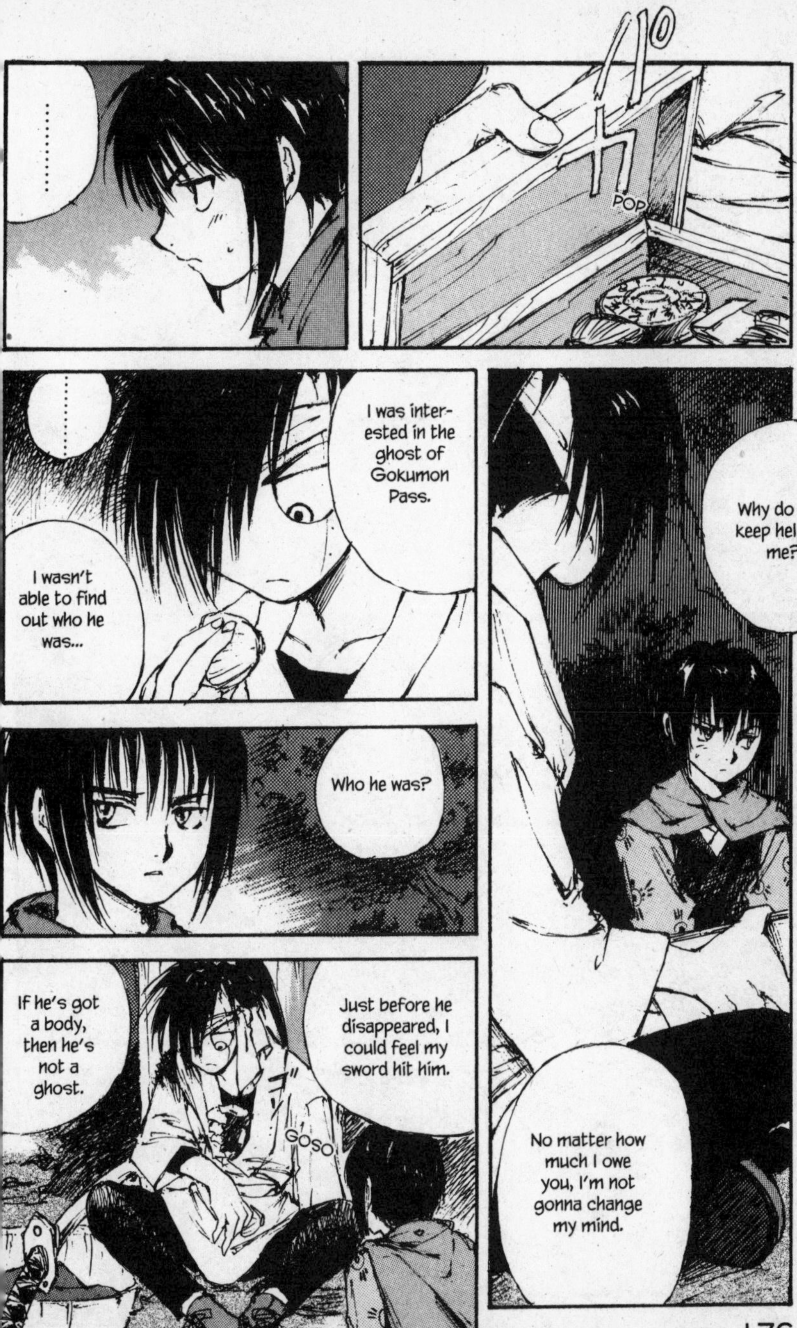
POP
......
Why do you keep helping me?
No matter how much I owe you, I'm not gonna change my mind.
......
I was interested in the ghost of Gokumon Pass.
I wasn't able to find out who he was...
Who he was?
Just before he disappeared, I could feel my sword hit him.
GOSO
If he's got a body, then he's not a ghost.

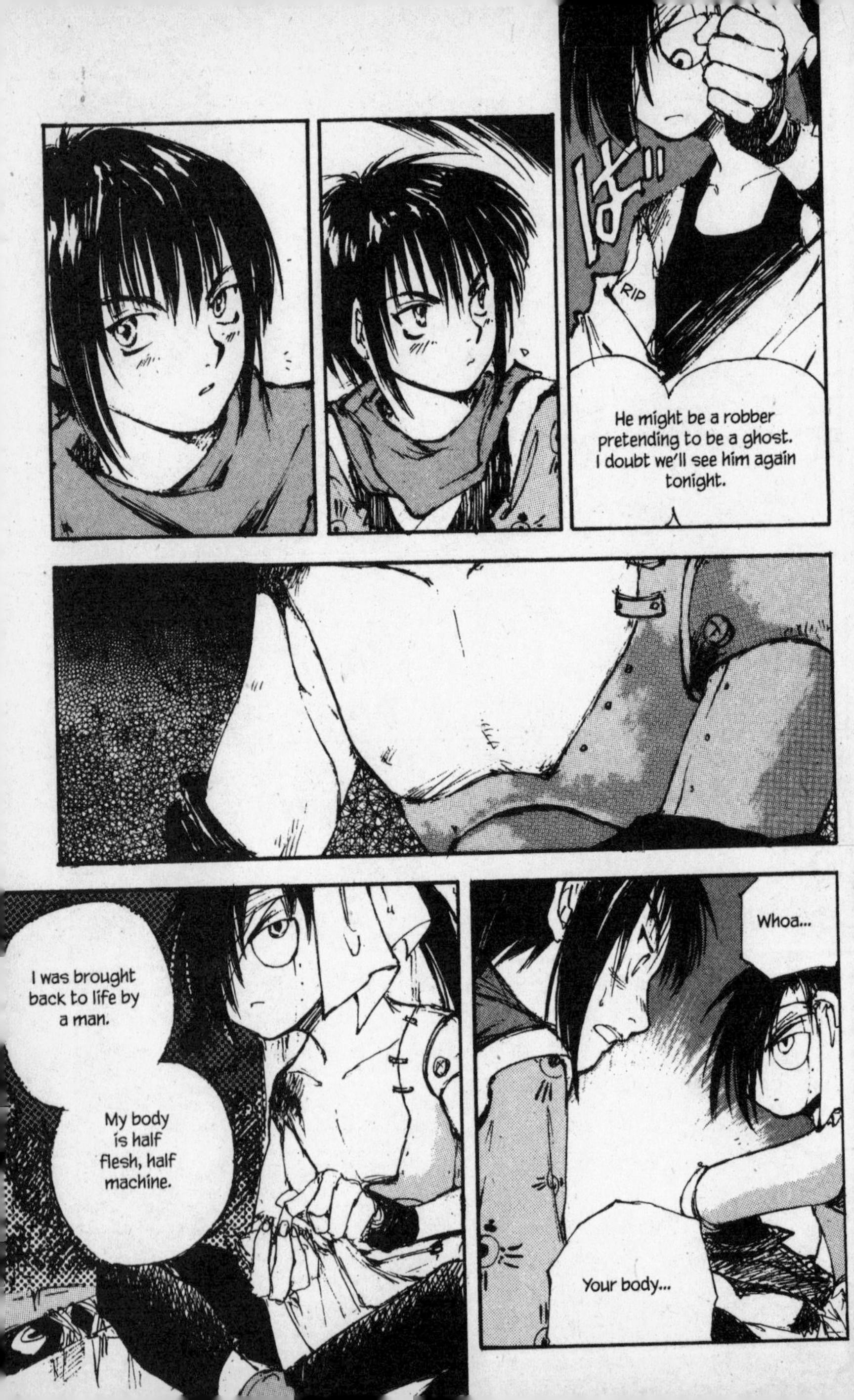
RIP
He might be a robber pretending to be a ghost. I doubt we'll see him again tonight.
Whoa...
Your body...
I was brought back to life by a man.
My body is half flesh, half machine.

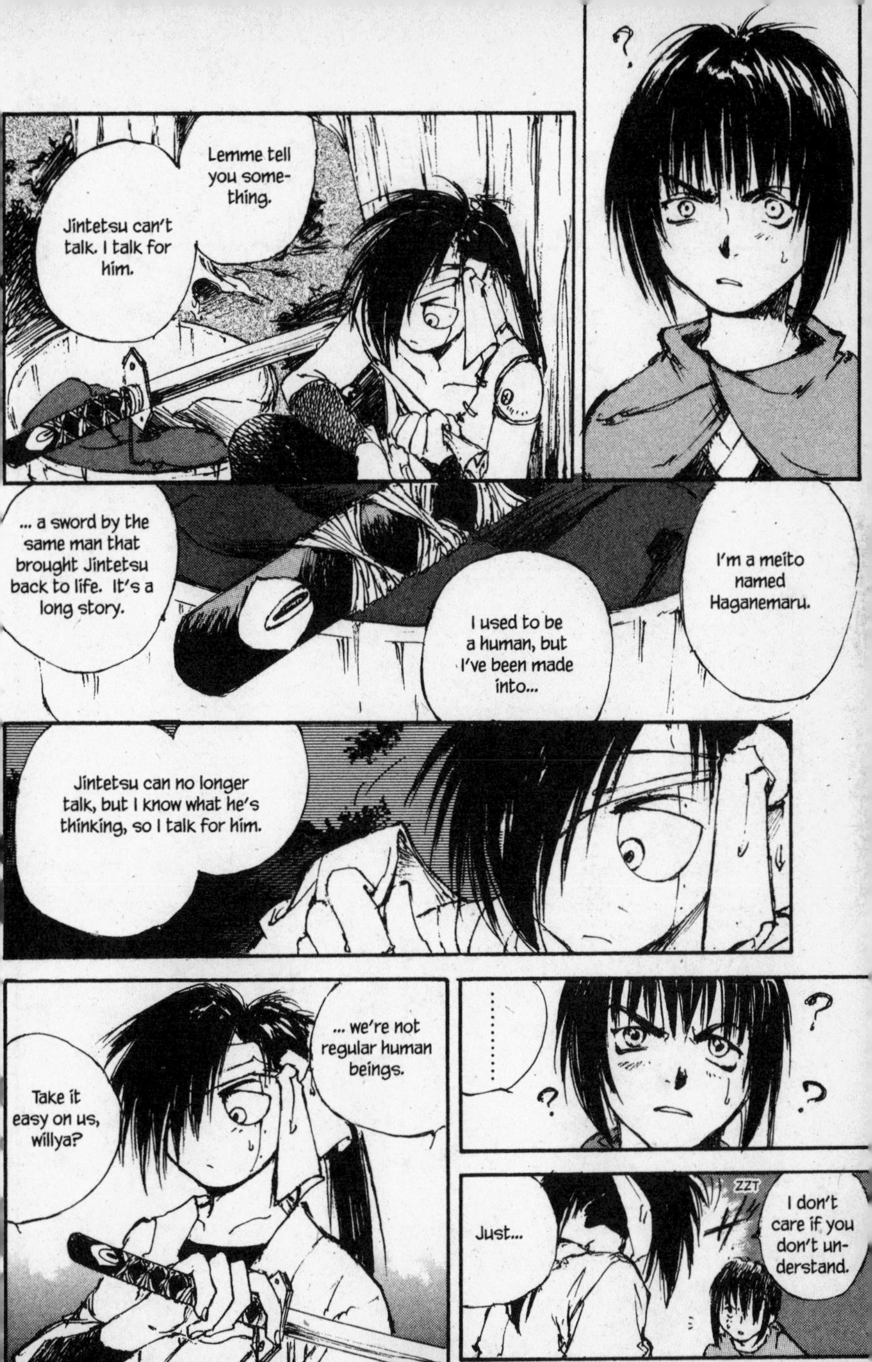
?
Lemme tell you something.
Jintetsu can't talk. I talk for him.
I'm a meito named Haganemaru.
I used to be a human, but I've been made into...
... a sword by the same man that brought Jintetsu back to life. It's a long story.
Jintetsu can no longer talk, but I know what he's thinking, so I talk for him.
?
......
?
?
I don't care if you don't understand.
ZZT
Just...
... we're not regular human beings.
Take it easy on us, willya?

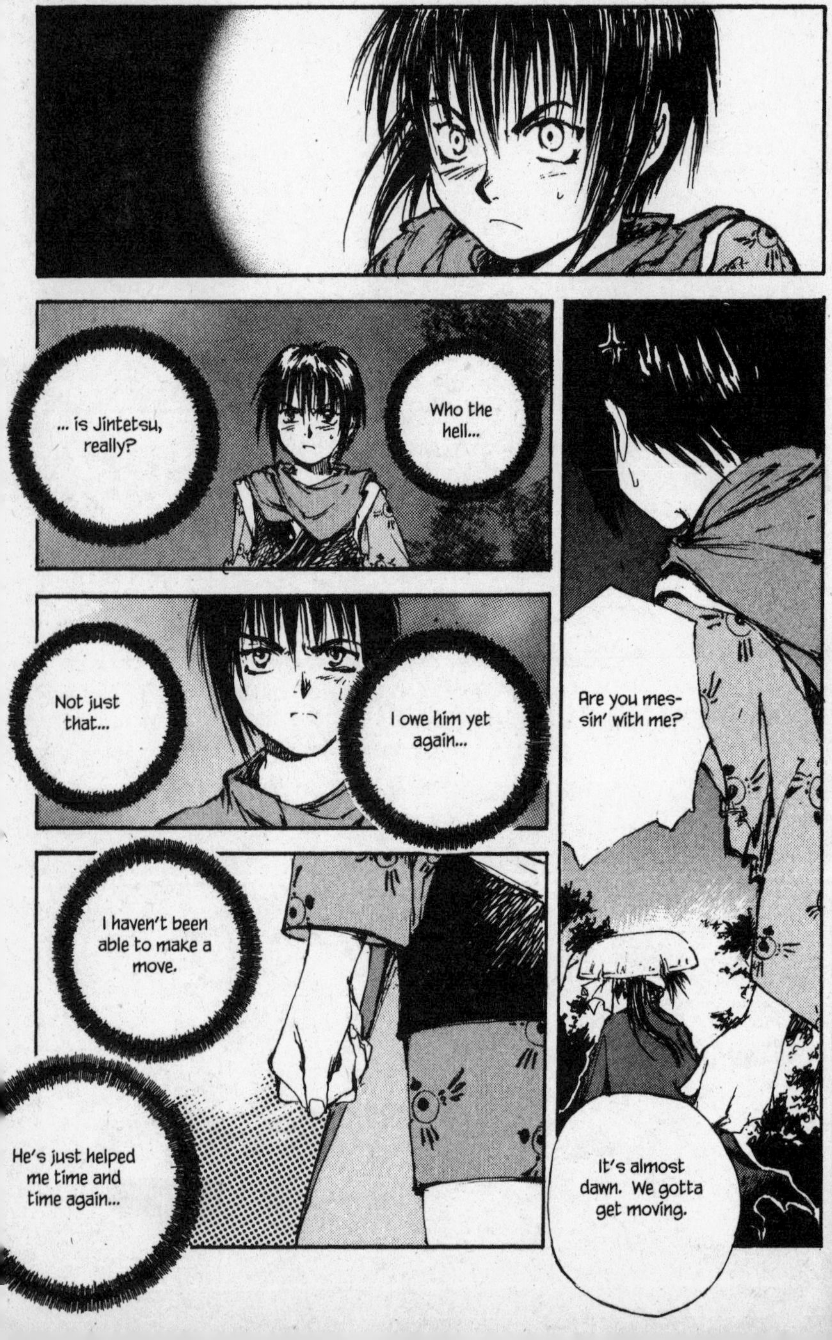
Are you mes-sin' with me?
It's almost dawn. We gotta get moving.
Who the hell...
... is Jintetsu, really?
I owe him yet again...
Not just that...
I haven't been able to make a move.
He's just helped me time and time again...

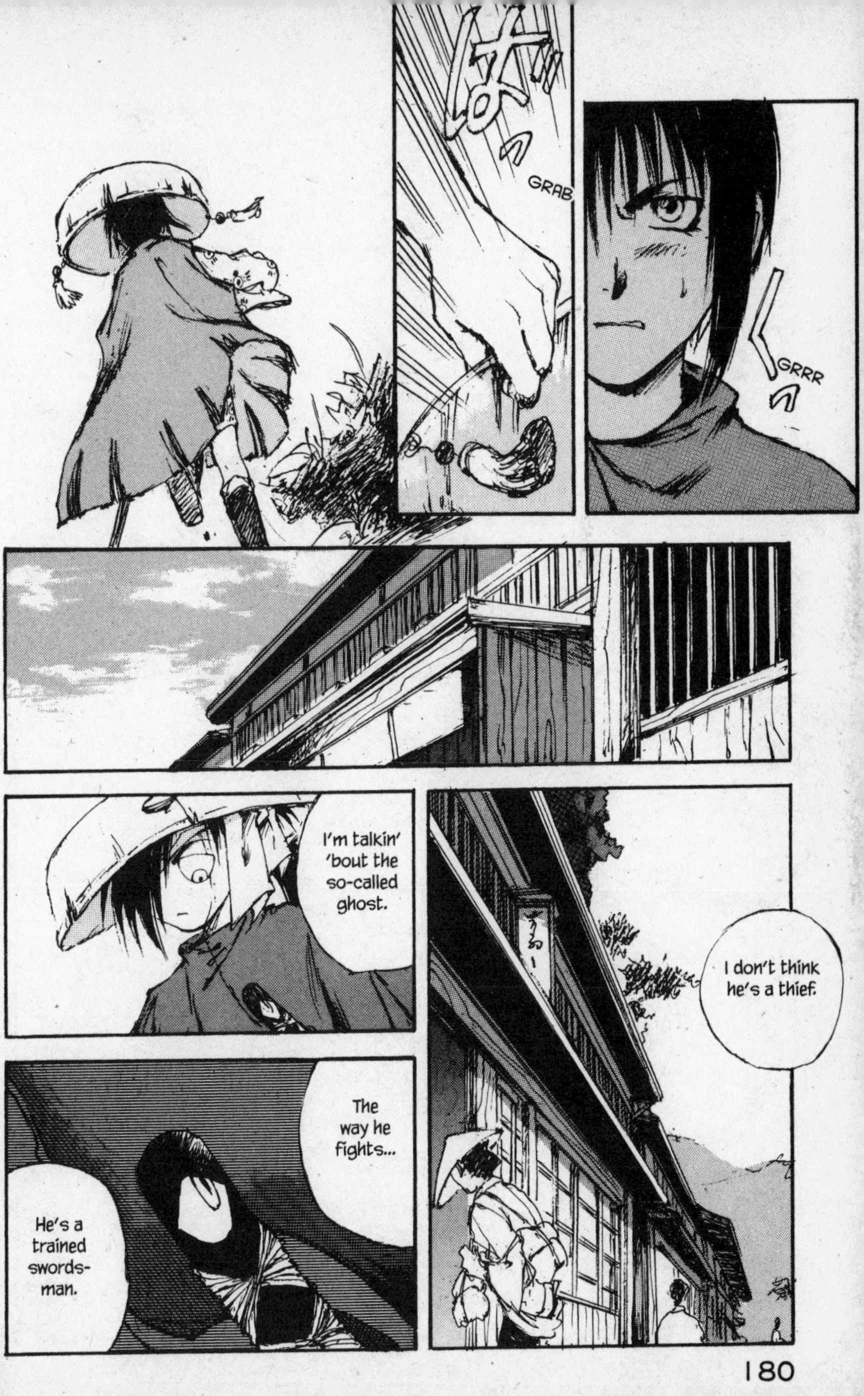
GRRR
GRAB
I don't think he's a thief.
I'm talkin' 'bout the so-called ghost.
The way he fights...
He's a trained swordsman.

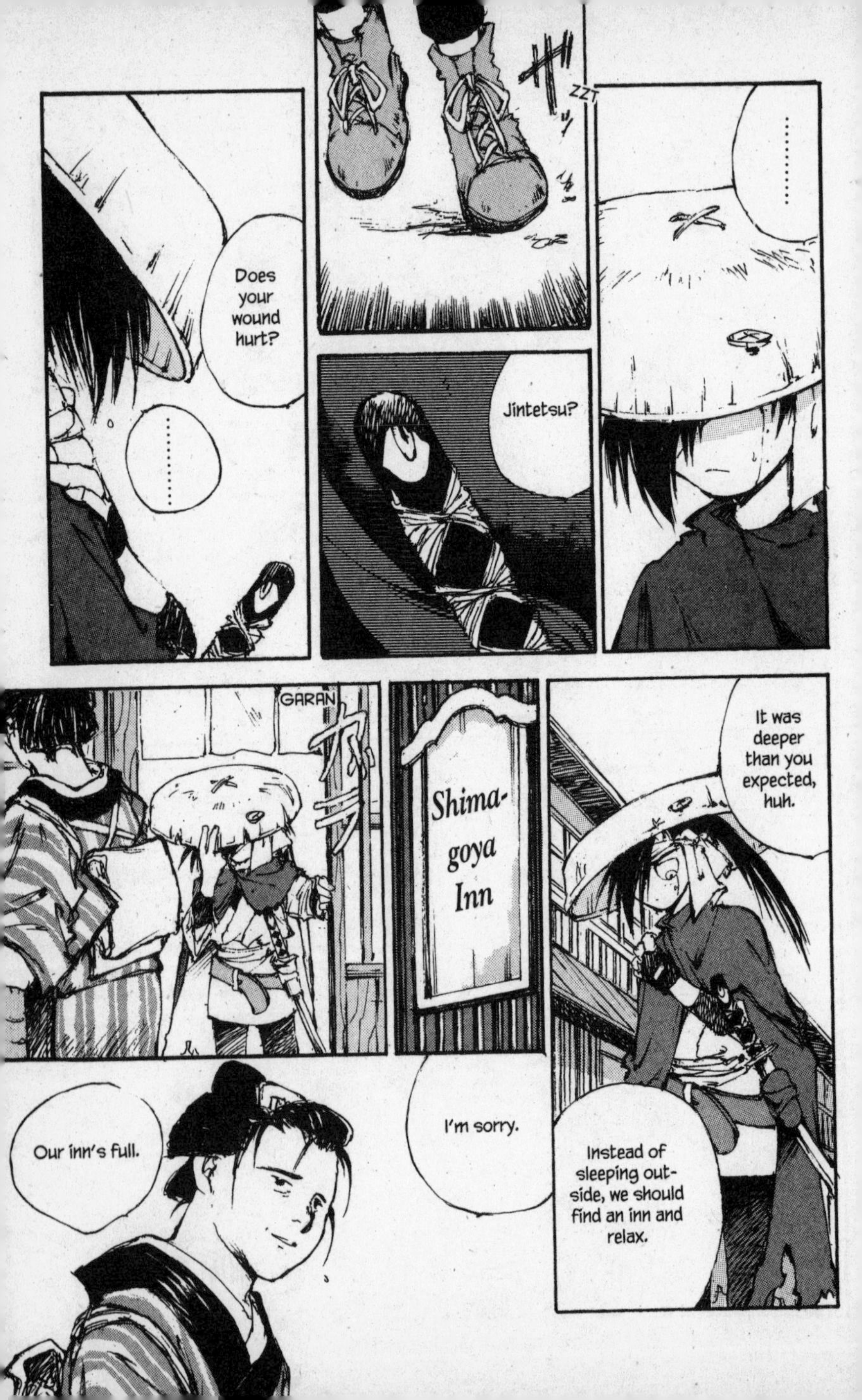

......
ZZT
Jintetsu?
Does your wound hurt?
......
It was deeper than you expected, huh.
Instead of sleeping out-side, we should find an inn and relax.
Shima-goya Inn
GARAN
I'm sorry.
Our inn's full.

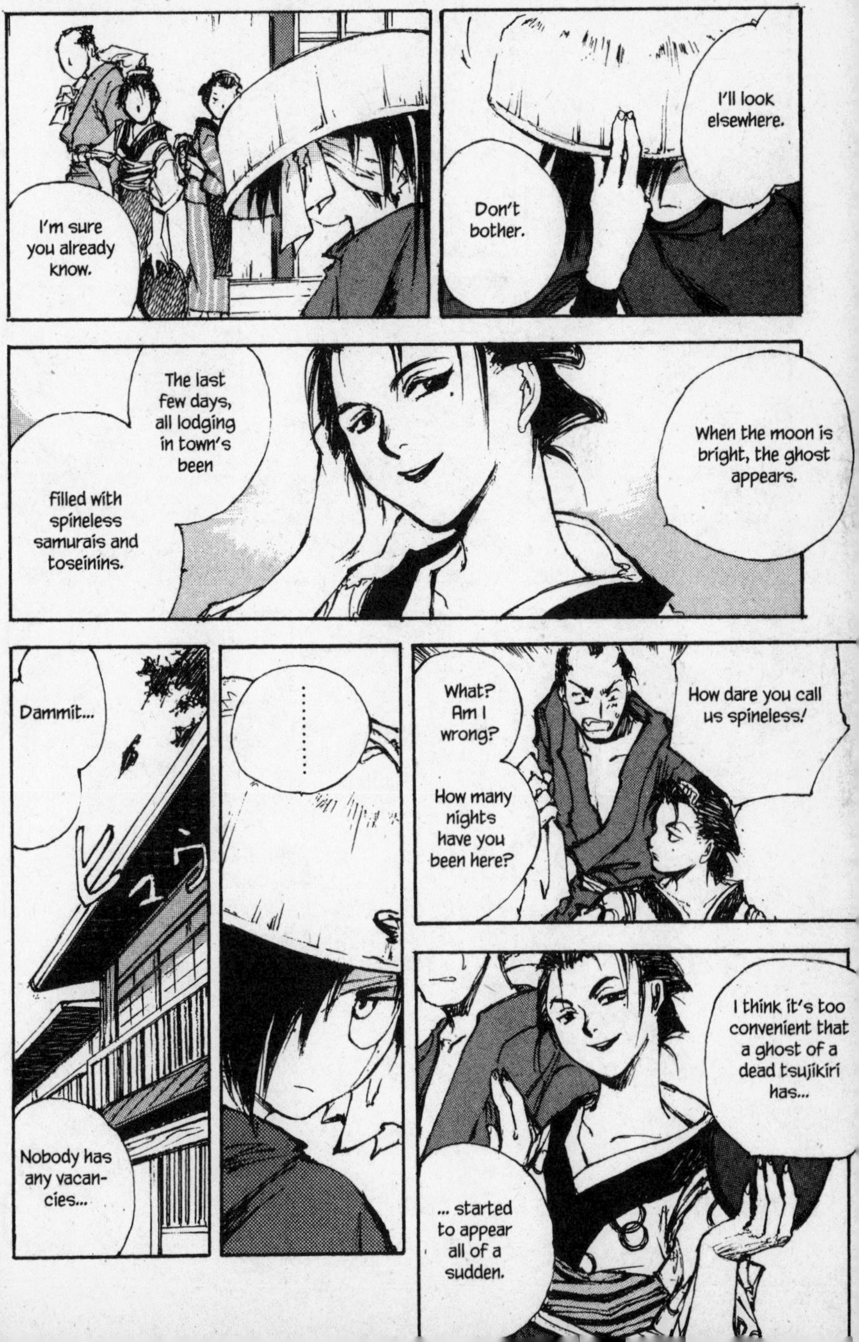
I'll look elsewhere.
Don't bother.
I'm sure you already know.
When the moon is bright, the ghost appears.
The last few days, all lodging in town's been
filled with spineless samurais and toseinins.
How dare you call us spineless!
What? Am I wrong?
How many nights have you been here?
I think it's too convenient that a ghost of a dead tsujikiri has...
... started to appear all of a sudden.
......
Dammit...
Nobody has any vacancies...

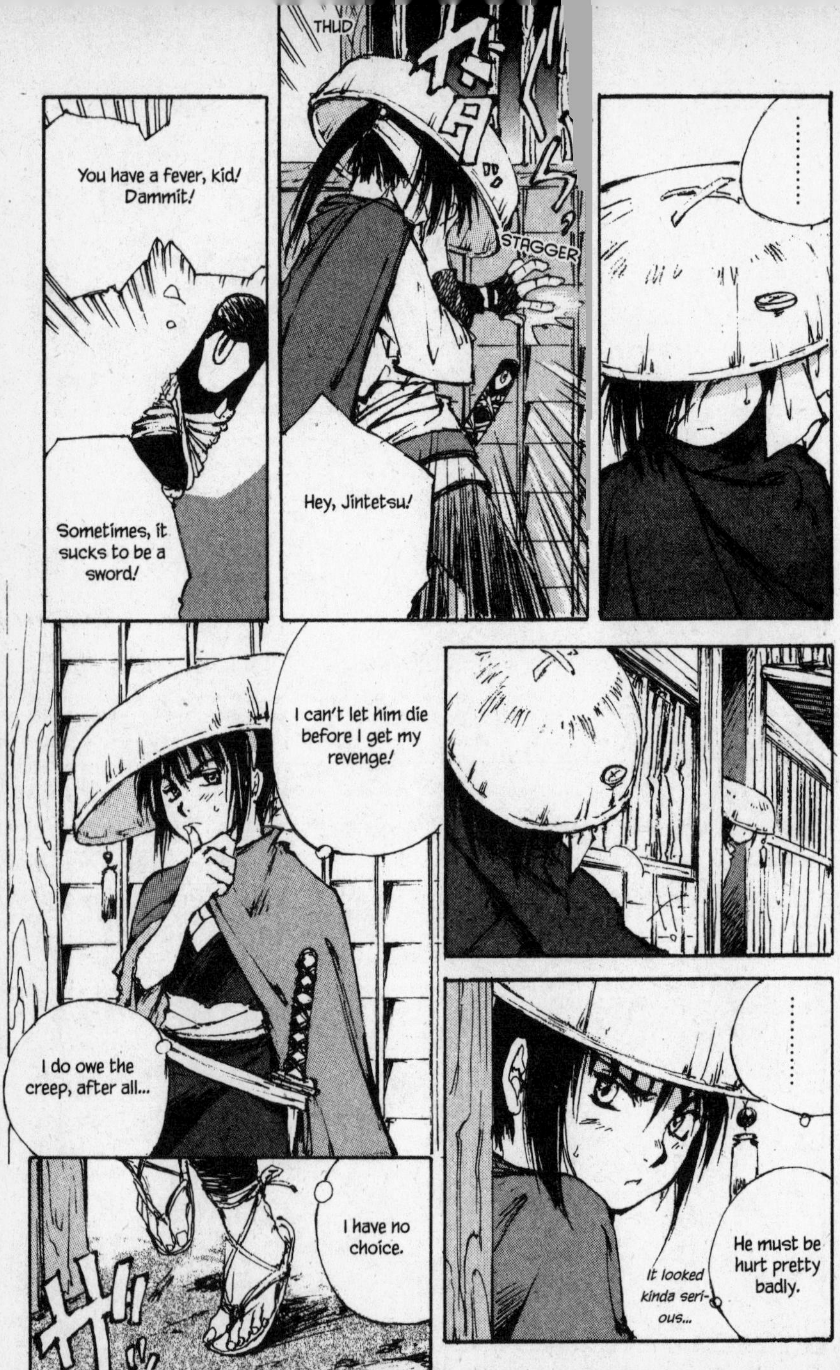
......
THUD
STAGGER
Hey, Jintetsu!
You have a fever, kid! Dammit!
Sometimes, it sucks to be a sword!
......
He must be hurt pretty badly.
It looked kinda seri-ous...
I can't let him die before I get my revenge!
I do owe the creep, after all...
I have no choice.
ZZT

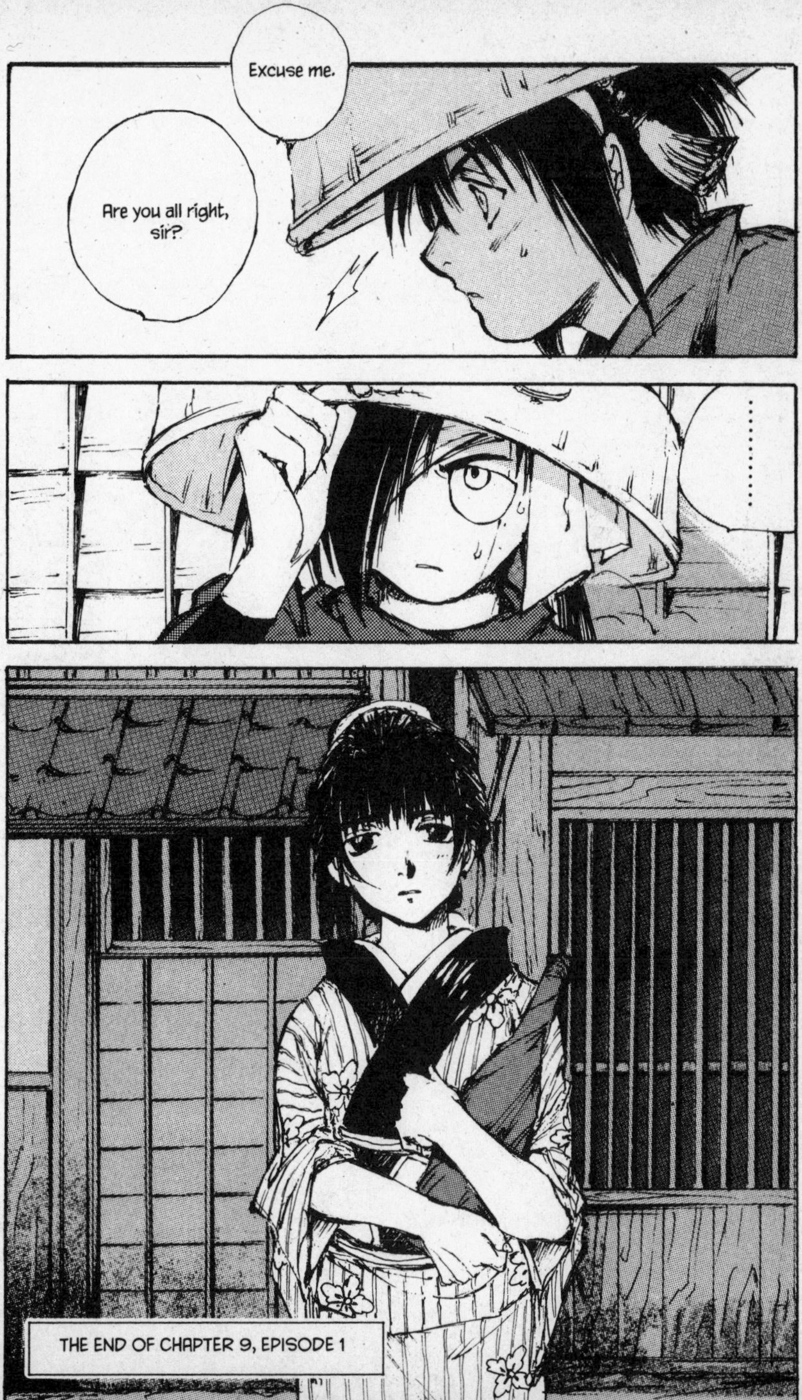
Excuse me.
Are you all right, sir?
......
THE END OF CHAPTER 9, EPISODE 1

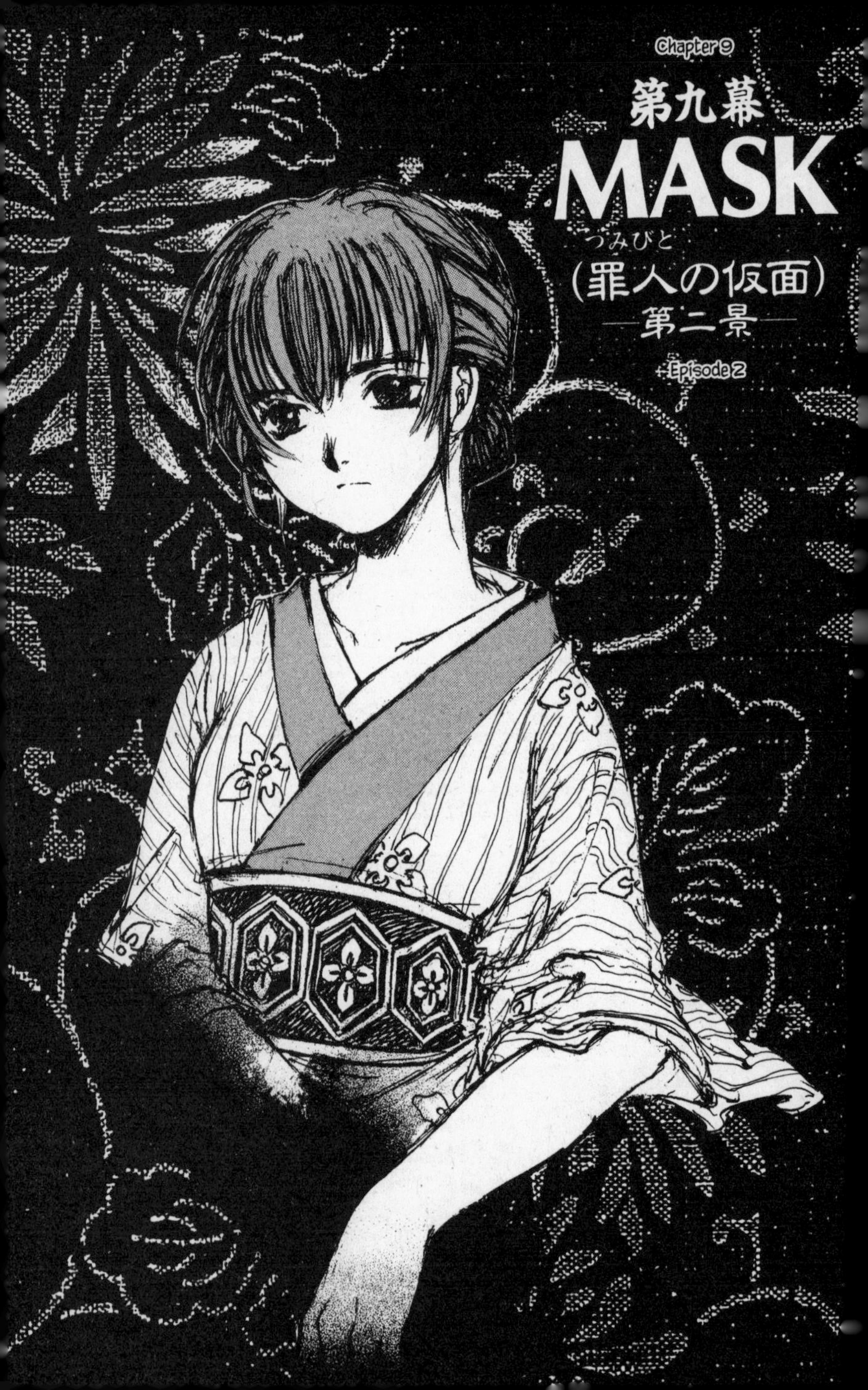
Chapter 9
第九幕
MASK
つみびと
(罪人の仮面)
—第二景—
Episode 2

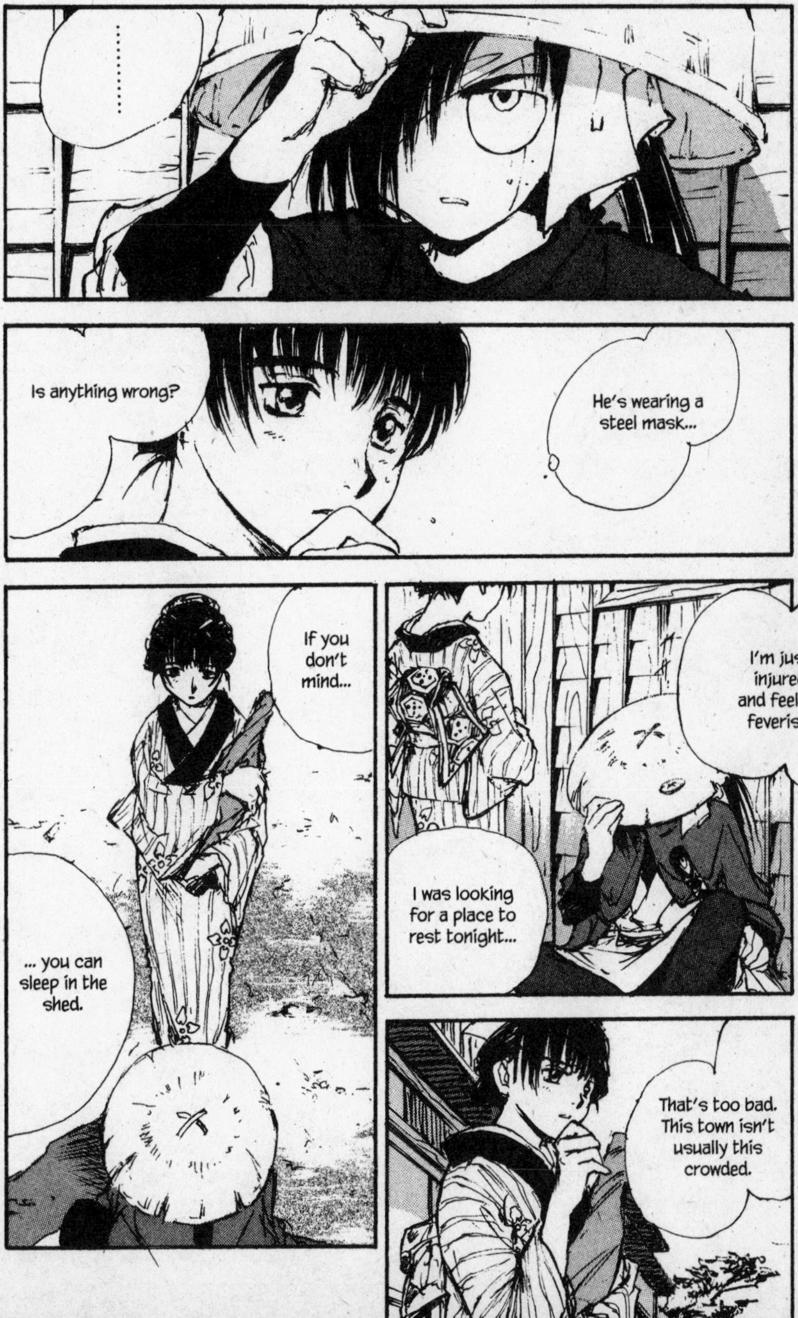
......
He's wearing a steel mask...
Is anything wrong?
I'm just injured and feeling feverish.
I was looking for a place to rest tonight...
That's too bad. This town isn't usually this crowded.
If you don't mind...
... you can sleep in the shed.

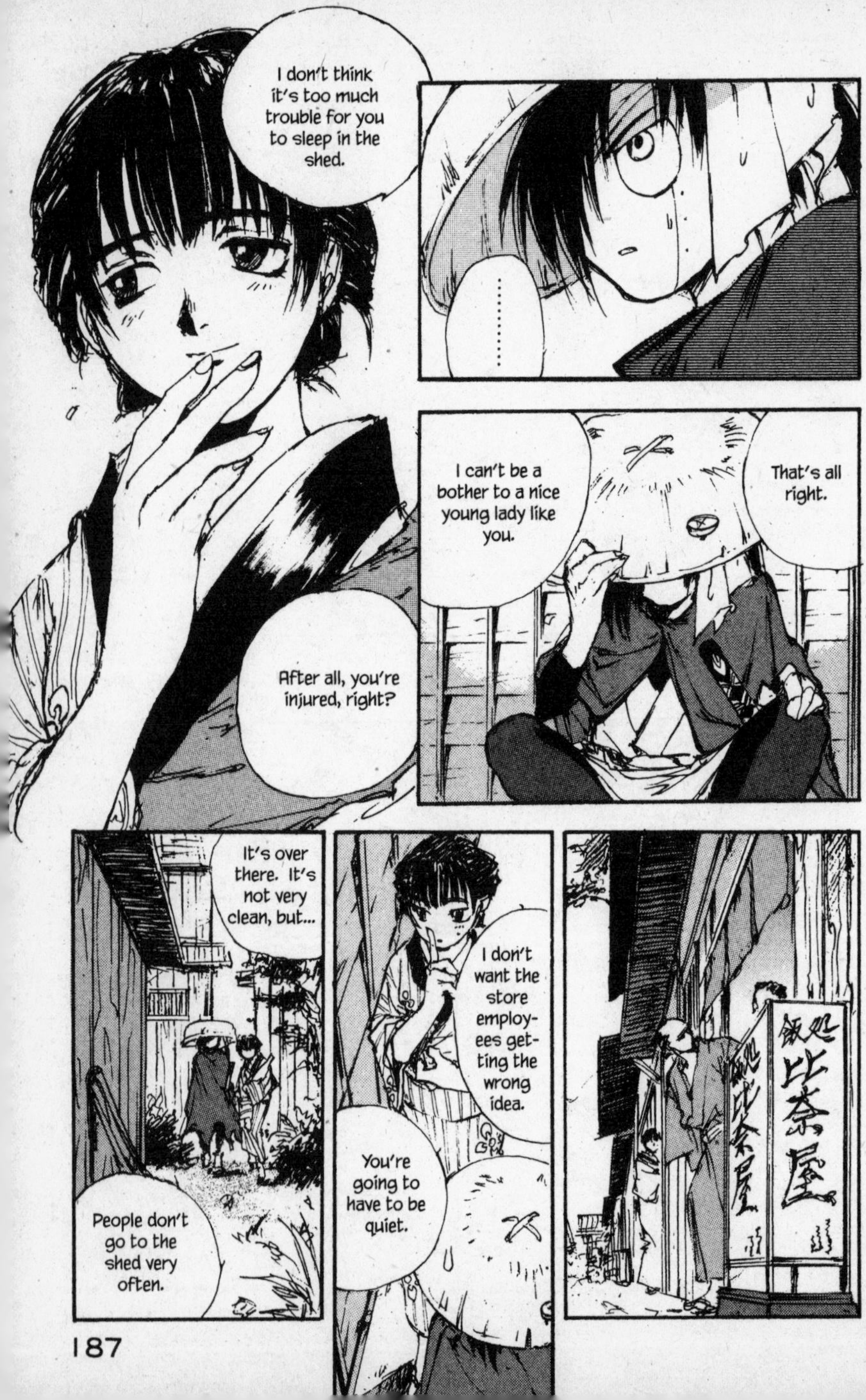
......
That's all right.
I can't be a bother to a nice young lady like you.
I don't think it's too much trouble for you to sleep in the shed.
After all, you're injured, right?
飯処
比奈屋
I don't want the store employees getting the wrong idea.
You're going to have to be quiet.
It's over there. It's not very clean, but...
People don't go to the shed very often.

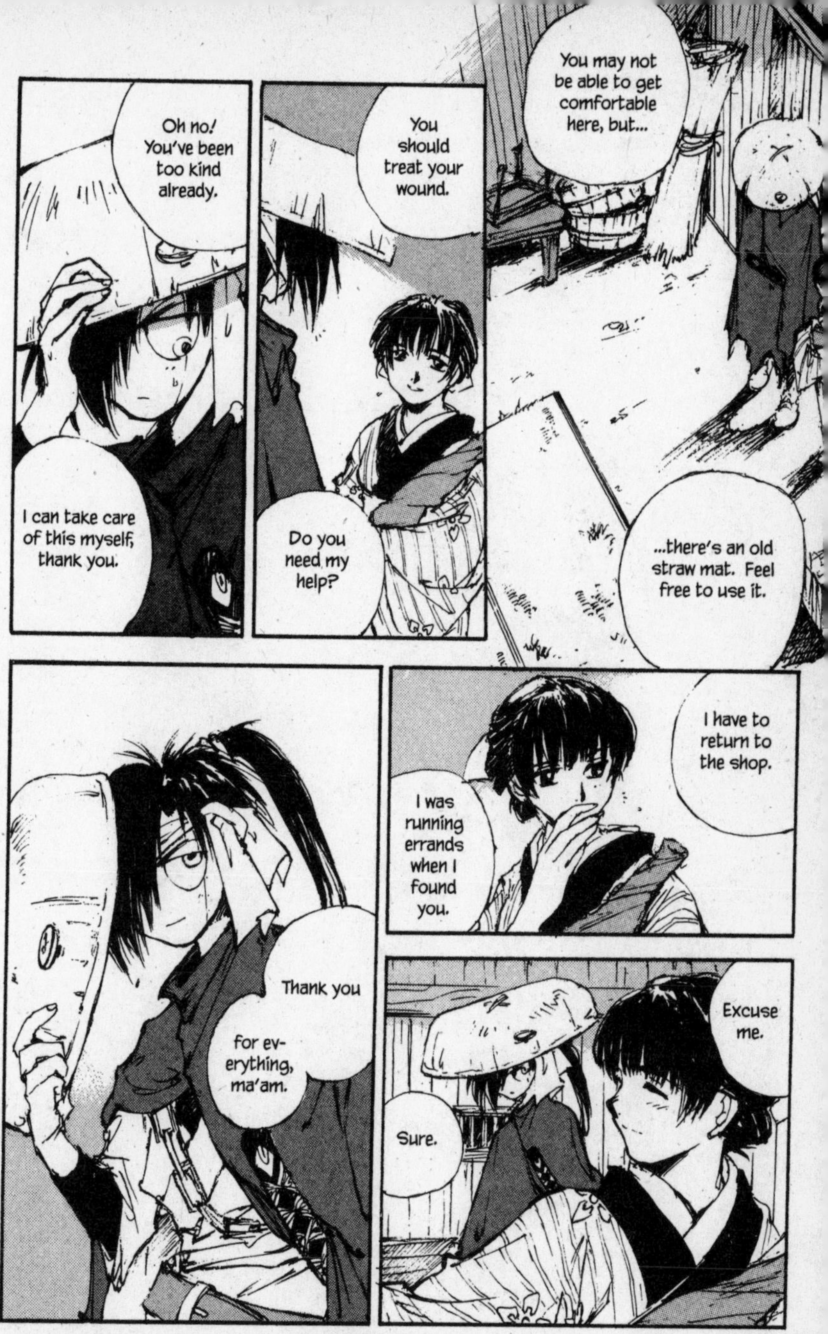
You may not be able to get comfortable here, but...
...there's an old straw mat. Feel free to use it.
You should treat your wound.
Do you need my help?
Oh no! You've been too kind already.
I can take care of this myself, thank you.
I have to return to the shop.
I was running errands when I found you.
Excuse me.
Sure.
Thank you
for everything, ma'am.

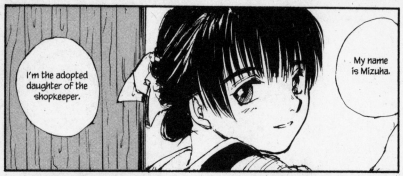

My name is Mizuha.

I'm the adopted daughter of the shopkeeper.

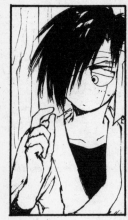

Are you still in pain?

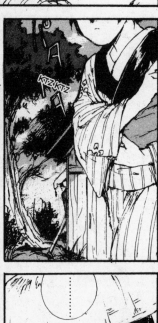

KIZ KIZ

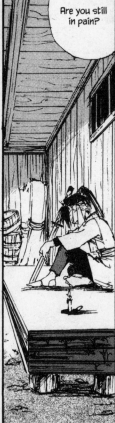

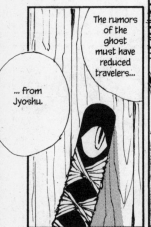

The rumors of the ghost must have reduced travelers...

... from Jyoshu.

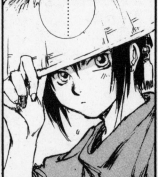

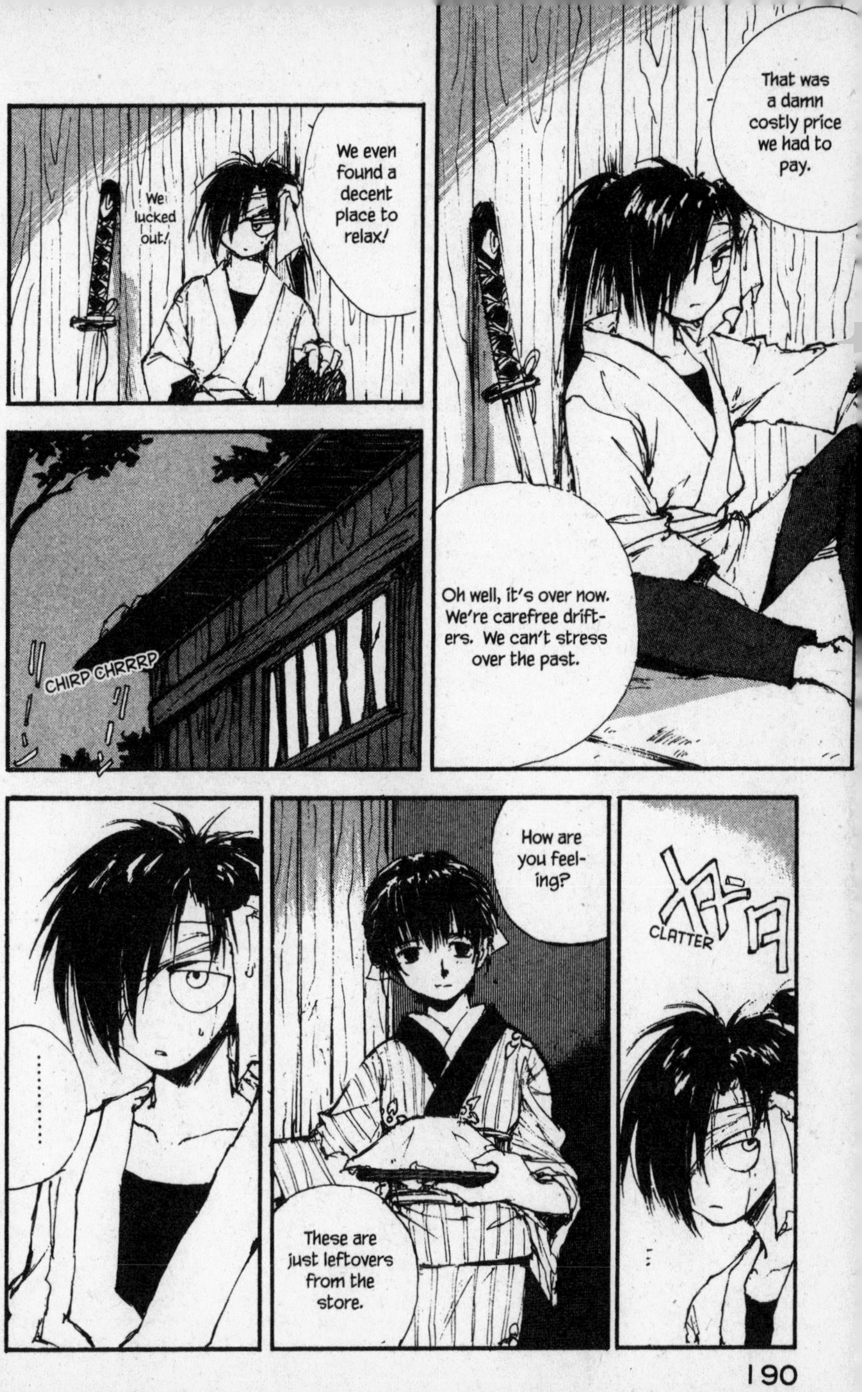
That was a damn costly price we had to pay.
Oh well, it's over now. We're carefree drifters. We can't stress over the past.
We even found a decent place to relax!
We lucked out!
CHIRP CHRRRP
CLATTER
...
How are you feeling?
These are just leftovers from the store.
......

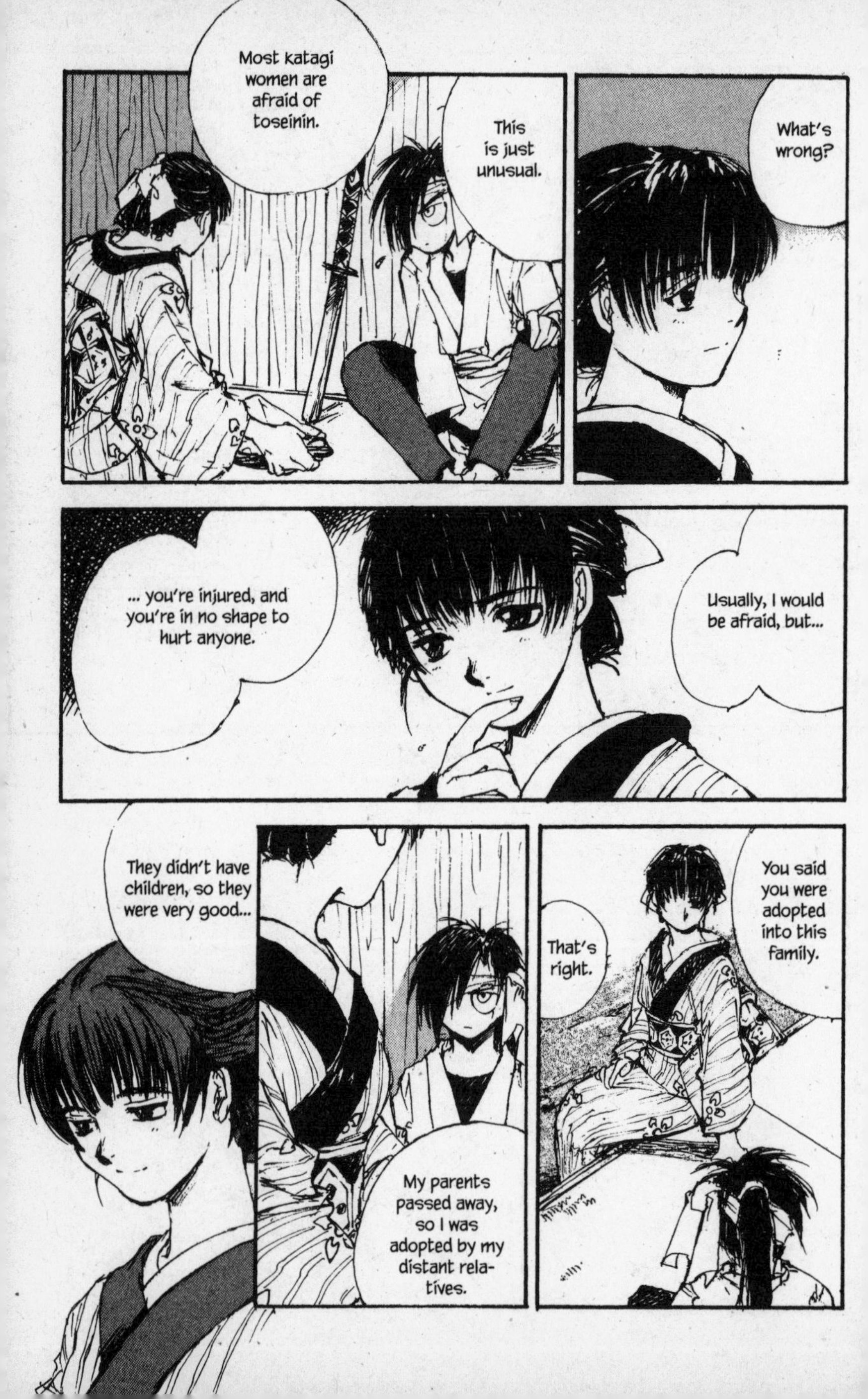
What's wrong?
This is just unusual.
Most katagi women are afraid of toseinin.
Usually, I would be afraid, but...
... you're injured, and you're in no shape to hurt anyone.
You said you were adopted into this family.
That's right.
My parents passed away, so I was adopted by my distant relatives.
They didn't have children, so they were very good...

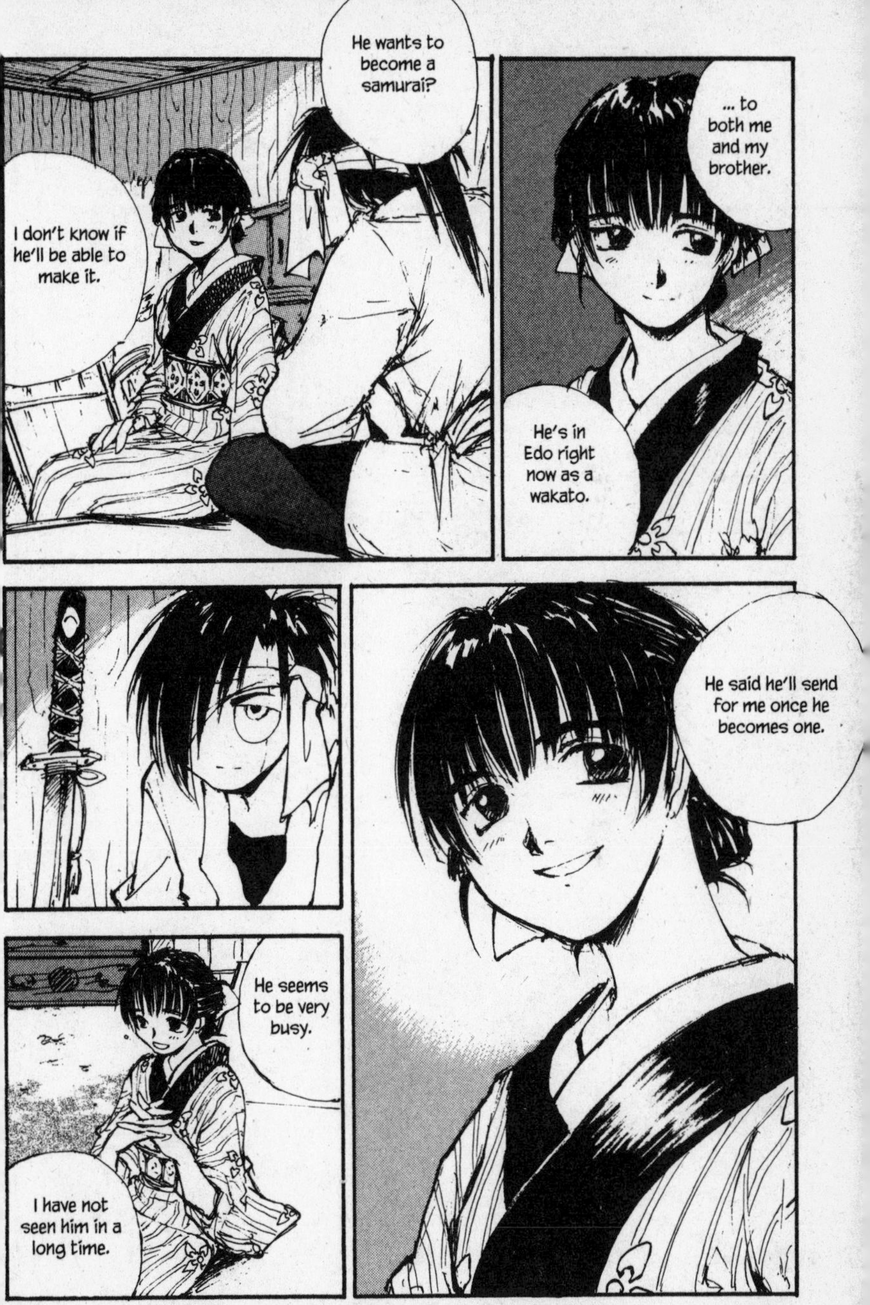
... to both me and my brother.
He's in Edo right now as a wakato.
He wants to become a samurai?
I don't know if he'll be able to make it.
He said he'll send for me once he becomes one.
He seems to be very busy.
I have not seen him in a long time.

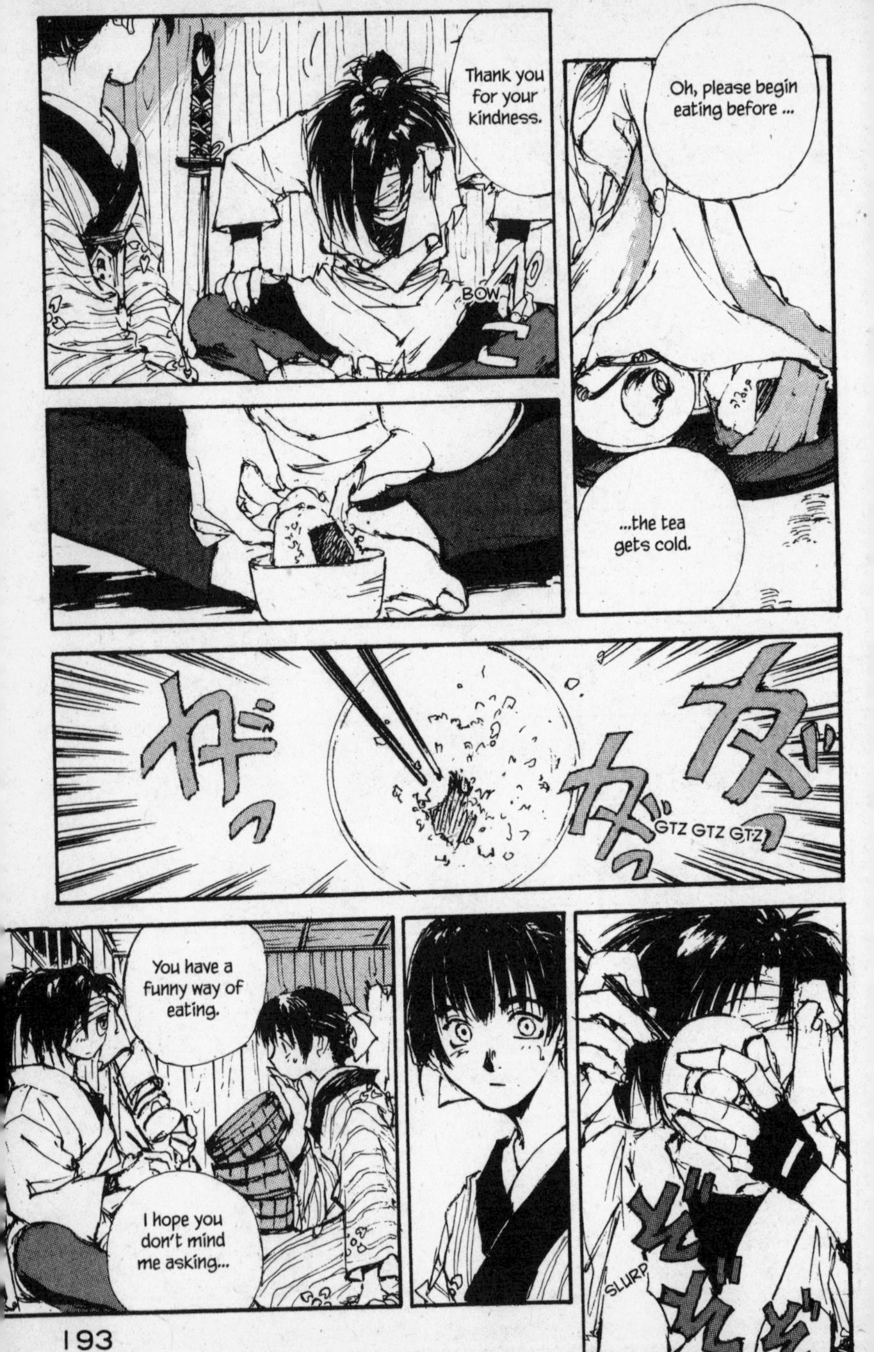
Oh, please begin eating before ...
...the tea gets cold.
Thank you for your kindness.
BOW
GTZ GTZ GTZ
SLURP
You have a funny way of eating.
I hope you don't mind me asking...

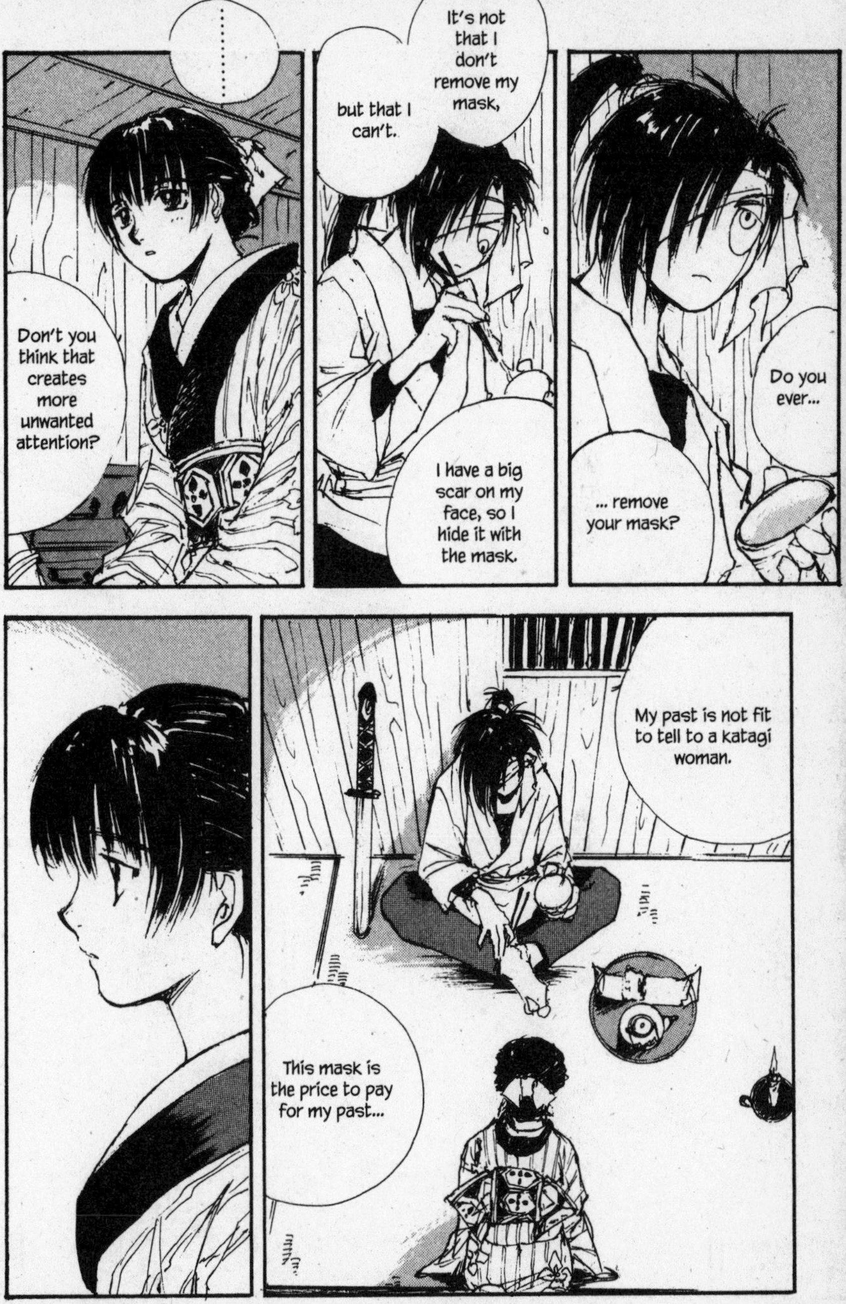
Do you ever...
... remove your mask?
It's not that I don't remove my mask,
but that I can't.
I have a big scar on my face, so I hide it with the mask.
......
Don't you think that creates more unwanted attention?
My past is not fit to tell to a katagi woman.
This mask is the price to pay for my past...

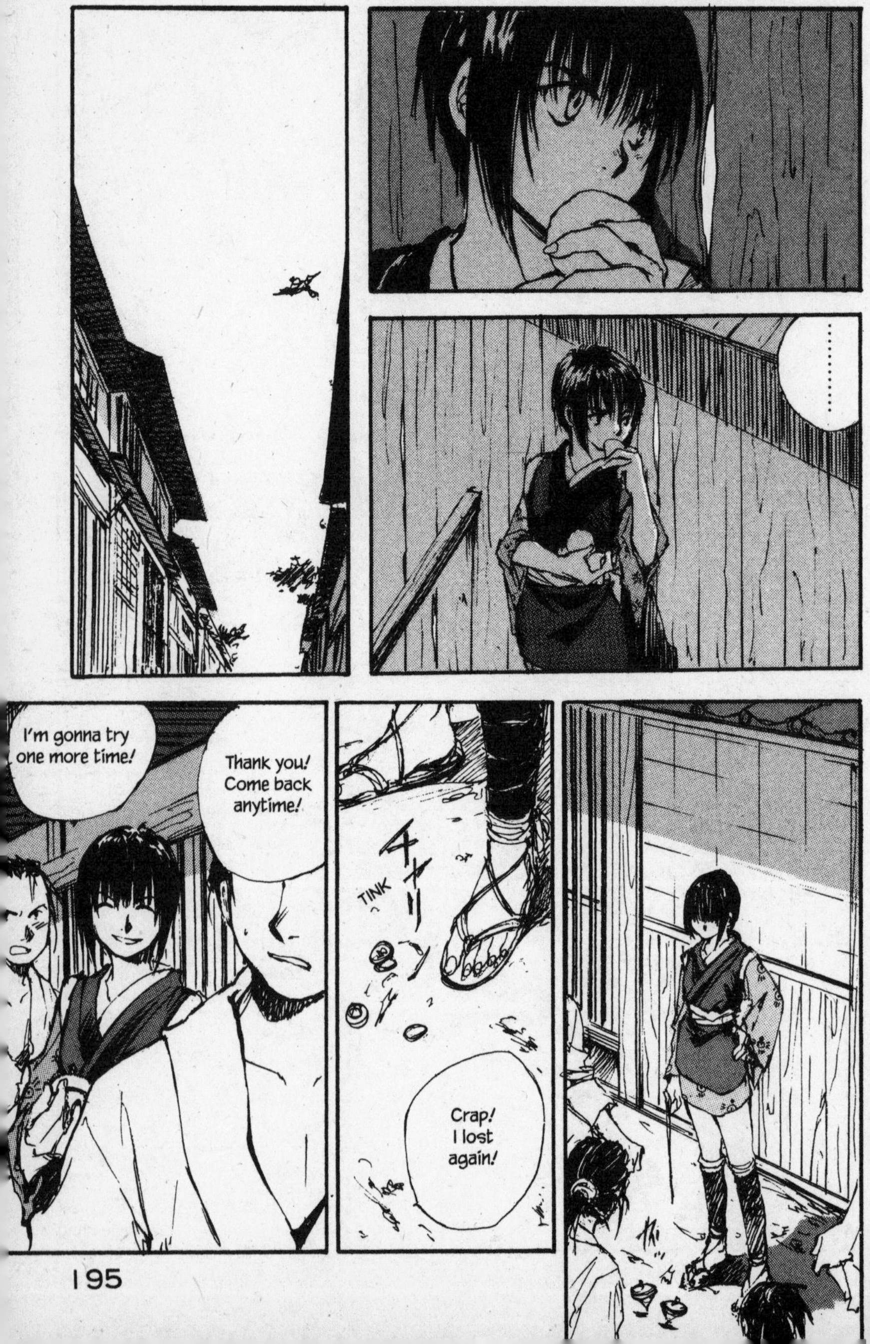
......
TINK
Crap! I lost again!
Thank you! Come back anytime!
I'm gonna try one more time!

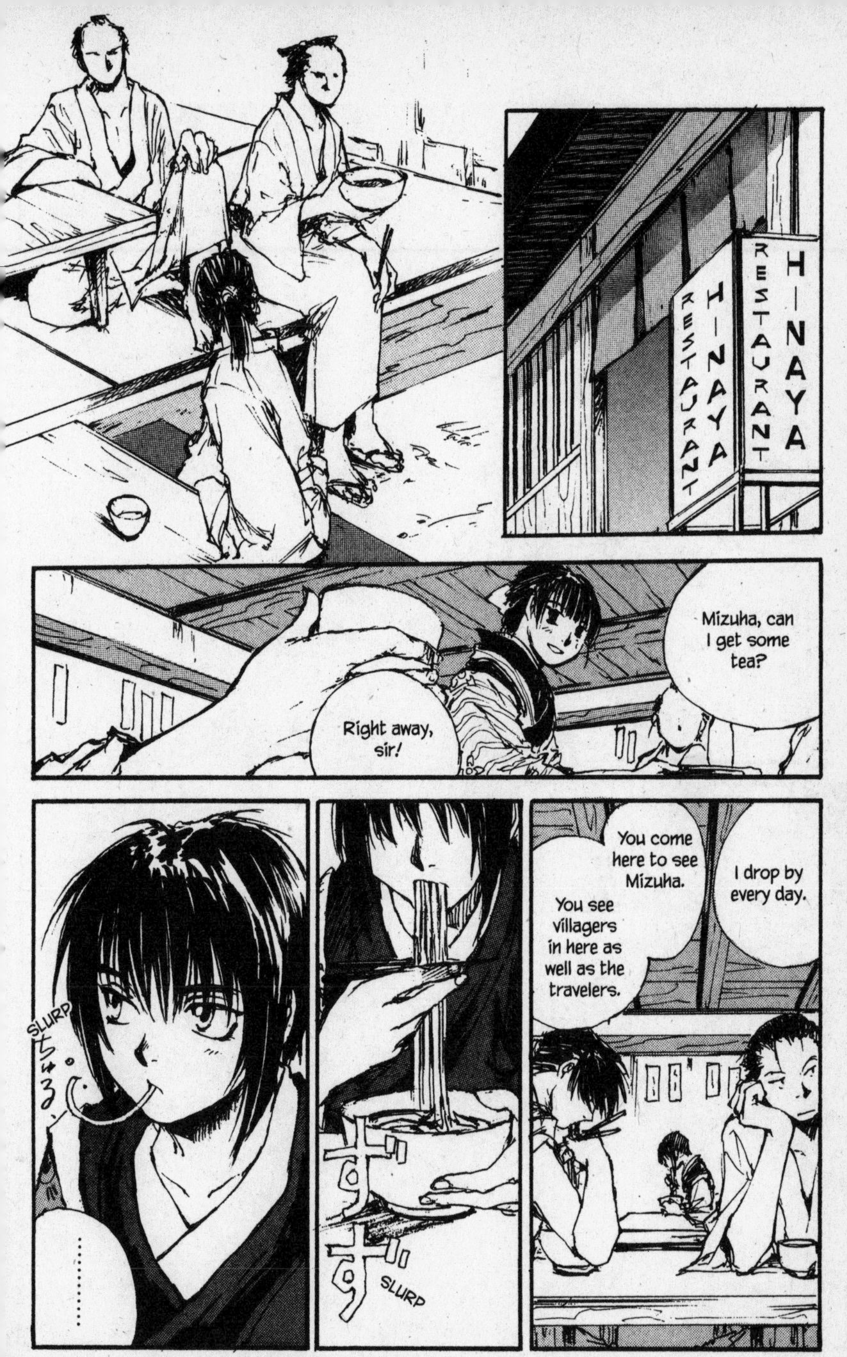
HINAYA
RESTAURANT
HINAYA
RESTAURANT
Mizuha, can I get some tea?
Right away, sir!
I drop by every day.
You come here to see Mizuha.
You see villagers in here as well as the travelers.
SLURP
SLURP
......

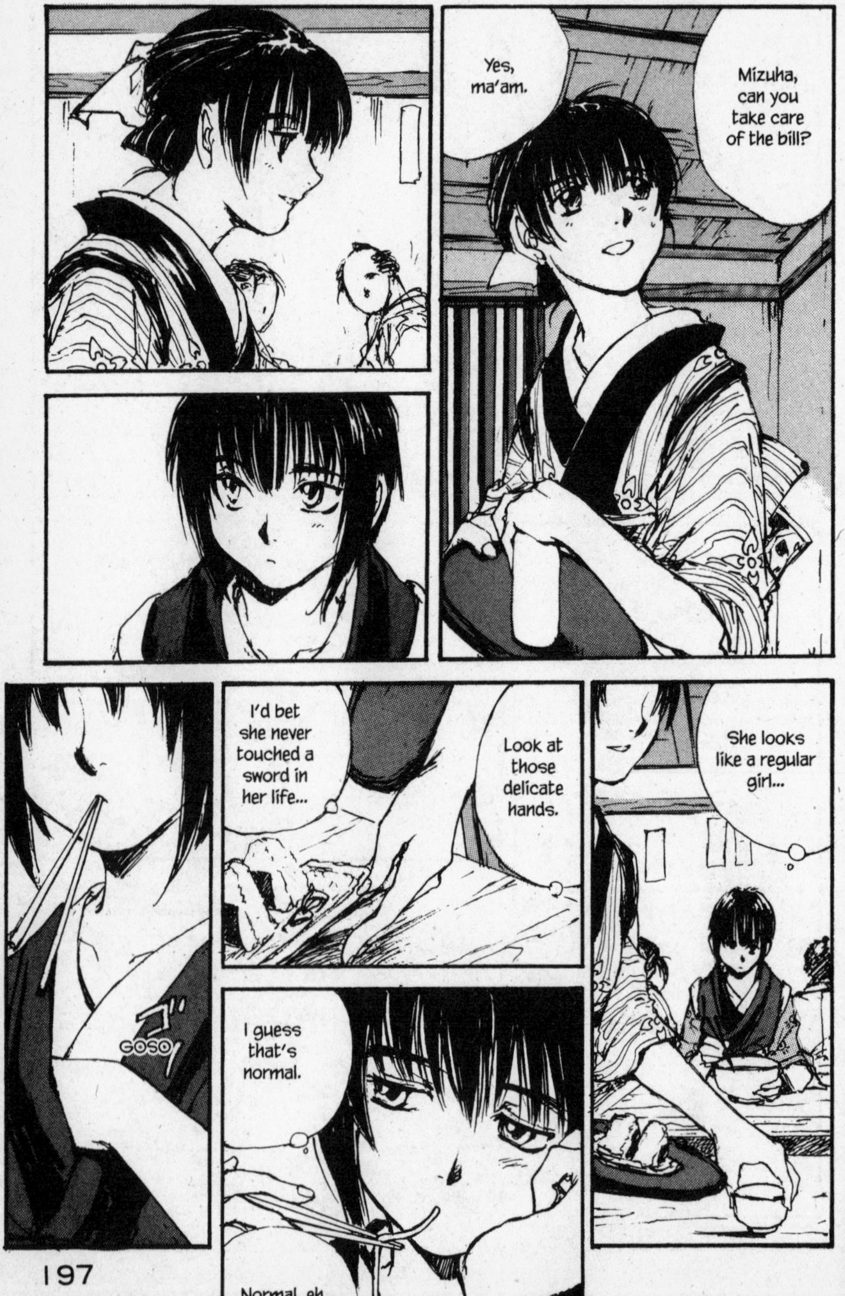

Mizuha, can you take care of the bill?
Yes, ma'am.
She looks like a regular girl...
Look at those delicate hands.
I'd bet she never touched a sword in her life...
I guess that's normal.
Normal, eh...
ゴソ
GOSO

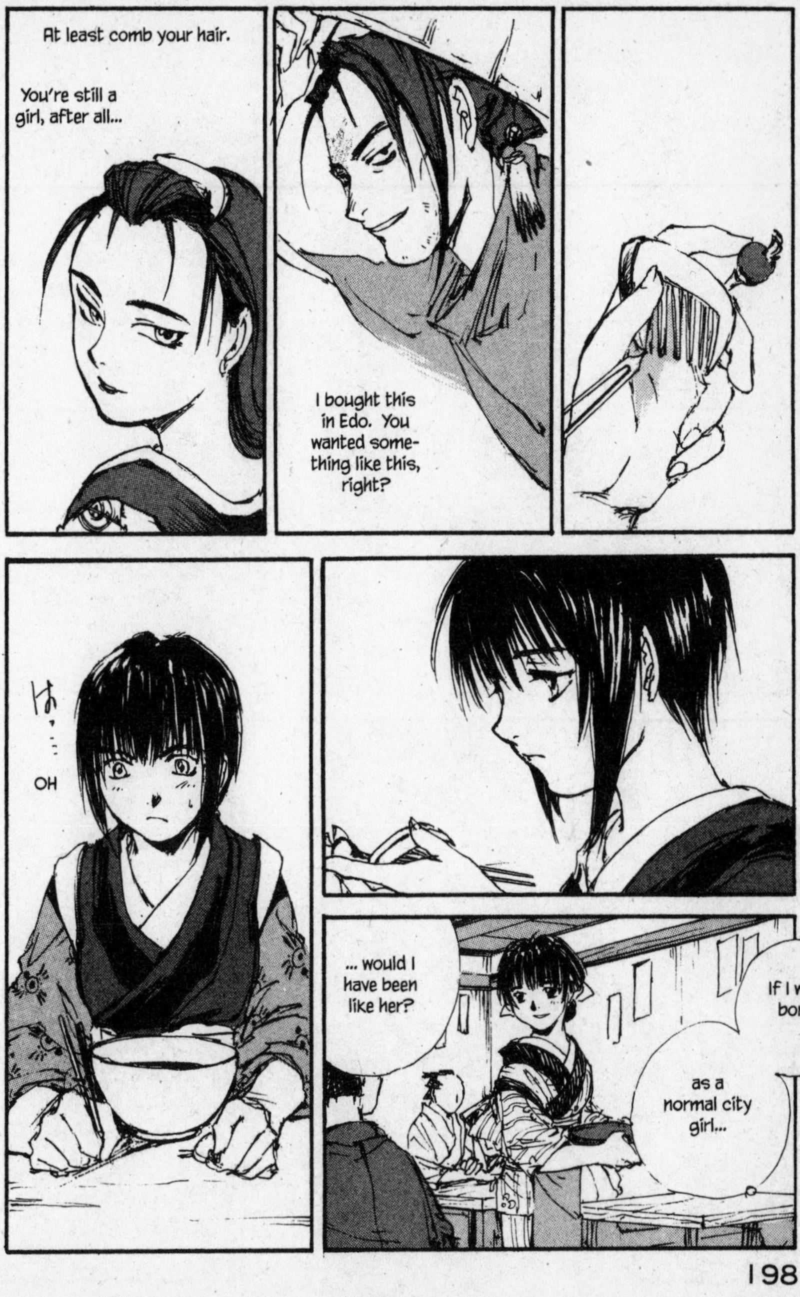
I bought this in Edo. You wanted something like this, right?
At least comb your hair.
You're still a girl, after all...
If I was born
as a normal city girl...
... would I have been like her?
は…
OH

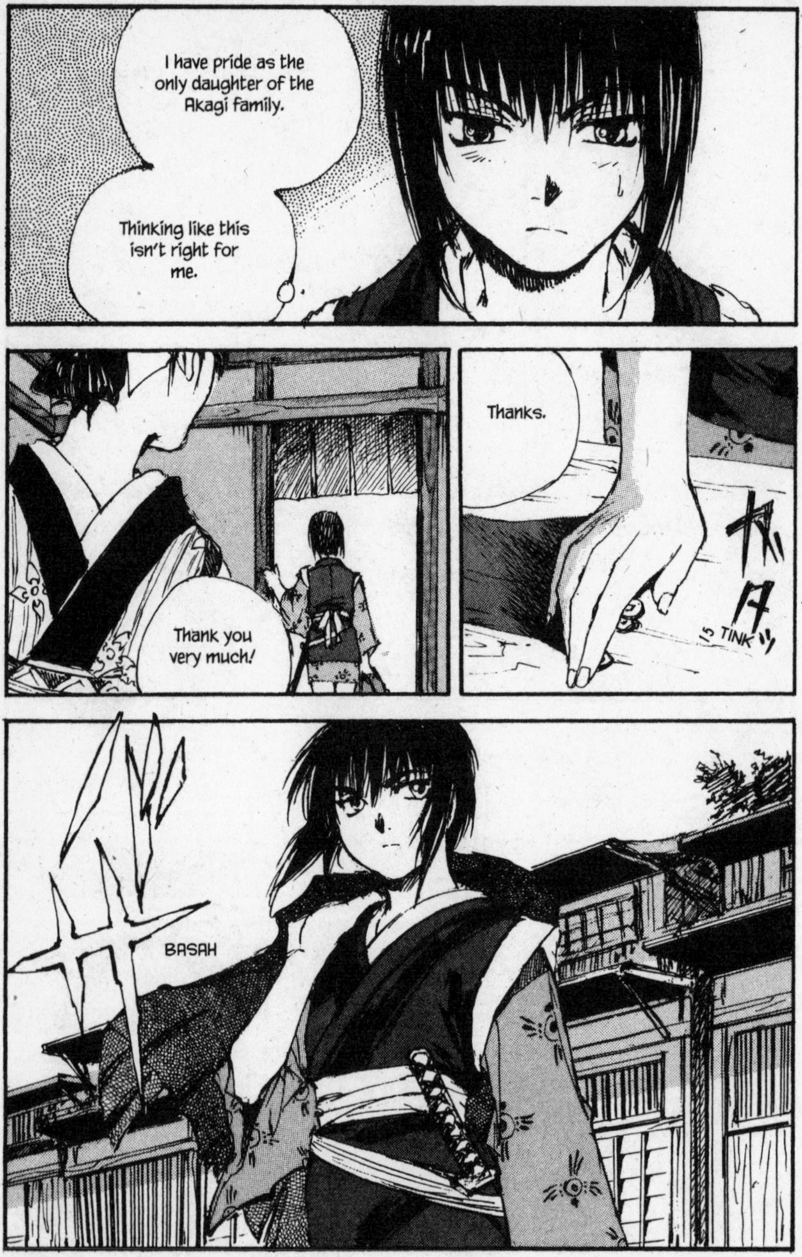
I have pride as the only daughter of the Akagi family.
Thinking like this isn't right for me.
Thanks.
TINK
Thank you very much!
BASAH

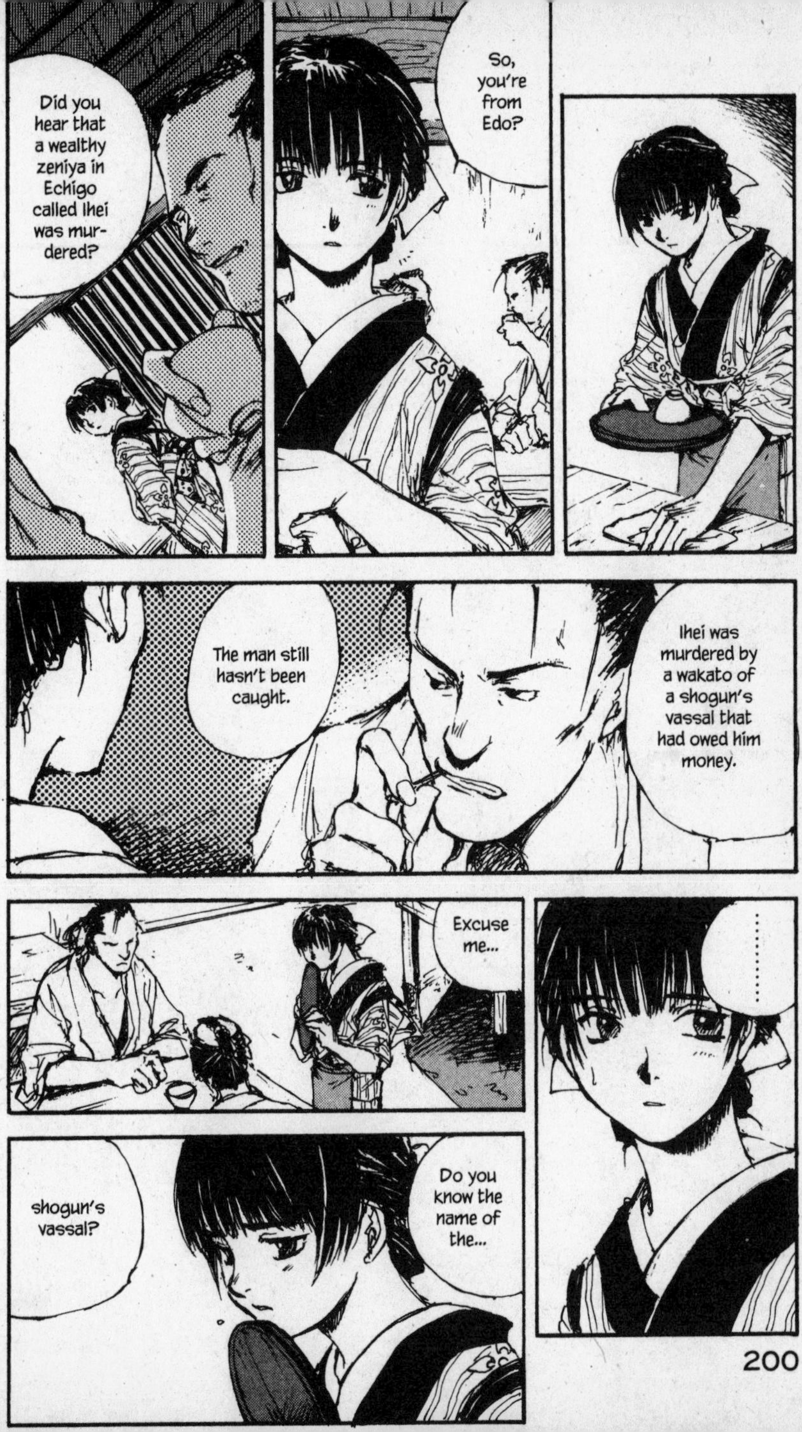
So, you're from Edo?
Did you hear that a wealthy zeniya in Echigo called Ihei was murdered?
Ihei was murdered by a wakato of a shogun's vassal that had owed him money.
The man still hasn't been caught.
......
Excuse me...
Do you know the name of the...
shogun's vassal?

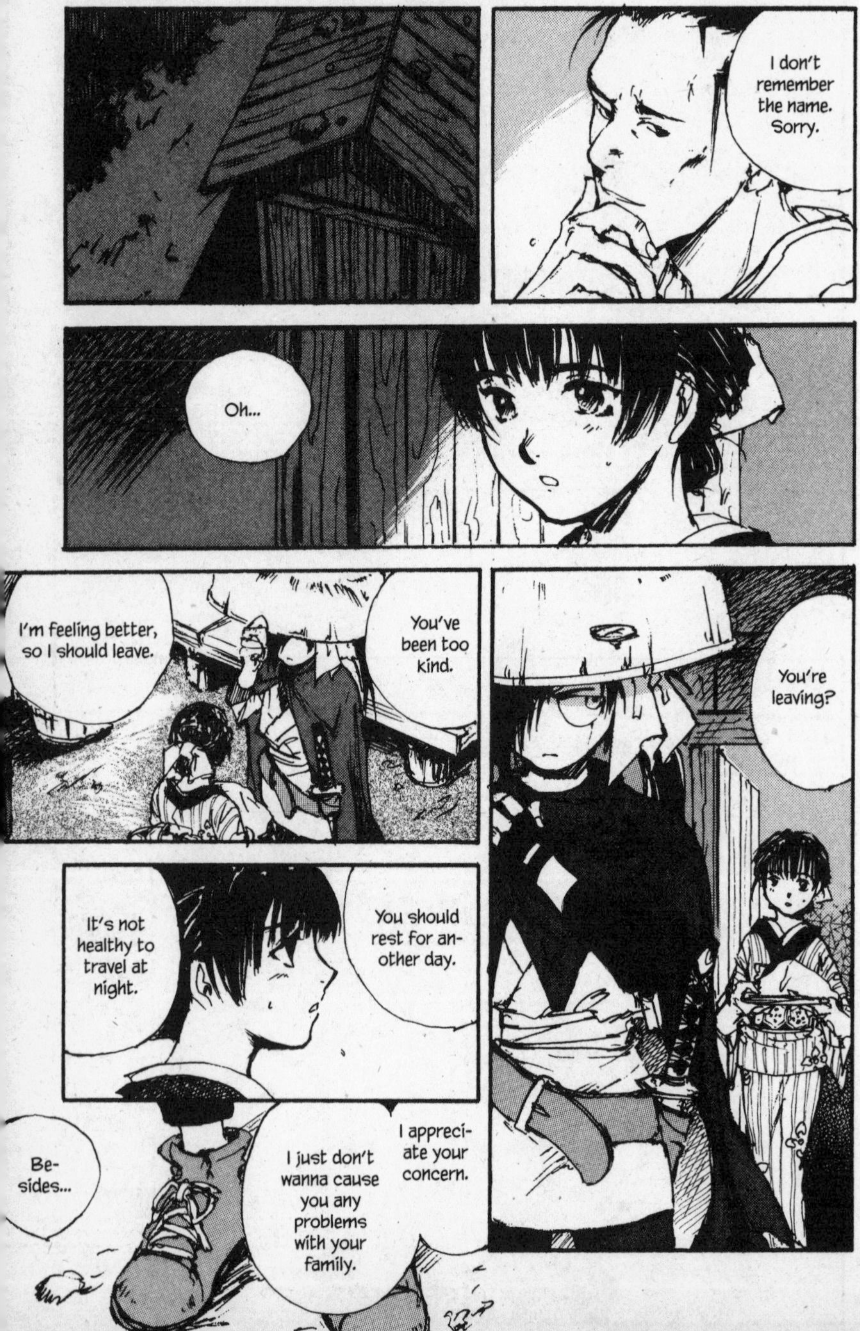
I don't remember the name. Sorry.
Oh...
You're leaving?
You've been too kind.
I'm feeling better, so I should leave.
You should rest for another day.
It's not healthy to travel at night.
I appreciate your concern.
I just don't wanna cause you any problems with your family.
Be-sides...

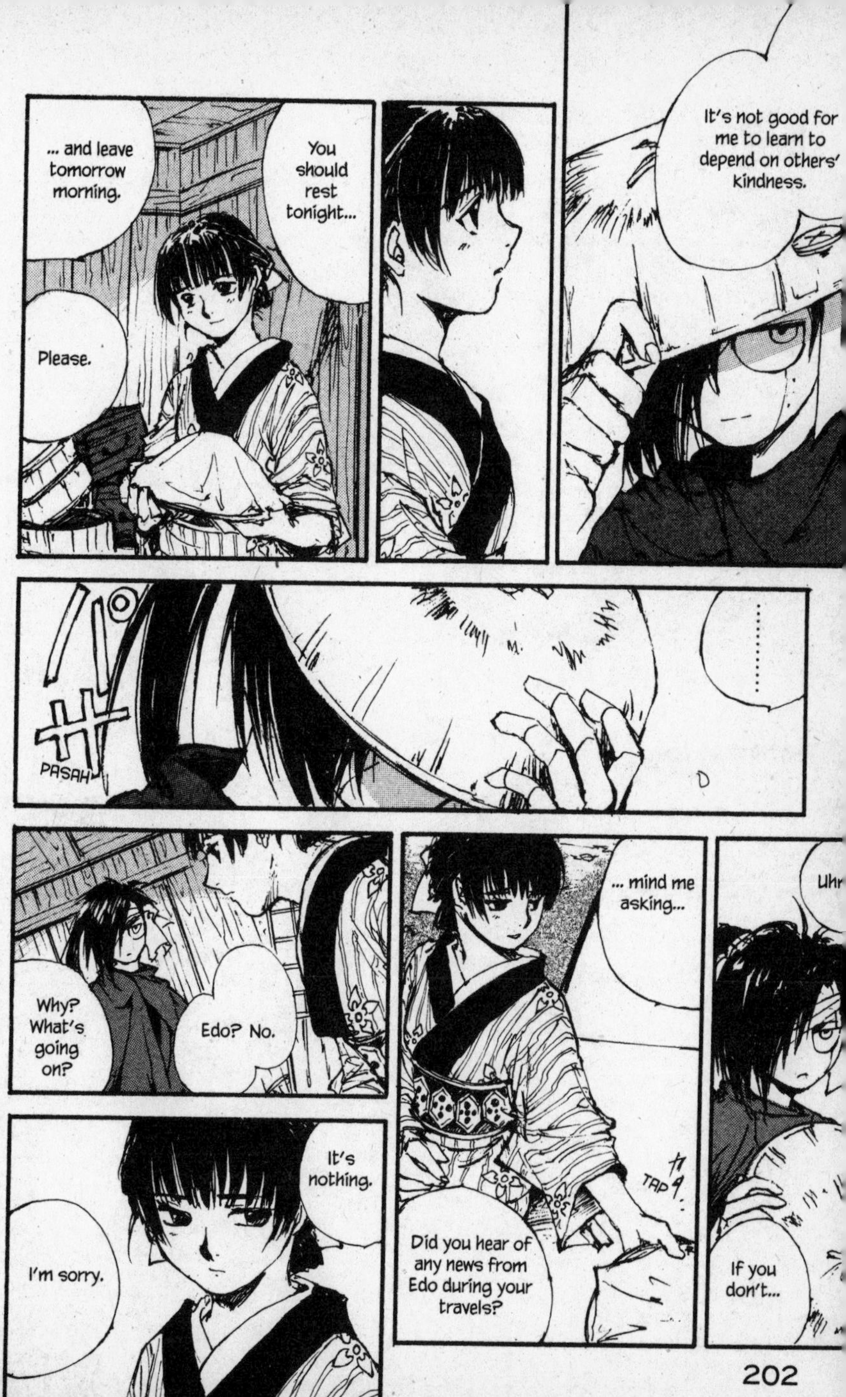
It's not good for me to learn to depend on others' kindness.
You should rest tonight...
... and leave tomorrow morning.
Please.
......
PASAH
Uh
If you don't...
... mind me asking...
TAP
Did you hear of any news from Edo during your travels?
Edo? No.
Why? What's going on?
It's nothing.
I'm sorry.

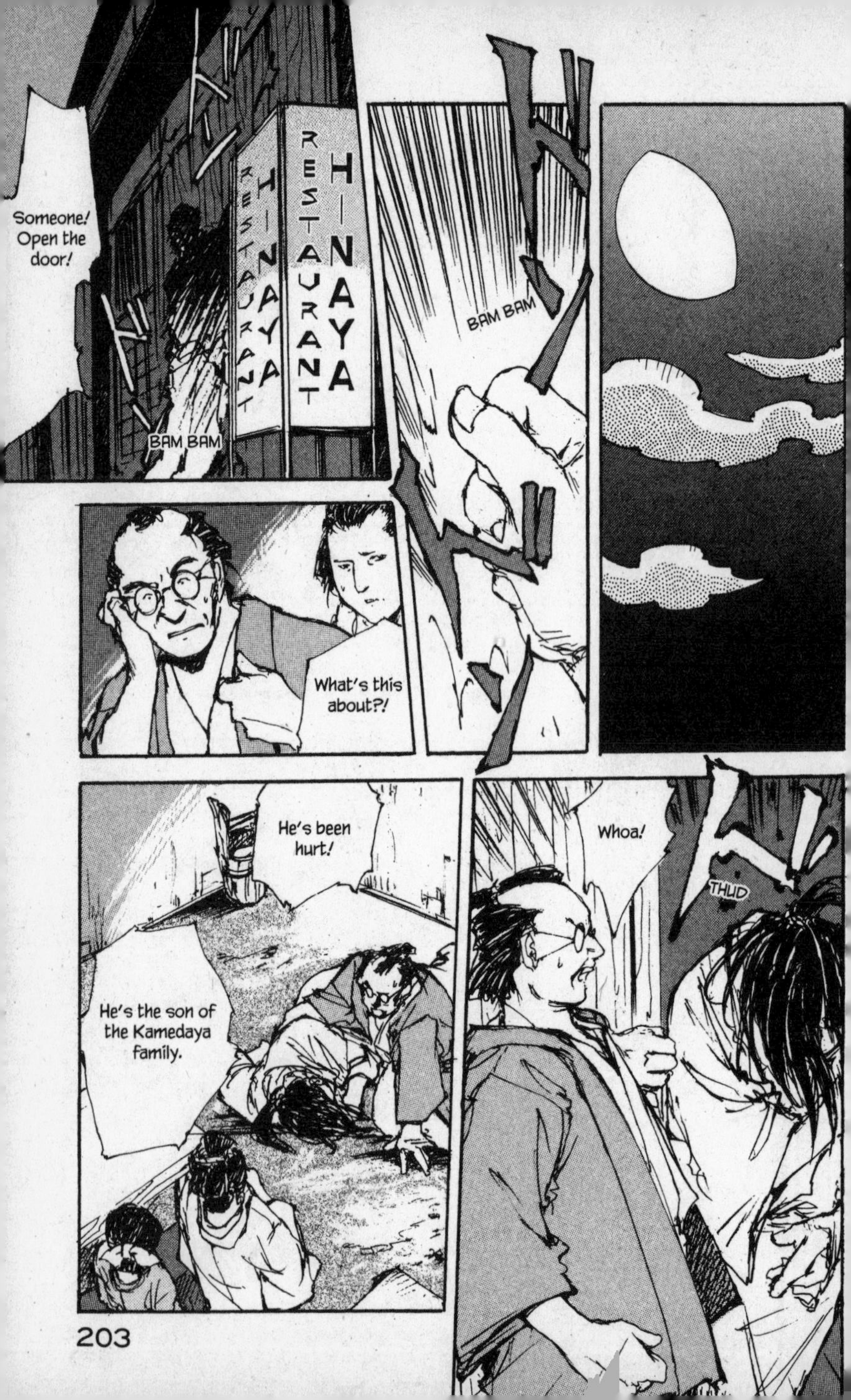
BAM BAM
HINAYA RESTAURANT
HINAYA RESTAURANT
Someone! Open the door!
BAM BAM
What's this about?!
Whoa!
THUD
He's been hurt!
He's the son of the Kamedaya family.

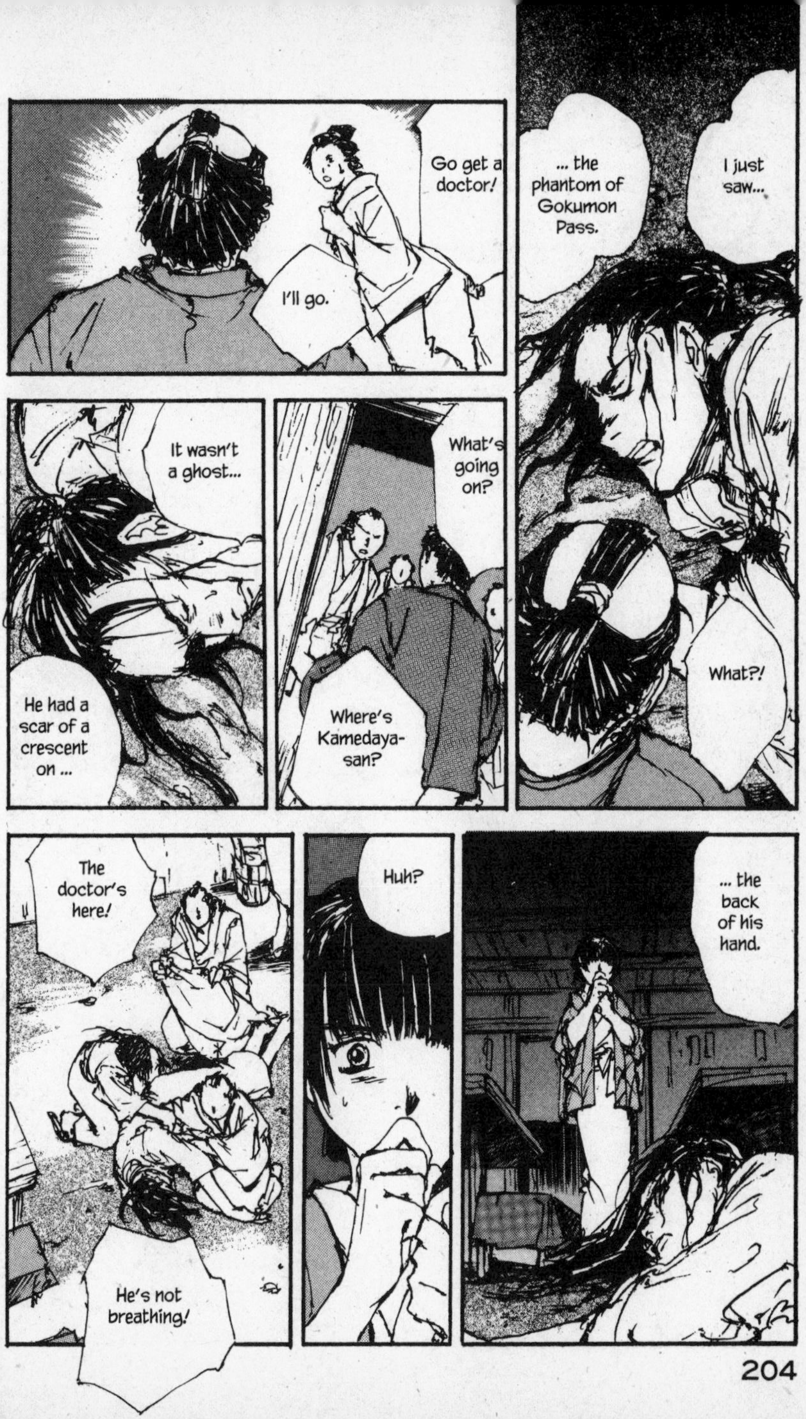
I just saw...
... the phantom of Gokumon Pass.
What?!
Go get a doctor!
I'll go.
What's going on?
Where's Kamedaya-san?
It wasn't a ghost...
He had a scar of a crescent on ...
... the back of his hand.
Huh?
The doctor's here!
He's not breathing!

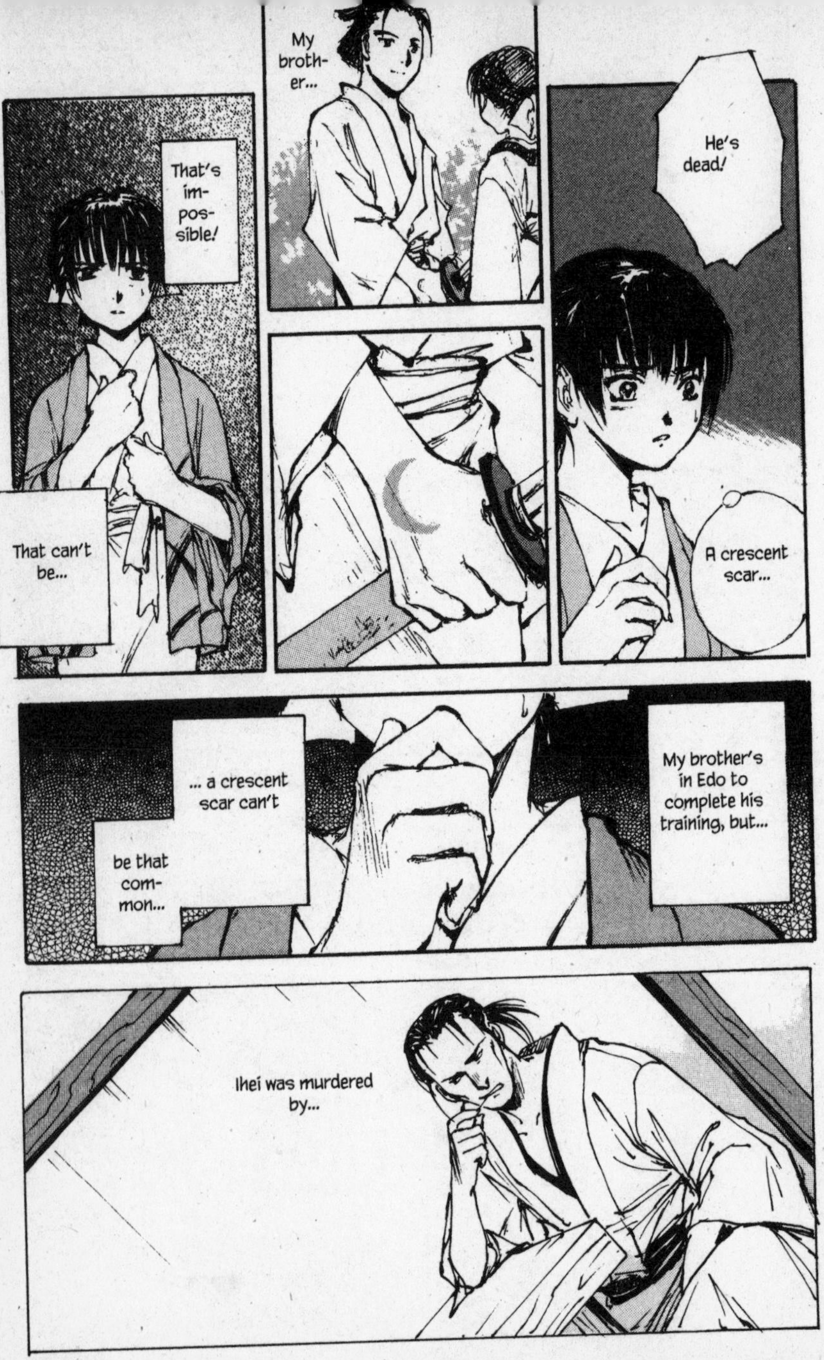
He's dead!
A crescent scar...
My brother...
That's impossible!
That can't be...
My brother's in Edo to complete his training, but...
... a crescent scar can't be that common...
Ihei was murdered by...

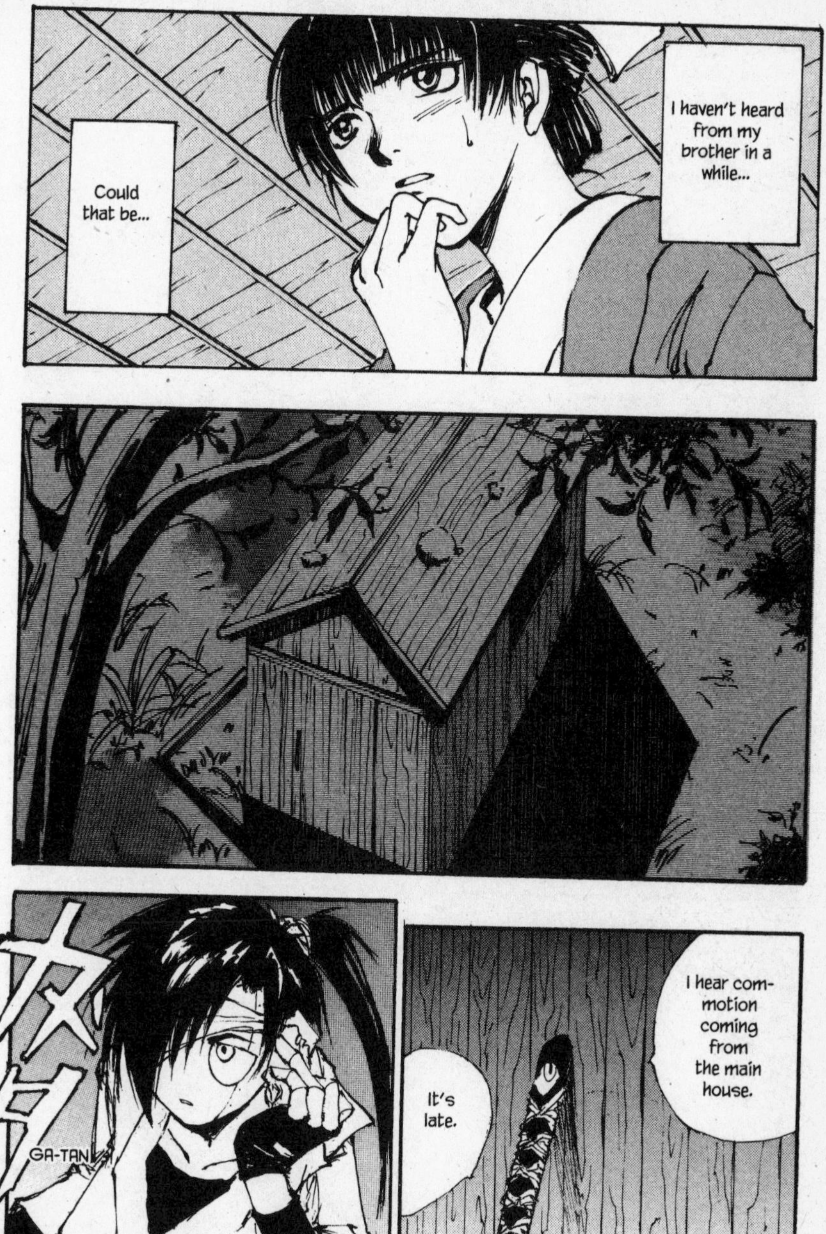
I haven't heard from my brother in a while...
Could that be...
I hear commotion coming from the main house.
It's late.
GA-TAN

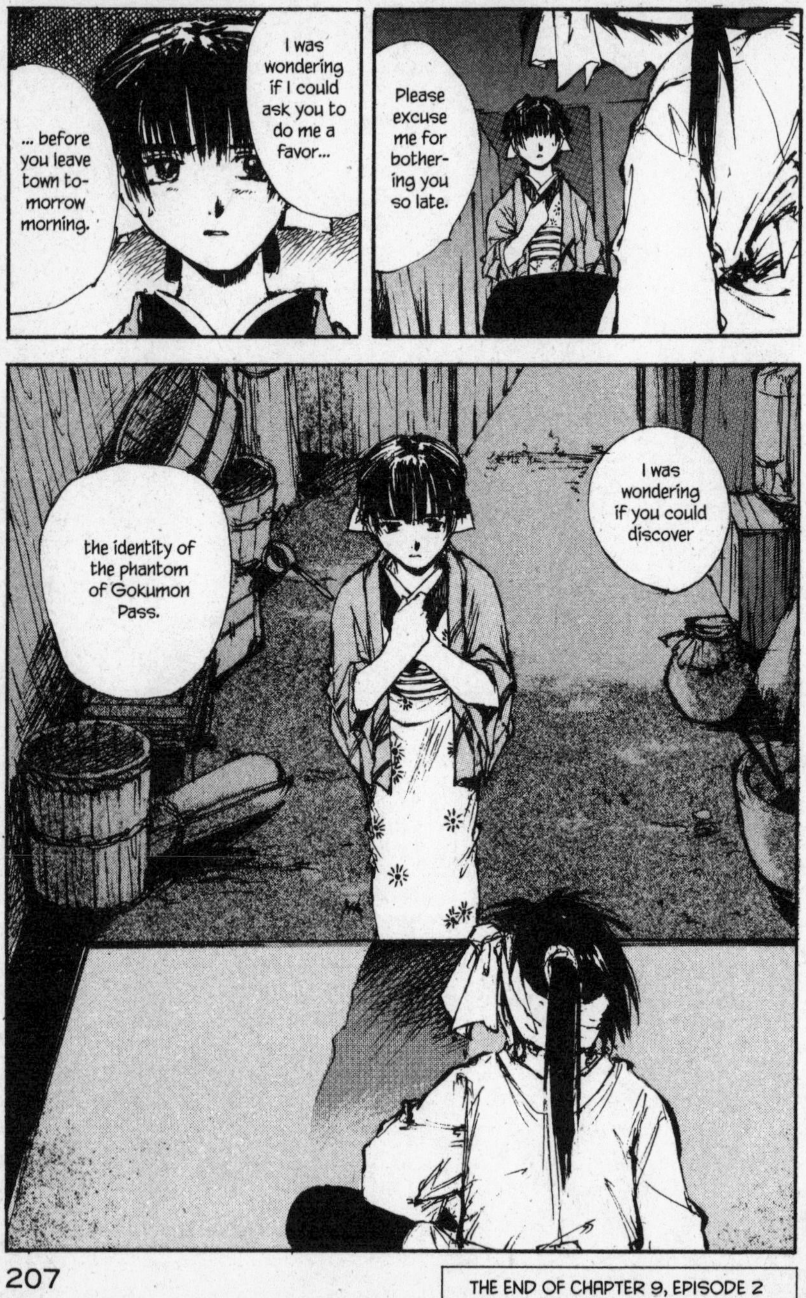

Please excuse me for bothering you so late.
I was wondering if I could ask you to do me a favor...
... before you leave town tomorrow morning.
I was wondering if you could discover
the identity of the phantom of Gokumon Pass.

THE END OF CHAPTER 9, EPISODE 2

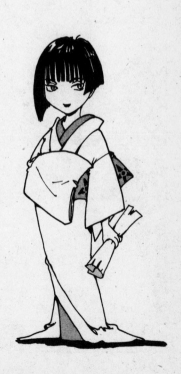

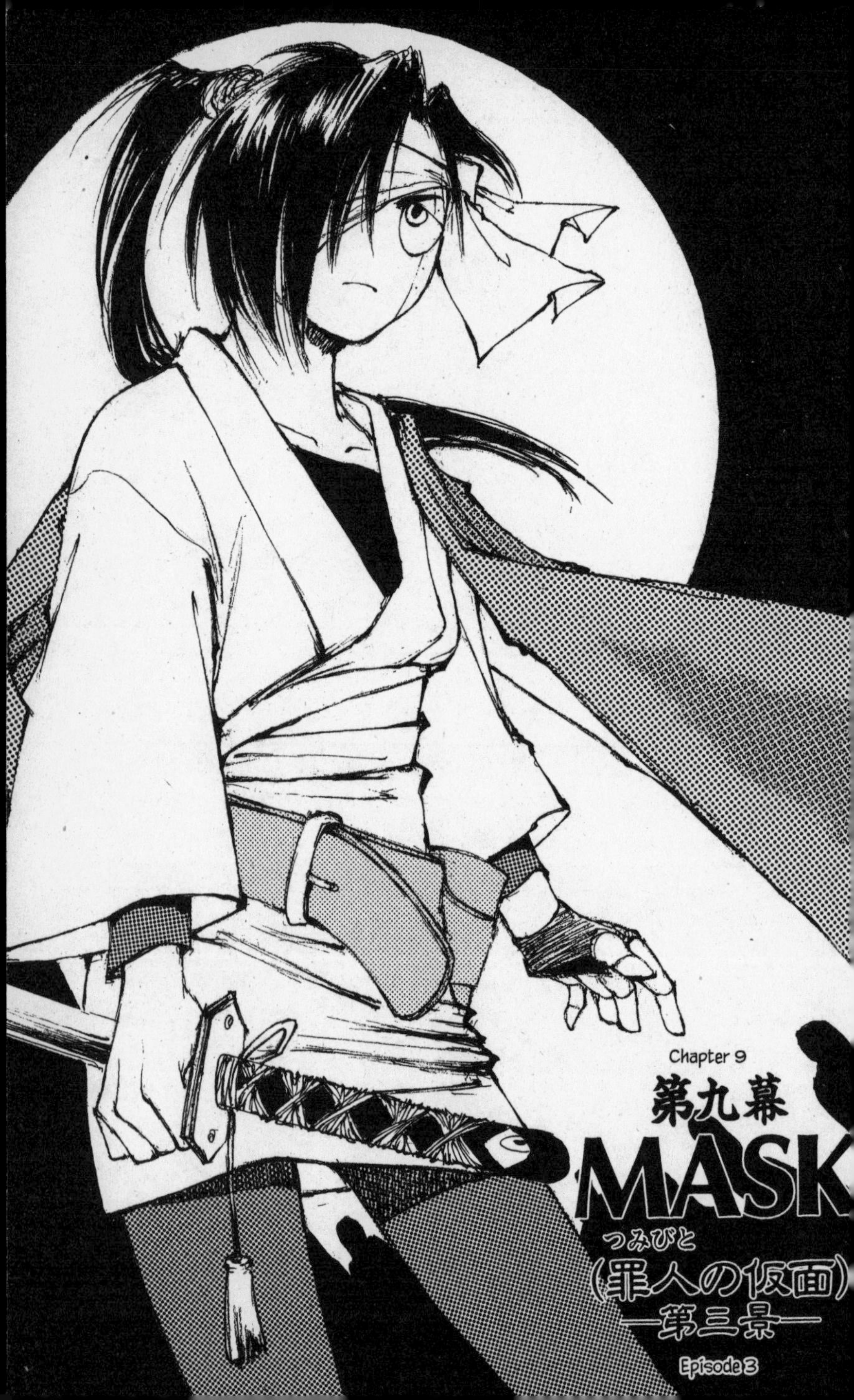
Chapter 9
第九幕
MASK
つみびと
(罪人の仮面)
—第三景—
Episode 3

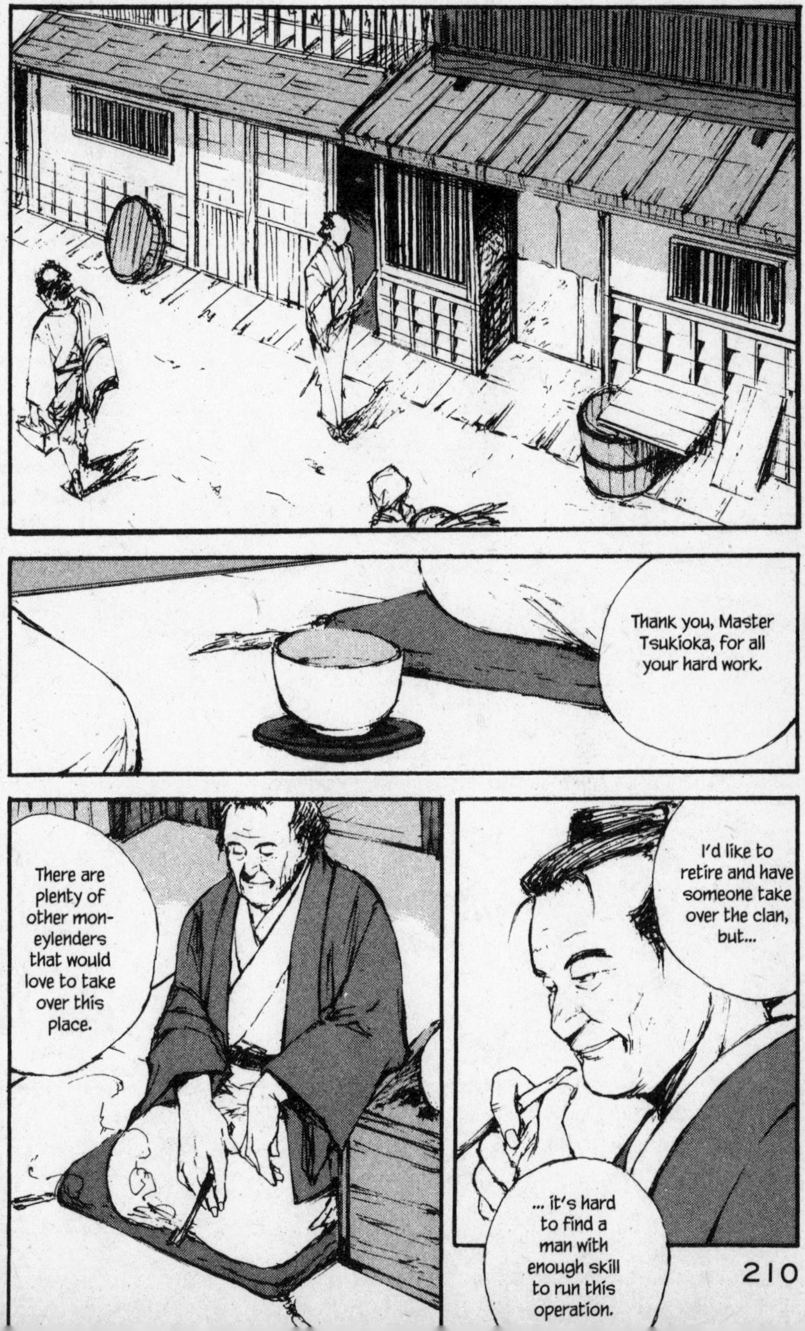
Thank you, Master Tsukioka, for all your hard work.
I'd like to retire and have someone take over the clan, but...
... it's hard to find a man with enough skill to run this operation.
There are plenty of other moneylenders that would love to take over this place.

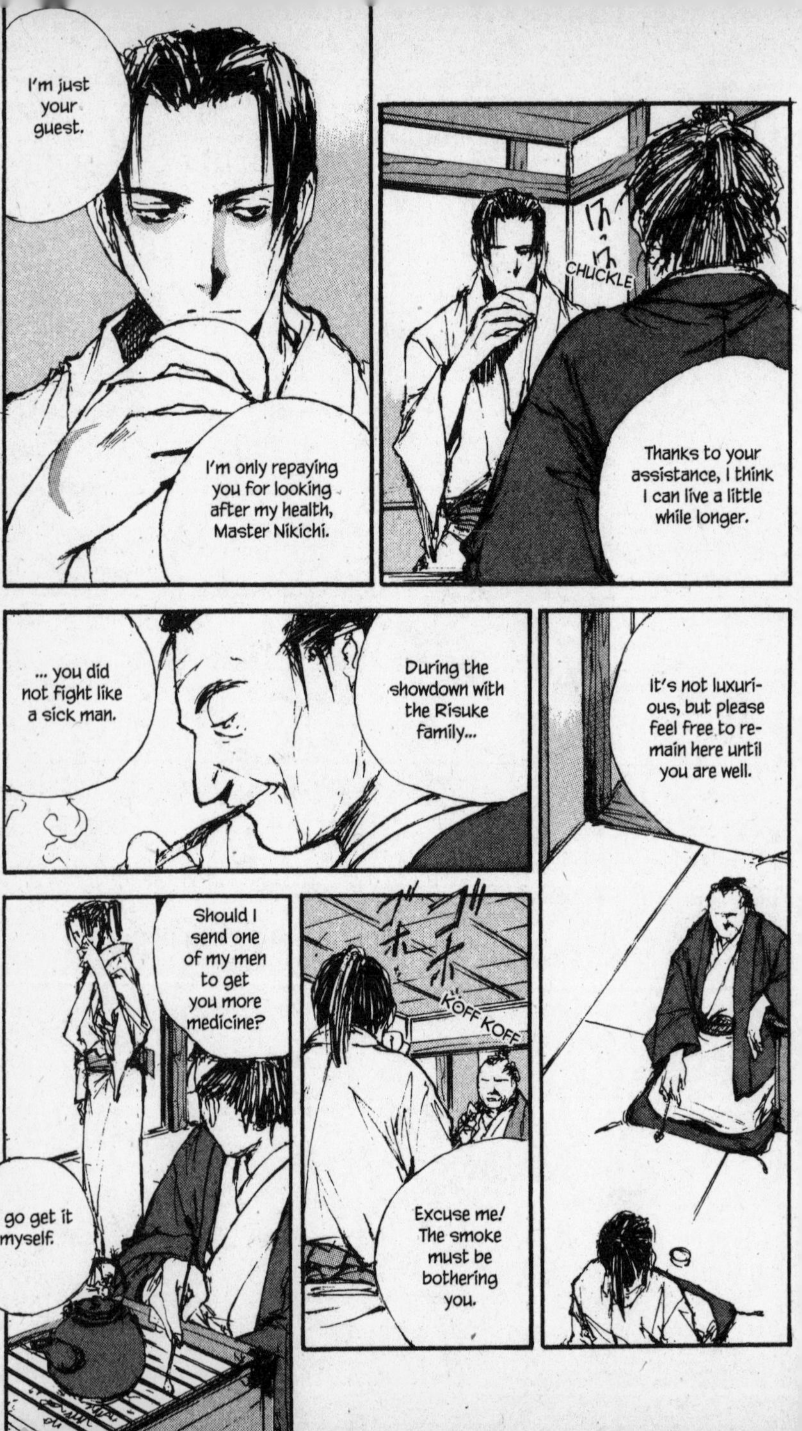
CHUCKLE
Thanks to your assistance, I think I can live a little while longer.
I'm just your guest.
I'm only repaying you for looking after my health, Master Nikichi.
It's not luxurious, but please feel free to remain here until you are well.
During the showdown with the Risuke family...
... you did not fight like a sick man.
KOFF KOFF
Excuse me! The smoke must be bothering you.
Should I send one of my men to get you more medicine?
I'll go get it myself.

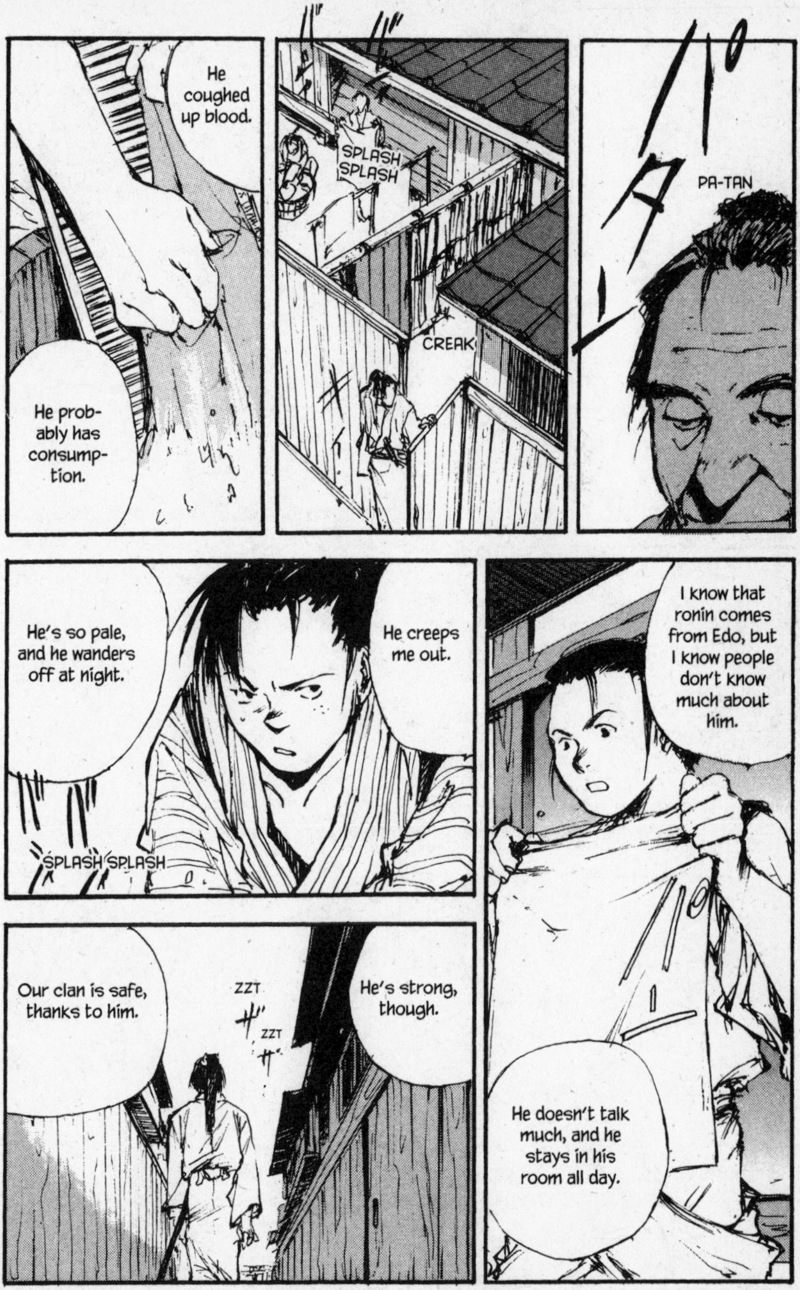
PA-TAN
SPLASH SPLASH
CREAK
He coughed up blood.
He probably has consumption.
I know that ronin comes from Edo, but I know people don't know much about him.
He doesn't talk much, and he stays in his room all day.
He creeps me out.
He's so pale, and he wanders off at night.
SPLASH SPLASH
He's strong, though.
ZZT
ZZT
Our clan is safe, thanks to him.

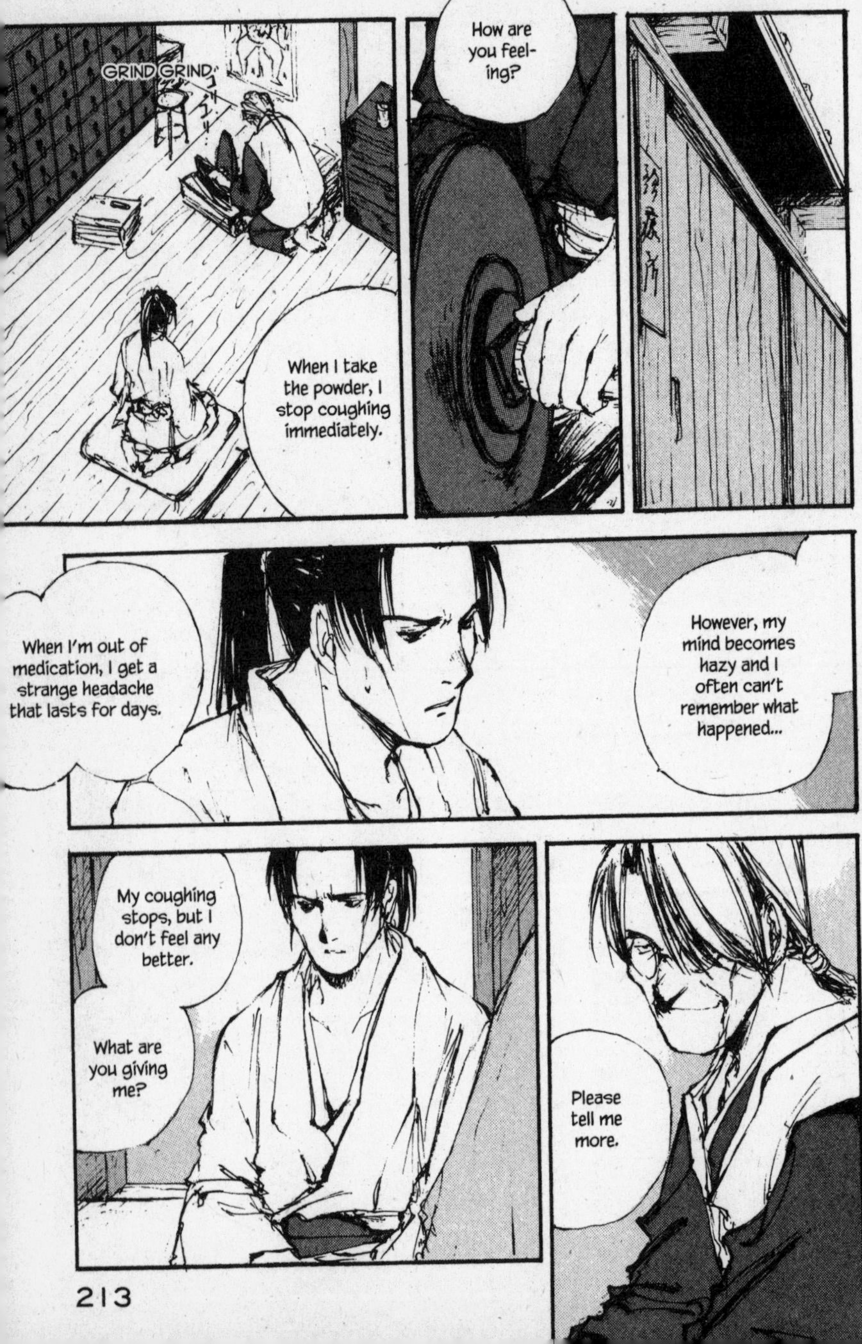
How are you feel-ing?
GRIND GRIND
When I take the powder, I stop coughing immediately.
However, my mind becomes hazy and I often can't remember what happened...
When I'm out of medication, I get a strange headache that lasts for days.
Please tell me more.
My coughing stops, but I don't feel any better.
What are you giving me?

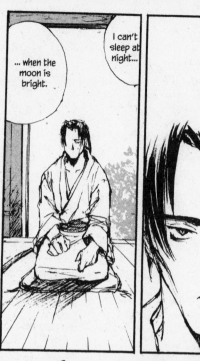

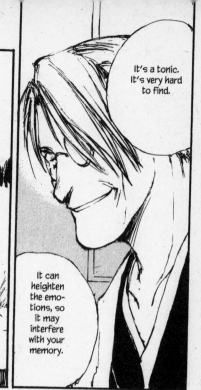

It's a tonic. It's very hard to find.
It can heighten the emotions, so it may interfere with your memory.
I can't sleep at night...
... when the moon is bright.
GRIND GRIND
Did your patient leave?
Ma-fon!
Call me Mako.
A shipment arrived from Nagasaki.

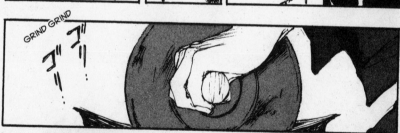

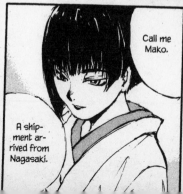

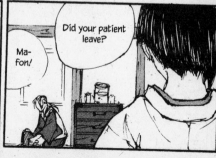

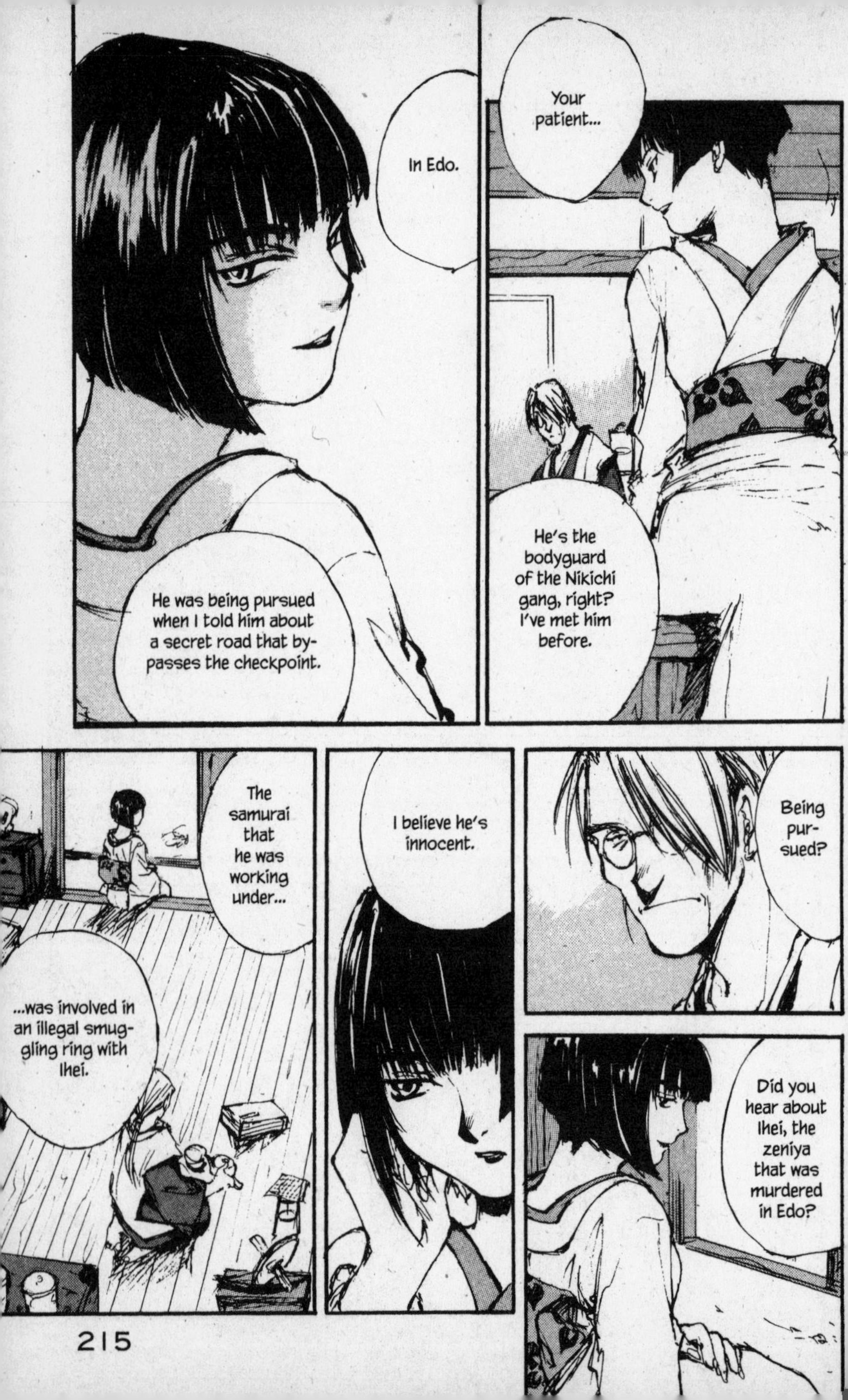
Your patient...
He's the bodyguard of the Nikichi gang, right? I've met him before.
In Edo.
He was being pursued when I told him about a secret road that by-passes the checkpoint.
Being pur-sued?
Did you hear about Ihei, the zeniya that was murdered in Edo?
I believe he's innocent.
The samurai that he was working under...
...was involved in an illegal smug-gling ring with Ihei.

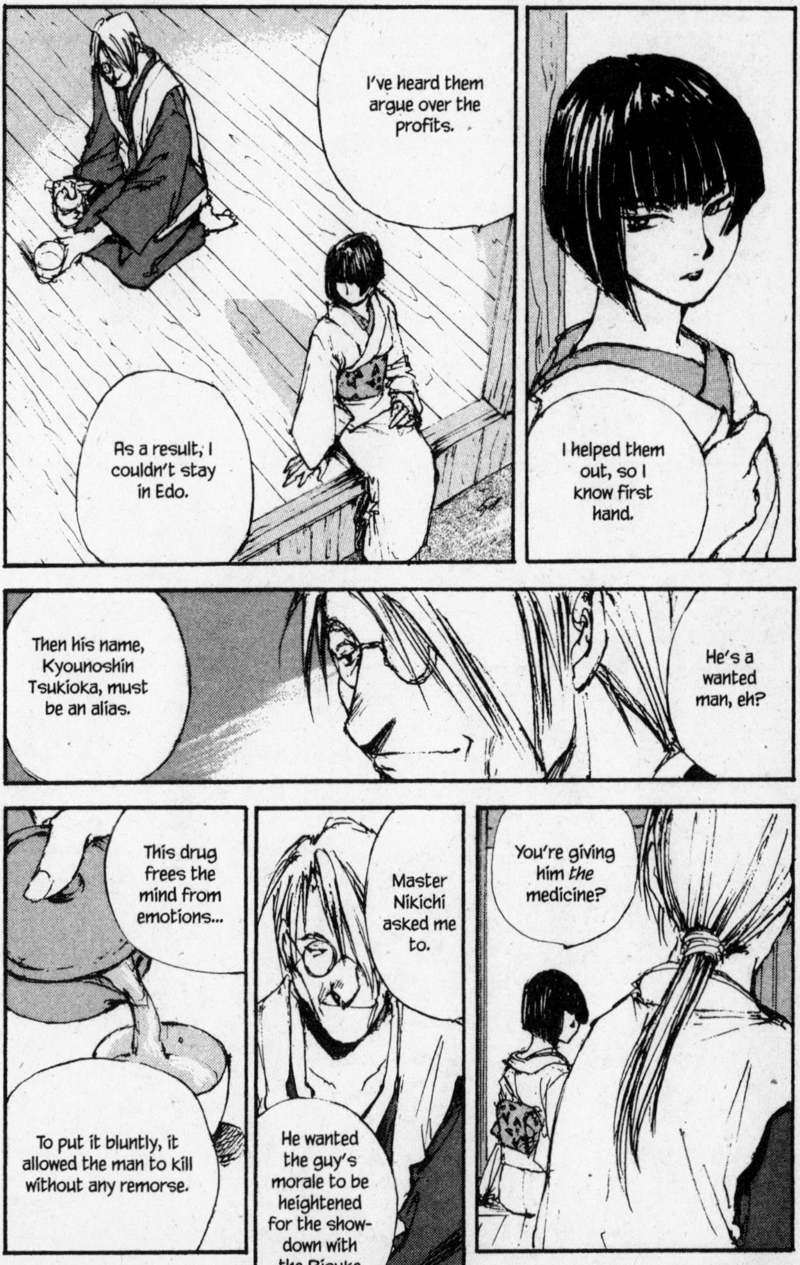
I helped them out, so I know first hand.
I've heard them argue over the profits.
As a result, I couldn't stay in Edo.
He's a wanted man, eh?
Then his name, Kyounoshin Tsukioka, must be an alias.
You're giving him *the* medicine?
Master Nikichi asked me to.
He wanted the guy's morale to be heightened for the show-down with the Risuke Family.
This drug frees the mind from emotions...
To put it bluntly, it allowed the man to kill without any remorse.

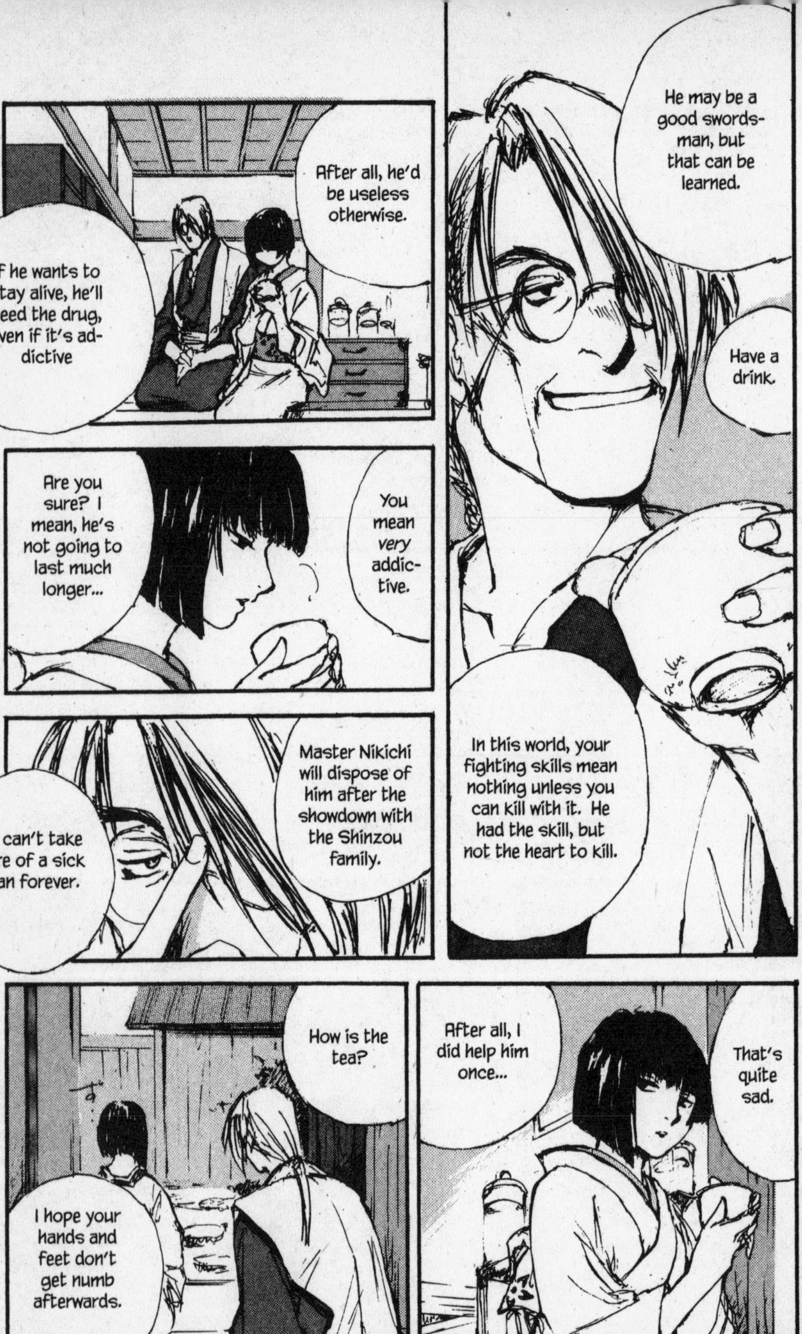
He may be a good swords-man, but that can be learned.
Have a drink.
In this world, your fighting skills mean nothing unless you can kill with it. He had the skill, but not the heart to kill.
After all, he'd be useless otherwise.
If he wants to stay alive, he'll need the drug, even if it's ad-dictive
You mean *very* addic-tive.
Are you sure? I mean, he's not going to last much longer...
Master Nikichi will dispose of him after the showdown with the Shinzou family.
He can't take care of a sick man forever.
That's quite sad.
After all, I did help him once...
How is the tea?
I hope your hands and feet don't get numb afterwards.

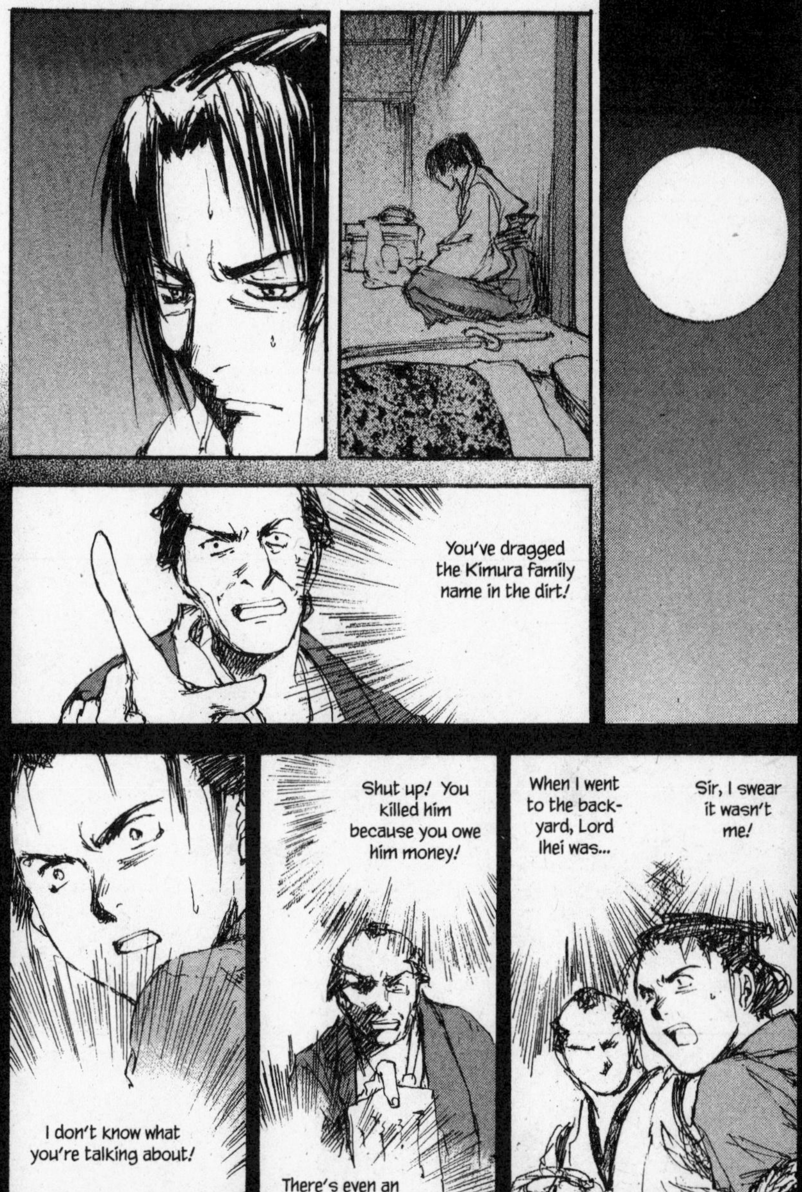
You've dragged the Kimura family name in the dirt!
Sir, I swear it wasn't me!
When I went to the back-yard, Lord Ihei was...
Shut up! You killed him because you owe him money!
There's even an IOU!
I don't know what you're talking about!

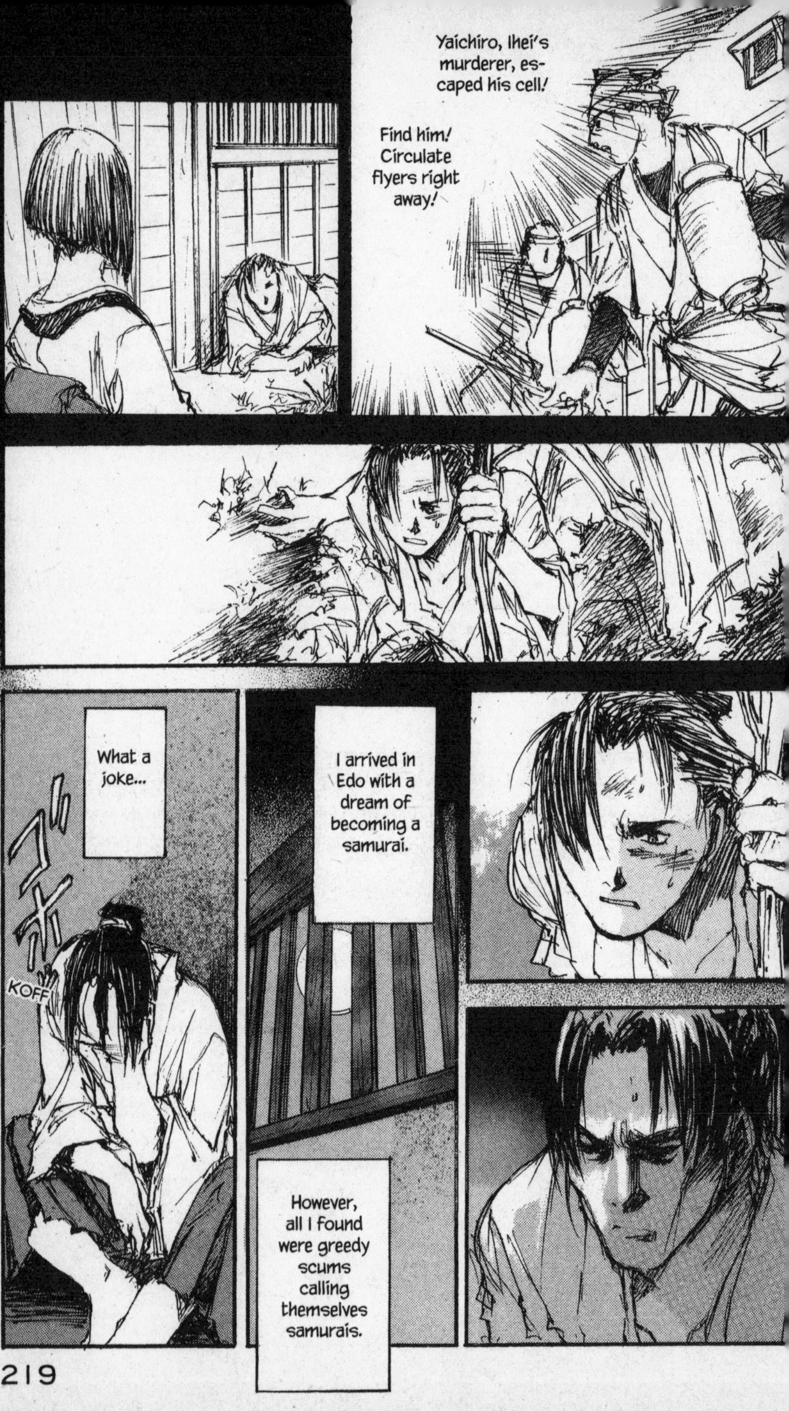

Yaichiro, Ihei's murderer, es-caped his cell!
Find him! Circulate flyers right away!
I arrived in Edo with a dream of becoming a samurai.
However, all I found were greedy scums calling themselves samurais.
What a joke...
KOFF

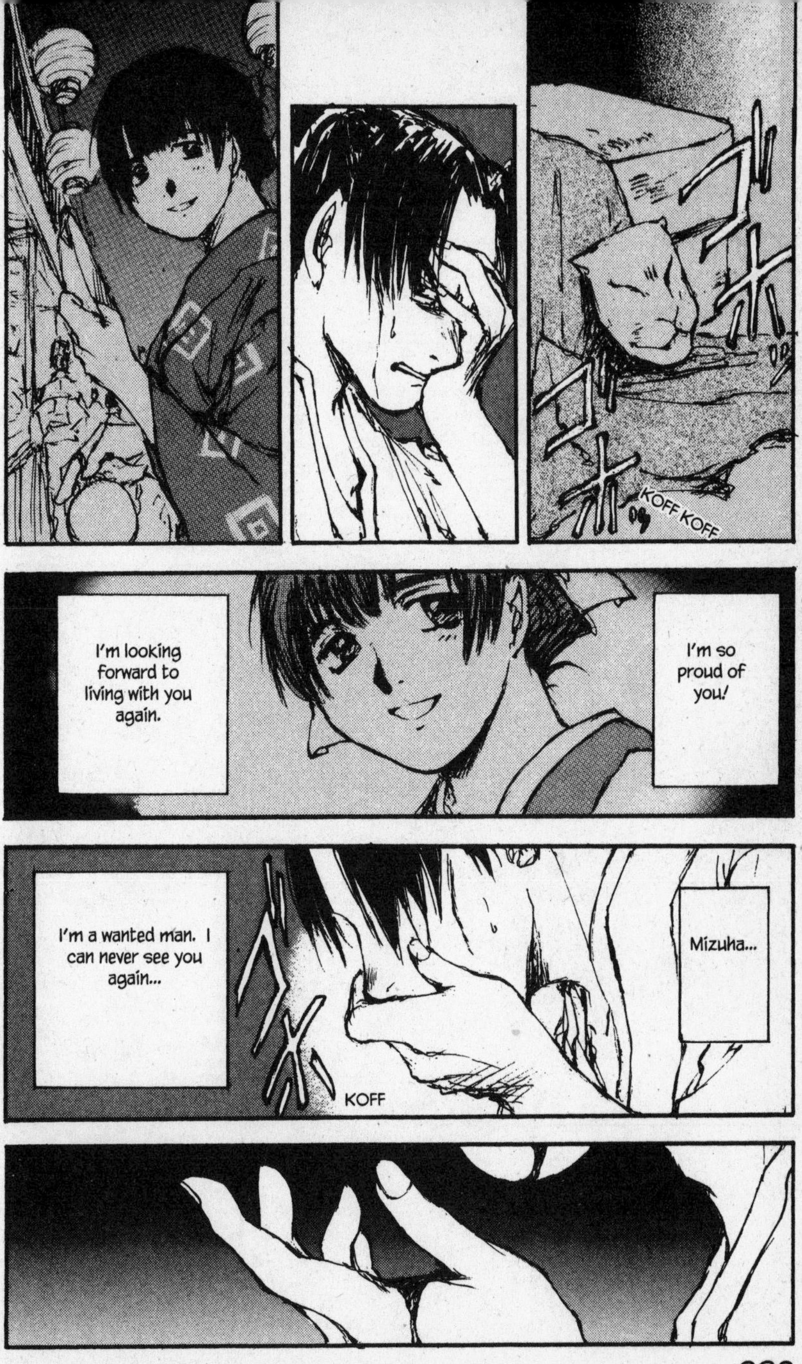
KOFF KOFF
I'm so proud of you!
I'm looking forward to living with you again.
Mizuha...
I'm a wanted man. I can never see you again...
KOFF

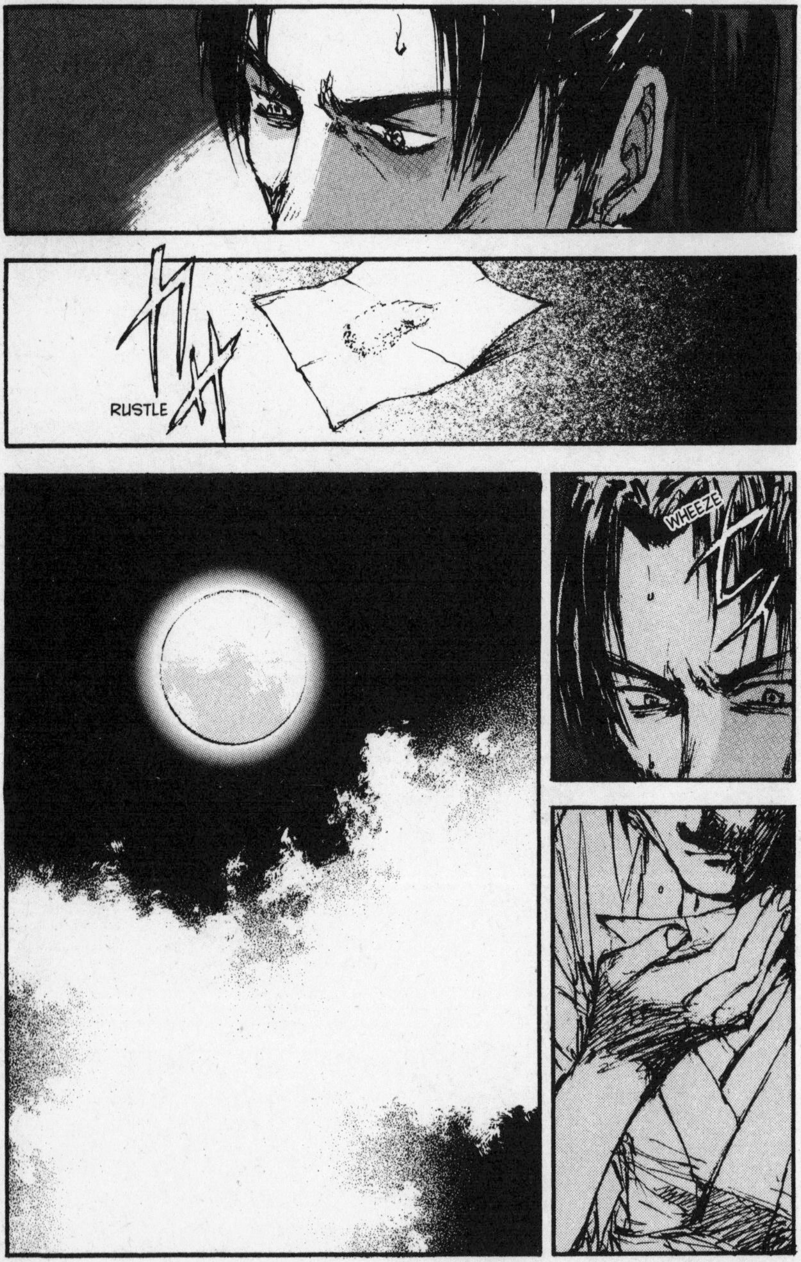
RUSTLE
WHEEZE

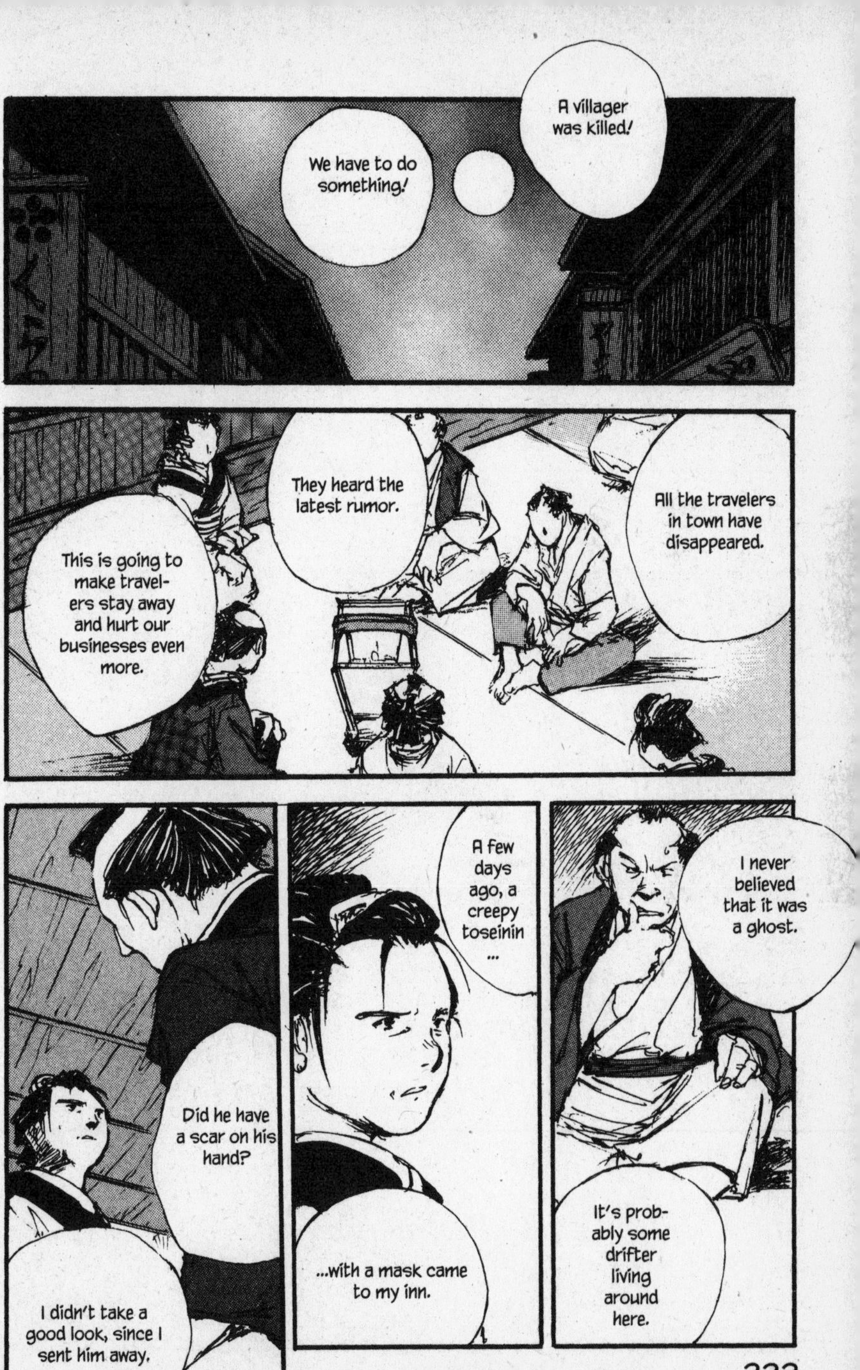
A villager was killed!
We have to do something!
All the travelers in town have disappeared.
They heard the latest rumor.
This is going to make travelers stay away and hurt our businesses even more.
I never believed that it was a ghost.
It's probably some drifter living around here.
A few days ago, a creepy toseinin ...
...with a mask came to my inn.
Did he have a scar on his hand?
I didn't take a good look, since I sent him away.

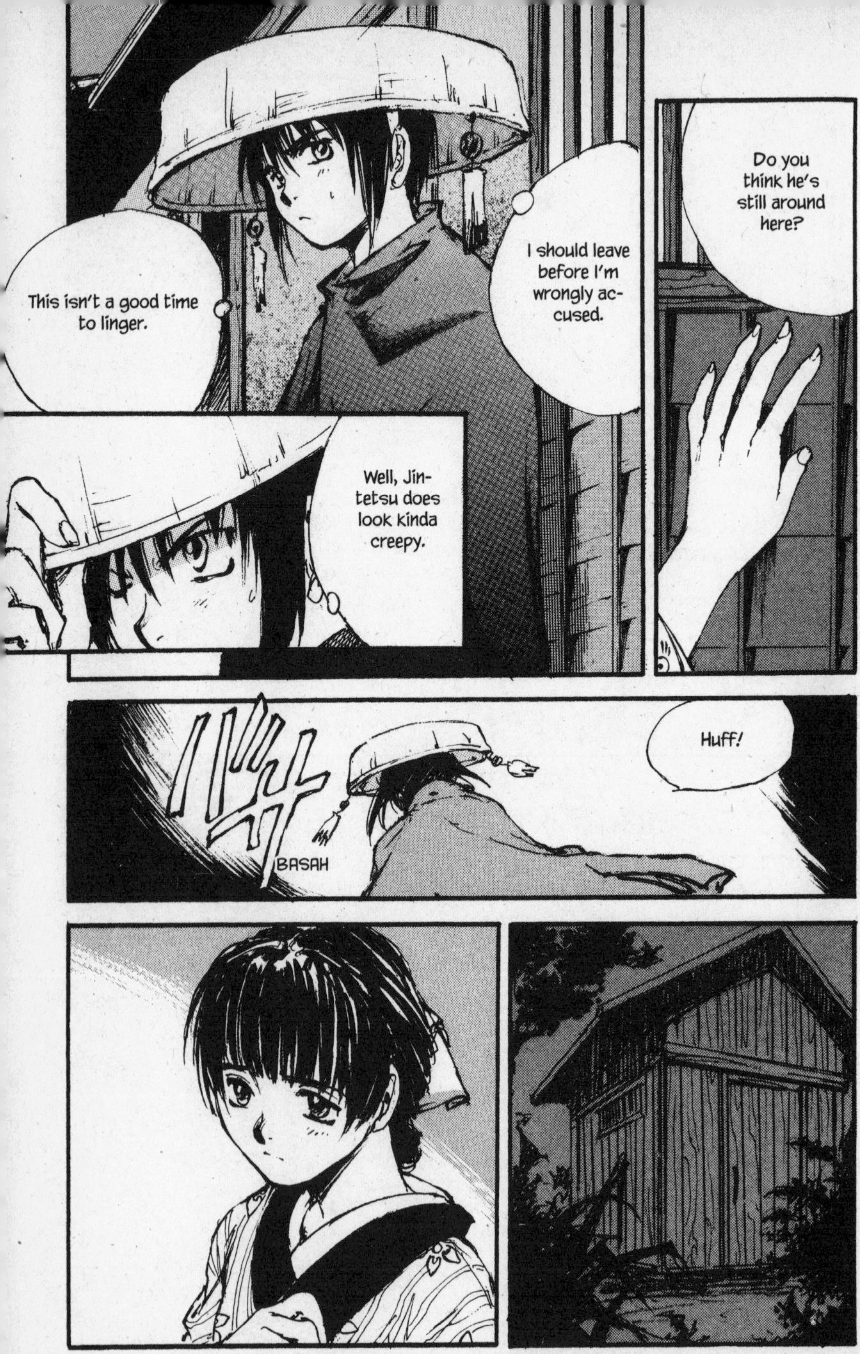
Do you think he's still around here?
I should leave before I'm wrongly ac-cused.
This isn't a good time to linger.
Well, Jin-tetsu does look kinda creepy.
Huff!
BASAH

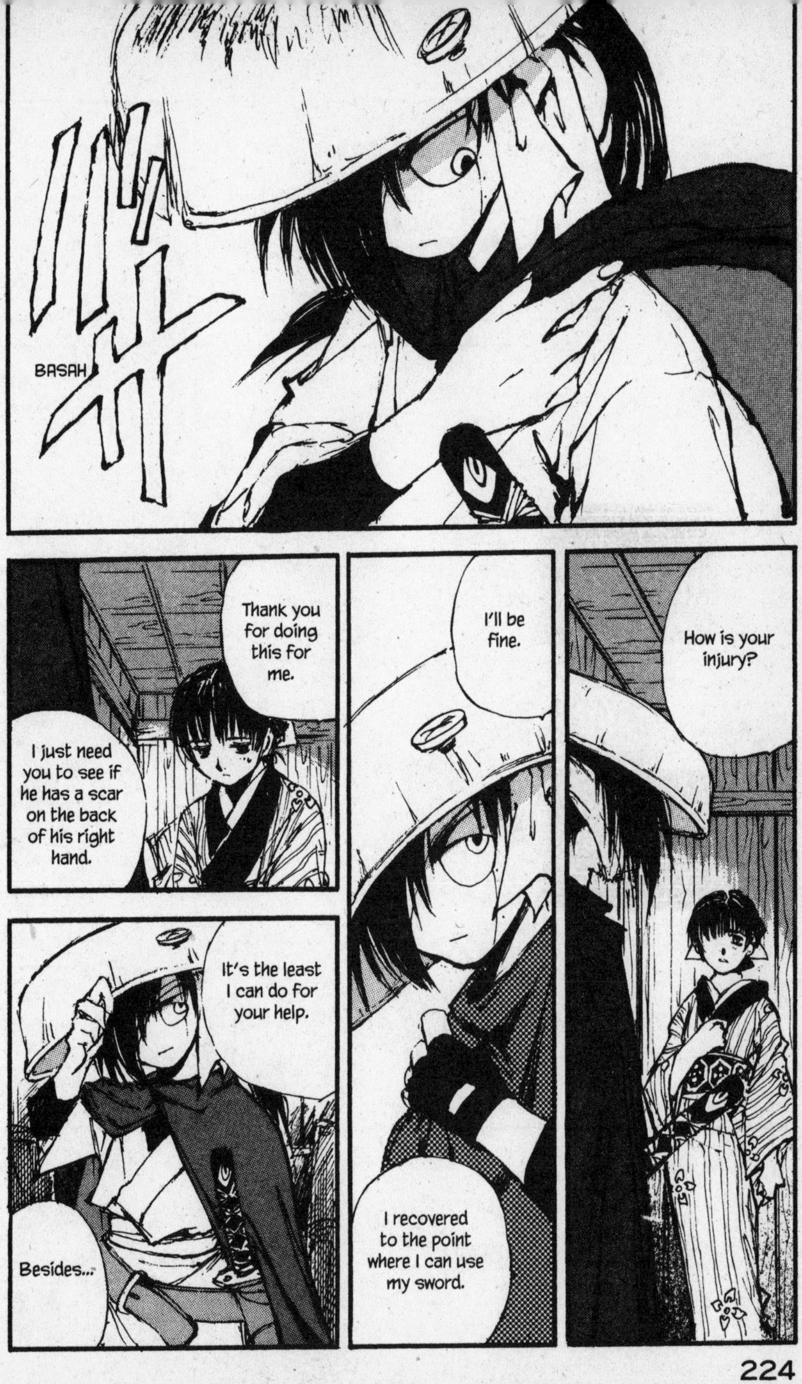
BASAH
How is your injury?
I'll be fine.
I recovered to the point where I can use my sword.
Thank you for doing this for me.
I just need you to see if he has a scar on the back of his right hand.
It's the least I can do for your help.
Besides...

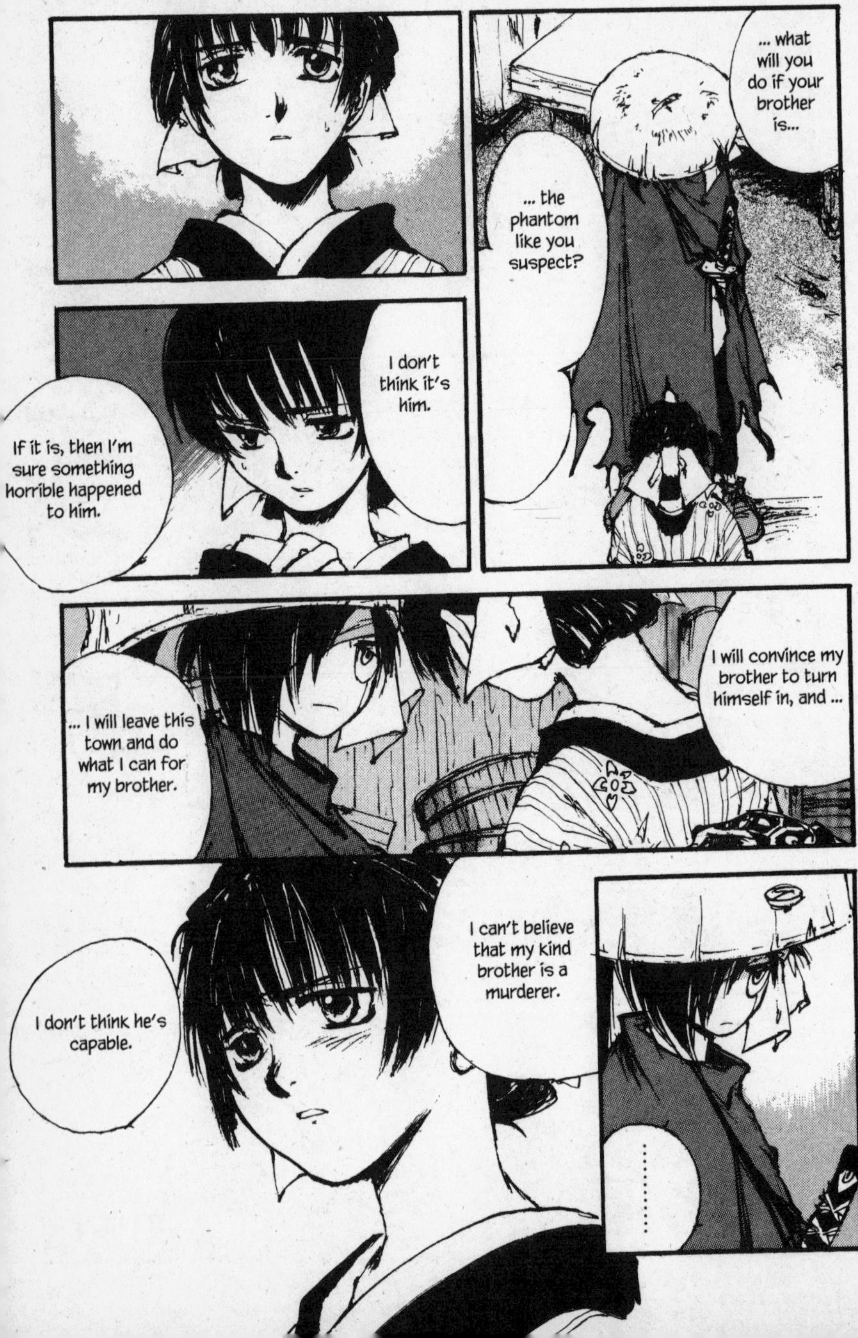
... what will you do if your brother is...
... the phantom like you suspect?
I don't think it's him.
If it is, then I'm sure something horrible happened to him.
I will convince my brother to turn himself in, and ...
... I will leave this town and do what I can for my brother.
......
I can't believe that my kind brother is a murderer.
I don't think he's capable.

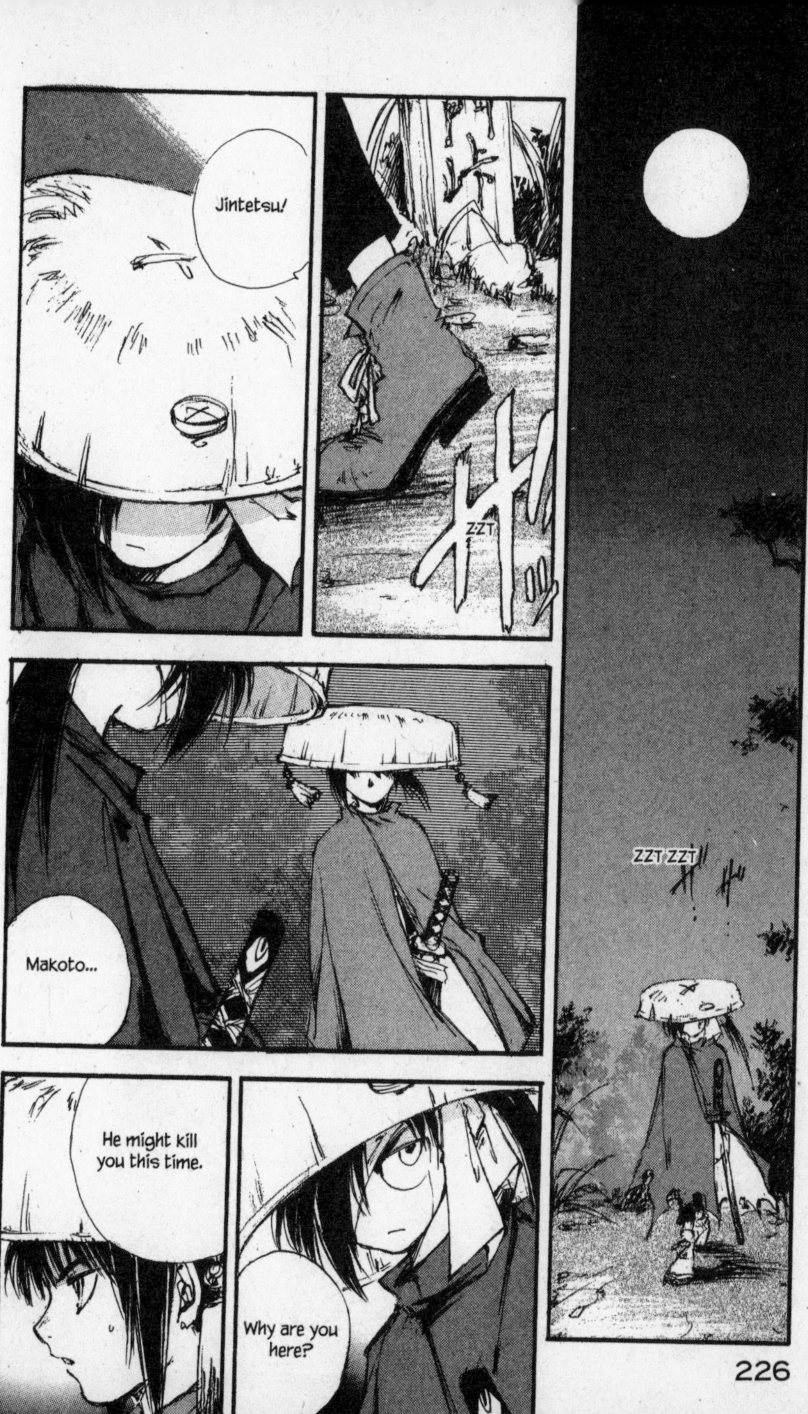
ZZT ZZT
ZZT
Jintetsu!
Makoto...
Why are you here?
He might kill you this time.

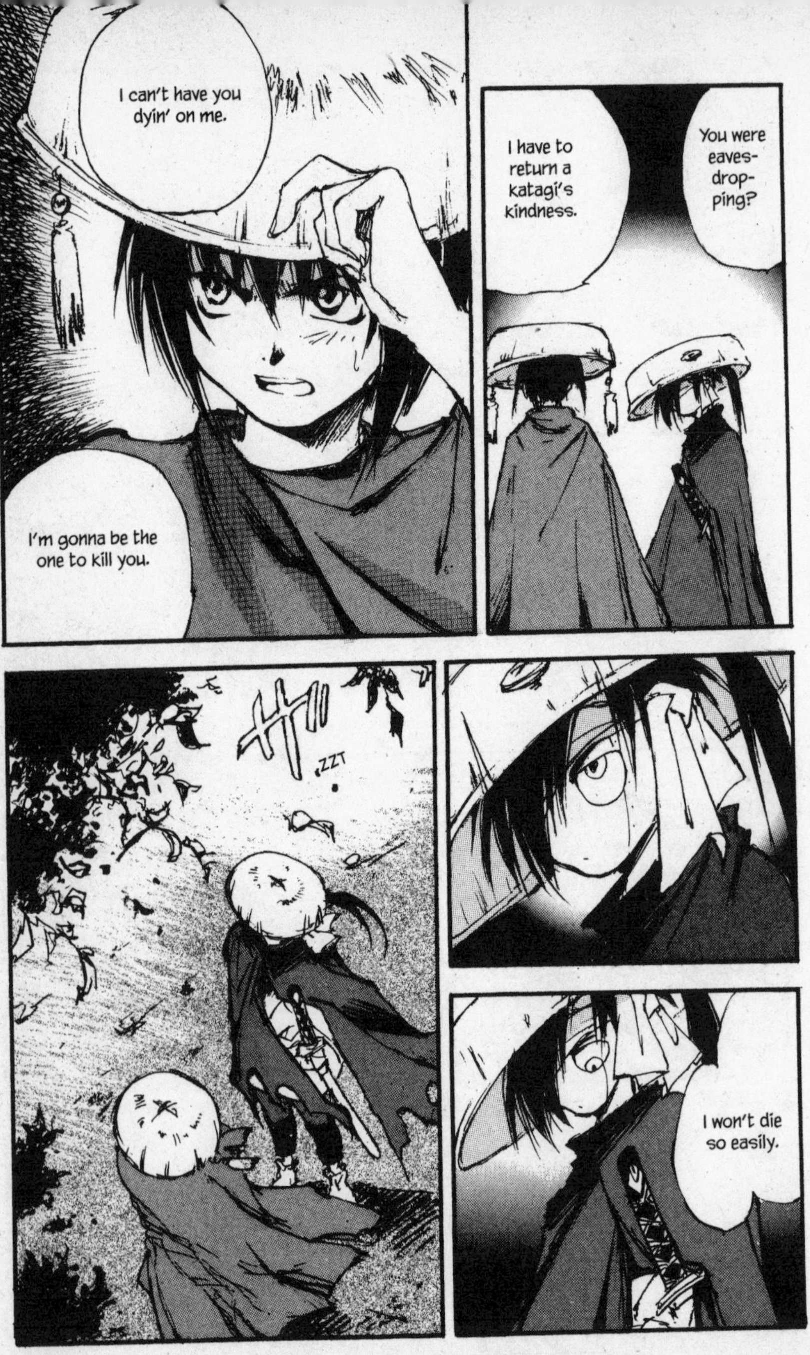
You were eaves-dropping?
I have to return a katagi's kindness.
I can't have you dyin' on me.
I'm gonna be the one to kill you.
I won't die so easily.
ZZT

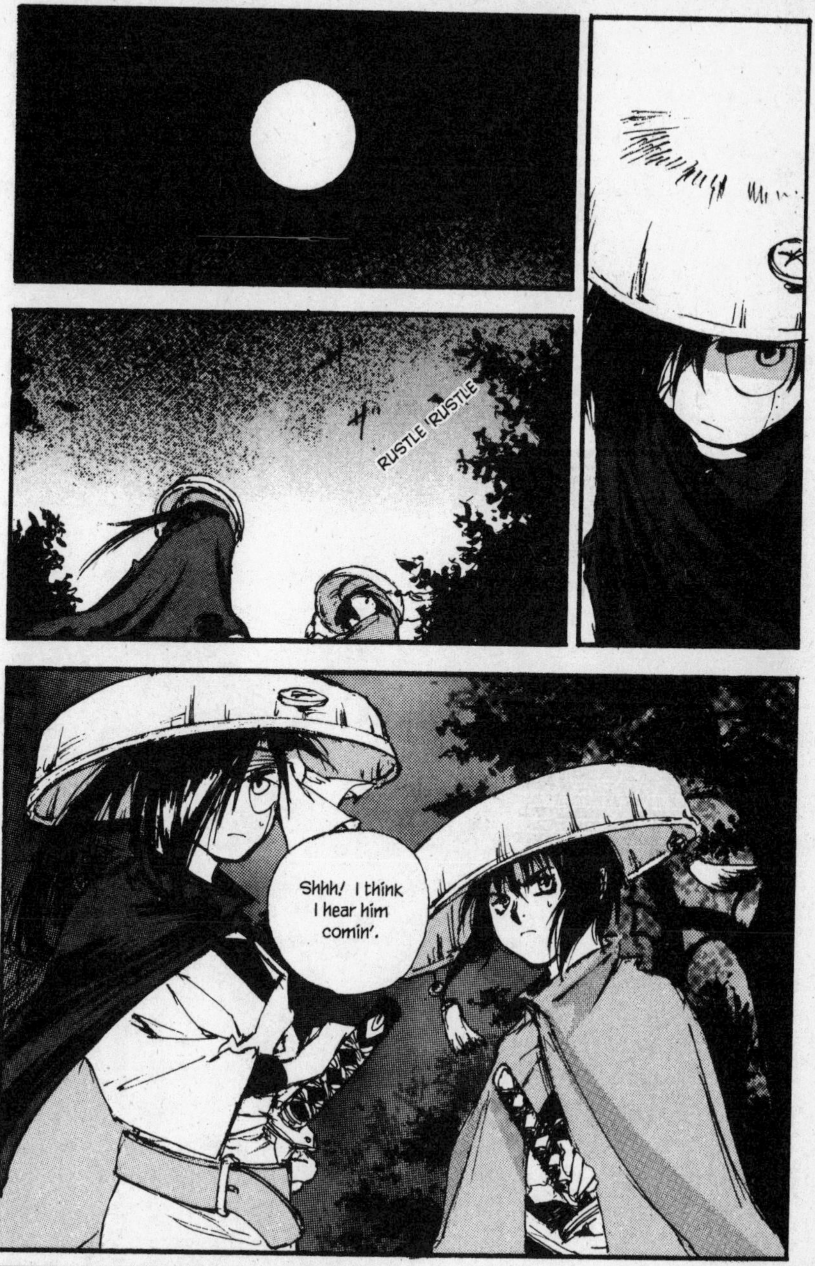
RUSTLE RUSTLE
Shhh! I think I hear him comin'.

THE END OF CHAPTER 9, EPISODE 3

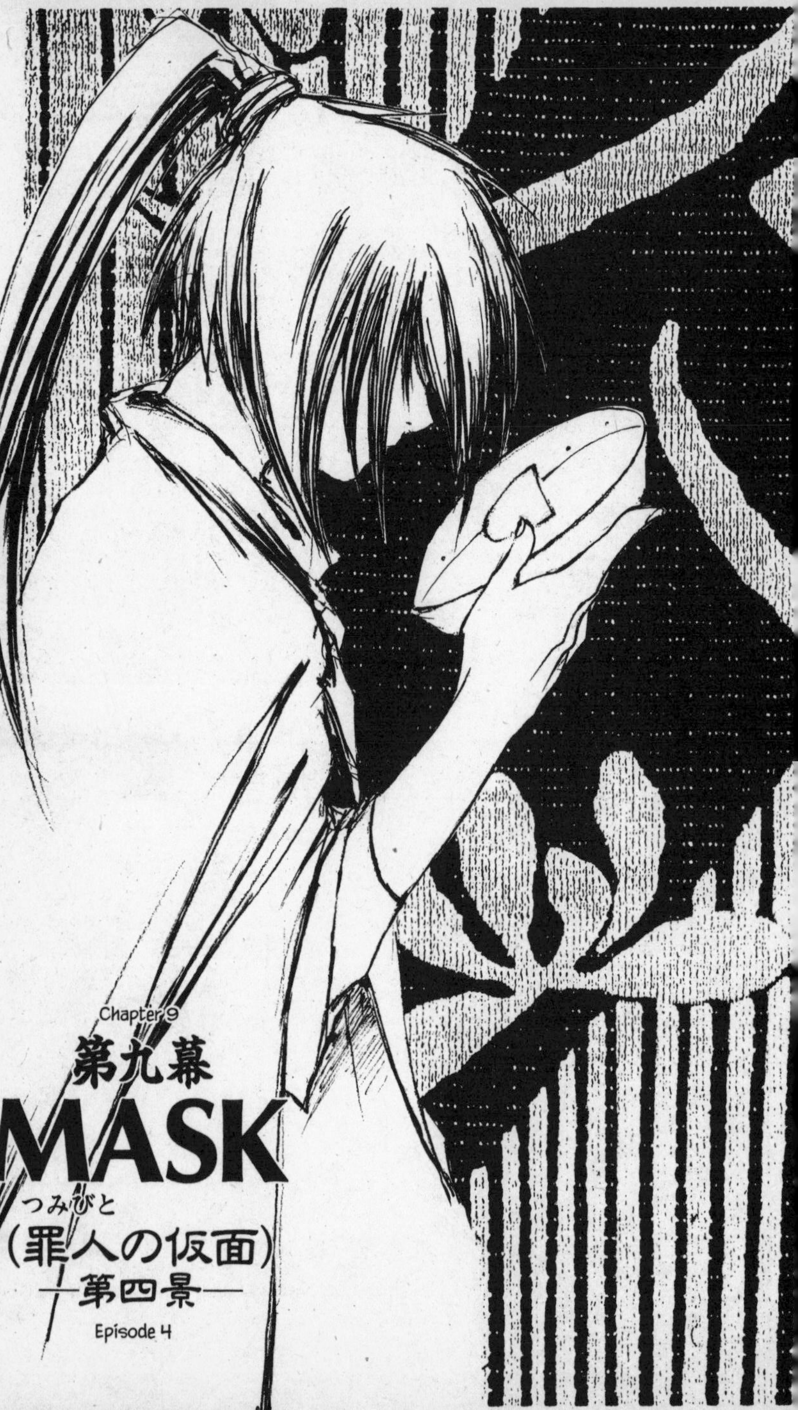
Chapter 9
第九幕
MASK
つみびと
(罪人の仮面)
—第四景—
Episode 4

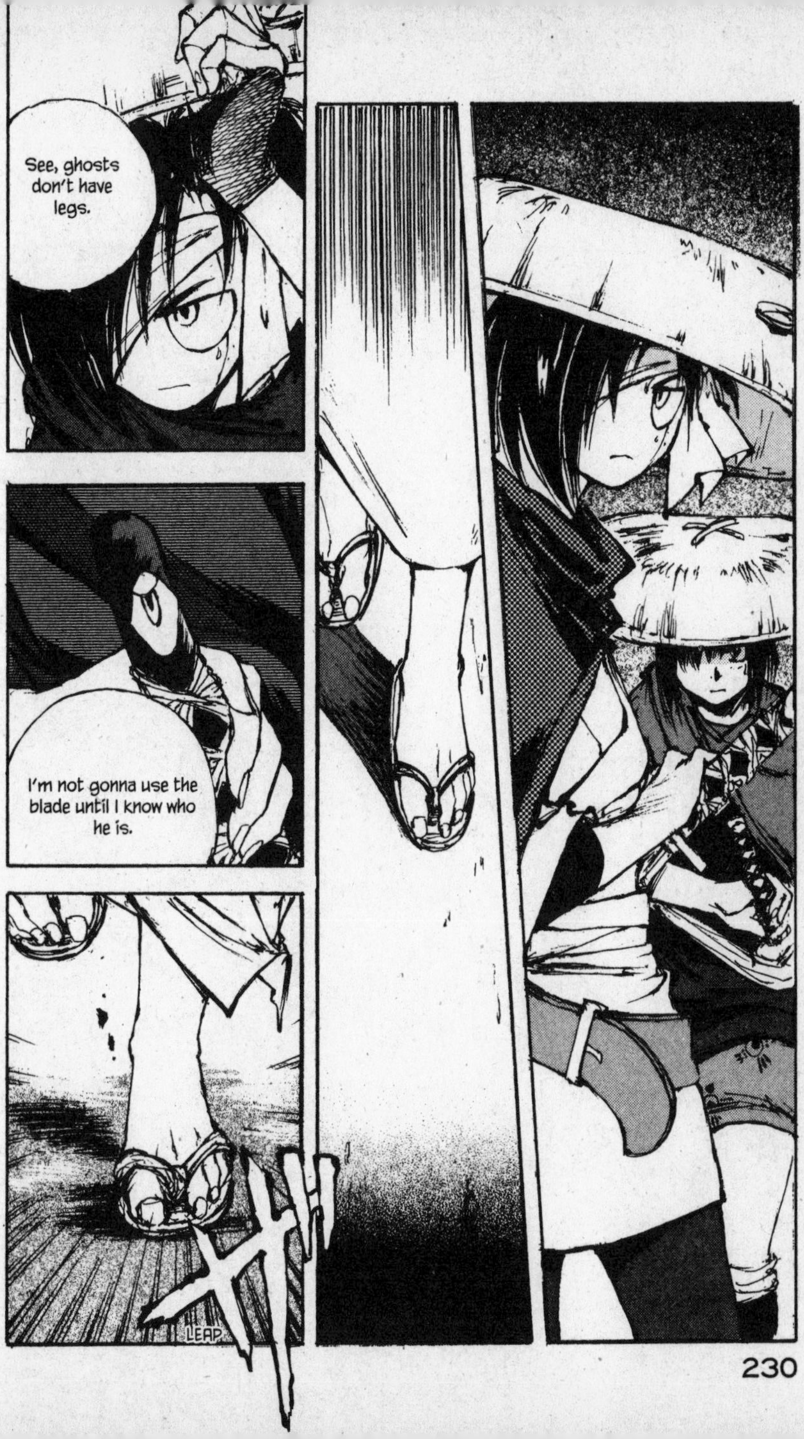
See, ghosts don't have legs.
I'm not gonna use the blade until I know who he is.
LEAP

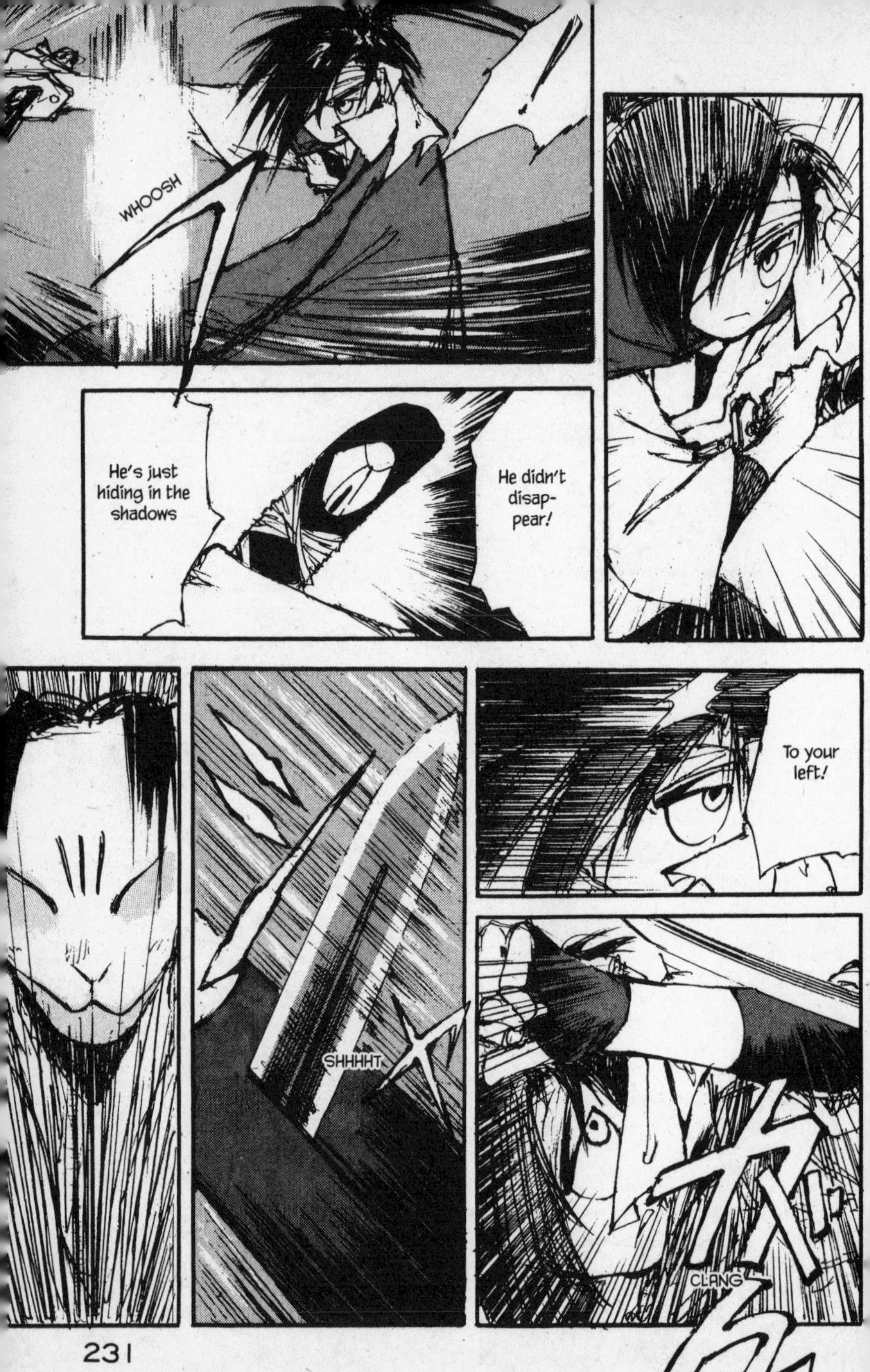
WHOOSH
He didn't disap-pear!
He's just hiding in the shadows
To your left!
CLANG
SHHHHT

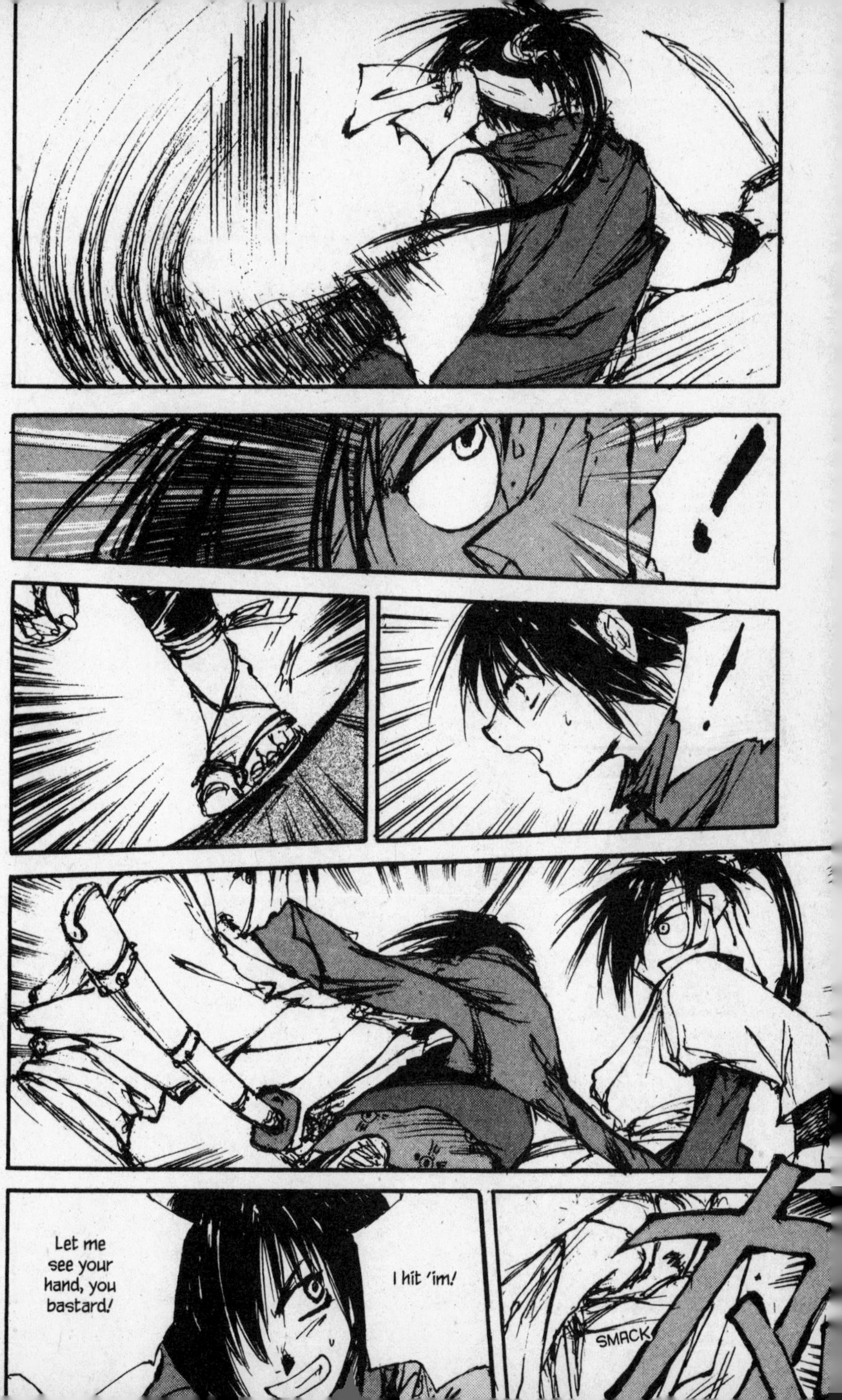
SMACK
I hit 'im!
Let me see your hand, you bastard!

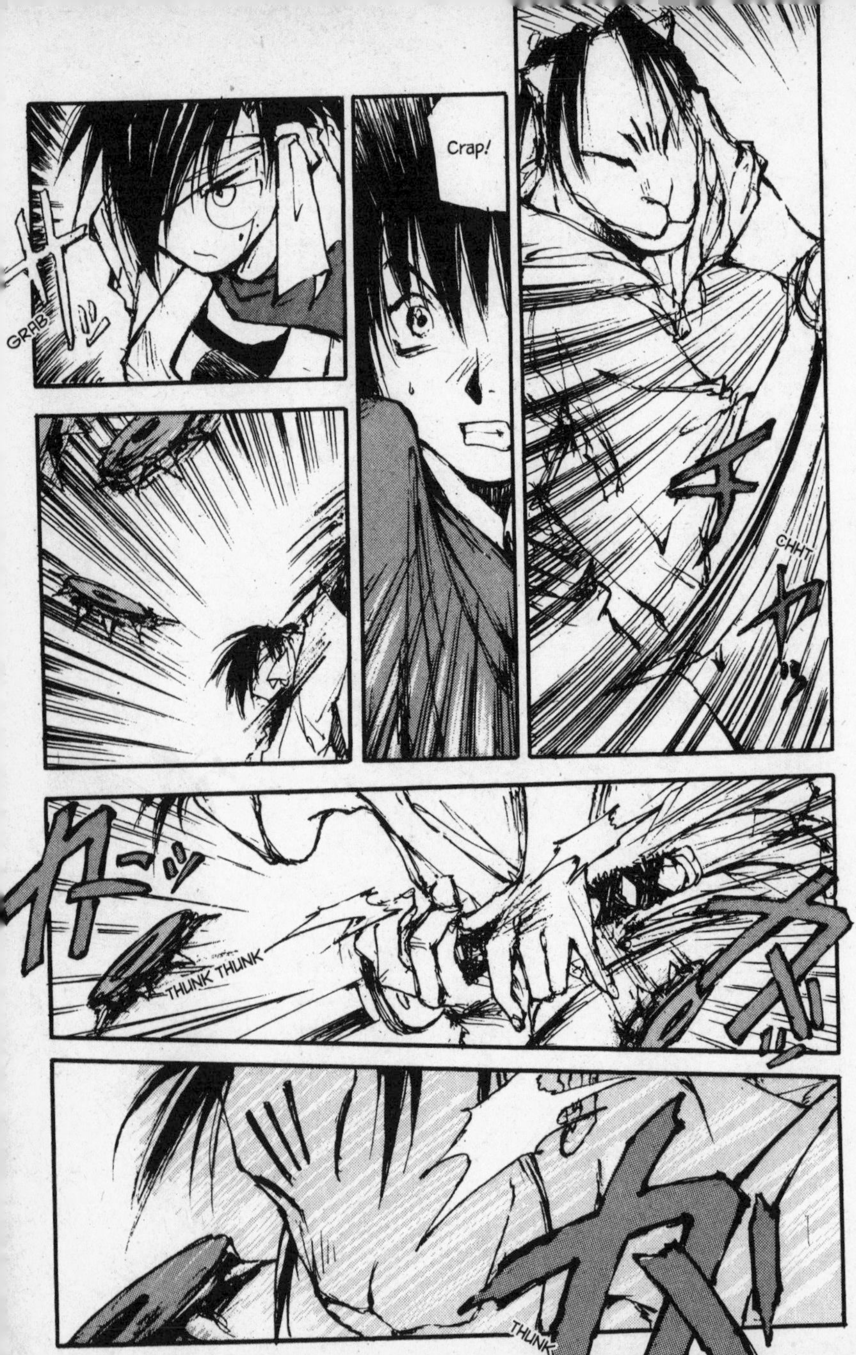
CHHT
Crap!
GRAB
THUNK THUNK
THUNK

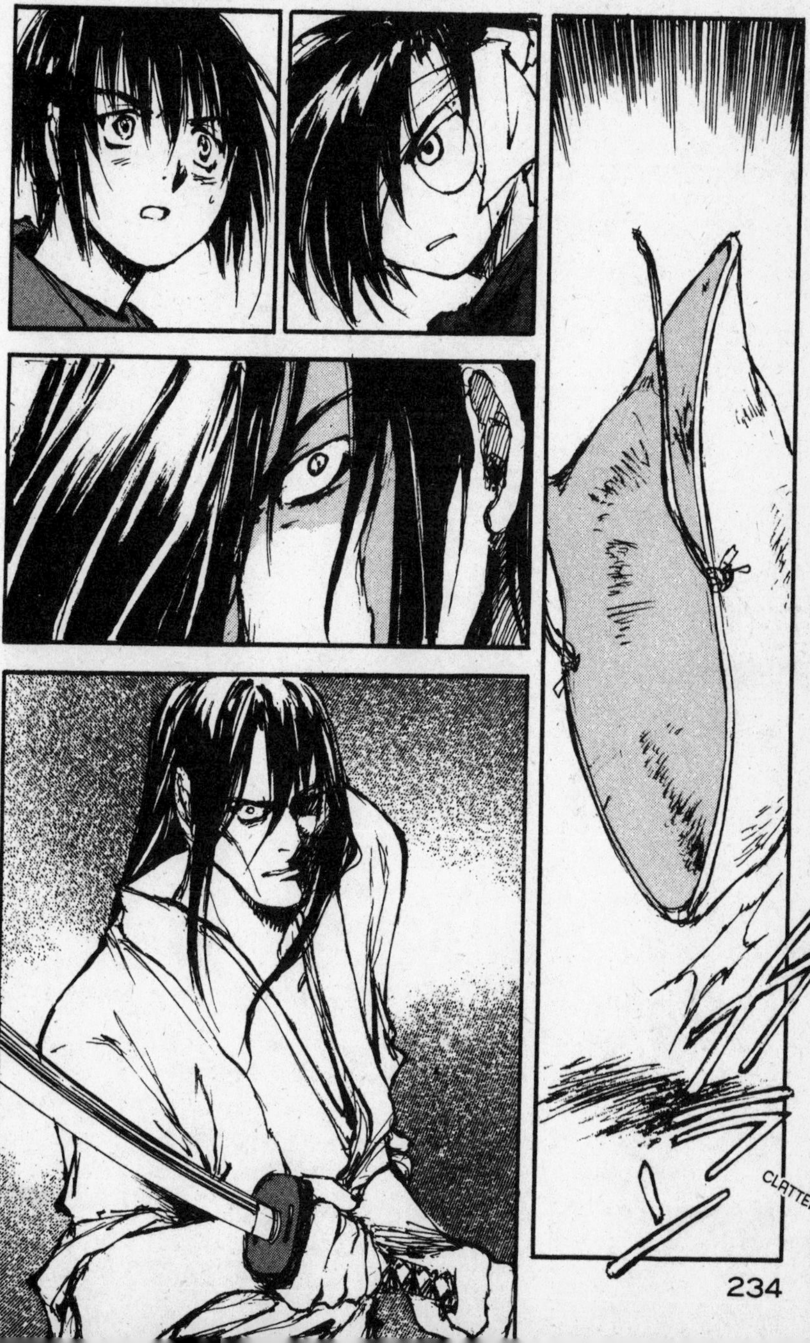
CLATTER

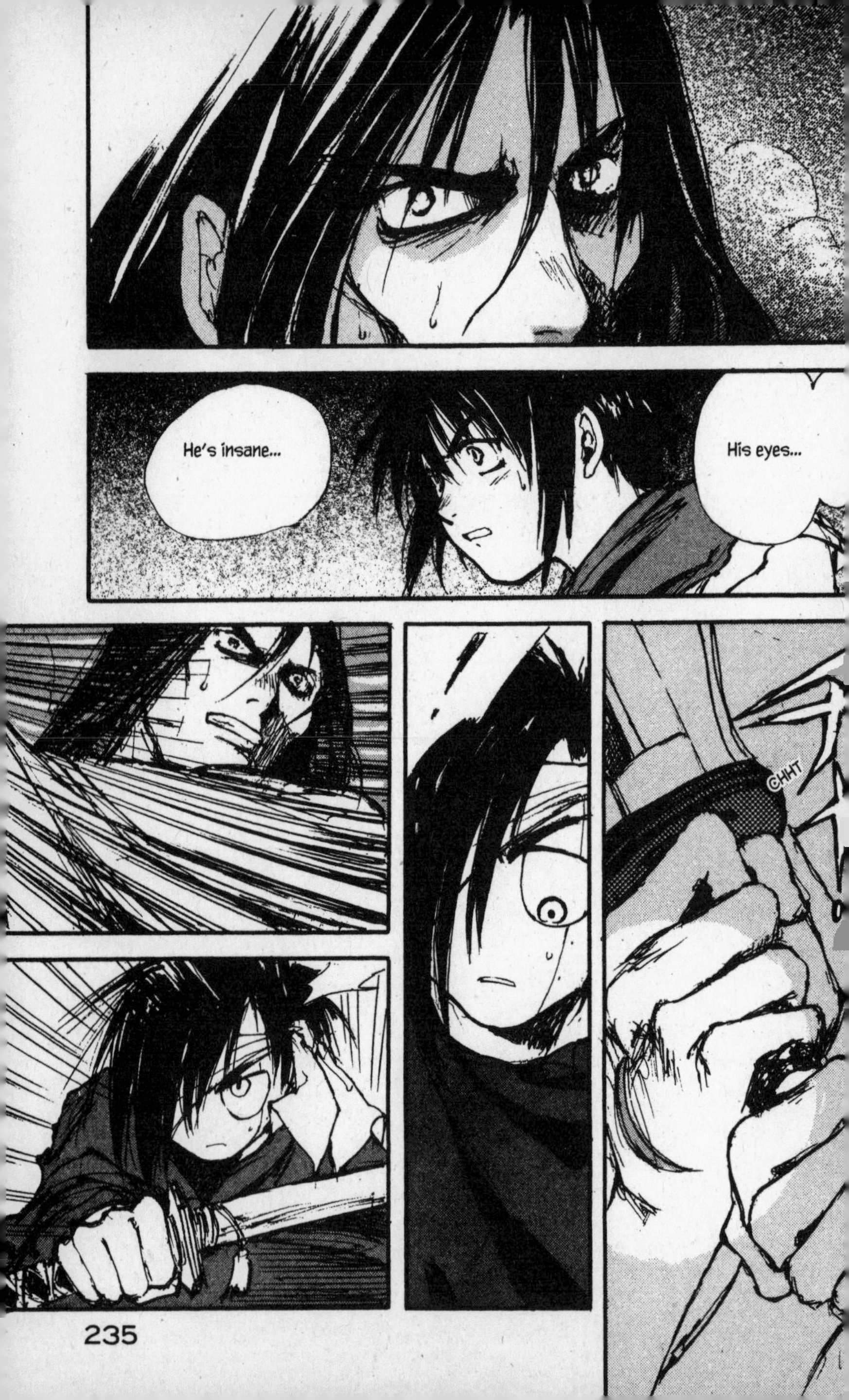
His eyes...
He's insane...
CHHT

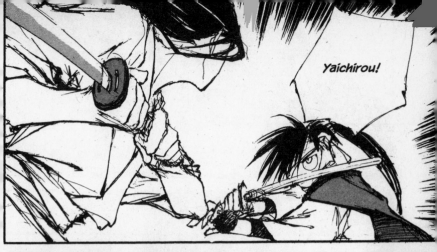

Yaichirou!

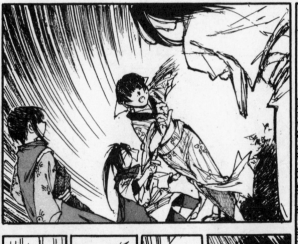

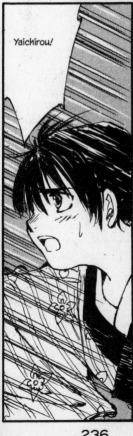

Yaichirou!

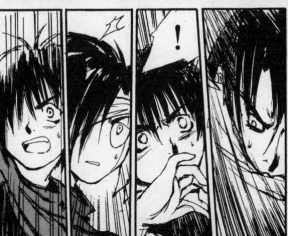

!

236

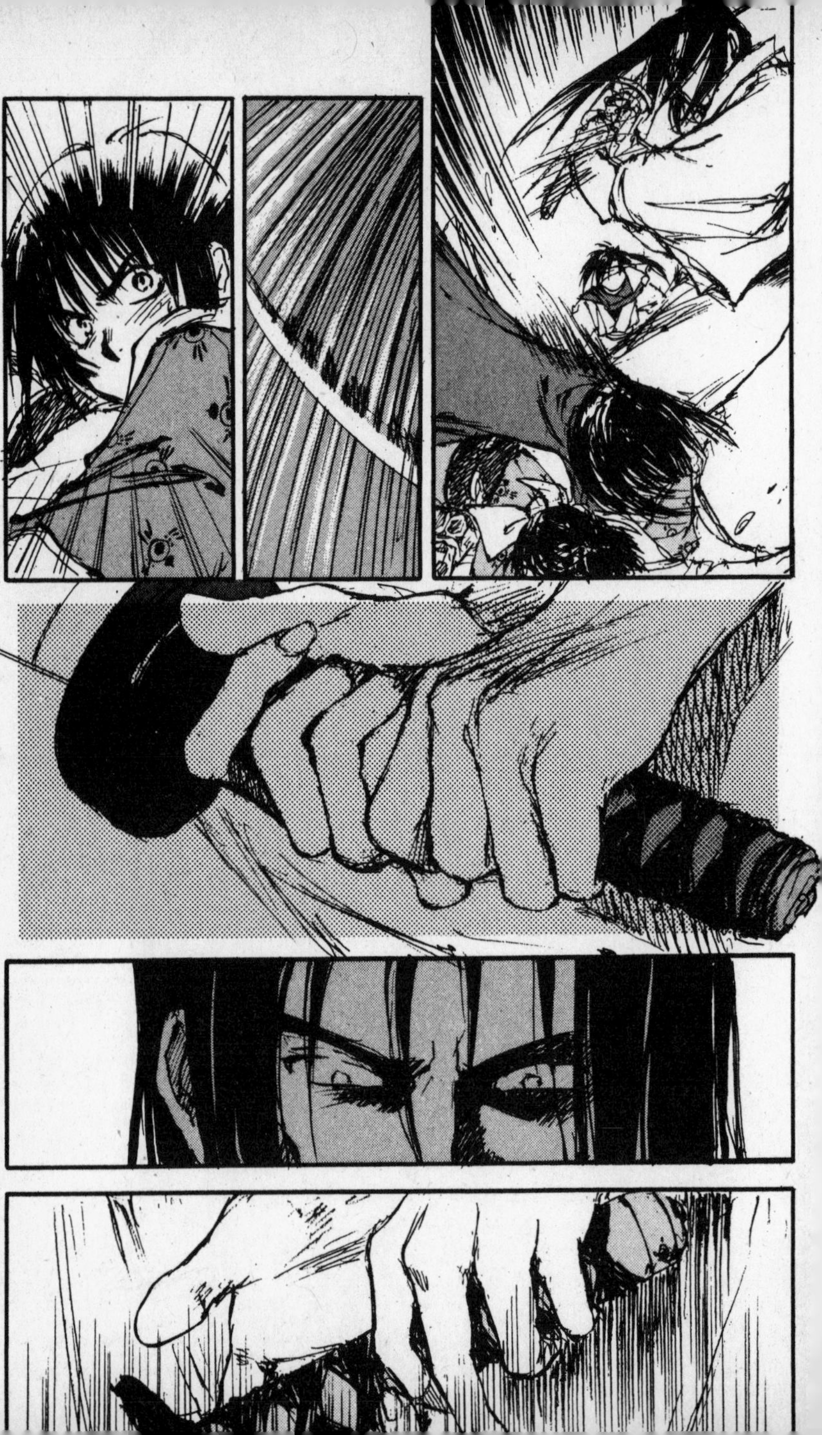

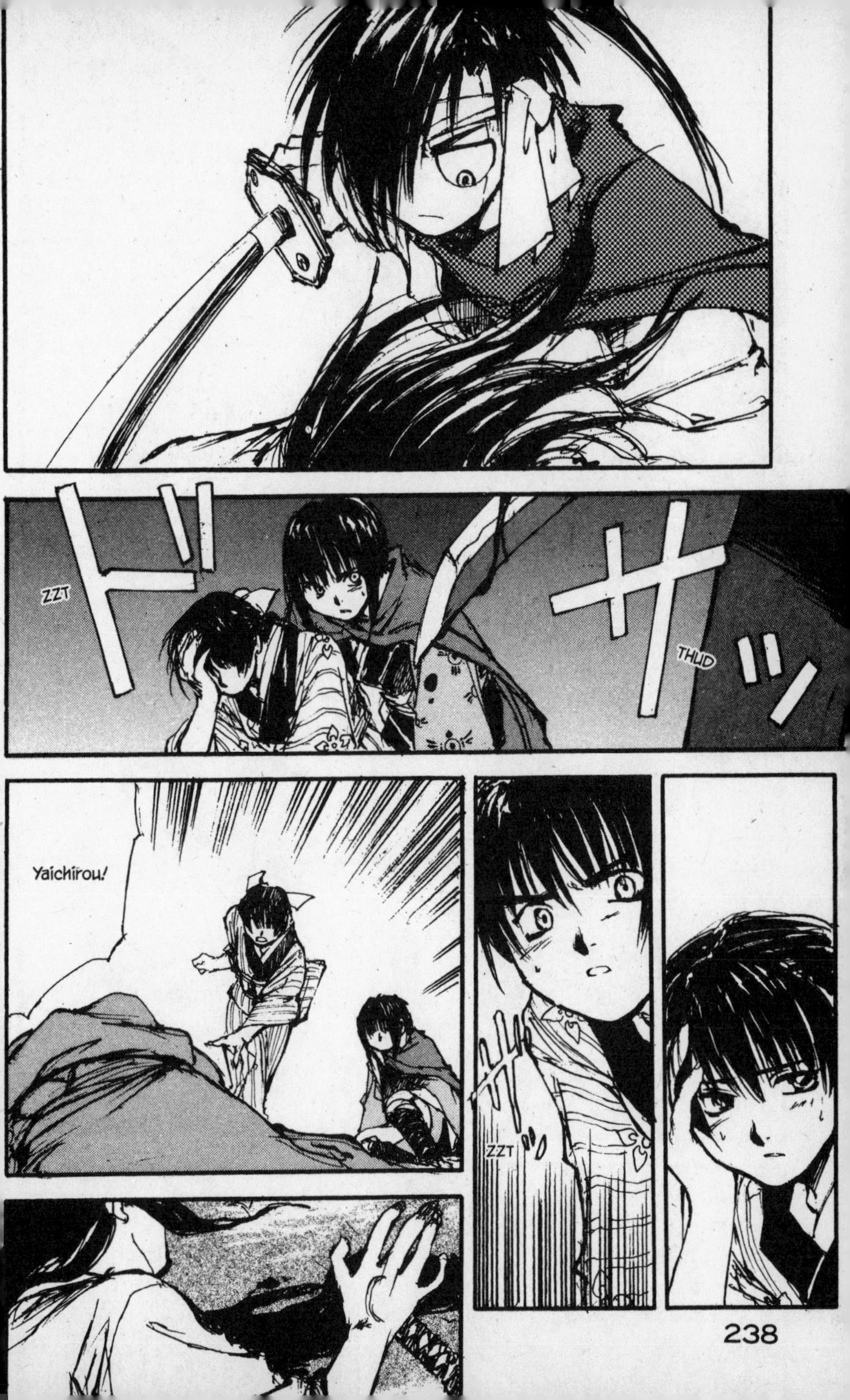
THUD
ZZT
ZZT
Yaichirou!

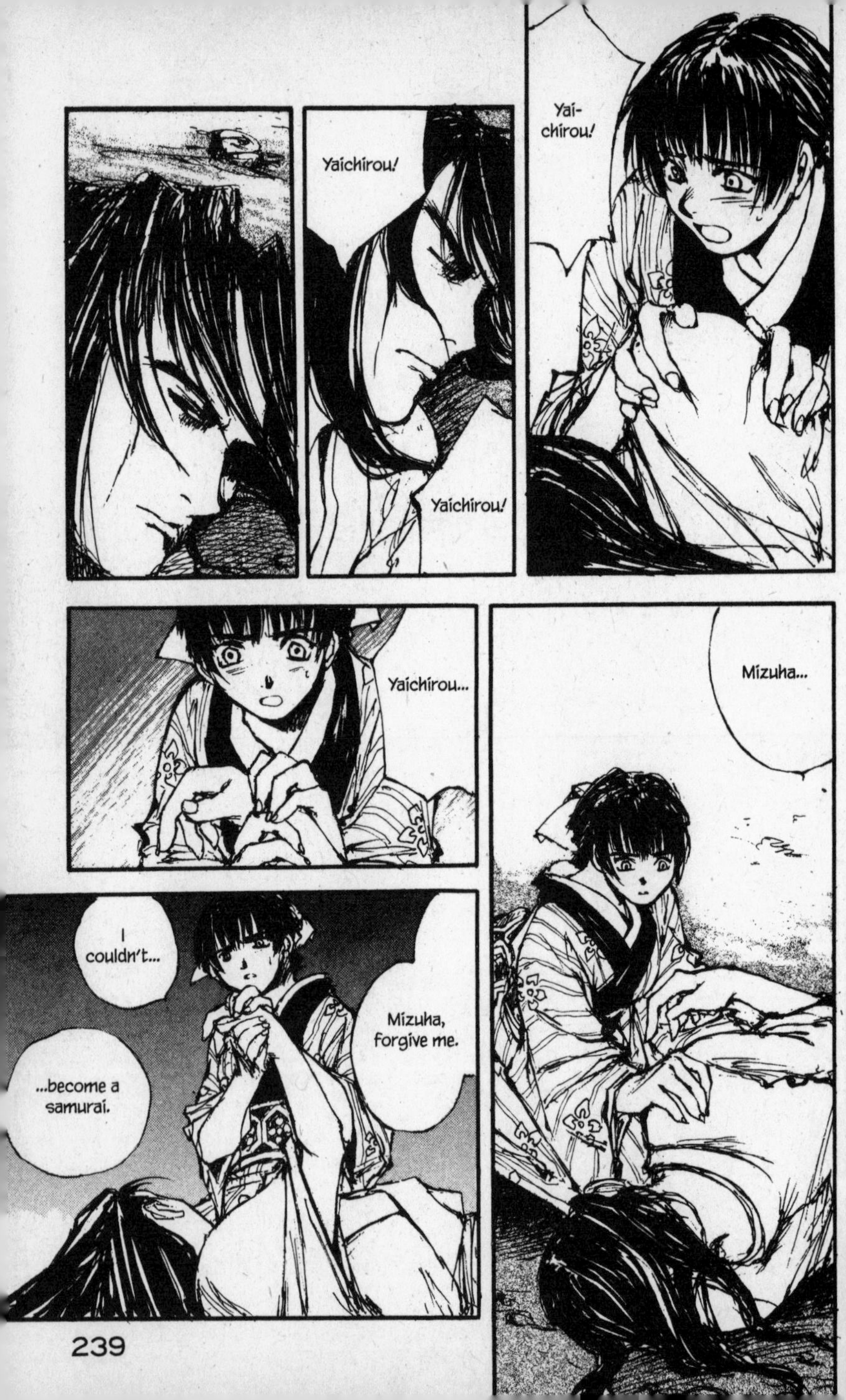
Yai-
chirou!
Yaichirou!
Yaichirou!
Mizuha...
Yaichirou...
Mizuha, forgive me.
I couldn't...
...become a samurai.

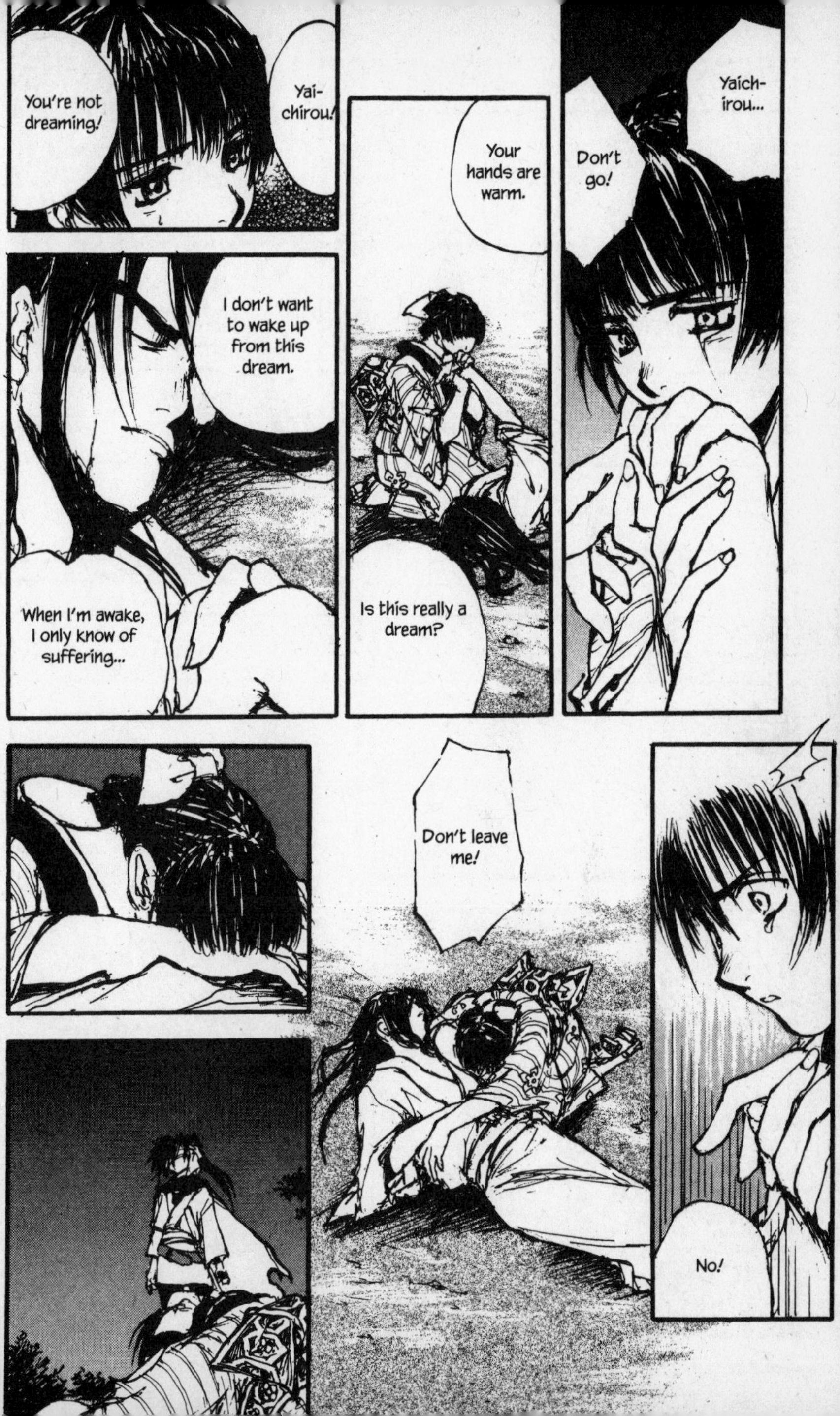
Yaich-irou...
Don't go!
Your hands are warm.
Is this really a dream?
Yai-chirou!
You're not dreaming!
I don't want to wake up from this dream.
When I'm awake, I only know of suffering...
No!
Don't leave me!

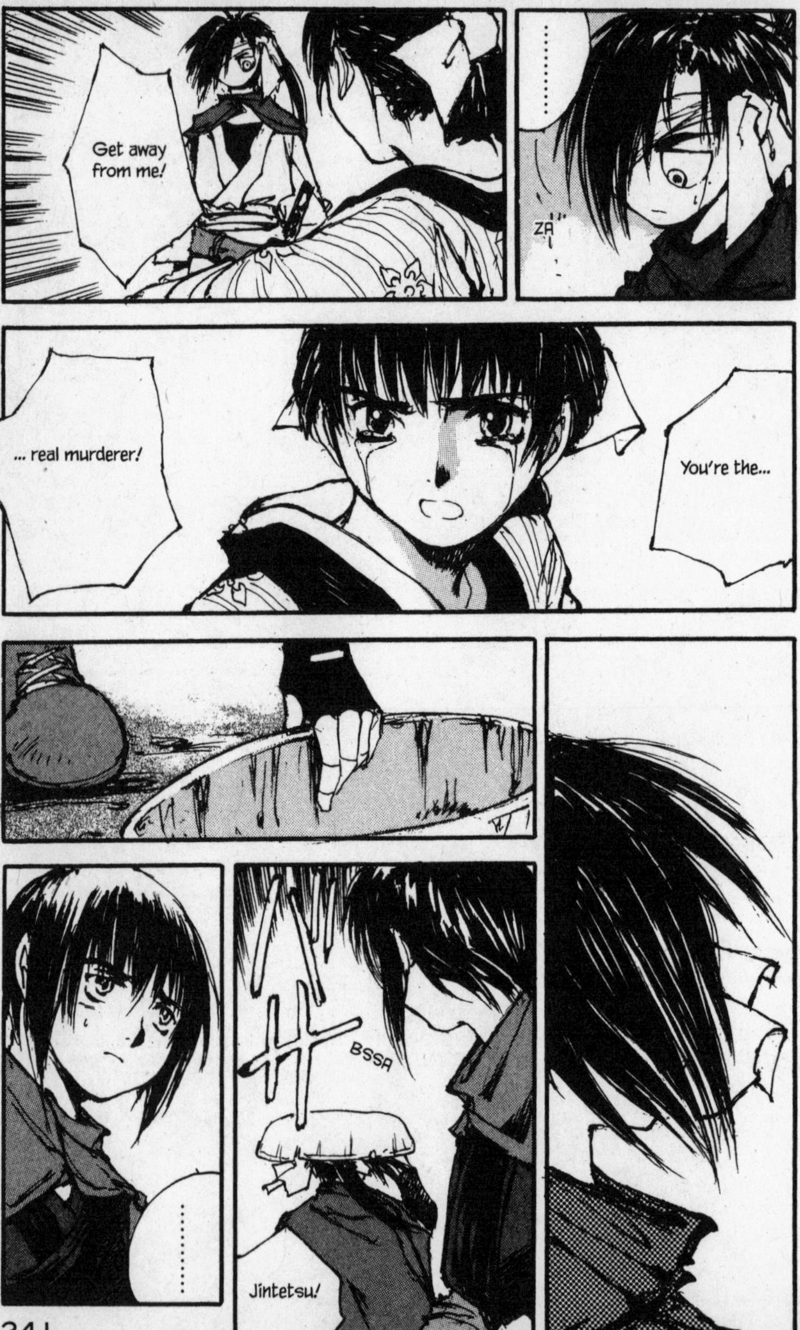
......
ZA
Get away from me!
You're the...
... real murderer!
BSSA
Jintetsu!
......

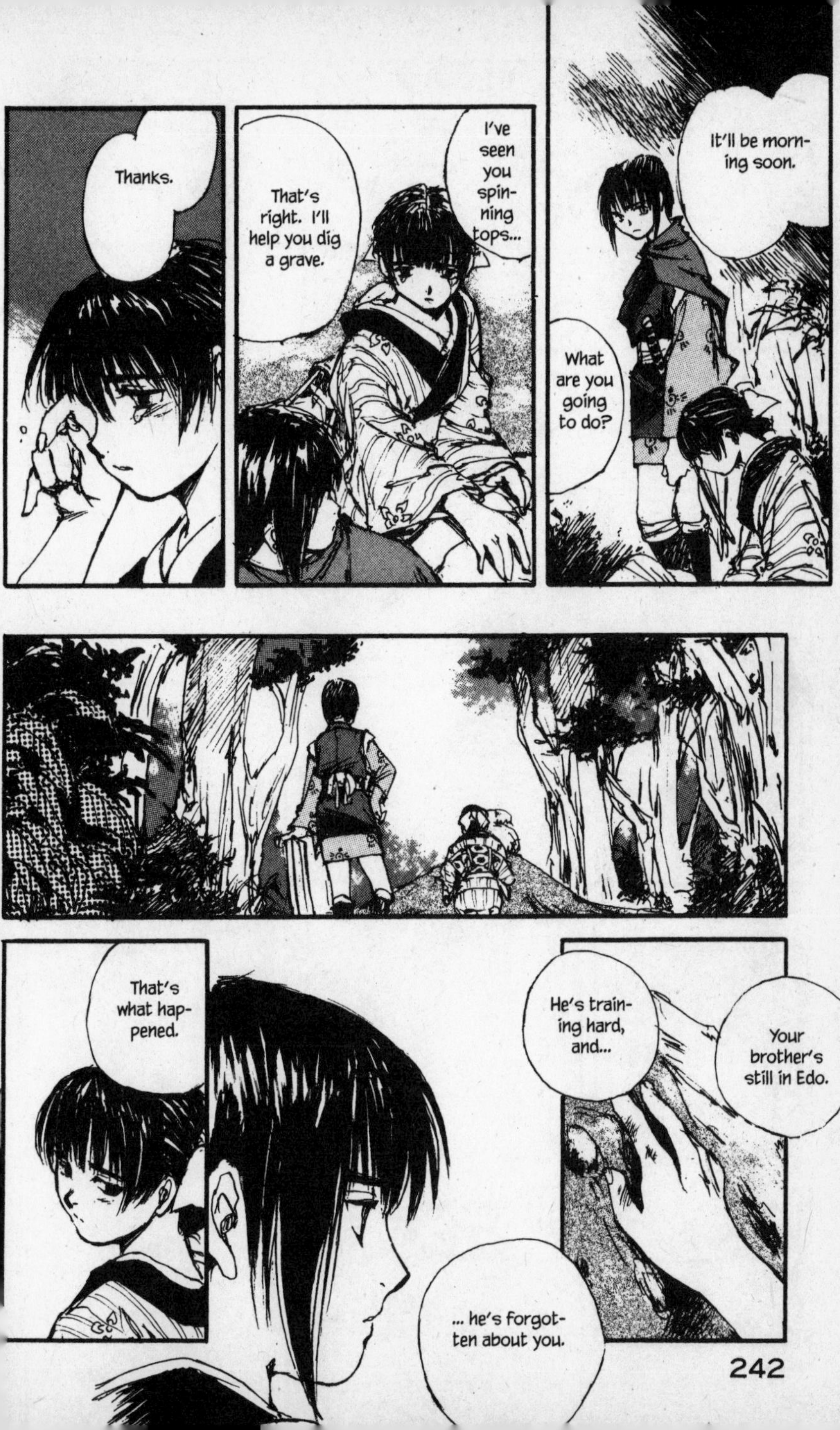
It'll be morning soon.
What are you going to do?
I've seen you spinning tops...
That's right. I'll help you dig a grave.
Thanks.
Your brother's still in Edo.
He's training hard, and...
... he's forgotten about you.
That's what happened.

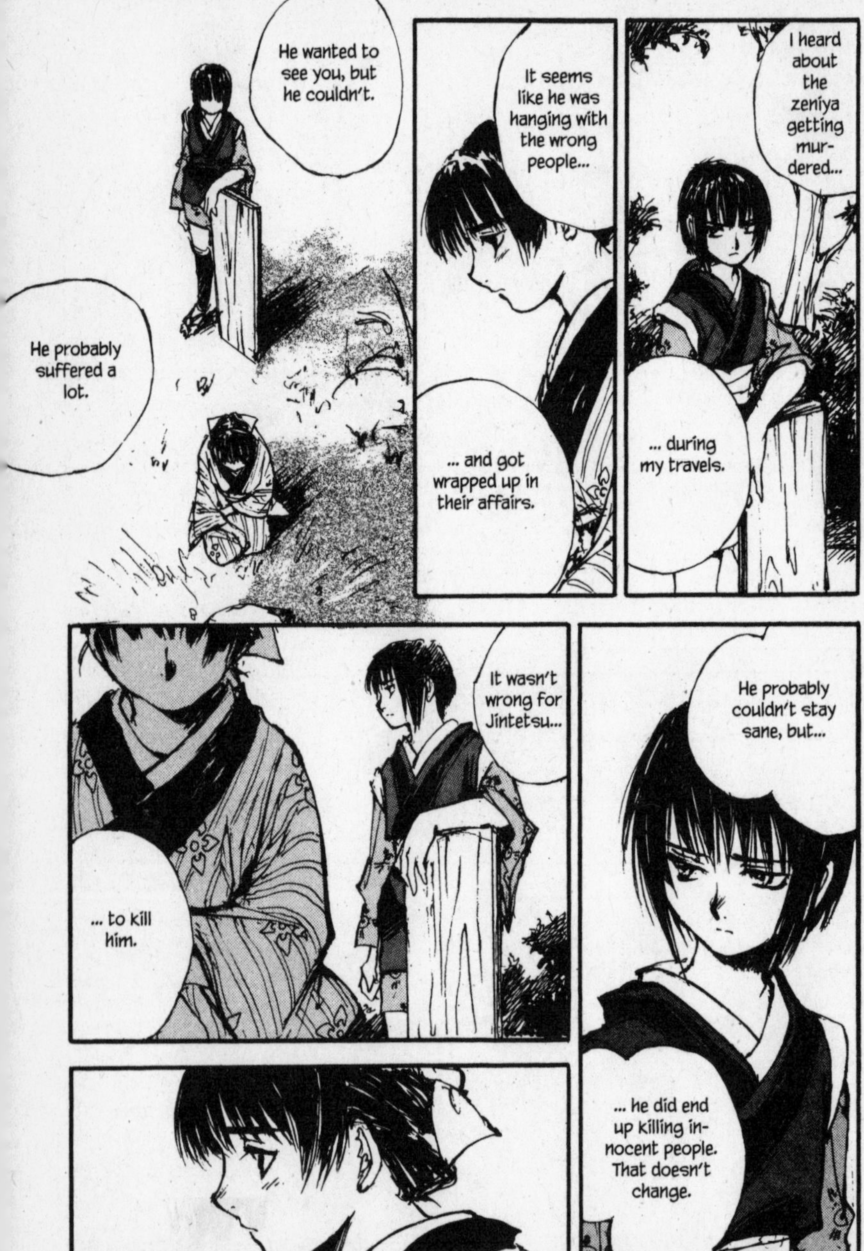
I heard about the zeniya getting mur-dered...
... during my travels.
It seems like he was hanging with the wrong people...
... and got wrapped up in their affairs.
He wanted to see you, but he couldn't.
He probably suffered a lot.
He probably couldn't stay sane, but...
... he did end up killing in-nocent people. That doesn't change.
It wasn't wrong for Jintetsu...
... to kill him.

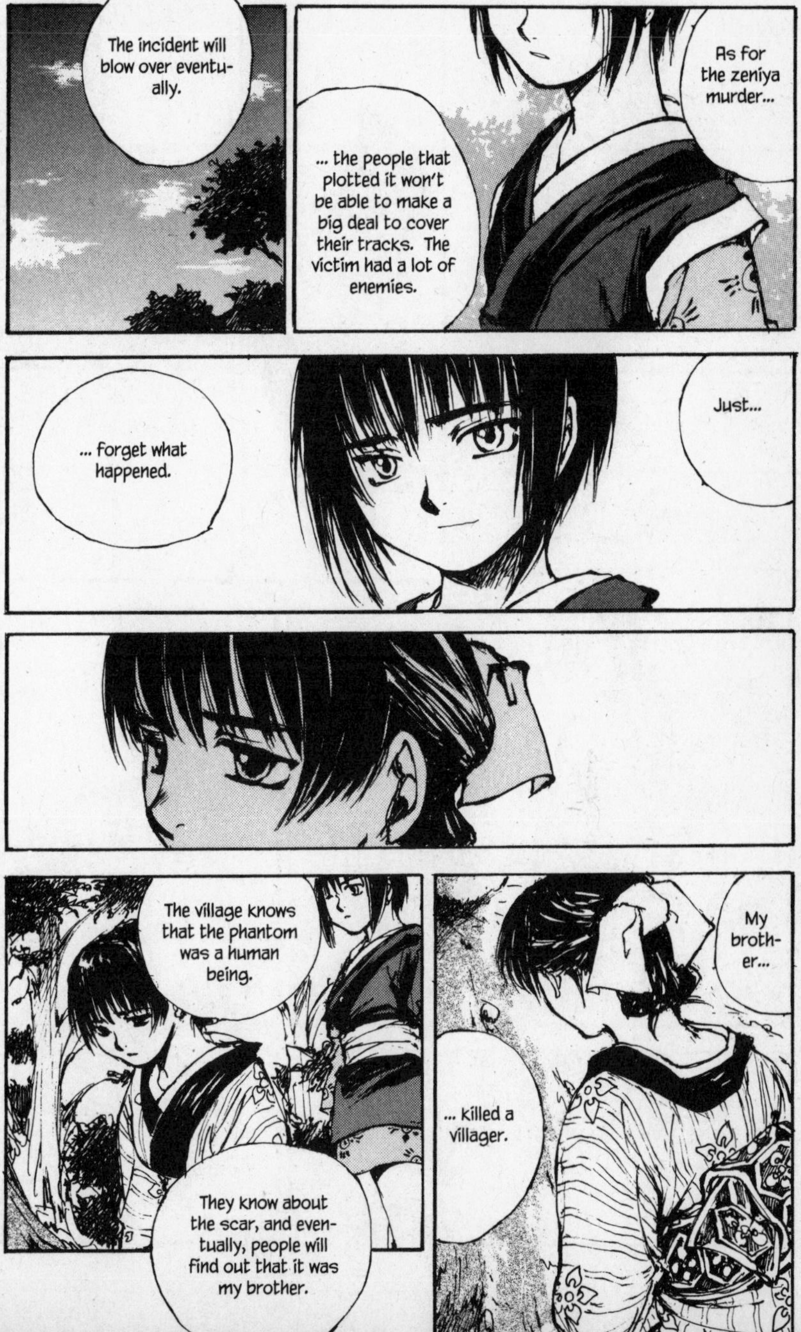
As for the zeniya murder...
... the people that plotted it won't be able to make a big deal to cover their tracks. The victim had a lot of enemies.
The incident will blow over eventu-ally.
Just...
... forget what happened.
My broth-er...
... killed a villager.
The village knows that the phantom was a human being.
They know about the scar, and even-tually, people will find out that it was my brother.

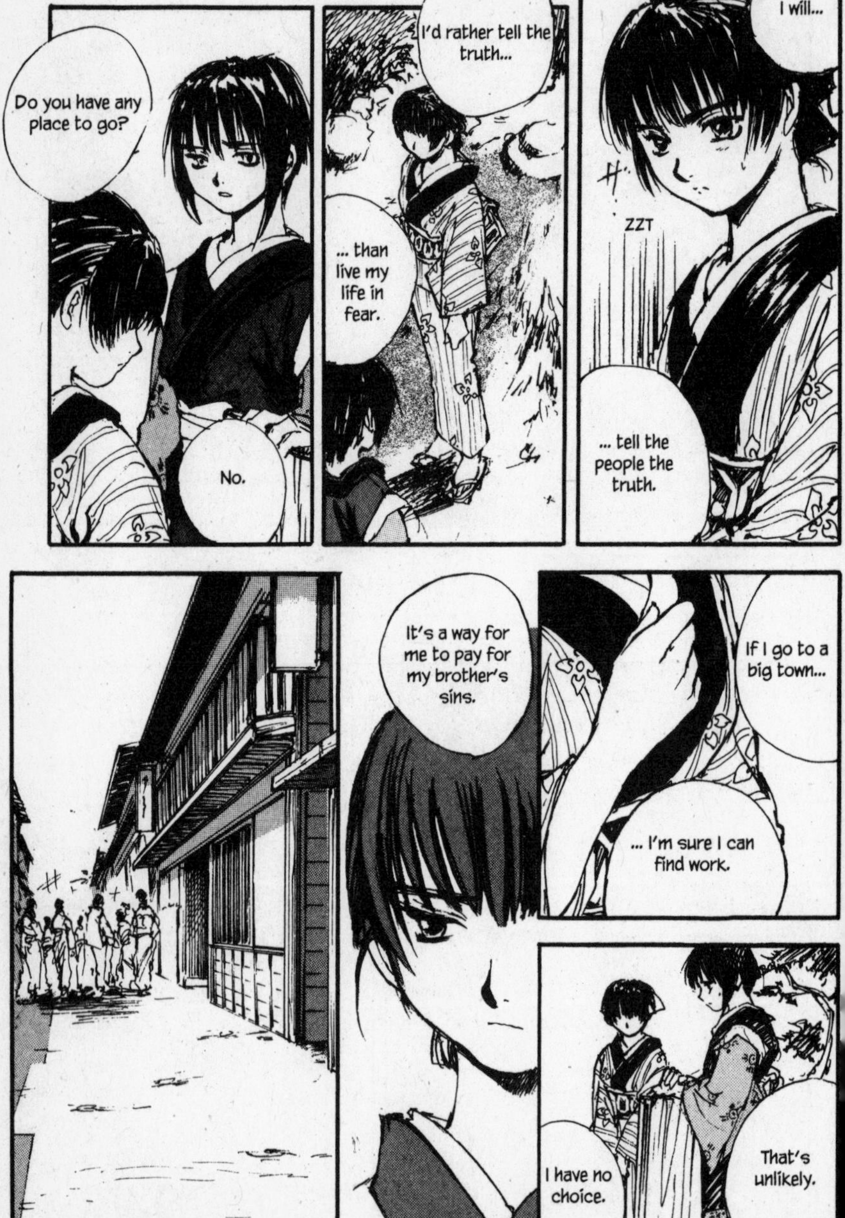
I will...
ZZT
... tell the people the truth.
I'd rather tell the truth...
... than live my life in fear.
Do you have any place to go?
No.
If I go to a big town...
... I'm sure I can find work.
That's unlikely.
I have no choice.
It's a way for me to pay for my brother's sins.

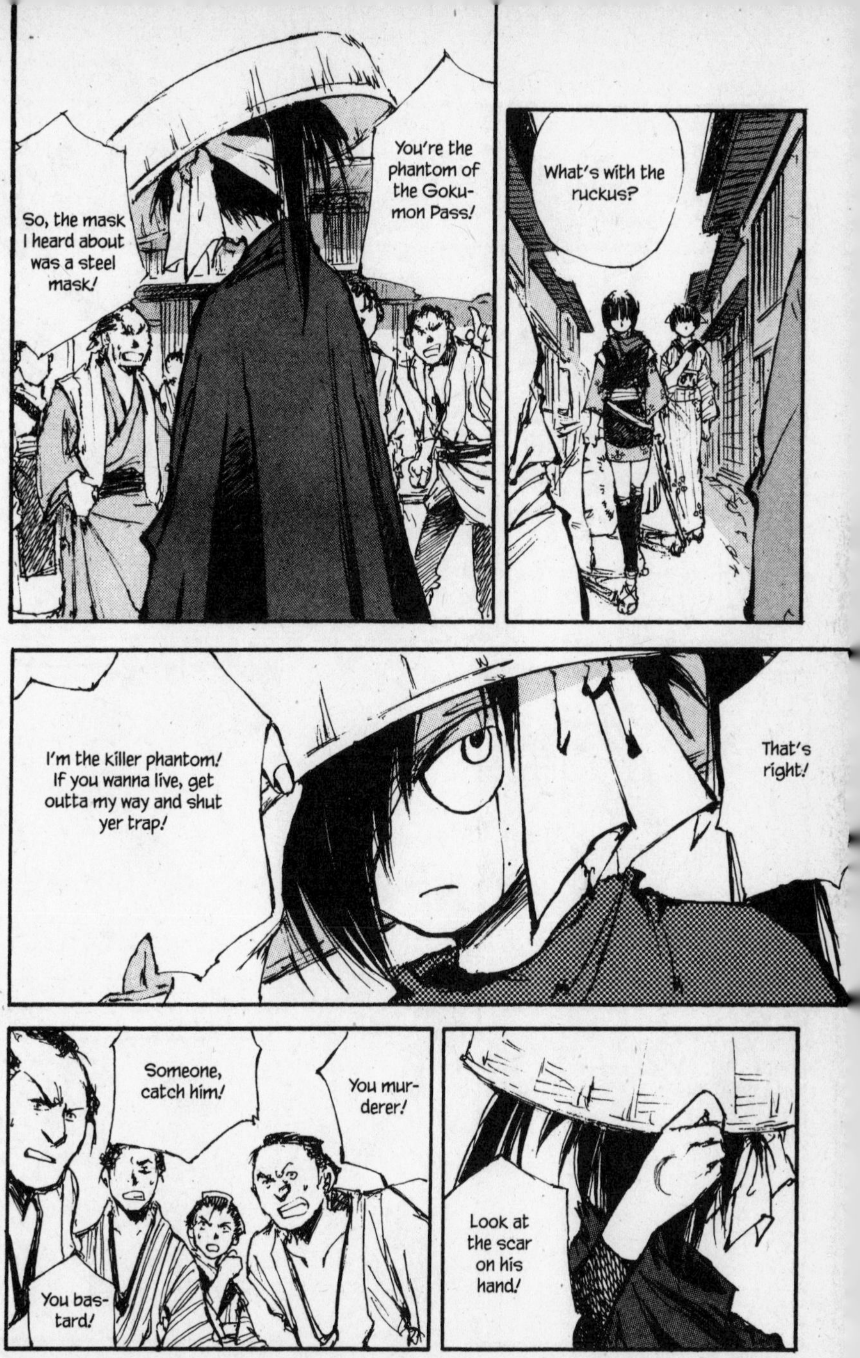
What's with the ruckus?
You're the phantom of the Goku-mon Pass!
So, the mask I heard about was a steel mask!
That's right!
I'm the killer phantom! If you wanna live, get outta my way and shut yer trap!
Look at the scar on his hand!
You mur-derer!
Someone, catch him!
You bas-tard!

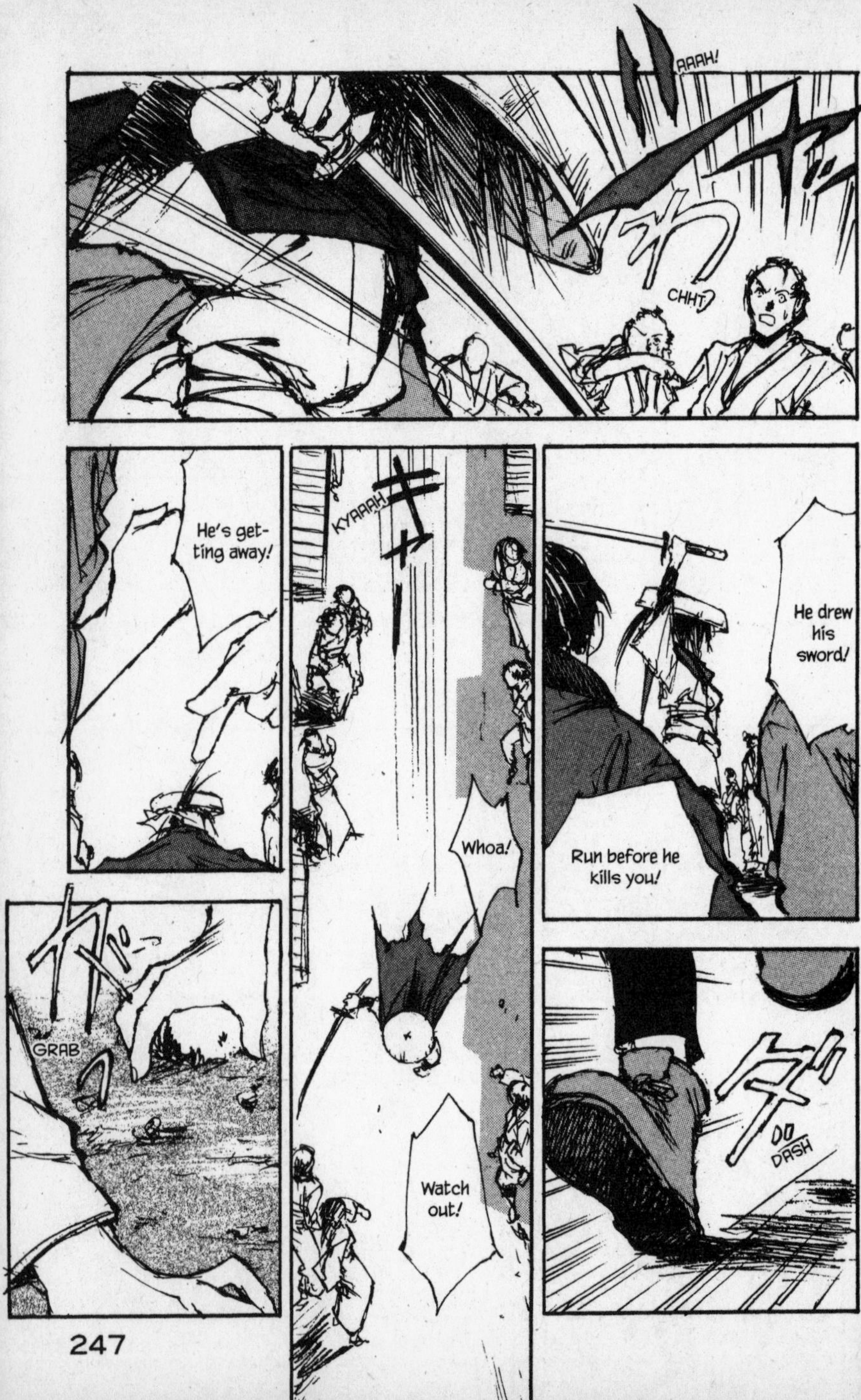
AAAH!
CHHT!
He drew his sword!
Run before he kills you!
DO
DASH
KYAAAH
Whoa!
Watch out!
He's getting away!
GRAB

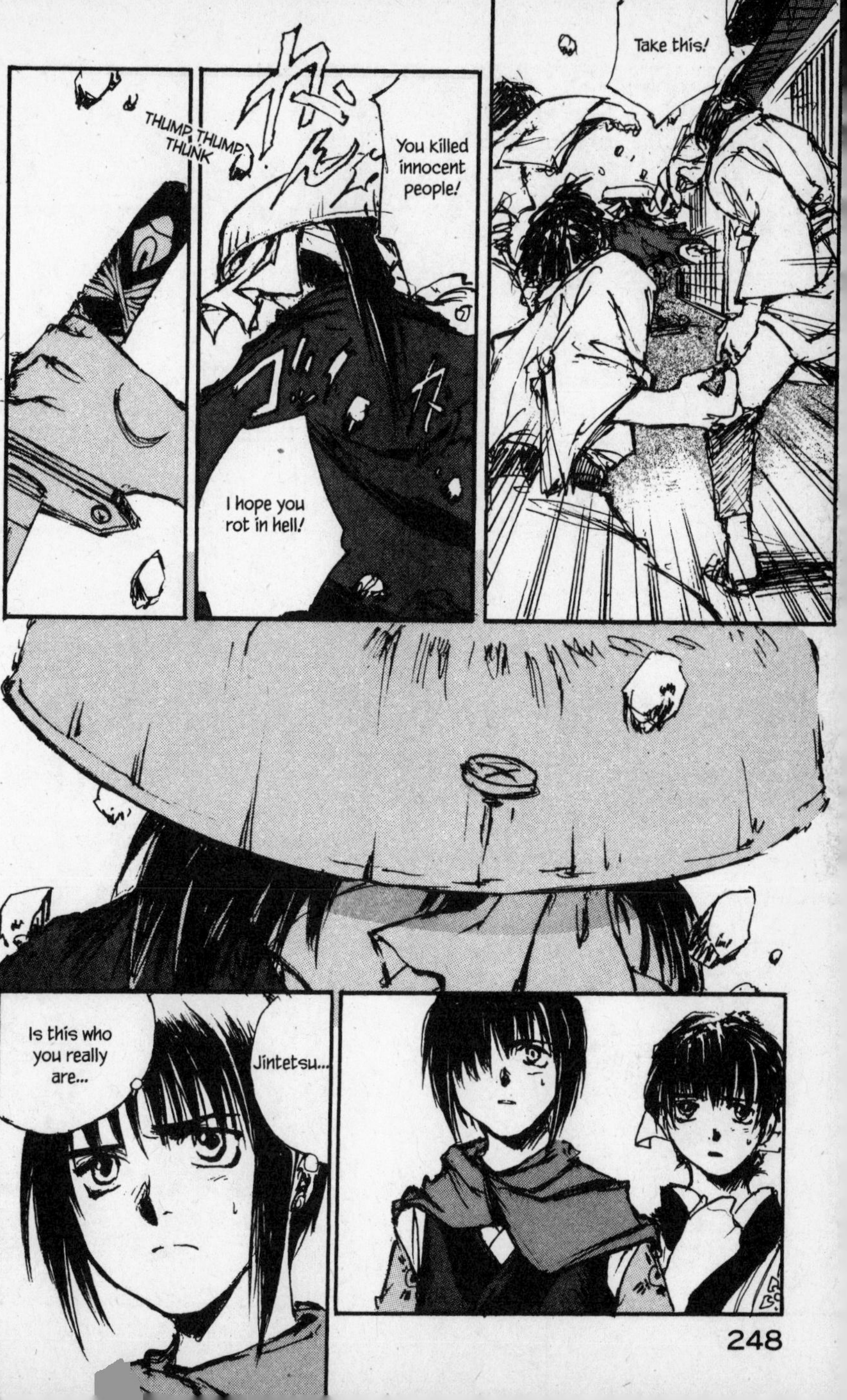
Take this!
You killed innocent people!
I hope you rot in hell!
THUMP THUMP THUNK
Jintetsu...
Is this who you really are...

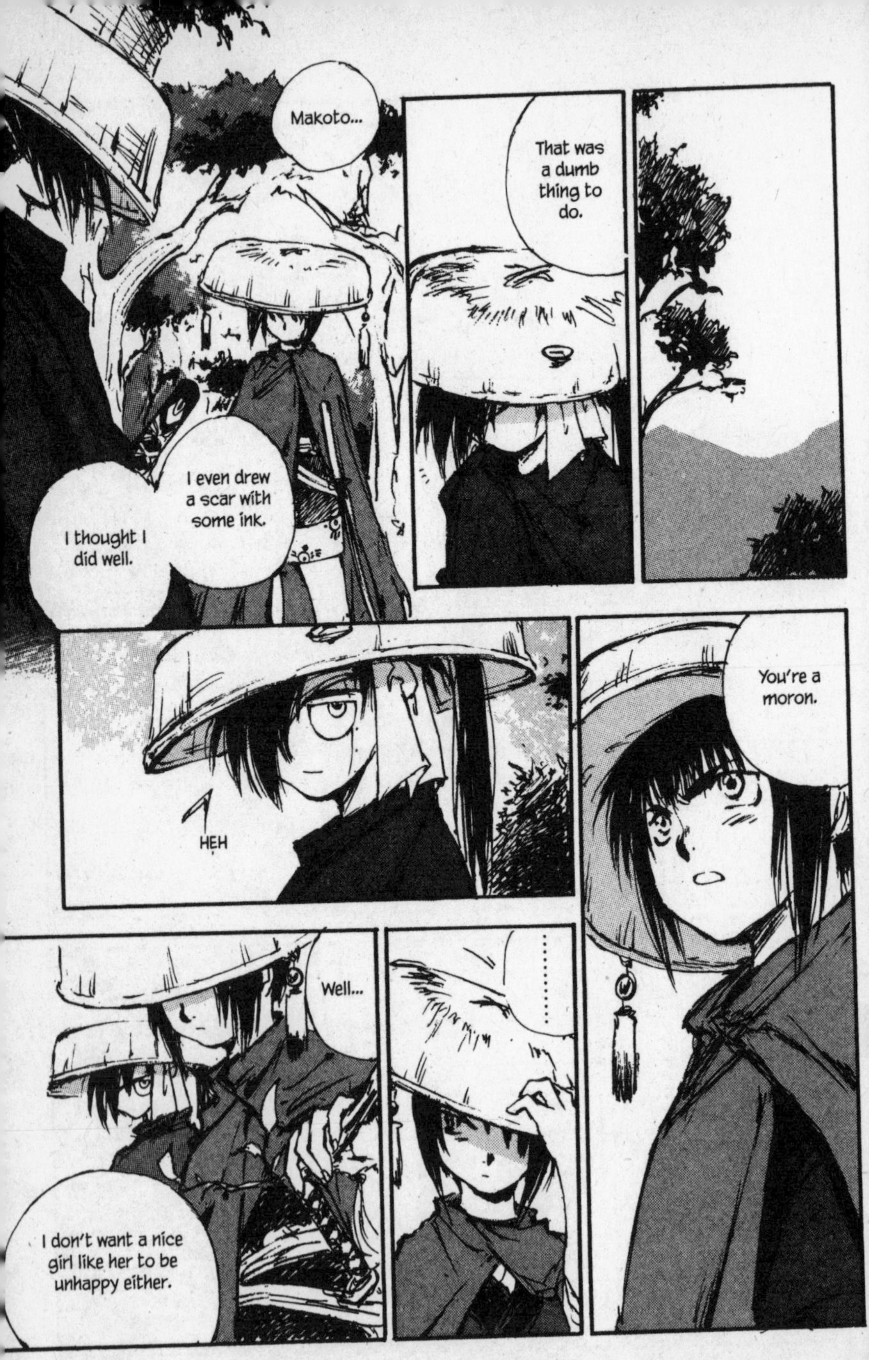
That was a dumb thing to do.
Makoto...
I even drew a scar with some ink.
I thought I did well.
You're a moron.
HEH
......
Well...
I don't want a nice girl like her to be unhappy either.

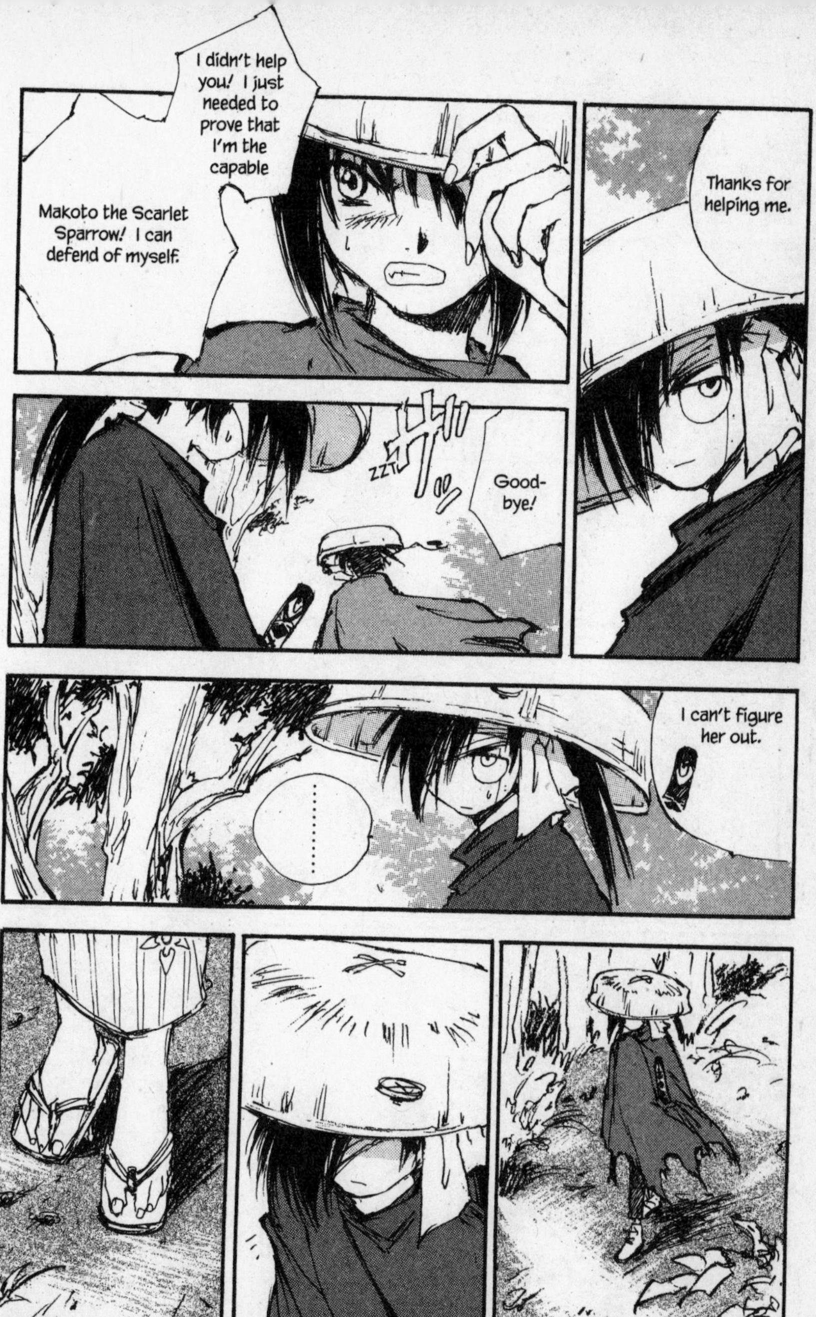
Thanks for helping me.
I didn't help you! I just needed to prove that I'm the capable
Makoto the Scarlet Sparrow! I can defend of myself.
Good-bye!
ZZT
I can't figure her out.
......

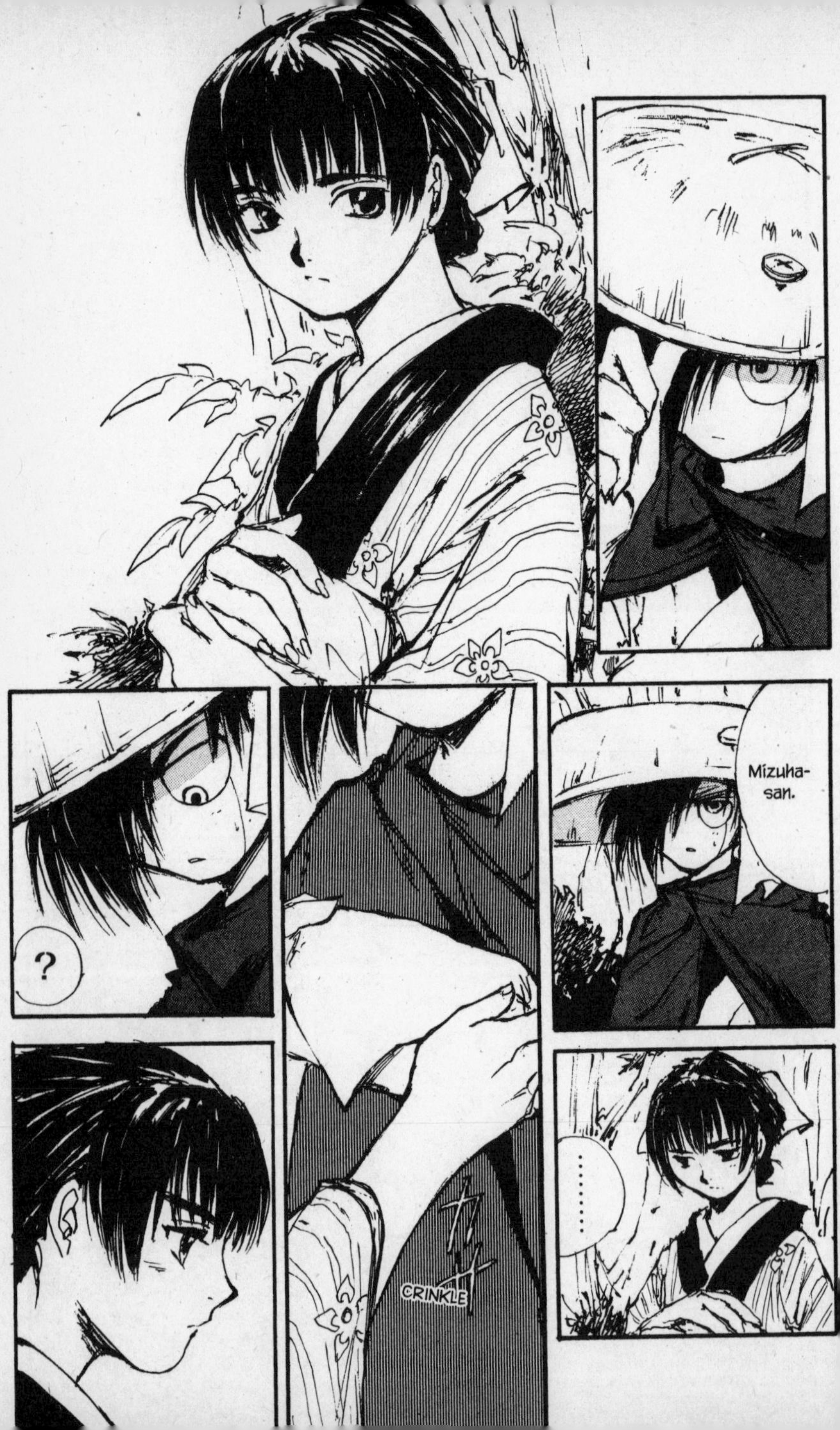
Mizuha-san.
......
CRINKLE
?

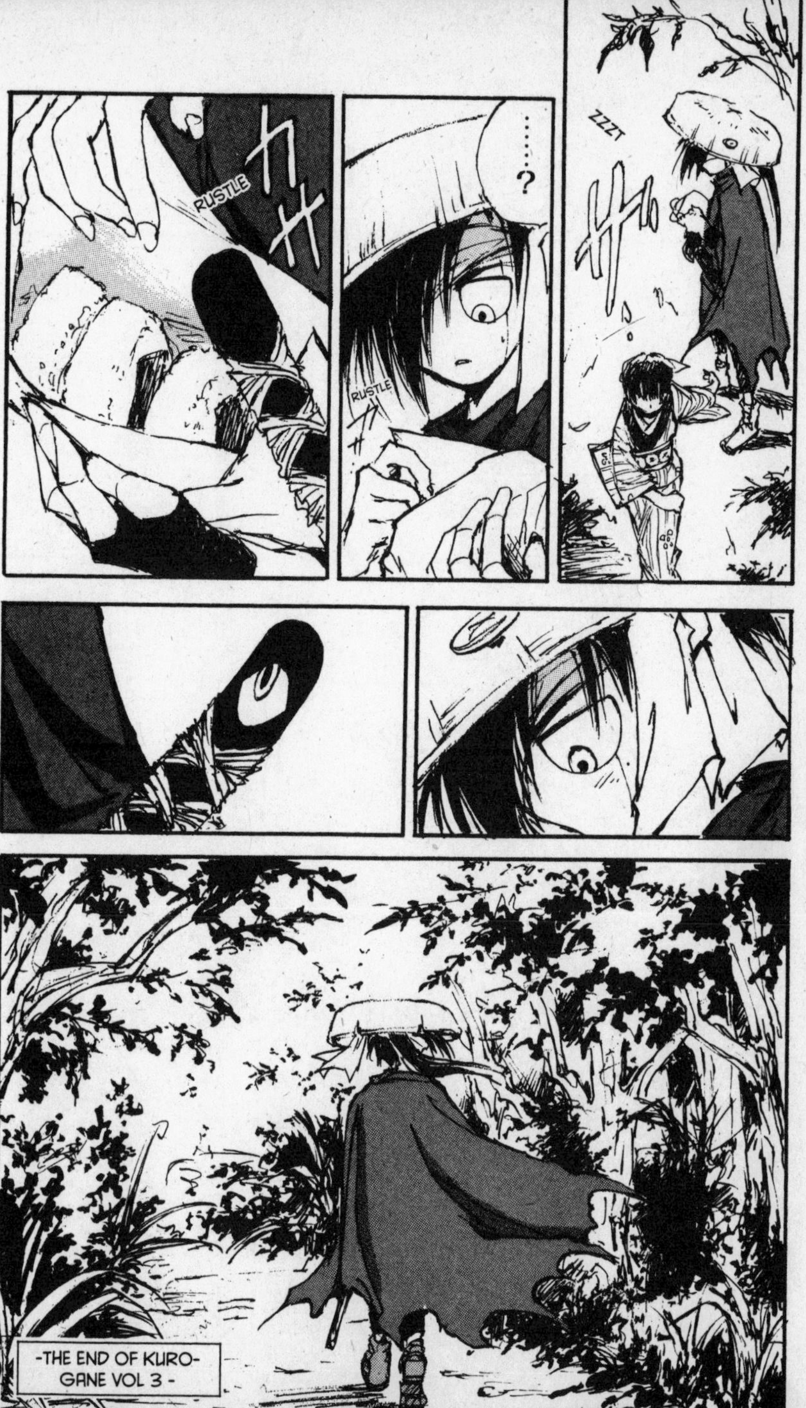
ZZZT
......?
RUSTLE
RUSTLE
-THE END OF KURO-GANE VOL 3 -

Translation Notes

Japanese is a tricky language for most Westerners, and translation is often more art than science. For your edification and reading pleasure, here are notes on some of the places where we could have gone in a different direction in our translation of the work, or where a Japanese cultural reference is used.

***Kitsune*, page 12**

Kitsune means fox in Japanese. Within the Shinto faith, *kitsune* is associated with Inari, the rice god. In Japanese folklore, *kitsune*, or fox spirit, possesses magical powers, including shapeshifting abilities. There are two major types of *kitsune*.The *myobu*, or celestial fox, associated with Inari, who are benevolent. The *nogitsune*, or wild fox (literally "field fox"), are often, though not always, presented as malicious. The most common human form of a *kitsune* is a beautiful woman. *Kitsunes* are known for tricking humans, which explains Jintetsu's comment on [12.7].

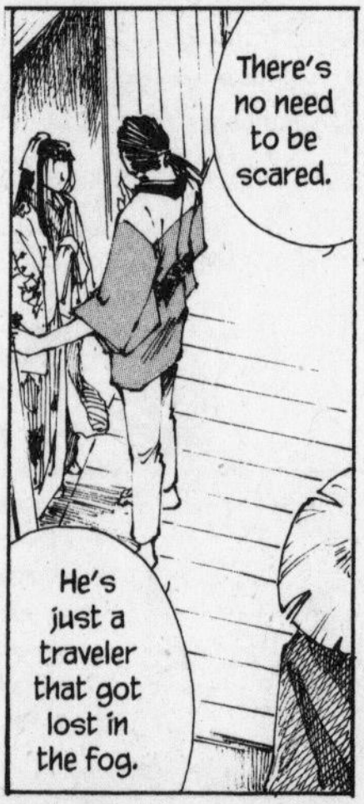
There's no need to be scared.
He's just a traveler that got lost in the fog.

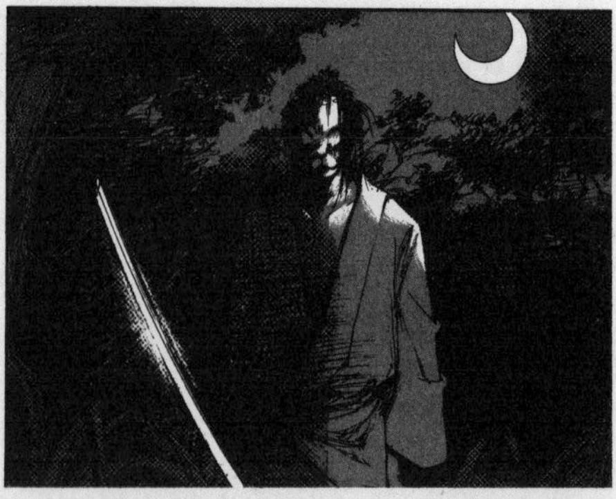

The mask that Yaichirou wears [168.4] is a mask of the *kitsune*.

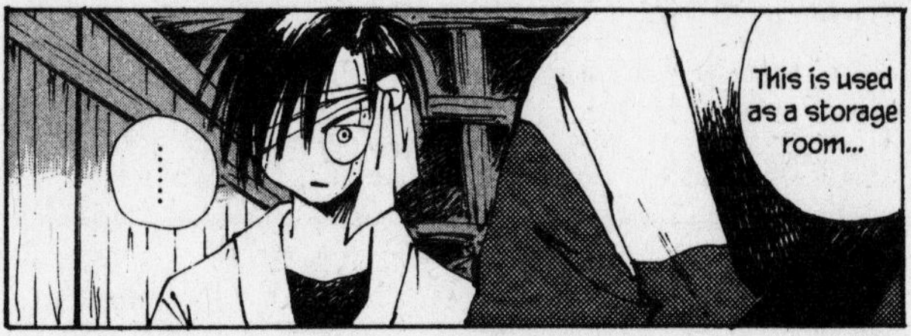
This is used as a storage room...
……

***Karakuri doll**, page 22*

Karakuri dolls are automated dolls that use various mechanisms to allow movement. Popular during the Edo period, *karakuri* dolls were created as entertainment for the feudal lords. The Zashiki *karakuri* is the most technologically complex and precious, using Western clockwork mechanisms, although some were powered by sand, mercury and even steam power.

***Gokumon**, page 161*

Gokumon means "prison gate" in Japanese.

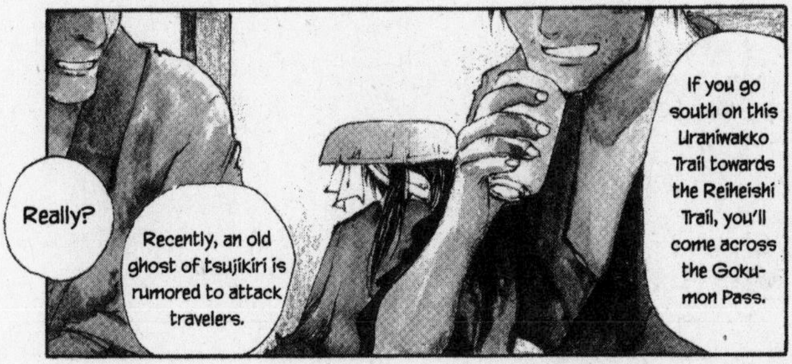
If you go south on this Uraniwakko Trail towards the Reiheishi Trail, you'll come across the Goku-mon Pass.
Recently, an old ghost of tsujikiri is rumored to attack travelers.
Really?

***Tsujikiri**, page 161*

Tsujikiri is a villain that kills innocent people with a sword, and sometimes strips the victim of all possessions (also called a phantom killer). It also refers to a villain that kills a passerby to test the sharpness of his new sword.

Meito, *page 178*
Meito is a sword inscribed with the name of the sword-smith.

Wakato, *page 192*
Wakato is a foot soldier or underling of a retainer or vassal. It also refers to a young samurai, or a lower-ranking samurai.

Zeniya, *page 200*
Zeniya is a money-exchanging business. It is also used as a title to refer to a person that is in the business. During the Edo period, jobs were stratified according to social class. Therefore, the title of *zeniya* would describe a man's profession as well as his class.

Order of birth, *page 203*
In the Japanese language, the order of birth is commonly indicated in the word used to describe a person. In the phrase, "He's the son of the Kamedaya family," the literal translation would be, "He's the second oldest son of the Kamedaya family." In Japanese, the word *cho-nan* refers to the oldest son, *ji-nan* refers to the second oldest, *san-nan* refers to the third son, *yon-nan* refers to the fourth son, etc. In English, it is common to refer to just the gender of your sibling, such as "he's my brother." However, in Japanese, when you refer to your siblings, the word will almost always indicate their order of birth in reference to you. For example, if you were to refer to your older brother, you would use the word *oni-chan*. A younger brother would be called *oto-to*.

Ronin, *page 212*
Ronin refers to a masterless samurai during the Edo period. In modern Japan, the word refers to students that have failed the entrance exam to the university of their choice, and is waiting for another chance. It is not uncommon for many students to retake an entrance exam several times before entering college

The following pages show art that was originally in the Japanese edition of *Kurogane* volume 3 as a double-sided fold-out mini-poster. Enjoy!

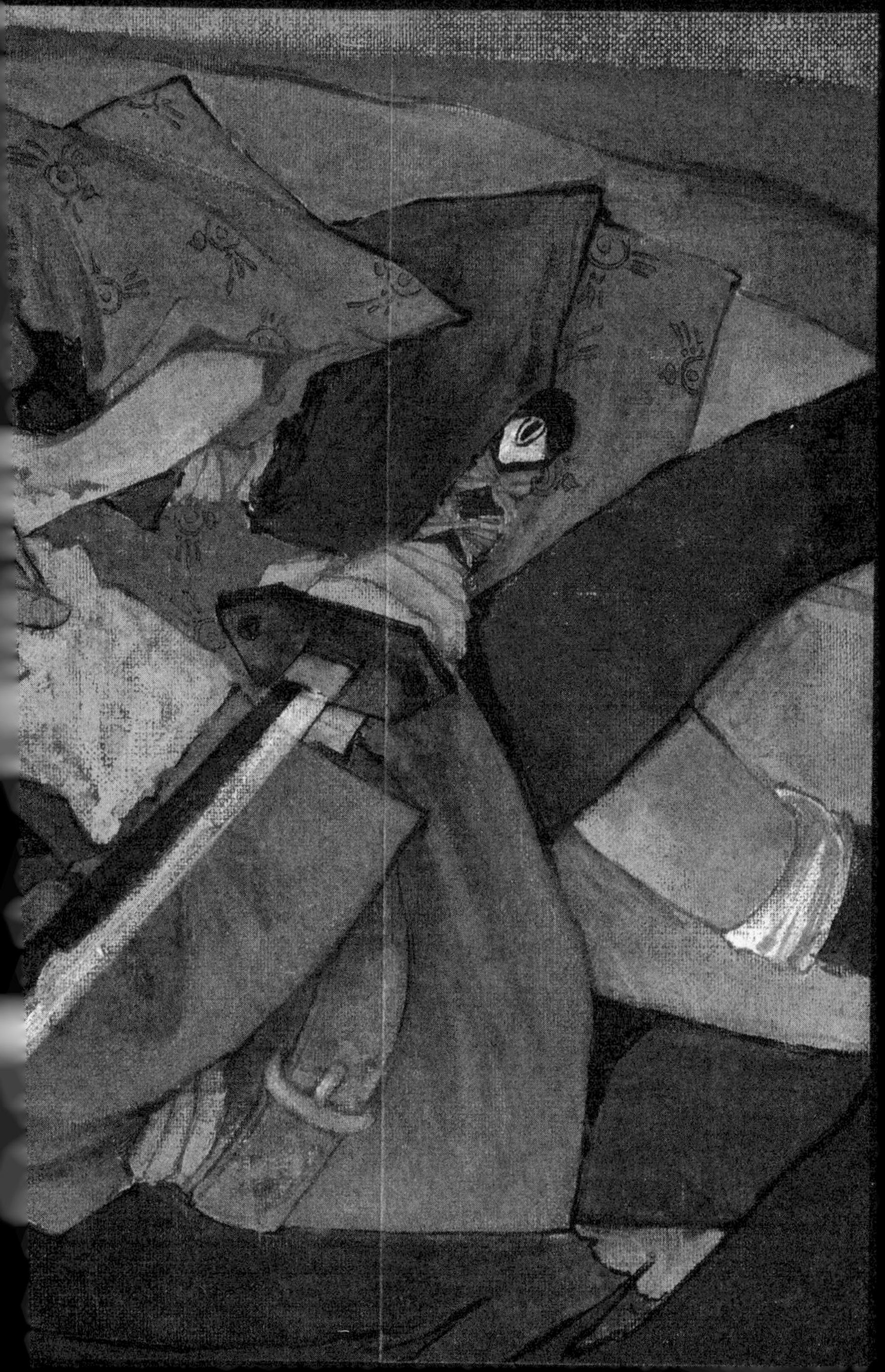

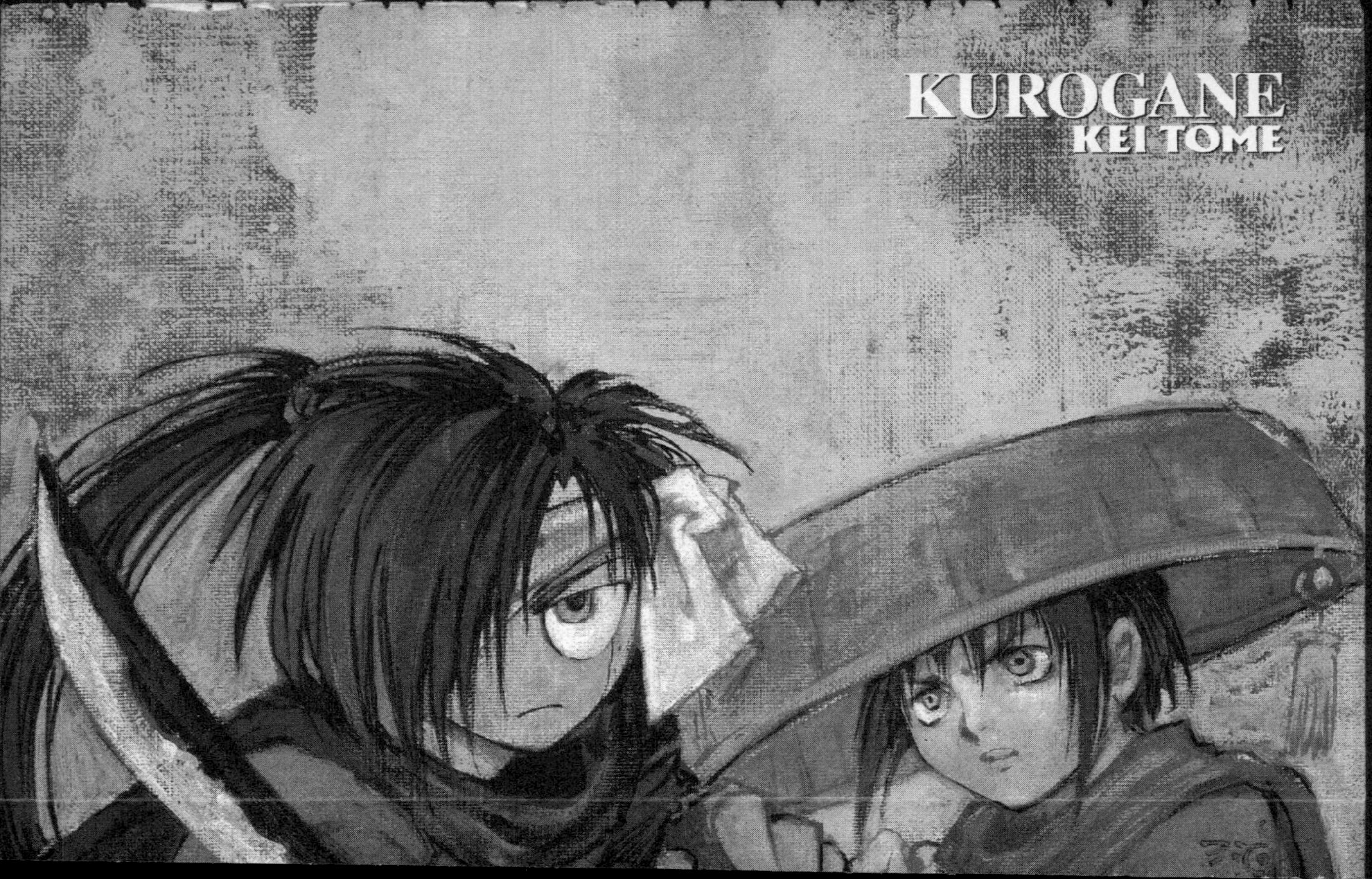
KUROGANE
KEI TOME

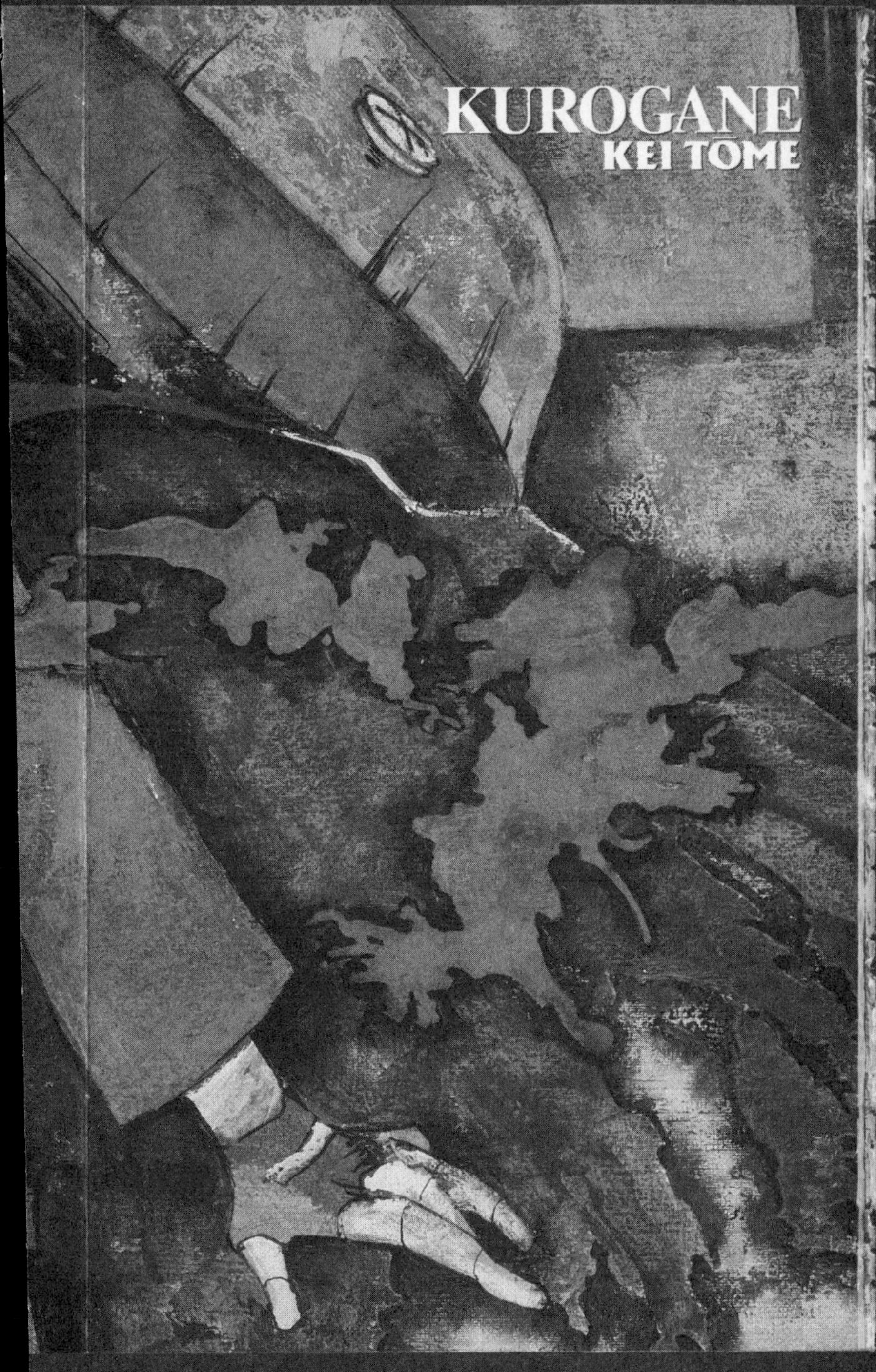
KUROGANE
KEI TŌME

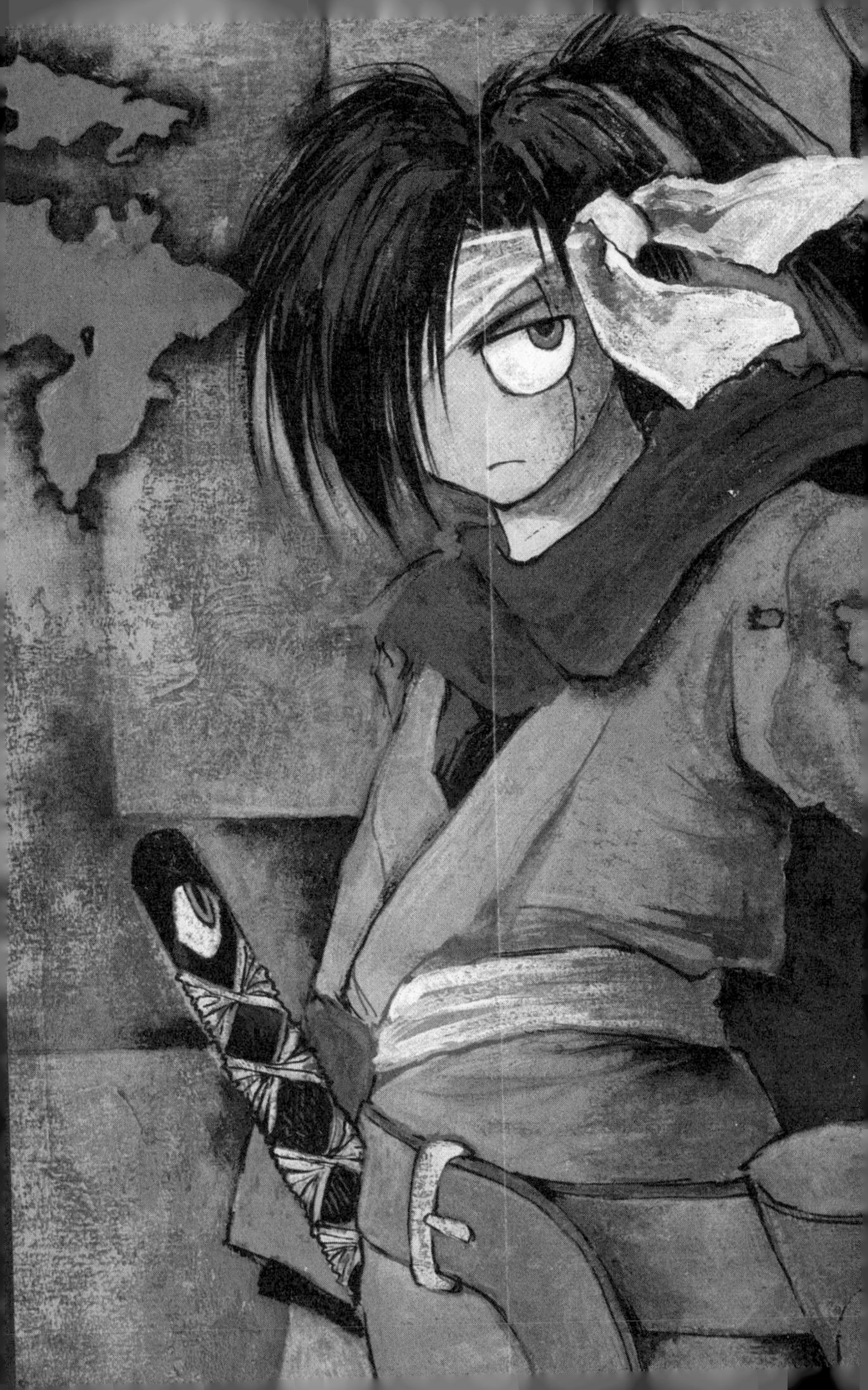

We're pleased to present you a preview from volume 4. This volume will be available in English on March 27, 2007, but for now you'll have to make do with Japanese!

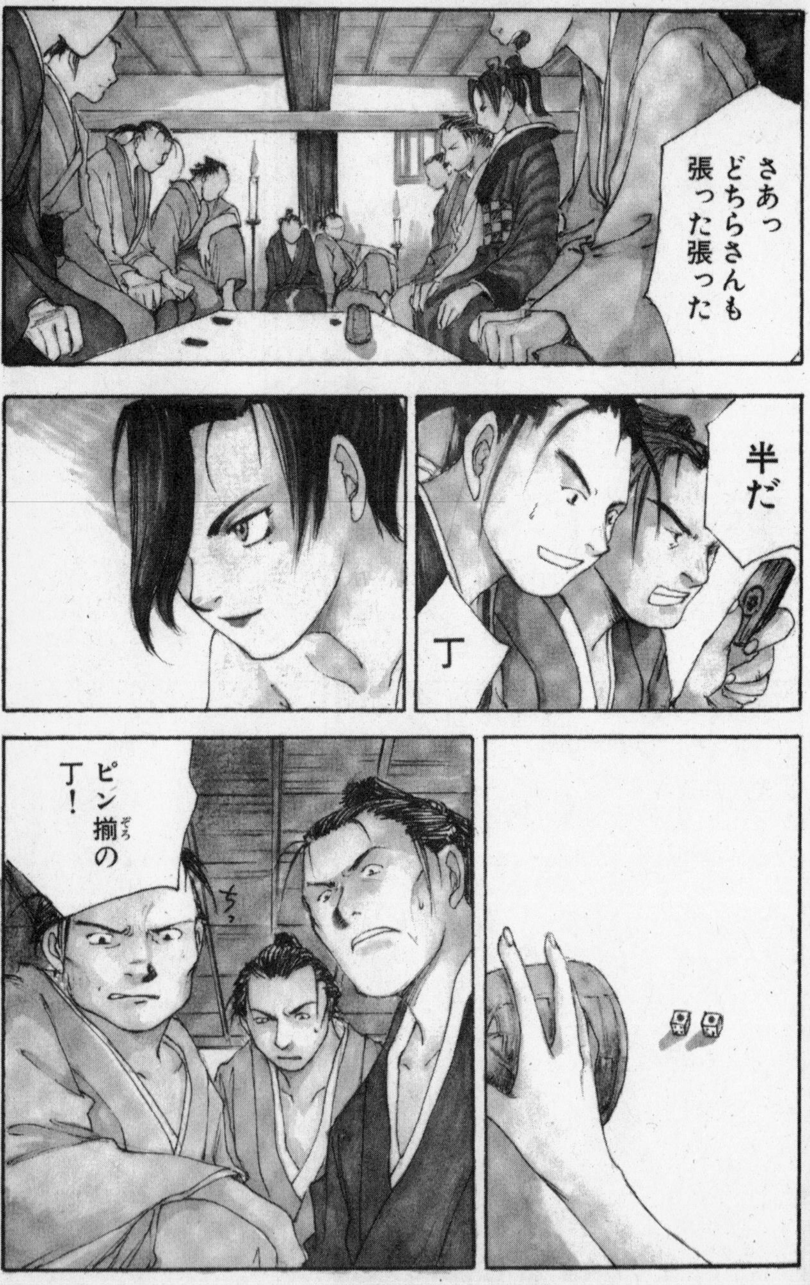
さあっ どちらさんも 張った張った
半だ
丁
ピン揃の丁！
ちっ

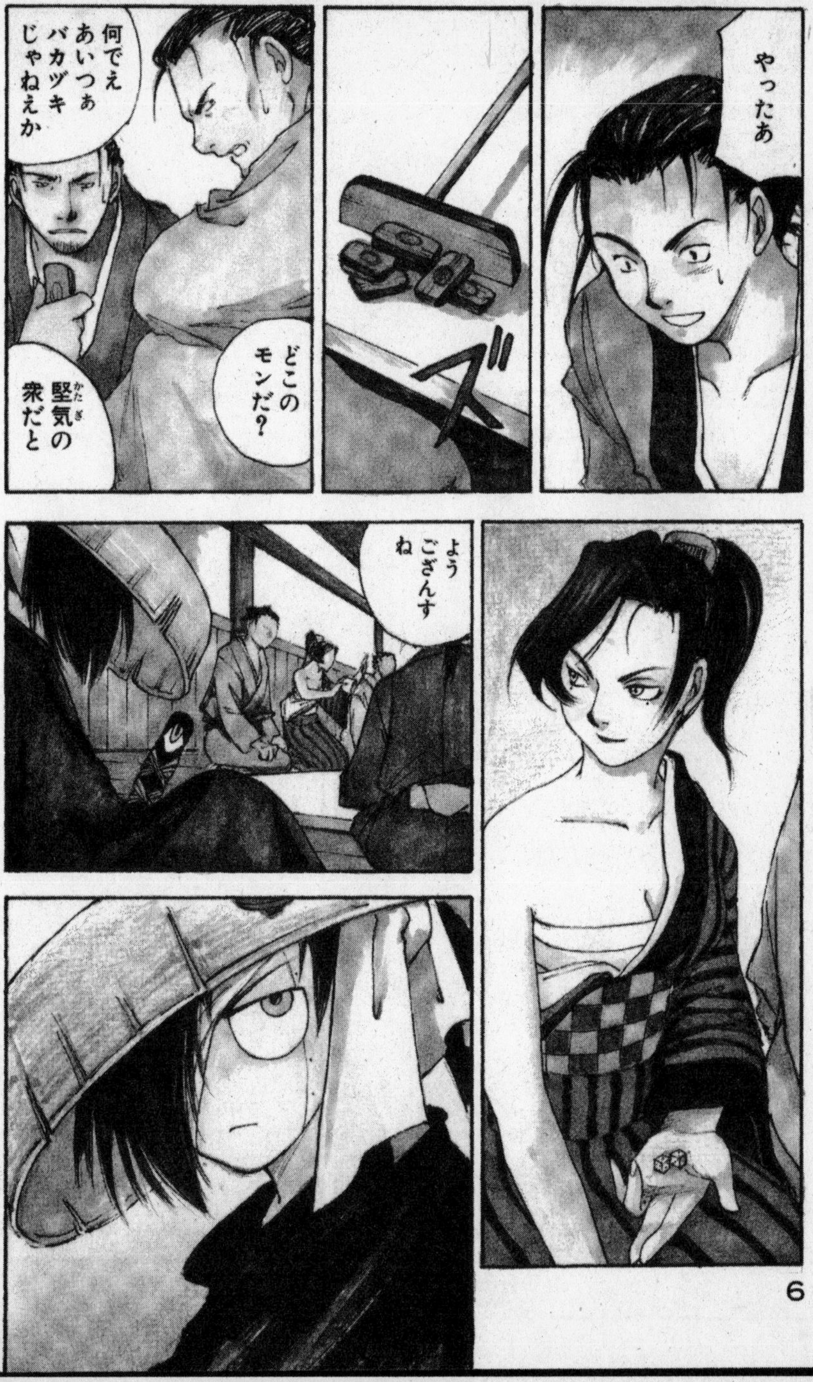
やったあ
ヅ
何でえあいつぁバカヅキじゃねえか
どこのモンだ?
堅気の衆だと
ようござんすね

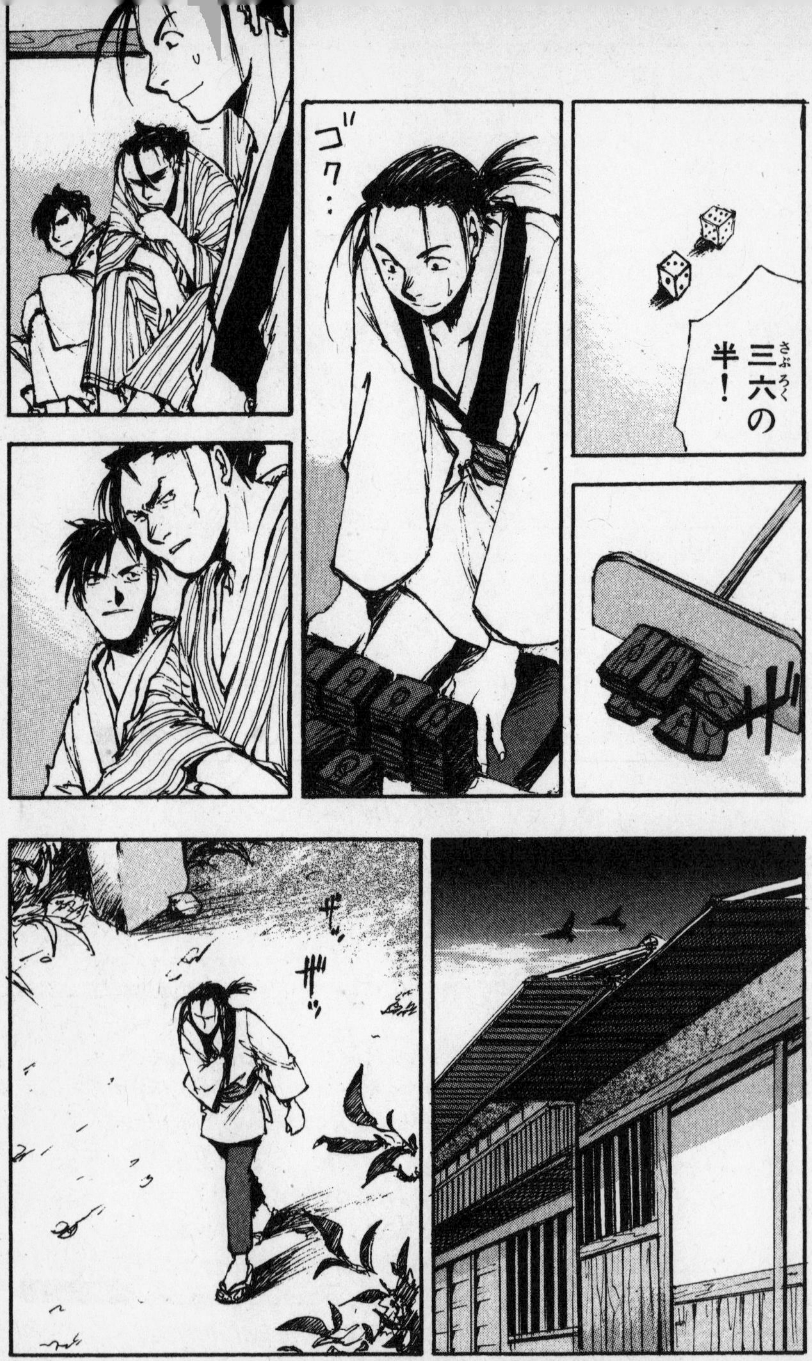
三六の半！
ゴク…
ザッ
ザッ
ザッ

Tomare!
[Stop!]

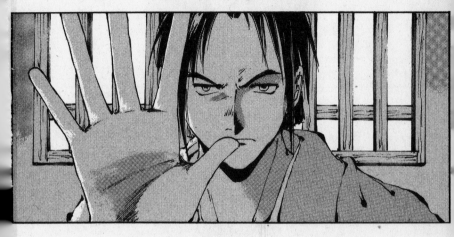

You are going the wrong way!

Manga is a completely different type of reading experience.

To start at the beginning, go to the end!

That's right! Authentic manga is read the traditional Japanese way—from right to left. Exactly the opposite of how American books are read. It's easy to follow: Just go to the other end of the book, and read each page—and each panel—from right side to left side, starting at the top right. Now you're experiencing manga as it was meant to be.